D0899060

HARVARD STUDIES IN URBAN HISTORY

Series editors
Stephan Thernstrom
Charles Tilly

IMMIGRANT MILWAUKEE, 1836-1860

Accommodation and Community in a Frontier City

WITHDRAW

Kathleen Neils Conzen

Harvard University Press

Cambridge, Massachusetts, and London, England   1976

Library of Congress Cataloging in Publication Data

Conzen, Kathleen Neils, 1942-
  Immigrant Milwaukee, 1836-1860.

  (Harvard studies in urban history)
  Includes index.
  1. German Americans—Wisconsin—Milwaukee. 2. Irish
Americans—Wisconsin—Milwaukee. 3. Milwaukee—Emigra-
tion and immigration. 4. Milwaukee—Social conditions.
I. Title. II. Series.
F589.M6C89   977.5'95'00431   75-37557
ISBN 0-674-44436-1

For Michael

Acknowledgments

Any project with a nine-year gestation period inevitably incurs a heavy burden of gratitude, which it is a pleasure to acknowledge. Eric E. Lampard, now of the State University of New York at Stony Brook, directed the work through its early stages at the University of Wisconsin; his probing questions, provocative suggestions, and the intellectual elbow room he provided, immeasurably enhanced both the scope of the work and the mental horizons of its author. Those who have had the opportunity of working with him will appreciate the extent of my gratitude. I also wish to thank Leo F. Schnore for his stimulating comments and for the office space and data processing funds which he channeled from his National Science Foundation Grant Number GS-921, Ecological Patterns in American Cities. Stephan Thernstrom, Morton Rothstein, David Ward, Philip Gleason, Margaret Walsh, Ann Orlov, Allan G. Bogue, J. Rogers Hollingsworth, Margaret E. Conners, and Elaine Neils Collins read all or parts of the manuscript at various stages of its preparation, and it benefited greatly from their suggestions. Its defects remain stubbornly my own.

Some of the material presented in Chapter 5 originally appeared in different form in my article, "Patterns of Residence in Early Milwaukee," in Leo F. Schnore, ed., *The New Urban History: Quantitative Explorations by American Historians* (Princeton: Princeton University Press, 1975), pp. 145-183, and is used by permission of the Center for Advanced Study in the Behavioral Sciences, Stanford, California; Tables 15 and 32 and Figure 11 are directly reproduced from that article. The State Historical Society of Wisconsin has granted permission to reproduce Figure 12 from its map collection. I also gratefully acknowledge permission from the Milwaukee County Historical Society to quote material from Harry H. Anderson, ed., *German-American Pioneers in Wisconsin and Michigan* (Milwaukee: Milwaukee County Historical Society, 1971).

I am also grateful to the University of Wisconsin for the fellowship aid which supported full-time research, and to the Research Committee of its Graduate School for making available computer time. Wellesley College provided generous aid for manuscript preparation. The staffs of the State Historical Society of Wisconsin, the Milwaukee County Historical Center, the Milwaukee Public Library, the Salzmann Library at St. Francis Seminary in Milwaukee, and the libraries of the University of Wisconsin at Madison and Milwaukee all helped smooth the path of research. For their hospitality during a summer of writing, I am grateful to Mary and Deryck Wardlaw, and particularly to my parents for support in so many ways. Most of all I thank my husband, Michael P. Conzen, for mapping assistance and the cartography which illustrates this project, for the critical sounding board which he has provided, and for the stabilizing confidence of a shared life.

Contents

TABLES

FIGURES

IMMIGRANT MILWAUKEE, 1836-1860

Introduction

It was a disparate group of midwives which assisted at the birth of Milwaukee's German community in early 1843. The infant city had decided to celebrate publicly the acquisition of federal funds to improve its harbor, and a number of its German-born residents concluded that the occasion warranted a special sort of participation on their part—"Resolved, that the German citizens of Milwaukee and surrounding country will show their interest of the concerns of the United States and Wisconsin, and especially of the Harbor Bill having passed Congress, by means in forming a procession, in connection with that of the native citizens, on Wednesday, the 22nd inst." Those working together on the elected arrangements committee included a Catholic priest, an Evangelical pastor, a Freethinking physician, an innkeeper, a shoemaker, a druggist, and a pioneer justice of the peace *cum* jack-of-all-trades. The committee did its work well. On the appointed day a contingent half a mile long joined the city's Harbor Parade under a banner proudly proclaiming "Die Deutschen Buerger von Milwaukee," with a militia unit, mounted riders, a train of sleighs, and "gentlemen on foot" marching to the music of the German brass band.[1]

It was an undoubtedly colorful event which served notice, as it was meant to, that the Germans were taking their place in public life as well as in the Harbor Parade alongside the other ethnic groups of the seven-year-old settlement, the native-born Americans, the Irish, and the French-speaking population. Even more important, however, the parade contingent marked the emergence of a slender community life among the motley crew of German-born strays, adventurers, and religious refugees who had been drifting into Milwaukee over the past half dozen years. That community was to grow and flower with the massive German in-migration of the late 1840s and early 1850s and would remain strong and vital for more than half a century thereafter.

The German community was to color Milwaukee's urban development and crucially mediate the adjustment of several generations of immigrant residents to American life. It was not only the numbers of Germans who settled there that gave Milwaukee its reputation as the most German of American cities nor their proportionate strength in the city's population but also the solidity and character of the community they created. This book will explore the achievement of that community in the first twenty-five years of Milwaukee's history, relating it to the accommodation patterns of individual German immigrants and contrasting it with the experiences of other groups in the city, particularly the Irish, but also the native born, the British, and other foreign-born pioneer residents.

My initial point of departure was a simple question: what happened when a large group of immigrants settled in a mid-nineteenth century frontier city? How did they come to terms with their new environment and, more broadly, what were the long-range implications of their initial solutions? Social scientists tell us that such contact between immigrants and a host society generates a long-term process of mutual reaction and accommodation whose eventual outcome can take numerous forms, ranging anywhere from complete assimilation of the immigrants into the host society through pluralism to a permanent caste situation. Significant stages in the process of integration include a period of initial accommodation, involving absorption of the immigrants into the economy of the host society, behavioral acculturation to its various roles, norms, and customs, and a satisfactory personal adjustment to the demands of coping with the new life; to be followed only later, if at all, by assimilation into the primary social structures of the host society with the disappearance of measurable behavior differences.[2] The manner and pace with which any given individual or group moves along the accommodation-assimilation continuum are influenced by a variety of factors. These include the selectivity of emigration—the personal attributes and skills of the immigrant, the motives and aspirations which accompany his move, his cultural and moral baggage—as well as the demographic composition of the emigration, its rate and pattern of settlement, and the character and attitudes of the receiving society.[3] In general, the more these factors combine to encourage immigrant isolation from the receiving society, under the assumption of adequate economic absorption, the greater the presumed ease of initial accommodation and the less the probability of rapid assimilation. Expectations widely different from the roles allowed by the host society, cultural differences in such areas as language or religion, relatively large numbers and rapid in-migration, even particular age and sex distributions or markedly deviant socioeconomic status may all tend to isolate immigrants and encourage the formation of separate cultures, neighborhoods, community institutions, either voluntarily or in reaction to exclusion from the host society. With such community activity, diverse individual immigrants become an ethnic group, sharing a sense of common belonging and origin, and the progress of the group conditions further individual integration.[4]

Historically, such ethnic communities, in Milton Gordon's analogy, have acted as a "decompression chamber in which the newcomers could, at their own pace, make a reasonable adjustment to the new forces of a society vastly different from that which they had known in the Old World," providing the "warmth, familiar ways, and sense of acceptance that prevented the saga of 'uprooting' from becoming a dislocating horror."[5] These communities were not and could never be direct recreations of Old World life but rather represented an adaptation of parts of the old culture to often vastly differing circumstances. Within the ethnic community, the immigrant found comfort, advice, and sometimes a job. He was often forced to take initiatives to found associations unknown in his homeland, thereby acclimatizing him to an important aspect of American life, and the existence of his community attracted the attention of vote-seeking politicians to draw him into the mainstream of political life. With the community thus filtering some of the trauma of personal adjustment, easing economic integration, and providing the institutional vehicles which gradually bore the message of acculturation while cloaking themselves in familiar forms, the immigrant—or his children—was set upon the path to wider interaction with the new society in which he had settled. Without that community, such contact would perforce have arrived sooner but with often far greater wrenching and disorientation.[6]

We can carry this chain of reasoning one step further and postulate that the more an ethnic community approached the character of true community in the fullest sense of the term, the more effectively it functioned to ease the transition from European to American life. Community in this sense refers, in Roland L. Warren's words, to "the shared interests and behavior patterns which people have by virtue of their common locality," or more technically, as Leo Schnore has suggested, to "the localized population which is interdependent on a daily basis, and which carries on a highly generalized series of activities in and through a set of institutions which provides on a day-to-day basis the full range of goods and services necessary for its continuity as a social and economic entity."[7] The full sense of community, so conceived, involves the notions of independence, interdependence, territoriality, and shared interest. While communities of interest can exist today without territoriality, in the period before improved transportation and communication a local base was a necessary prerequisite for effective interaction. It could be argued, indeed, that the term is best reserved for precisely those interactions which result from propinquity. The greater the "intersection of locality and interest," the stronger the community.[8]

This notion of community underlines the significance of a shared neighborhood and institutional completeness for the nineteenth century ethnic group but also suggests that an effectively functioning ethnic community would not require a single-minded sense of belonging or internal unity. Rather, the more it approached the diversity inherent in full community status, the greater its impact on the accommodation and assimilation of its members. The greater the employment opportunities within the ethnic community, for example, the less the need for extensive and possibly difficult outside contact. Yet such employment implies the creation of internal class divisions between employer and employed. In fact, to the extent that the ethnic community reproduced the class structure of the broader community, it could fulfill its members' status aspirations without ejecting them, and would have little need to rely upon outsiders to provide services. A larger ethnic community would have a greater opportunity to develop the wide range of organizations necessary to fulfill the wants of all segments of the group without reliance upon extra-community assistance, but thereby also widening internal differences. The ethnic community, it can thus be argued, may have functioned most effectively to cushion the process of integration when it was sufficiently large and diverse to demand no more of its members than a general sense of sharing a similar fate, permitting the development of more intense communality of interest at the subgroup level.[9]

In the light of these considerations, what can we expect from that German community which announced its presence so dramatically in Milwaukee on Washington's Birthday in 1843? How all-inclusive and internally differentiated would it become and what status would it achieve for and through its members? Frederick Jackson Turner long ago theorized that the equality generated by the economic opportunity of the frontier promoted rapid Americanization of immigrants in the west, though he was never very specific about the mechanics of integration; a more recent variant by Stanley Elkins and Eric McKitrick suggests that it was rather the shared experience of a "time of troubles" in the early days of an unstructured community which provoked widespread participation and acceptance of any man who could help, including, presumably, the foreign born.[10] From a Turnerian perspective, moreover, the lack of preexisting economic, political, or social institutions on the frontier meant greater opportunity for all, while the extra difficulty of travel from port of arrival to the frontier may have selected the more ambitious or moneyed immigrant in the first place.[11] If ethnic community formation were solely the product of deprivation, either economic or social, such a frontier perspective would suggest that in Milwaukee we would find not only rapid acceptance of the Germans and rapid economic advance, but also a weak and short-lived ethnic identity. However, a major shortcoming of such environmental interpretations is their failure to take into account cultural baggage—in this instance, such factors as the natural desires of both immigrant and native-born to associate with those who spoke their language and shared their values, the lesser familiarity of the Germans with the process of new settlement formation, distinct life styles and notions of authority—as well as those differences in capital and skills which constituted a more tangible estate.

The frontier status of Milwaukee, founded in 1836, only a few years before the massive German in-migration, was not irrelevent. We could anticipate, in fact, that the "unassigned" space of the new city, as well as its primitive social and economic organization, encouraged ethnic community formation on a territorial base; that the Germans, because of their numbers and the selectivity of their emigration, were able to take advantage of this situation to develop a particularly complete and independent ethnic community, which aided adjustment and economic integration while encouraging only gradual acculturation and minimal structural assimilation; and that other groups, lacking either their size or their particular selectivity, failed to develop similar communities but rather responded more immediately as individuals to the opportunity of the frontier city. While this model of the initial experience of Milwaukee's immigrants cannot be more exactly specified or more rigorously tested, measures of economic and occupational status for the city's population as well as more specific consideration of the experiences of individuals in various trades can be used to delimit the nature of the immigrants' economic integration. The measurement of residential clustering will help clarify the way in which associations, institutions, and political units generated both the cooperation and the conflict through which community goals and character evolved, while some consideration of immigrant backgrounds and family situations will help assess the nature of the immigration itself. Federal manuscript censuses, city directories, newspapers, and early city histories provide the main data for this analysis, which concentrates, as I have sought to emphasize, upon the immigrant community as a whole rather than upon the assimilation or mobility of its individual members.

The model I have sketched suggests that the Milwaukee German experience does not coincide neatly with the standard wisdom on immigrant accommodation and assimilation in nineteenth century America, which stresses the pitiable economic situation of the immigrant, his prejudiced exclusion from native society, his social and personal disorganization, and the pathological conditions of the central slums in which he dwelled, while also postulating his long-term rise in socio-economic status and movement out of the ghetto to ultimate assimilation into some kind of nonethnic society. This so-called ghetto process of immigrant assimilation, drawn largely from the experiences of immigrants in large industrialized cities and given almost poetic expression in Oscar Handlin's *The Uprooted*,[12] is now under attack from several directions. It is clear, for example, that the mixed residential pattern of earlier nineteenth century mercantile cities precluded ghetto formation, and that even when ghettos developed, they often contained such a mixture of nationalities and exhibited such rapid population turnover that complete isolation within a single culture was impossible. Critics have stressed the positive, healthy adjustment functions of ghetto institutions while questioning the necessarily pathological character of all slums. Finally, it is clear that America still remains an ethnically divided society, that the ghetto elevator has not functioned to fully assimilate all groups or individuals into a homogeneous single culture. Thus the incidence, the quality, and the functions of the ghetto have been questioned, and Sam Bass Warner, Jr., and Colin B. Burke have suggested that it is in fact only a "limited case" in the experience of urban immigrants.[13]

Rather than simply dismiss the notion of a ghetto altogether, however, or exclude from theoretical consideration instances where an ethnic group is able to concentrate in nonpathological conditions or where several groups share a neighborhood, it would seem more fruitful to treat these as varieties of accommodation which deserve systematic analysis and comparison. Thus, in the Milwaukee case, I am analyzing the accommodation process for a skilled and sizable immigrant group and for a city whose birth roughly coincided with the beginnings of mass immigration. Such a situation, I am hypothesizing, permitted the sort of spatial congregation and economic, political, and cultural participation which encouraged painless adjustment and good living conditions for many but which also encouraged the postponement of assimilation—in effect, a middle case between the ghetto model and its critics.

Milwaukee's reputation as a preeminently German city would make its early ethnic history worth exploring. In the recent concern over the relative merits of assimilationist versus pluralistic approaches to the history of immigrant groups in America,[14] the case of the Germans has received little specific consideration. Yet their numerical primacy, the lengthy duration of their migration, and the wide extent of their settlement patterns,[15] all suggest that the German experience should form a test of any model of immigrant accommodation. Despite, or perhaps because of, a well-laid foundation of early chronicles which culminated in the work of the generation of historians represented by Carl Wittke, John Hawgood, and Joseph Schafer, scholarship until recently has been content to rest with Wittke's interpretation of the German experience as a "normal fusion process" interrupted only be the shock of the First World War, or Hawgood's essentially contradictory view of a German retreat into the "tragedy" of unassimilated group life in reaction to antebellum nativism, ended only by the equally traumatic World War I period.[16] But as the "new" social and political historians have begun to explore more carefully such issues as social mobility, changing urban life and work styles, and the determinants of voting behavior, they have encountered the Germans time and again[17]—sufficiently often, in fact, to warrant studies that attempt to place the "German as worker" or the "German as voter" within a broader context involving the reexamination of the entire German immigrant experience.[18]

If a case study such as the present one is to contribute to the emergence of such a new synthesis, it is necessary to weigh the extent to which the Milwaukee situation was representative of conditions elsewhere. Antebellum Milwaukee's ethnic composition did, in fact, represent an extreme version of a pattern shared by other midwestern and western New York cities, characterized by generally low native and high German proportions in their populations (Figure 1). Milwaukee had a lower proportion of other foreign born (largely Irish) than most

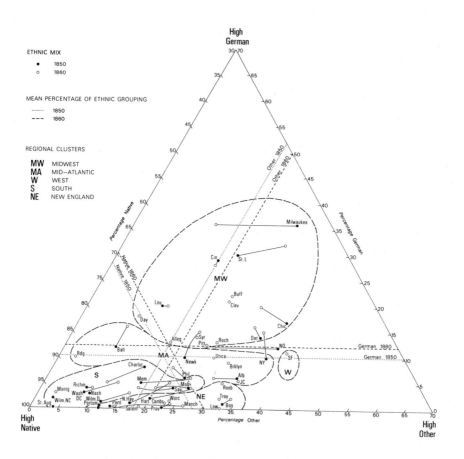

Figure 1   Ethnic composition of major American cities, 1850-1860

Source: J. D. B. DeBow, *Mortality Statistics of the Seventh Census of the United States 1850* (Washington, D.C.: A. O. P. Nicholson, 1855), 41; Joseph C. G. Kennedy, *Population of the United States in 1860* (Washington, D.C.: Government Printing Office, 1864), *xxxi, xxxii.*

of the other cities in its category by 1860, as well as a smaller native and larger German component. It was also the youngest of these mid-western cities, and one of the smallest, surpassing only Cleveland, Dayton, and Syracuse in size.[19] It may be that Milwaukee's distinctiveness in these respects will have the advantage of isolating processes of immigrant accommodation underway elsewhere in less evident form; full assessment of the place of the community prodded into being in Milwaukee by the Harbor Parade arrangements committee in the schema of immigrant and particularly German immigrant assimilation patterns, however, must wait for further comparative analyses of a variety of communities, institutions, and issues.

Milwauky Is All the Rage

1 Among the first Germans to arrive in Milwaukee was a nameless shoemaker, lured to the pioneer settlement from Chicago in 1836 by one of Milwaukee's founding fathers. As early legend has it, he was so frightened by the Indians he saw upon landing that he quickly returned south and advised his countrymen to avoid the new Wisconsin town if they valued their scalps.[1] But if any heard his advice, it had little effect in stemming the flow of foreign born into the bayside community in the ensuing months and years, a flow that was to make Milwaukee the most immigrant of antebellum American cities. The immigrants were drawn by the coincidence of the opportunities Milwaukee offered with their own backgrounds and aspirations, elements that constitute an essential point of departure for understanding the lives they created for themselves in Milwaukee.

Urban Foundations

"Milwaukee is a pleasant town, a very pleasant town," wrote Anthony Trollope in 1860; "Why it should be so, and why Detroit should be the contrary, I can hardly tell; only I think that the same verdict would be given by any English tourist." Trollope, in fact, was simply echoing a judgment passed many times by travelers, settlers, and local boosters in the quarter century following the precipitate departure of the nameless German shoemaker. Unlike Trollope, most of those who made any attempt to sort out their impressions gave due credit to Milwaukee's "charming situation on elevated ground, between Lake Michigan and Milwaukee River." "Its Lakefront rivals in Beauty that of Naples," gushed a local booster; its protected location near the center of a bay nearly seven miles wide and two and a quarter deep made it as admirable "for commercial purposes, as it is for beauty and salubrity."[2]

It was to the bay and especially to the rivers that Milwaukee owed its existence. Here, wave action over long centuries had breached the morainic ridge which kept the southward flowing Milwaukee River captive. Where the river escaped to meet Lake Michigan at the breach, longshore currents deposited a sandbar across the estuary, and the lagoon behind gradually filled and became swamp. Through it wound not only the Milwaukee but also the Menomonee and Kinnickinic rivers, with bluffs bounding the swamp along the watercourses (Figure 2).[3] The estuary provided one of the few safe havens for ships on the smooth western coast of Lake Michigan, and the rivers had long acted to channel inland trade to its shore. The area was a locus of Indian

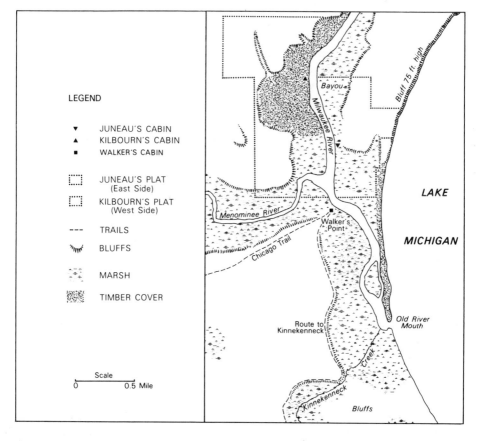

Figure 2   The site of Milwaukee. Based upon "Map of Milwaukee in 1826 as Recalled by Early Settlers," in Still, *Milwaukee*, 16.

settlement for hundreds of years before the arrival of its first white resident, a French fur trader, in the mid-1700s. By the early 1830s Milwaukee had become a flourishing trading post of the American Fur Company under the direction of Canadian named Solomon Juneau.[4]

When southeastern Wisconsin was opened to American settlement in 1833, after Indian land cessions following the Black Hawk War, land speculators filtering into the region soon noted the advantages of the Milwaukee area for harbor and millsite development. The peculiar topography of the site influenced its original development as three separate speculative ventures. A Green Bay land speculator, Morgan L. Martin, entered into partnership with Juneau to develop the area between the river and the lake as a townsite. The western bank of the river, with its direct access to the Wisconsin interior, attracted a Michigan assistant surveyor, Byron Kilbourn. The third developer was George H. Walker, a young Virginian, who established a trading post south of the river junctions to form the last of Milwaukee's triple nuclei. Though squatters flooded into the area, these three speculators were able to maintain title to their respective sections when the townsite lands were opened for sale by the federal government in July 1835. In the fall of that year they proceeded to file plats for the east and west side settlements, and their rivalry to attract settlers and trade was to exert a continuing influence on the settlement's growth.[5]

The new townsite grew quickly. As the Green Bay *Intelligencer and Democrat* reported in September 1835, "Land speculators are circumambulating it and Milwauky is all the rage." Many of the early pioneers soon moved on to other pastures, but permanent settlers mingled with the transients and speculators from the beginning. The frontier town's "unusually large number of bachelors" was leavened by a considerable number of women the following year, and Milwaukee's 1836 population of perhaps 700 reportedly included "a great company of 'solid men,' who, while they intended to make as much money as possible, were determined to make the place their home and throw their influence in behalf of its future prosperity."[6]

By fall, however, money began to grow scarce and business slowed down until the "financial revulsion" was unmistakeable the following spring. A settler arriving a July of 1837 later recalled that "I found Milwaukee with a population of about 1,000, the west side of the river mostly under water, many of the houses built on stilts, abandoned, and doors open, most of the population of 1836 having left the place by reason of the panic."[7] Milwaukee was experiencing the effects of the national financial panic and reaping the consequences of premature development in advance of its hinterland. New settlers were "few and far between," and Milwaukee could claim a population of only about 1,700 by 1840.[8] Recovery was well under way by 1842 or 1843, however, and rapid population growth characterized most of the remaining antebellum years, with the exception of additional periods of recession in the late forties and late fifties (Table 1).

This population surge was supported largely by the commercial functions of an entrepot city for one of the nation's fastest growing frontier regions. Even in its earliest years, the euphoria of land speculation had been mixed with the more prosaic yet profitable provisioning of the Wisconsin hinterland, and the post-1837 depression underlined the dependence of Milwaukee's business life on the continued immigration to Wisconsin which provided a market for its goods and services. As late as the immediate pre-Civil War period, some Milwaukee businessmen were still highly conscious of this dependency.[9] Manufactured goods were imported from the east and sold to city dwellers, farmers, and retailers throughout the state, while Milwaukee merchants in turn shipped the products of Wisconsin to eastern markets. Such urban functions created jobs in wholesaling, retailing, transportation, and finance. The need to house these businesses and the men whom they employed produced a heavy demand for labor in the construction trades, while various other craftsmen and persons employed in service industries could likewise make a good living meeting the needs of the "city-building" sector of the economy. The active canal, harbor improvement, and railroad campaigns of antebellum boosters attest to the continuing efforts to maintain and improve the city's commercial strength. In such a business climate, manufacturing played a relatively subsidiary role. In 1850, census-defined manufacturing activities occupied only 7.3 percent of the population and only 7.6 percent ten years later. Although Milwaukee accounted for about a quarter of all Wisconsin manufacturing during the years before the Civil War, it ranked only twenty-seventh among all American cities in manufacturing in 1860, at a time when it was the nation's twentieth city in size.[10]

As the settlement grew and prospered, it also acquired the political accoutrements of its urban status. Early petitions for incorporation as a single village, divided into three wards reflecting the three original settlements, were denied, but east and west side residents were able to

Table 1   Size and origins of Milwaukee's population, 1835-1860

Year	Total	Nativity	N	Percent of total	Percent of foreign born
1835	125				
1840	1,692				
1842	2,730				
1843	5,669				
1846	9,508				
1847	14,067				
1848	16,521	*Native*	*6,969*	*42.2*	-
		Foreign	*9,552*	*57.8*	-
		British	1,051	6.4	11.0
		Irish	2,487	15.1	26.0
		German	5,708	34.5	59.8
		Other	306	1.8	3.2
1850	20,061	*Native*	*7,181*	*36.0*	-
		Foreign	*12,782*	*64.0*	-
		British	1,457	7.3	11.4
		Irish	2,816	14.1	22.0
		German	7,271	36.4	56.9
		Other	1,238	6.2	9.7
1855	30,447	*Native*	10,812	35.5	-
		Foreign	19,635	64.5	-
1857	44,004	-	-	-	-
1860	45,246	*Native*	*22,398*	*49.5*	-
		Foreign	*22,848*	*50.5*	-
		British	1,640	3.6	7.2
		Irish	3,100	6.9	13.6
		German	15,981	35.3	69.9
		Other	2,127	4.7	9.3

Sources: James S. Buck, *Pioneer History of Milwaukee* (Milwaukee: Swain & Tate, 1890) I, 159, 69-70, 81-84; 1840 federal ms. census schedules; 1842 territorial ms. census schedules; Rudolf P. Koss, *Milwaukee* (Milwaukee: Herold, 1871), 143; 1846 territorial ms. census schedules; 1847 territorial ms. census schedules; school census, cited in James S. Buck, *Milwaukee under the Charter* (Milwaukee: Symes, Swain & Co., 1884) III, 198; J. D. B. DeBow, *The Seventh Census of the United States: 1850* (Washington: Robert Armstrong, 1853), 922; *Annual Report of the Secretary of The State of The State of Wisconsin for the Year 1855* (Madison, 1856), 71; school census, cited in Buck, *Milwaukee under the Charter* (1886), IV, 240; Joseph C. G. Kennedy, *Population of the United States in 1860* (Washington, D. C.: Government Printing Office, 1864), 538-539.

organize separate governments in 1837 under a Wisconsin general act for the incorporation of towns. The initial division thus created was to endure as an important factor in Milwaukee politics and government. Even after the two towns were united in 1839 (Walker's Point was finally added in 1845), the trustees of each ward retained a great degree of autonomy and power, particularly with regard to the levying and spending of revenue collected within the wards, the proceeds of which were largely devoted to street improvements.[11]

Sectionalism was therefore an important factor in weakening village government, and in an attempt to remedy the situation a new charter was requested, which became law on January 31, 1846. The charter created a city of five wards nearly eight square miles in area but retained the ward fiscal autonomy which had vitiated village government. In consequence, a system of government would in time develop in which the local committees of alderman rather than the council as a whole became the controlling financial power.[12]

The Peopling of Milwaukee

The inhabitants of the new settlement were a diverse lot almost from the beginning. The original French-speaking settlers and Yankee pioneers were soon joined by British adventurers, Irish navvies, would-be farmers from the states of the German Confederation. By 1848, when the first figures on ethnic background became available, immigrants constituted over half of Milwaukee's residents, increasing to almost two thirds of the 20,000-odd population two years later (Table 1). Despite the inflation of the native proportion of the city's 1860 population by the inclusion of American-born children of immigrant parents, the continued growth of the immigrant presence in Milwaukee is evident from a sample of adult heads of household in the federal census manuscript schedules (Table 2).[13]

Throughout the antebellum period, the Germans were the predominant but by no means the only major immigrant group. It is impossible to detail the arrival of Milwaukee's immigrants before 1848. A search for names of obvious foreign origin in the 1840 federal manuscript census schedule yielded 22 which appeared Irish, 32 German. If it can be assumed that those living in such households generally shared the ethnic background of the heads, then a minimal 6.5 percent of Mil-

Table 2   Origins of sample heads of household (percentage of total population)

Year	N	Native	Foreign	British	Irish	German	Other
1850	1,020	22	78	10	19	41	8
1860	2,266	16	84	6	16	52	10

waukee's population was Irish, slightly over 7 percent German. This crude estimate undoubtedly understates the size of the Irish population particularly but has some value in suggesting the relatively low visibility of the Germans in 1840, as well as the comparatively early arrival of the Irish.[14]

This becomes evident when the 1840 estimates are compared with the ethnic distribution of the city's population in the three later antebellum census years for which detailed data are available. The Germans throughout the period remained the most numerous among the foreign born, followed by the Irish, the British, and other nationalities (largely Dutch, Canadians, Scandinavians, and other western and central Europeans). The Irish contributed their maximum proportion to the city's population in 1848, the British and other groups reached proportionate peaks in 1850, while the Germans continued to increase their predominance to 1860. Between 1848 and 1850 the foreign-born population increased at a faster rate than the total population. Among the foreign born, the most rapidly increasing segment was the British, while Irish population growth was already leveling off. In the decade between 1850 and 1860, the British joined the Irish in a considerably reduced growth rate, while migrants from German-speaking areas and other European states continued to arrive in Milwaukee at relatively high rates throughout the 1850s.

Contemporary accounts and later memoirs flesh out the statistical skeleton of Milwaukee's peopling. The earliest years of the city's history belonged indisputably to the native born. Those who flocked to Milwaukee in the late 1830s and early 1840s came in great part from New York and New England. For example, among the Americans in a group of 214 biographical subjects in a late nineteenth century local history who had migrated to Milwaukee before 1860, 40 percent were born in New England, 46 percent in New York. The proportions were roughly similar if only those arriving during the years of native dominance before 1845 are considered: 45 and 52 percent respectively.[15] The heads of household samples from 1850 and 1860 federal censuses confirm this pattern. In 1850, 36 percent of the American-born household heads were New England natives, a percentage which dropped to 32 percent in 1860, while the 45 percent representation of New York-born household heads in 1850 increased to 49 percent ten years later. Thus the native born settlers of early Milwaukee were not a random mix of Americans, but were, in the words of the city's biographer, "New York and New England, once, twice, or thrice removed."[16] From all indications, Milwaukee remained an essentially "Yankee-Yorker" village with a leavening of Irish and British until some time in the mid-forties.

Nevertheless, the German contingent which would displace the dominant Americans at least numerically could trace its roots back to the earliest period of settlement. There are several candidates for the title of "first German to settle in Milwaukee in 1835," including the contemporary nominee, Johann Jakob Meyer, a baker from Oldenburg; a certain Wilhelm Strothmann, who walked up from Chicago and was so delighted with his reception that he settled on a government grant in nearby Greenfield; and Henry Bleyer, a Hanoverian wood turner who left his family in its Detroit home while he established himself in Milwaukee. Many of those who contributed to the "quite noticeable" influx of Germans in the following year reportedly were young bachelors who came to look over the settlement and claim land before leaving either temporarily or permanently, but others remained to form the tiny nucleus of a German community. Most of these had previously settled elsewhere in America, as was to be expected of immigrants in a new and little known interior settlement; most were reputedly artisans, farmers, or farm laborers in origin, as were those who followed in the next few years. Their ranks numbered such later pillars of the community as Eduard Wiesner, a shoemaker, and his wife, who had first settled in Chicago, and George Abert, then nineteen, who after five years on his own in America found a place as Kilbourn's right-hand man in laying out the new settlement.[17]

One of the more colorful of the 1837 arrivals was Christian Schwartz, a Saarbrücken carpenter who was to change his name to the more aristocratic Schwartzburg and become a perennial dissenter in the German community; another was the almost legendary Matthias Stein. Stein, born in Saxony in 1807 or 1808 and trained as a carpenter, had emigrated in 1831, first to Baltimore and a year later to Washington, D.C. There he worked as an instrument maker for three years and, as he told it, made the acquaintance of President Andrew Jackson through a mutual penchant for early morning exercise. He then moved west, sampling St. Louis before coming to Milwaukee. He had no intention of remaining but when boiler trouble delayed his boat, Juneau talked him into settling, and he became the archetypal pioneer in the eyes of later German settlers.[18]

Figurative battalions began to tread on the heels of such single spies by 1839. About a hundred German families arrived in early summer, for example, reportedly with "bags of gold some of them having $20,000 and upwards." By the following summer, Germans were arriving "in droves—sometimes 200 to 300 in one week," and the volume had so increased by 1843 that a local commentator could note that "the public houses and streets are filled with new comers, and our old citizens are almost strangers in their own town." However, few of the newcomers remained in the city. "The final location of a vast majority is settled upon before they arrive here by the forerunners who have been sent on for the purpose. A vessel load lands and in a few hours their effects are loaded upon wagons, and the whole are moving for the interior."[19]

The growth of Milwaukee's German population thus can be viewed best as a byproduct of the great influx to the farming frontier which was channeled through the city until railroads enabled settlers to bypass the lake port. A farm of one's own was the goal, and those who remained behind in the early years tended to be in large part craftsmen, manual laborers, tradesmen, occasional professionals—men who were unsuited to farming or who lacked the means to buy land. Many first tried farming and then moved back to the city, many others planned to work in Milwaukee only as long as it would take to earn the purchase price of a farm but in the end remained.[20]

Such was the small group of Old Lutherans who arrived in 1839, religious dissenters from Mecklenburg, Pommerania, and other parts of Prussia. When the Prussian king in 1817 had ordered a union of Protestant churches, some Lutherans refused to accede, and by the late 1830s several such groups decided to pool their resources and emigrate in the face of government threats. Of the thousand or so Old Lutheran emigrants—in the main petty craftsmen and rural day laborers of little means—about half settled near Buffalo; the remainder passed through Milwaukee on their way to rural areas to the north. Some twenty families, most penniless, since their funds had been donated to the common

purse, remained behind in Milwaukee to form a tight-knit contrast to
the other pioneer Germans, most of whom reportedly were Catholics
from the south German states. Some members of other groups of Old
Lutherans who fled to Wisconsin in 1843 and 1845 also remained in
Milwaukee to augment the small settlement.[21]

The middle years of the 1840s brought a certain change in the character of the German immigration as well as an increase in its size. Quite a
number of men who would later become prominent in the city's affairs
began arriving as early as 1841 so that by mid-decade, as one who
arrived in 1844 later recalled, "The entire physiognomy of the German
population changed. Men of enterprise began to arrive."[22] The revolutions of 1848 in Europe, however, were generally given credit for stimulating the major recasting of the population:

> The most important epoch in the history of Milwaukee's German population
> was the revolution in Europe in 1848 . . . When the revolution was suppressed
> a flood of immigrants from all parts of the German empire, from Austria and
> other German countries began, and quite a number of highly cultivated men
> drifted to Milwaukee.[23]

While there were settlers of the earlier period with comparable backgrounds and motives for emigration, Milwaukee attracted a significant
group of political refugees in the late 1840s and early 1850s.

Despite the arrival of the advance guard of political refugees, however, 1848 and the years immediately after were a period of reduced
German in-migration. The deluge came in the first half of the 1850s.
Declining numbers were beginning to be noted again in 1856, but it was
a general opinion that the continued German immigration of the decade
postponed the effects of the depression of the later 1850s in Milwaukee,
when "there were more 'Kronen,' 'Gulder,' and 'Kreuzer' in circulation
than American money."[24] Contemporary impressionistic evidence thus
points to the early years of the 1840s as the crucial turning point in the
German settlement of Milwaukee, followed by generally high in-migration rates thereafter, with downturns at the ends of both prewar
decades and a peak in the first half of the 1850s.

The arrival of Milwaukee's Irish settlers was less heralded. Given the
absence of evidence for further growth in the original French-speaking
settlement, the establishment of Milwaukee's first Roman Catholic
church in 1839, with its services in English, suggests the early presence

of a sizable Irish population. While the 1840 census yielded an estimate of only 22 Irish household heads, with a total of 112 persons in the households they headed, a local historian's listing of the arrival of noted members of the early Irish community found that 33 of the 59 mentioned were already present by 1840. According to Henry Bleyer, historian of the Milwaukee Old Settlers' Club, many Irish arrived between 1839 and 1841 after cotton mills in Fall River, Massachusetts, failed in the 1837 panic. When a German observer in 1843 estimated that about 400 Irishmen were eligible to vote, he was doubtless indulging in exaggeration, but his estimate nevertheless suggests the visibility of the Irish in Milwaukee at that time.[25] Thus, although little specific information is available, a core group of Irish in Milwaukee clearly was established well before the 1845 famine in Ireland.

Remaining immigrant groups are equally difficult to trace (Table 3). The largest groups in 1850 were the British, Canadians, Dutch, French,

Table 3   British and other immigrant groups in 1850 and 1860 samples

Origin of head of household	1850		1860	
	N	Percent of sample	N	Percent of sample
England	77	7.5	103	4.5
Scotland	23	2.2	32	1.4
Wales	2	0.2	12	0.5
Canada	17	1.7	19	0.8
Netherlands	18	1.8	45	2.0
France	14	1.4	14	0.6
Norway	8	0.8	27	1.2
Switzerland	7	0.7	20	0.9
Austria	2	0.2	31	1.4
Bohemia	6	0.6	38	1.7
Denmark	5	0.5	4	0.2
Sweden	-	-	4	0.2
Poland	1	0.1	3	0.1
Belgium	2	0.2	1	-
Hungary	-	-	5	0.2
Luxembourg	1	0.1	2	-
Portugal	-	-	1	-
Russia	-	-	4	0.2
Unknown	4	0.4	1	-

Norwegians, and Swiss. By 1860 the Dutch, Norwegians, and Swiss had increased their representation; the Austrians and Bohemians also became more important, but the British, Canadians, and French declined proportionately, the latter absolutely as well. Biographical information makes it clear that both Scots and Englishmen were among Milwaukee's earliest settlers and suggests a fairly steady but unspectacular flow into the city thereafter.[26] The Norwegian settlement appears to have grown slowly from 1838, when the first Norwegians in Wisconsin passed through Milwaukee on their way to Muskego, and various records indicate a scattering of Scandinavians throughout the city by 1847, many of them engaged in seafaring activities.[27] Thanks to the memoirs of an early Dutch settler, the beginnings of the settlement from the Netherlands can be dated to 1846.[28] Austrian and Bohemian settlement undoubtedly responded to the same forces stimulating general German immigration during the 1850s and followed a similar rhythm; many of the French also had German names and indicated Alsatian origins. The lessening Canadian proportion is owing to the gradually declining importance of the original fur traders and their families, as well as to the same factors which lessened the importance of native in-migrants.

A final word is in order about one population element not yet considered, the Negroes. The first black settler arrived in 1835, a cook on a lake schooner who was employed for a time by Juneau. Milwaukee's early black historian, William T. Green, estimated that about twenty Negro families lived in Milwaukee in 1845, most having arrived since 1840.[29] By 1850 there were still only 23 households headed by blacks or mulattoes (although a few of these households contained more than one family), and only 25 such households ten years later. Total black and mulatto population in 1850 amounted to 89 persons, and in 1860 to 92.[30] Thus Negroes played a comparatively minor role in antebellum Milwaukee, but were at least present in sufficient force to add a racial dimension to Milwaukee's ethnic mixture.[31]

Such then was the composition of Milwaukee's population during its first quarter century. First a "Yankee-Yorker" village with a small and picturesque French-Canadian element, it acquired a sizable Irish population within a few years of its founding. Rising numbers of native migrants were joined by English and Scots in the early 1840s, while the seeds of the German community, planted at the same time, bore fruit especially after the middle of the decade. During the 1850s the Germans were Milwaukee's dominant ethnic group. In the same decade, the Dutch created their own settlement, and small numbers of central Europeans were harbingers of changes to come.

The Push from Europe

The timing and volume of Milwaukee's foreign born settlement depended, of course, not only on conditions in Milwaukee itself, but on the European circumstances which induced emigration. Those circumstances, in turn, influenced the kinds of persons who ultimately chose to make a home for themselves in Milwaukee, and the sorts of intangible baggage which they brought with them. Their training and skills, their reasons for leaving and the knowledge and dreams that shaped their attitudes toward the new homes they hoped to create, all were to condition their reactions to life in Milwaukee. Ideally, each immigrant's cultural baggage should be individually assessed, yet few of Milwaukee's early residents bequeathed much information to a later generation. Scraps of biographical reminiscence and scattered letters provide clues that can be generalized with a certain amount of trepidation. In the main, however, it is necessary to rely upon broader descriptions of the motives and processes of mid-nineteenth century emigration in order to illuminate not only the pace of Milwaukee's peopling but the backgrounds and attitudes with which Milwaukee's newcomers approached their uprooting and replanting.

The city's founding coincided with the beginnings of large-scale European immigration, particularly from Ireland and Germany, which continued, with significant fluctuations, through the following decades (Table 4). Milwaukee received a disproportionately large share of the German immigration and a correspondingly smaller share of that from Great Britain and Ireland. The explanation lies both in the character of the emigrations and the pull of Milwaukee.

The wave of migration whose flow peopled Milwaukee was, in the words of Brinley Thomas, "essentially a Malthusian evacuation," in which severe rural crisis and the pressures of impending industrialization brought rising population pressures to a head in Europe and ejected "surplus" population overseas. By the 1830s and 1840s improvements in transportation and communication made the prospect of mass emigration to America possible. Popular education, and the spread of newspapers, books, and postal services brought word of American

Table 4 European immigration to the United States by decades

	Total	Great Britain		Ireland		Germany	
		N	Percent	N	Percent	N	Percent
1820-29	99,291	26,336	26.5	51,617	51.9	5,753	5.8
1830-39	422,779	74,350	17.6	170,672	40.4	124,726	29.5
1840-49	1,369,304	218,562	15.9	656,145	47.9	385,434	28.2
1850-59	2,619,774	545,322	20.8	1,129,486	43.1	976,072	37.3

Source: United States Bureau of the Census, *Historical Statistics of the United States: Colonial Times to 1957* (Washington, D. C.: Government Printing Office, 1960), 57.

opportunities to the smallest peasant communities. Cheap ocean transport, a byproduct of the growing Atlantic commerce in which immigrants provided a profitable ballast on the westbound voyage for vessels carrying raw materials to Europe, made emigration economically feasible. On the other side of the ocean lay a developing nation which needed and, with the exception of certain periods of economic recession, seemed able to absorb unlimited numbers of those who saw no opportunity for themselves in Europe. And finally, the political revolutions which periodically convulsed Europe may well have made Europeans more familiar with the notion of opportunity, of change; when the desire, once aroused, was thwarted, many were all the more willing to seek a good life abroad.[32] Most of those who arrived in Milwaukee in the years before 1860 probably left their homes at a point when economic changes were breaking up the old community forms of life and making mobility desirable, yet before those changes had proceeded to the point of providing sufficient alternative opportunities in their homelands.

Such pressures were particularly severe in Ireland, whose cultural evolution had produced an agricultural system of absentee landlords, small farmers with insecure tenure and high rent, and a large number of landless cotters who rented barely enough land to grow the potatoes which kept them and their families alive. Population growth ultimately threatened the collapse of the whole system, but the more immediate scourge by the 1820s was the farm consolidation which followed the entrance of Irish agriculture into the British market, stimulated by legislation in the following decades. As Irish agriculture groped its way toward rationalization, numerous farmers and farmers' sons saw in emigration a way to exchange a whole catalog of evils—exorbitant rents, insecure tenure, competition from cotters, agrarian unrest, the unprofitability of farming on the Irish scale, outright redundancy—for ownership of their own farms in the American west. These farmers, mainly from Ulster where custom gave them the means to finance their trip through the sale of their improvements, were joined by artisans and other city folk attracted by the opportunity of America or displaced by changes in craft industries.[33]

As emigration continued, however, it created an impetus of its own. Older emigrants sent back news of conditions in America with remittances for passage, and greater traffic brought lower fares. The emigration contagion increasingly affected the peasants for whom eviction often became the prelude to departure. The shift in source of migrants was signified in changes in advertisements for shipping lines, which began to stress America's need for labor rather than its free land. The change also meant that Ulster lost its predominance as emigrant supplier, and with the shift of emigration to the south by the early 1840s, the Catholic proportion among Irish emigrants increased. The way was thus prepared for the great exodus stimulated by the potato famine, when one and a third million Irish left the country in the eight years following 1848. The total economic dislocation resulting from successive crop failures led to enormous increases in evictions, and for those evicted, there remained unreasoned flight in the hundreds of ships which brought grain to Ireland from America, flight financed perhaps by relatives in America, by savings and sale of what little they had, by landlords relieved at their departure. Emigration continued even after famine abated, declining during the depression of the late 1850s in the United States but becoming "an accepted fact of life" for those with no future in Ireland and increasingly numerous relatives beckoning across the sea.[34]

Milwaukee undoubtedly received a share of the earlier, less desperate Irish emigration. John Furlong of Cork, for example, was the son of an educated gentleman-farmer of considerable means who had lost his money in the post-Napoleonic agricultural crisis. The father brought his family to Quebec in 1821, where they farmed a large tract of land. John, in turn, moved from Quebec to a farm near Detroit in 1832 and then to infant Milwaukee four years later. The Riggs family, who arrived in Milwaukee in 1843, had emigrated from the north of Ireland in 1831 to a farm in western Ontario. Men of such origins, however, had the best chance of making their mark in Milwaukee and the relatively few biographies of Irishmen in the local histories bear mute witness to the background more typical of the majority of Milwaukee's Irish. The outlines of Patrick Duffy's story were perhaps representative. His father died in Ireland in 1848 at the age of 45, his mother a year later in Canada following a post-famine emigration. Patrick himself must have emigrated with her; he settled in Boston the year of her death and came to Milwaukee four years later as a 22-year-old shoemaker.[35]

Because a census taker for Milwaukee's fourth ward in 1860 exceeded instructions by noting exact birthplaces, his returns suggest the origins of Milwaukee's Irish population. Of the 749 persons of Irish birth in his ward, 41 percent came from the old province of Munster, 24 percent from Leinster, 15 percent from Connaught, and only 11 percent from Ulster, which had provided the majority of the pre-1836 emigration. The counties which contributed the largest numbers formed a contiguous block of seven counties in southern Ireland, providing 57 percent of Milwaukee's fourth ward Irish population (Figure 3). The fourth ward Irish may not have been representative of their countrymen in Milwaukee, but their origins suggest that most of Milwaukee's Irish by 1860 were probably Roman Catholic and products of lower-class agrarian flight.[36]

British immigration to the United States before 1860, by contrast, included a significant proportion of skilled industrial workmen, although the majority were farmers and agricultural laborers attracted by the availability of American land. For the small farmer or the ambitious farm laborer, particularly in the more isolated areas of Britain where local alternatives were less evident than elsewhere, emigration was a way to avoid facing an inexorably changing British economy which had little place for small scale agriculture; for the skilled workman, America offered the lure of good wages, particularly in the periods of cyclical unemployment which characterized the early phases of industrialization. The poorest stayed behind while those with much to lose and much to gain fueled the steady emigration which reached antebellum peaks during periods of recession and crop failure, particularly in the early and late 1830s and at midcentury. Lowland Scots and the Welsh were influenced by the same fear of a poor agricultural future, while in the Highlands the process of land consolidation which had been producing impoverished emigrants for a century continued.[37]

The British who left biographies in Milwaukee were generally not of

Percent of 4th Ward Irish

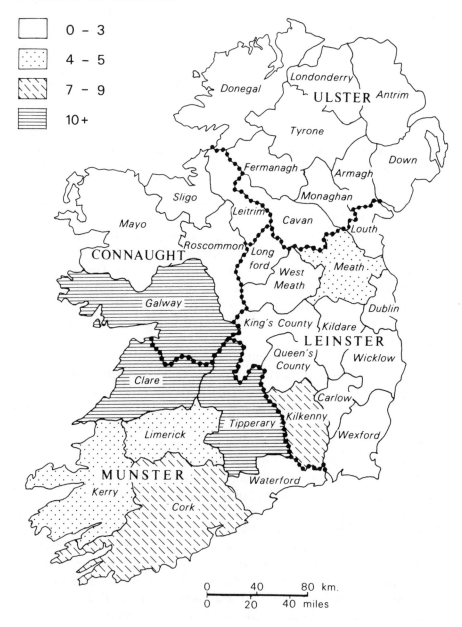

Figure 3   Origins of Milwaukee's fourth ward Irish, 1860

farming backgrounds. They were commonly young men who had left home after completing apprenticeships. Of sixteen for whom more than minimal biographical information was found, nine were Scots, two were Welsh. Six had completed a craft apprenticeship and three had legal or mercantile training; two had owned their own firms, two were the sons of gentlemen and educated as such. A strictly rural background was evidenced by only three, one who came of "sturdy yeoman stock," another of a family of "limited means" anxious to farm in America and the third an orphaned Welsh farm laborer. A growing city like Milwaukee drew a good portion of those with skilled backgrounds, and they could be expected to succeed there. Despite their backgrounds, however, at least six of these men had tried farming in America before settling in the city.[38]

In the broadest sense, the promise of a better material future in America was their lure. A Scot reported that he was "inspired by the financial opportunities of America," an Englishman "having only limited means, decided to seek his fortune in the United States." Two young Scots, more fortunate than their compatriots, were brought over directly to work in a Milwaukee bank. Many more personal reasons undoubtedly influenced decisions as well, as in the case of the young man who came not only "to better his financial condition" but to "indulge his liking for field sports with gun and rod, which were legally restricted in England" or the Englishman who was able to fulfill in America the religious vocation thwarted by his father's "temporary estrangement" from his local church.[39] These are the types of motive one could expect that those who proved successful would later recall; nevertheless they suggest that Milwaukee's British representation was in many ways undoubtedly reflecting wider trends.

The motives expressed by German settlers, as could be anticipated for a larger group, were more varied in their reflection of the complex forces which led to the massive German immigration of the antebellum period. "Germany" in the mid-nineteenth century was a term applied to some three dozen loosely allied states, not all of which were experiencing the same social changes at the same pace. The states of southwestern Germany—Rhenish Prussia, the Rhenish Palatinate, Bavaria, Baden, and Württemberg—were the first centers of German emigration. Much of the area was characterized by a dense population of freehold farmers with extremely fragmented holdings, the result of generations of division among heirs. In such a situation, poor harvests created an acute crisis for both the farmers and the small shopkeepers and artisans dependent upon them. The area had good transportation connections and an eighteenth century history of emigration. Thus, when crops failed in 1816, the "year without a summer," thousands poured out to America, pioneering the nineteenth century German emigration. While the tide of emigration quickly receded, it turned again in the early 1830s and gathered momentum in the wake of economic and social change, spreading north and east from the core area in overpopulated southwestern Germany to neighboring Hesse-Darmstadt and Hesse-Kassel, as well as to Franconia, Westphalia, Hanover, and Oldenburg. Of those who left many were still small farmers with their families; others were home manufacturers and artisans suffering from factory competition and the decline of the old lifestyle of the guilds. Like their British fellows, the German emigrants of these years were persons with something left to lose, as well as skills or property which could be converted to cash to salvage their future overseas.[40] As a Stuttgart observer commented in 1846, "Those who have nothing are stuck too deeply to be able to leave, but heads of families with several thousand Gulden worth of property are afraid that even this will have to be broken up, leaving their children beggars, if they remain any longer."[41]

By the mid-forties, however, the spread of the potato rot and resulting local famine conditions, combined with the economic depression of the following years, meant that many of the emigrants came from lower classes than formerly and from parts of central Germany previously untouched by the emigration fever. The 1848 revolutions apparently had little direct effect on emigration. Their imminence may have induced some conservatives to leave and delayed the departure of some liberals; their success did make emigration legally more simple; their failure to "make everything right" may have been a factor in the decisions of many. After a peak in 1847, volume sank again until 1851, probably for economic reasons: the famine was over and the preceding heavy emigration made land difficult to sell while encouraging higher wages. Harvests, however, were poor between 1850 and 1853, and between 1852 and 1854 over half a million Germans emigrated. The majority were, as before, southwestern Germans of the lower middle and peasant classes, but new momentum came from such areas as Saxony, the Thuringian states, Brunswick, Hanover, Schleswig-Holstein, Pommerania, Posen, and especially Mecklenburg, areas where agricultural reorganization in a period of increasing population set adrift poor, usually unmarried, day laborers or apprentices, who took far less money with them than previous emigrants.[42] In 1854 a Wisconsin agent in Bremen noted of Germans that the United States "has been 'opened' to them and there are but a few families in Germany who have no relatives in America."[43] By the following year, however, the American economic recession triggered an abrupt decrease in emigration, which was not to resume again until after the American Civil War.

The composition of Milwaukee's German population generally reflected the broader patterns of German emigration. The arrival in 1839 of the Old Lutherans from northern Germany has already been noted; otherwise, most of the early pioneers reportedly came from Rhenish Prussia, Bavaria (especially its western regions), Baden, and Saxony; most were Roman Catholics.[44] Census returns for some wards in 1850 provide the earliest statistical estimate of the origins of Milwaukee's Germans (Table 5 and Figure 4).[45] Prussia provided by far the

Table 5 Birthplaces of sample German heads of household (by number with identified birthplaces and percent of total number with identified birthplaces in census year)

	1850		1860	
State	N	Percent	N	Percent
Prussia	91	45.2	294	31.1
Bavaria	35	17.4	144	15.2
Hesse-Darmstadt	17	8.5	69	7.3
Saxony	12	6.0	71	7.5
Hanover	11	5.5	42	4.4
Württemberg	8	4.0	36	3.8
Baden	7	3.5	41	4.3
Mecklenburg	3	1.5	120	12.7
Hesse-Kassel	3	1.5	12	1.3
Saxe-Weimar	3	1.5	2	0.2
Pommerania[a]	-	-	48	5.1
Schleswig-Holstein[a]	- -	-	7	0.7
Other	11	5.5	59	6.2
Total	201		945	
Germany (unspecified)	213		233	
	414		1,178	

[a]Category coded for 1860 only.

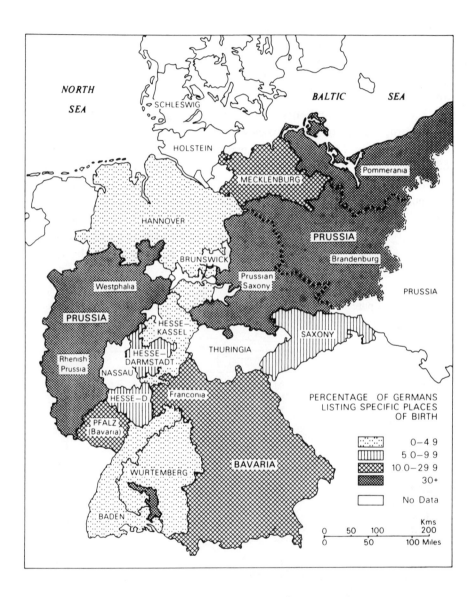

Figure 4   Origins of Milwaukee's Germans, 1860

greatest number of emigrants, although the census unfortunately did not differentiate between the major districts of Prussia. Bavaria sent the second greatest number to Milwaukee, followed by Saxony, Hanover, and Hesse-Darmstadt. Ten years later, similar statistics suggest the continued dominance of these two groups, although they declined relatively in the face of a strong increase of Mecklenburgers. Because Mecklenburgers were concentrated in the areas of Milwaukee added to the city after 1850, they probably represent the post-1850 Mecklenburg emigration. The census figures suggest that Milwaukee perhaps received fewer persons from extreme southwestern Germany than expected, although in the absence of comprehensive statistics from either Germany or the United States this cannot be estimated accurately. The sources of Milwaukee's German immigration suggest that the city drew most heavily from those areas whose emigrants included not only farmers but artisans, the kinds of persons whom a city like Milwaukee would attract, of lower middle class backgrounds. However, the strong Mecklenburg representation also suggests that during the 1850s Milwaukee's German newcomers may have included a good share of the relatively less well-endowed rural migrants of that period.

The only specific information on pre-migration careers of Milwaukee's German residents comes from biographical information about those who did well in Milwaukee. Among a group of about 90 such biographical subjects who recorded pre-immigration backgrounds in sufficient detail to permit generalization, over two fifths had been apprenticed as artisans, over a third had university or professional backgrounds, around 13 percent had mercantile training, and only 7 percent indicated a farming background. German origins of the 105 indicating birthplace were likewise somewhat skewed: 31 percent (including 7 percent who specified Rhenish Prussia and 5 percent from Westphalia) were Prussians, 17 percent were Bavarians, almost 10 percent Hanoverians, 8 percent from Hesse-Darmstadt, and 6 percent from Württemberg, with no other state contributing as much as 5 percent; there were no Mecklenburgers in the group.

The predominance of economic factors among their recorded motives for emigration suggests the extent to which at least this elite group of Milwaukeeans had responded to the changing nature of opportunity in Germany. For Jacob Best and his four sons, for example, the move from Rhineland to Milwaukee represented a deliberate relocation of the family brewery from a depressed agricultural region to a new area where better profits to support the rising generation could be anticipated. For Gottlob Bossert, emigration provided an alternative when his uncle refused to retire and vacate a place for him in the family mercantile firm. Few others left such specific explanations of why they decided to try their fortune in America, to find advancement in the land of opportunity where they could begin a business, do better, or earn a better living, but the facts that at least eight clearly emigrated upon completion of apprenticeship or their journeyman's *Wanderjahre*, or other training, eight after completing their academic education, four at marriage, and two each following completion of military service and family deaths suggest the close association of emigration with the assessment of future chances made at a normal period of life cycle change.[46]

The very youth of most upon emigration—over a quarter ($N=118$) were in their late teens, almost two thirds in their twenties, and only three over 40—suggests the spirit of adventure that often accompanied economic calculation, as in the case of the young man who desired "to make a change to better his condition, or at least to see more of the world."[47] The pull for many was intensified by friends or relatives already in America, whom they wished to join or who had sent back glowing reports. For two at least, emigration was also a means of avoiding military service.

Milwaukeeans also emigrated for political motives—ten directly stated that they were political refugees, and a half dozen others implied that the contrast between the German and American political situations was the reason for their flight. They included not only such prominent refugees as Hans Balatka, Peter Engelmann, and Mathilde and Fritz Anneke, but also young men perhaps peripherally drawn into the revolutions who responded as much to the pull of American opportunity as to the push of German repression—men like Pius Dreher, a young butcher who returned from republican Switzerland to fight in the revolutionary army of his native Württemberg and after release from Prussian captivity emigrated again, this time to America, or like William Frankfurth, whose revolutionary ardor so irritated the uncle for whom he clerked that he decided to make his own way in America. There were doubtless many like Frankfurth for whom the years of revolution and reaction catalyzed long-standing disquiet about the future of German society. John Kerler, for one, had spent a good part of his life making a

sufficient fortune to sell his brewery and retire to the gentlemanly existence that would qualify him for a magistrate's position; yet when the
time came, society had so changed that he was unable to enjoy his
hard-won honors, and the "unpleasant occurrences" of the revolutionary year led him to seek a quieter life in America. His future
son-in-law, August Frank, also saw emigration as both a way to escape
the "unbearable political situation of 1848 and the social ills" as well as
a way to satisfy his "vague urge for improvement of the present
condition."[48]

To an aspiring Austrian clerk, the revolutions "suggested the desira-
bility of carrying out forthwith a plan long entertained" and a young
doctor made his decision partly because of the "repressions of the
regime," partly owing to "heavy family misfortunes." Similarly mixed,
undoubtedly, were the motives of the Rhenish-Prussian farmer who in
1847 "having tired of the oppression and misrule of some Government
subordinates" decided to emigrate; it is difficult to guess whether he
was demanding liberty or, more likely, objecting to high taxes or a
personal vendetta. It has to be remembered, as well, that emphasis on
political motives for emigration was a response to the mythology of life
in a democratic society, often after the fact. More than one so-called
forty-eighter may have been similar to Charles Quentin, a high-placed
Prussian official whose biography noted that he left during the post-
revolutionary reaction when "his sense of independence induced him to
quit the Prussian service" but to whom a contemporary evidently
referred when he discussed the Prussian official "who was motivated to
move to America not because of politics nor because of love of the
wilderness nor from any weariness of Europe, but from the much more
real passion for the dollar"—for a rate of return of 25 cents on the
dollar, in fact.[49]

The available evidence thus suggests that a desire to improve one's
lot in life, often showing itself at a time when a young man was
required in any case to look around and make certain decisions about
his future, induced many of Milwaukee's later German business and
professional leaders to emigrate. Discontent with the German political
situation, love of adventure, and the attraction of American institutions, were sometimes other factors; but it seems clear that for most,
emigration was undertaken to achieve a better life than the one possible
in Germany.

The Pull of Milwaukee

To explain why the emigrants left Europe, however, is not to clarify what drew them to Milwaukee. The great majority of German immigrants, particularly, came to America in search of land. Thus the Milwaukee German settlement was in many respects a consequence of the greater migration to the Wisconsin farmlands, and the attraction of the former was, to the Germans, largely defined by the latter.[50] Milwaukee benefited from historical accident, in that its founding and the opening of Wisconsin to settlers coincided with the major flow of German emigration. It was "all the rage" at a time when Germans followed the fashion in frontier settlement. "Such an area suddenly gets a reputation, everybody talks about it, they all flood there, until it is all explored and the best lands have been sold," noted a German observer in 1847. "For the past three years it has been Texas, Iowa, and Wisconsin that have drawn the immigrants."[51] Immigrants hoping to earn funds to buy their own farms, those who tried farming and failed, those who saw opportunity for themselves in providing urban services for their farming compatriots, those who realized, instinctively perhaps, that a booming urban frontier provided opportunity in conjunction with the expansion of the agricultural frontier, all would gravitate to Milwaukee, the entrepot of one of the latest areas to experience a land boom.

The German movement to Milwaukee benefited as well from the orientation of transportation routes. For immigrants who wished to settle in the West but had no particular destination in mind, readily available transportation helped channel their journeys. "The main roads to the West are thickly bordered with Germans," Franz Löher observed, "since our immigrant must check his journey wherever the boat captain suddenly demands money for the river or lake trip."[52] Milwaukee in the 1840s and 1850s was one of the end points on the northern route that led west from New York, and as that port increasingly dominated in terms of immigrant arrivals, so did the number of potential Milwaukeeans increase.[53]

The most common antebellum route from New York to Milwaukee involved a steamboat journey up the Hudson to Albany, then by rail to Buffalo, and by steamboat on the lakes to Milwaukee, a trip which lasted about ten days. In the years before 1842 the trip between Albany and Buffalo was often made via the Erie Canal, but as it took a week, compared with the day's rail trip, and could be equally costly owing to the need to buy food for the longer period, later immigrants were advised to avoid the canal route. It was possible to go by rail all the way from New York to Lake Erie by 1851, and by 1853 immigrants were also advised to go by train from Detroit to Chicago, and then by steamer to Milwaukee; costs were the same either way and the journey by rail was shorter. Itineraries suggest the increasing popularity of the railroad during the 1850s not only from Detroit to Chicago, but also through Canada to Detroit.[54]

The combination of urban frontier opportunity, beckoning farms, and accessibility had much to do with attracting the city's first German settlers, who in turn became magnets for later comers. Many of the earliest Germans to arrive had previously lived in other lake cities such as Buffalo or Detroit like the pioneers mentioned earlier. Some were undoubtedly attracted by the need for labor on a new townsite, men like John Pritzlaff, who spent two years laboring on New York and Pennsylvania canals before coming to Milwaukee in 1841, when construction was underway on the abortive Milwaukee and Rock River Canal, or the young man who decided to see if Milwaukee could improve upon the five years of casual labor he had spent in Detroit. The attraction for August Greulich, as for so many others, was Wisconsin land: after arriving in America at the age of 21, the former seminarian wandered from Boston to Cleveland to Detroit, from factory labor to hod carrying to a series of profitable businesses, marriage, and an alderman's seat, until he decided to try Wisconsin farming in 1841. Finally, three years later, after ten years in America, he settled in Milwaukee where a good friend of Detroit days (his wife's guardian) was the Catholic pastor.[55]

This early, almost accidental German attraction to the city soon took on a more purposeful cast. By the 1840s, guidebooks, pamphlets, and published letters carried to Germany the message of Wisconsin's excellent soil, good transportation, healthy climate, light tax load, and inexpensive land, and many included a favorable mention of Milwaukee. Several gave a great deal of attention to careful description of German life in the city and provided reasoned estimates of German chances of business success.[56] Milwaukee also benefited directly from advertisements by two men who settled there in the early 1850s and reportedly "exercised great influence" on the emigration of families from the Rhineland and Hessen. These were Karl Quentin, the Prussian official mentioned earlier, and Ludwig von Baumbach, a former minister of the prince-elector of Hesse-Kassel, who attributed his emigration to his concern for the future of his children. Both opened real estate and commission businesses, and both wrote books praising their adopted city and state both for settlement and for investment.[57]

It is impossible to know how many read this literature carefully, but the prospective emigrant who used it to guide his decision had before him the picture of Milwaukee as a pleasantly situated and healthful, rapidly growing community in a developing agricultural area. As German settlement increased, he was presented as well with the prospect of a rich social and cultural life and political participation, of an environment more German than American. Some later commentators, to be sure, stressed that Germans were not at the top of Milwaukee's economic structure and often lived in poor and unhealthy parts of town, but by that time emigration was declining in any case, and the educated reader could discount the applicability of such comments for his own case.

If the prospective emigrant were religiously inclined, his church also may have played a role in attracting him to Milwaukee. When two Old Lutheran leaders traveled back to Germany in 1853, their reports stimulated the emigration of entire congregations, some of whom probably settled in Milwaukee with their coreligionists. Both the European visits of John Martin Henni, Milwaukee's first Roman Catholic Bishop, in the late 1840s and his reports to the Vienna and Munich missionary societies, which helped support his diocese, are credited with stimulating the emigration of "numbers of Catholic clergymen from Austria, Bavaria, and Switzerland, and thousands of Catholics from these and the Rhenish states," many of whom settled in the port city. The strength of the religious appeal is reflected by the comment of a new Milwaukee resident in 1846: "Thank God, we have the Christian religion here as in Germany."[58]

Finally, the series of public and private efforts devoted to attracting German settlement to Wisconsin could not help promoting Milwaukee as well. Private efforts included the circulation of leaflets in coastal Germany in the early 1840s (a venture of some speculative Yankees); the promotion of German settlement in articles in Milwaukee newspapers, aimed at exchange papers or for clipping and mailing to potential immigrants; as well as an original booster effort on the part of Milwaukee's first German newspaper in 1846. The *Banner* sold sheets of letter paper imprinted with a "brief and true" description of Wisconsin and the conditions of immigrants in the territory. Letter writers were reassured that the printed form covered only the first and a small part of the last sheet, leaving the second and third sides for private messages. The *Banner* sold the letter paper for six cents apiece and reported sales of over 300 within a few weeks.[59]

Such private efforts were climaxed by the establishment of the state office of the Commissioner of Emigration by the Wisconsin legislature in 1852. The office functioned until nativist opponents gained its repeal in 1855. The commissioner's task was both to publicize the state in the United States and abroad and to assist immigrants on their route west. The effectiveness of the office is difficult to assess. Since the two most active commissioners, Hermann Haertel and Frederick Horn, had Milwaukee connections, they would have tended to stress the advantages of the city as well as of the state in general. Contemporary opinion concerning the value of the agency was demonstrated when one of the assistants was engaged as an emigrant agent in New York by Wisconsin private citizens after repeal of the public office and continued in that task as late as the spring of 1857.[60]

Other private efforts to encourage immigrants to settle in the state and city continued sporadically in the following years. A German *Einwanderungs- und Handels-Zeitung* (Immigration and Commerce Journal) was published briefly in Milwaukee in 1857.[61] In June of 1859, some 50 Milwaukeeans, mostly Germans, met to discuss means of enticing more Germans away from competing states. Deciding that it was too late in the season to send an agent to New York (which suggests that the private agency had been discontinued sometime in the interim), they agreed that a brochure describing the advantages of the state could have great success if circulated in Germany and the United States. Wisconsin, they felt, had to meet the competition of newer states; if immigrants could be induced to settle in large numbers, both they and the city would benefit materially, "not to speak of the consequences of the strengthening of the German element in the northwestern part of the Union." By December, however, although a formal Society for the Promotion of Emigration to Wisconsin had been organized and the brochure written, the project was apparently aborted through lack of funds.[62]

The most important publicity for Wisconsin and Milwaukee, however, was found in the unsolicited testimonials which filled the letters to those left behind in the old country. "I thank God for giving me the idea to emigrate," one Milwaukeean wrote. "One must work hard with all one's strength and zeal, but one has hopes that his labor will be rewarded. I believe that if William were here, he and his family would fare better than in Germany."[63] Such a measured judgment from a relative would be carefully considered back home and could be expected to bear more weight than a guidebook or other publicity to one conscientiously weighing emigration. In writing specifically about Milwaukee, newly arrived immigrants tended to stress its rapid growth and pleasant appearance, as well as the healthfulness of the region and the business opportunities for certain trades. German society and Yankee peculiarities such as the Sunday "blue laws" as well as the natural beauty of the site were sources of comment. Drawbacks to Milwaukee life were sometimes mentioned—"the finer culture, the true aesthetics are not to be found"—but on balance Milwaukee came out positively. John Kerler, Jr., explained why:

> You have the choice between Wisconsin and Michigan. I was in both states, and my preference was for Wisconsin, namely Milwaukee, because my father was mainly looking for a place in which Germans had settled and where one could manage better with his own language . . . Milwaukee is the only place in which I found that the Americans concern themselves with learning German, and where the German language and German ways are bold enough to take a foothold. You will find inns, beer cellars and billiard and bowling alleys, as well as German beer, something you do not find much of in this country. The Dutchman (the Americans call the Germans this name by way of derision) plays a more independent role—has balls, concerts and theaters—naturally not to be compared to those in Germany and has even managed to get laws printed in German. His vote carries a heavy weight at election time. You will find no other place in which so much has been given the Germans, and if you value *this*, you may safely prefer Wisconsin, and especially Milwaukee, to other places.[64]

With the added inducement of a business opportunity and Kerler's well-dowered sister, his friend ultimately joined him in Milwaukee, one of many who arrived as the result of such direct solicitation. The father of Frederick Pabst was another, as was Henry Starke, a twenty-year-old railroad laborer who emigrated with his brother, "being encouraged to make this move by the reports of a former fellow citizen who had returned to his native town on a visit from Milwaukee." Many of the letters that traveled from Milwaukee to Germany no doubt bore not only encouragement but remittances for the voyage to strengthen the direct migration to the Wisconsin city.[65]

Others responded after their arrival in America to the gravity exerted by Milwaukee's German population. It was the glowing reports of Milwaukee and its rich German life, heard in Buffalo, that drew the young wine merchant, John P. Kissinger, traveling in America to satisfy his curiosity, and friends persuaded both Charles Julius Munkwitz and Joseph Sidler to give the Wisconsin city a try before giving up on America in disgust. Also attracted were Germans carefully scouting for a business location. Henry Stern, for example, disliking the position his excellent letters of recommendation had obtained for him with a Boston merchant, peddled dry goods in New York and New Jersy to familiarize himself with American customs and language. After a few months he found a position with a New York importer, spent some time in New Orleans for his firm, and on his return to New York met a friend who spoke so favorably of the West that they decided to set up a business in Milwaukee. They chose that city "after careful consideration . . . principally because the German emigration was directed there at that time." Solomon Adler had spent six years in the clothing business in New York before moving his establishment to Milwaukee in 1848; "an occasional trip west" as a clerk in a New York import firm had drawn him to "the idea of establishing himself in Milwaukee." Similar business trips to Milwaukee and Chicago for his cousin's Buffalo tannery led Frederick Vogel to interest this cousin and a partner in financing a tannery in Milwaukee in 1848.[66]

There is no satisfactory way of estimating the proportion of Milwaukee immigrants whose indirect migration paths had provided them with experience elsewhere in the United States before arriving in Milwaukee. The recording of children's birthplaces in the federal manuscript census, however, provides clues to the migration paths of those heads of household who migrated with their families and had several children.[67] By this measure, sample German households were far more apt to exhibit relatively direct paths to Milwaukee than the Irish or the British, owing, perhaps, to the family character of much of the German emigration. By contrast, the Irish propensity for stage migration was evident.[68]

Milwaukee tended to draw most of its German stage-migrants from New York or Ohio (Figure 5); by 1860 Pennsylvania and Illinois were also favored way-stations. Since the 1850 sample contained a greater proportion of persons who settled early in the city, before its reputation abroad was sufficient to attract direct migration and who therefore of

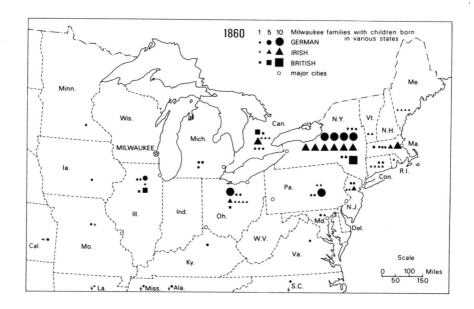

Figure 5   Migration paths to Milwaukee

necessity migrated in stages, one could expect that the proportion of such migrants would drop by 1860, but this was clearly the case only for the Irish. For the German paterfamilias, the careful choice of destination while still in Germany must have been an important part of his decision to emigrate.[69]

In contrast, these data suggest that a smaller proportion of Milwaukee's Irish responded in a conscious decision to any direct pull exerted by the city. Like their early Yankee and German counterparts, Milwaukee's pioneer Irish most likely drifted into the settlement from elsewhere around the Great Lakes, attracted by the opportunities of a newly opened area. For them, as for later Irish settlers, the trip west involved a series of moves, from job to job and place to place. For many, such movement in stages was a matter of neccessity. A Wisconsin agent in New York in 1854 found when he questioned newly arrived Irish that:

Most all were ready and willing to go to Wisconsin if they had the means of getting there. They either remain here or go to some other city not far off or to some railroad or canal about to be built in order to get the means to buy in future a home in the West. By inquiring among our Irish population in Wisconsin hardly one in twenty will be found who came directly from Ireland to Wisconsin for the reasons before stated while with the German and Norwegian population it is just the other way.[70]

It was the need for labor to clear the townsite, level the hills, fill the swamps, and build streets which undoubtedly first drew large numbers of Irish to Milwaukee, as word of the new settlement spread. The canal construction, plank road laying, and harbor improvements of the forties, railroad construction in the fifties, provided continued sources of unskilled employment. While some were induced to the area through direct advertisements and recruiting, in other cases a casual letter to an eastern newspaper could have the result of sending swarms of Irish westward.[71] But once the Irish established a core settlement and some began to enjoy at least limited success, they could then follow the well-established custom of sending for those left behind in the East or in Ireland, who would themselves take a more direct route to Milwaukee. The demand was sufficient by 1841 to induce Milwaukee steamship agents to advertise directly to Irishmen that they could "receipt fare for passengers from any port in Ireland, thro' to Milwaukee or Chicago. Those Irishmen that wish to send home for their friends, can make arrangements with the subscriber to have them here by the first of October next, by making application soon." Others who came directly may have been drawn in the early 1850s by the advertising of John Gregory, whose American Emigration Co-Operative Association hoped to attract Irish farmers to Wisconsin land and whose books sang the praises of Wisconsin to the literate Irishman.[72]

Many of the British who settled in Milwaukee were undoubtedly also attracted by the farmlands of Wisconsin, described in guidebooks and advertisements in Britain; some were drawn directly by the activities of such organizations as the British Temperance Emigration Society.[73] Many, however, followed the more indirect migration paths indicated by children's birthplaces. Among the immigrants in the biographical sample, 50 percent of the 22 British had stopped elsewhere in the United States, for an average of 7.8 years (as compared with the 65 Germans in the sample, 47 percent whom had migrated indirectly, but with an average interval between their arrival in the United States and settlement in Milwaukee of only 3.9 years).[74] Some of the British migrated in stages because, like the Irish, they could afford no other way, others because they had settled elsewhere before hearing of Wisconsin, others because of their intent to farm. New York and Canada were the most popular way-stations for the British as for the Irish, and to a lesser extent Illinois and Ohio (Figure 5).

Stability and Mobility

The attraction of Milwaukee for its immigrant residents was, of course, not necessarily a permanent one. The German shoemaker fearful for his scalp was not the only newcomer to become a statistic of out-migration. Discussions of population growth and immigration may imply the accretion of one layer of permanent population upon the next, yet this was certainly not the case. Milwaukee's citizens shared the restlessness characteristic of Americans elsewhere during the same era. The aggregate community of 1860 was not simply the community of 1850 with new additions. Only 39 percent of those present in the 1850 heads of household sample could still be found in the 1860 city directory.[75] This crude rate of persistence is generally consistent with findings for other older and more settled, although also rapidly growing, American cities.[76]

It is necessary, however, not only to point out the large turnover within Milwaukee's population as a whole, where out-migration as well as in-migration played a crucial role but also to stress the ethnic differences in crude persistence that existed. Among the Irish, 49 percent of those present in 1850 remained in 1860, compared with 44 percent for the native born, 40 percent for the British, 33 percent for the Germans, and 26 percent for other nationalities.[77] Those groups which had first established themselves in Milwaukee were by 1860 the most stable; occupying an intermediate position were the British once again; and the Germans and other nationalities, who poured into Milwaukee at increasing rates during the 1850-60 decade, maintained greatest mobility. This is consistent with other findings which suggest that the probability of further moves is greatest in the years immediately following an individual's first move into an area and decreases with time.[78] Thus greater mobility could be expected within those ethnic groups that contained the largest proportion of newcomers within the decade considered. Differences in persistence in Milwaukee may also have been related to patterns in the migration paths of the different ethnic groups.

Persistence can be considered both an indicator of successful adjustment and a sine qua non for community formation; thus these differential rates not only require clarification but may themselves further an understanding of the accommodation of immigrants to Milwaukee life. Their different backgrounds and migration paths, the timing and volume of their settlement, and the nature of the city as they found it— its economy, its political structure, its population mix—were all ingredients which went into that accommodation, even if they can only be lightly sketched rather than precisely measured. They suggest, in sum, a city of great potential for autonomous community formation, and at least one group—the Germans—of sufficient size, diversity, and motivation to take advantage of it.

Building Blocks of Community

2   When the Remeeus family—husband, wife, and five children—landed in Milwaukee late one afternoon in the summer of 1843, they had less than a dollar left. They saw their baggage unloaded and soon found themselves in a quandary: the friend whom they had expected to meet no longer lived in Milwaukee, and while they had relatives nearby, they discovered that it was 18 miles to the place where they had settled. A fellow Hollander who offered to help them quickly disappeared when he found that they were virtually penniless. Finally a 15-year-old boy from their native Zealand offered to take them to his home, and there they remained until the brother-in-law could come and fetch them.[1]

Their difficulties that first day obviously became part of a family mythology, encapsulating the tribulations and the generous comradeship which marked the first days of adjustment for so many of the city's immigrant settlers. Milwaukee offered the familiar series of obstacles and aids which greeted the arriving traveler in most cities of the period. Before 1842, when the first lake piers were built, arrival usually meant a damp ride in a small lighter from the steamboat anchored in the bay to the river docks in the center of the city. Construction of the piers permitted direct embarkation but generated the further hazard of exorbitant charges for unloading baggage—charges that provoked frequent complaints and led Milwaukee's Germans to form the city's first Emigrant Protection Society. Then there were the runners. They waited, spyglasses in hand, in a shanty on the bluff overlooking the piers. When passenger boats "hove in sight and were recognized, these watchmen took to their heels to advise the hotels, which in turn would scurry and bob away to the pier to solicit patronage from homeseekers and pilgrims bound for this great unknown country." The hotels kept omnibuses to meet the boats, but most immigrants probably rented carts to carry the baggage which they had shepherded so far already. Beset by draymen urging their patronage in colorful and sometimes violent Irish accents, they must have felt fortunate to get family and goods off the pier in one piece and with cash still in pocket.[2]

Fortunate immigrants found friends waiting to welcome them and help them to settle in. The others had their choice of increasing numbers of hotels and boarding houses catering specifically to persons of particular nationalities. The Irish newcomer, for example, could find not only "cheap fare" and "comfortable accommodations" but also "a genuine Cead Mille Faltha" at O'Brien's Travellers' Home, while Barley Stimson offered "a regular English Tavern" atmosphere to his traveling compatriots at the Brass Keys. The Steamboat Hotel went him one better in catering specially to emigrants from Lincolnshire. These and other Irish and British establishments were joined by numerous German inns, the successors to Louis Trayser's pioneer Zum Deutschen Little Tavern. If a newcomer could afford room and board at 75¢ a night or $4.00 a week, he could register at Theodore Wettstein's Deutsches Haus, described by one contented patron in 1853 as perhaps the finest German inn in America, but German *Gemutlichkeit* could also be had for $2.50 to $3.00 a week in numerous lesser establishments.[3]

Many eschewed such quarters for the less expensive expedient of a rented room or house for temporary shelter or storage of belongings while looking for work, scouting for land, or waiting for friends to arrive. The search for friends and acquaintances among earlier settlers could lead to inquiries at the various immigrant taverns and consultation of city directories. Many families cut their ties with Milwaukee as soon as possible once they found land, buying a wagon, hiring a carter, or hitching a ride with a farmer from their new district for the move to the countryside. Others, after a preliminary search, decided that farming was not for them and returned to the city to find jobs and permanent homes.[4]

For them, and for those who had planned to remain in Milwaukee, the real task of adjustment was upon them. For only a few families do surviving personal documents permit us to assess the fund of knowledge, the emotions, and the strength of character with which new Milwaukeeans set about that task.[5] But there are personal attributes whose aggregate distributions we can measure—age, sex, family status, literacy—which likewise influenced adjustment. The 21-year-old youth who stepped off the boat alone, burdened only with his tool kit, had a different prospect before him than did an anxious father with a large family like John Remeeus, while in contrast to both were the expectations of a grandmother enjoying a tearful reunion with her family. Any generalizations about the accommodation of such persons to their new lives or their roles in the creation of an immigrant community, must take such demographic variation into account. Moreover, variations over time in age structures, family relationships, and educational background not only shed further light on the selectivity of Milwaukee's peopling but also provide preliminary indications of ways in which different immigrant groups coped with life in the city which they found waiting at the foot of the pier.

Youth is Served

Frontier Milwaukee was a young man's town. It was built by young men, and the continued arrival of young migrants retained for it a youthful complexion. Almost two thirds of the business and professional leaders included in one of Milwaukee's biographical compendia, for example, were in their twenties when they arrived in the city. Only in the late 1850s, as the new city matured, did the proportion of newcomers over 30 years old increase markedly, and that increase was restricted to the native born. The German group, in fact, included greater proportions of younger men as time passed.[6]

Milwaukee exhibited the characteristic age structure of a frontier area initially peopled by such young adults (Figure 6).[7] The excess of 20 and 30 year olds and the dearth of adolescents in the 1840 population evolved into a pattern less deviant from the national norm by 1850 but one still characterized by a marked bulge in the years of young adulthood. By 1860, for which it is necessary to rely on county figures in the absence of aggregate age statistics for the city, it was the 30 year olds and their children who were proportionately more numerous than in the nation as a whole. This pattern reflected the declining rate of new immigration, and possibly an older average age for newcomers, as well as the maturing of the small cohort of children produced in the frontier period.

The masculine preponderance in most age categories, proportionately stronger than in the nation as a whole, was also a product of the frontier. A visitor to Milwaukee in 1847 complained that it was "Certenly . . . the d—mdst place for Old maids that ever it has been my lot to see before. They go in such droves along the side walks that it kept me a dogeing all the time to keep clear of dresses or being struck by

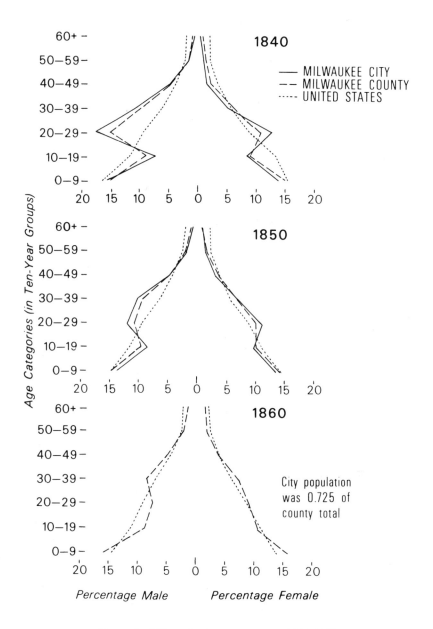

Figure 6   Milwaukee's age structure, 1840-1860

Source: U.S. Bureau of the Census, *Historical Statistics of the United States, Colonial Times to 1957* (Washington, D.C.: Government Printing Office, 1960), 10; U.S. Department of State, *Compendium of the Enumeration of the Inhabitants and Statistics of the United States, Sixth Census* (Washington, D.C.: Blair and Rives, 1841), 92-93; J. D. B. DeBow, *Statistical View of the United States . . . Compendium of the Seventh Census* (Washington, D.C.: A. O. P. Nicholson, 1854), 192; Joseph C. G. Kennedy, *Population of the United States in 1860* (Washington, D.C.: Government Printing Office, 1864), 526-27.

a bustle when they are a swinging them along."[8] The visibility of Milwaukee's spinsters notwithstanding, adolescent women were the only age group to really outnumber their male counterparts in either 1840 or 1850 (Table 6). While the national sex ratio increased with continued immigration, however, that of Milwaukee declined, so that by 1860 the city definitely reflected an urban rather than a frontier sex pattern, with females outnumbering males.[9] It was again adolescents and particularly young women in their twenties who swelled the female proportion, women who came to the city seeking employment or husbands—or whose brothers left the city for newer frontiers.

Table 6   Sex ratios of Milwaukee's white population

	1840	1850	1860
Place			
Milwaukee	1,335	1,097	980
Milwaukee county	1,254	1,118	1,016
Rural Milwaukee county	1,214	1,157	1,116
United States	1,036	1,043	1,047
Age specific sex ratios (city 1840, 1850; county 1860)			
0-9	1,116	1,041	1,006
10-19	853	873	879
20-29	1,404	1,038	852
30-39	2,034	1,441	1,161
40-49	3,000	1,413	1,325
50-59	1,235	1,292	1,287
60-69	1,000	951	1,201
70+		1,102	1,000
Sex ratios by ward			
1	1,334	989	919
7			843
3		1,215	1,059
4	1,331	1,085	952
2		1,099	1,061
6			1,021
9			1,004
5	1,324	1,175	1,017
8			1,023

Sources: Figure 6 and *Historical Statistics*, 9; *Compendium*, 1841, 92-93; DeBow, *Seventh Census*, 914; Kennedy, *Population*, 538-539.

The maturing of Milwaukee's frontier population is also reflected in its net fertility ratio, a census-based estimate of reproduction using the ratio of children under five years of age per thousand women in their childbearing years. This estimate went from 972 in 1840 to 846 in 1850 as the immigrant wave approached its peak, and then to 973 in 1860, compared with national ratios of 1,055, 892, and 905 for the same years.[10]

While the peopling of Milwaukee thus created distinctive demographic patterns, the contributions of the different groups of foreign born are more difficult to isolate. Census data were not aggregated by place of birth, but sex ratios calculated for the city's individual wards (Table 6) permit some inferences concerning foreign-born sex distribution, since two thirds of the second ward heads of household in 1850 were German, as were over 70 percent of the householders in wards two, six, eight, and nine in 1860. The greater male preponderance in these German wards (which were exceeded in this respect only by a downtown ward with large numbers of young resident clerks as well as a heavy Irish population) and the low sex ratios of the first, fourth, and seventh wards favored by native-born residents suggest that it was strong stabilization in the native population that accounted for changes in citywide trends, whereas immigrant areas retained the male surplus characteristic of recent migration.[11]

At least among heads of household, however, there was little significant difference in age distributions by nativity (Table 7).[12] The overall age trend was upward from 1850 to 1860, as could be anticipated. The modal category for all nativity groups in both census years was the 31-40 age group; however, in both decades the Irish and Germans had slightly larger proportions forty and under than did the native born. There was likewise little significant difference by nativity in the age distributions of females 15 and over, according to a separate sample taken from the 1860 census.[13]

Age not only reflected the history of group migration to Milwaukee, but may well have influenced adjustment patterns. The relative youth of most Milwaukee householders may have left them psychologically better prepared for the new life than their older compatriots who, on the other hand, may have come better equipped with capital and skill.[14] But the lack of significant variation in age patterns by nativity suggests that age differences played relatively little role in influencing differing accommodation patterns from ethnic group to ethnic group.

Table 7   Percentage of household heads in each age group by nativity

Age group	Native	British	Irish	German	Total
			1850		
	(N=226)	(N=102)	(N=192)	(N=414)	(N=1,020)
0-20	2	1	0	1	2
21-30	30	31	35	35	34
31-40	38	42	44	41	40
41-50	19	19	13	16	16
51-60	8	6	7	6	7
61+	3	1	1	1	1
			1860		
	(N = 359)	(N = 147)	(N = 361)	(N = 1,178)	(N = 2,266)
0-20	1	1	1	0	1
21-30	25	17	26	21	22
31-40	37	46	37	47	43
41-50	26	28	24	21	23
51-60	8	8	8	7	8
61+	3	1	4	4	3

Family and Household

In 1846 Milwaukee's German newspaper reported the drowning of a butcher driven to drink when his wife and children refused to leave Germany and join him in Milwaukee.[15] His was an extreme case, but the man who was accompanied to Milwaukee by his family or who could at least look forward to shortly greeting them at the pier, undoubtedly viewed his adjustment in different terms than did the bachelor free of dependents. He must have felt less mobile, less free to pick and choose his job or residence, but probably had greater psychological security and stronger incentive to immediate success. "Do you not know of a wife for him?" wrote August Frank to his parents in Germany deploring the wasteful and unambitious habits of his younger brother Ernst.[16] Young Ernst did settle down once he was married, and most of Milwaukee's household heads, immigrant and native alike, evidently also possessed this incentive, although the proportion of married household heads declined by 1860 among the British and the Irish.[17] The increasing stability in native patterns suggested once again by these figures contrasts with the clear increase in households headed by single persons among the Irish as well as with the consistently large proportion of married household heads which their tendency to family migration apparently encouraged among the Germans.

Households headed by single persons varied considerably in both character and in their potential threat to the stability of a community life oriented around the family. Some of these households simply consisted of one or more young men living in or near their place of employment. Others were headed by women; indeed, the increase in female-headed Irish and German households between 1850 and 1860 was more than sufficient to account for the decline in the proportion of married heads in these groups and was experienced also by the native born (Table 8). The Germans had the smallest proportion of female-headed households in both years; the Irish had by far the largest proportion by 1860. Although these households could and did involve single women as well as widows and women deserted by their husbands or living temporarily apart from them for a variety of reasons, the majority had children of the same name living with the household heads. This was particularly true for the Irish, while the incidence of female heads of household without children was greatest among the Germans in 1850 and the natives in 1860.

Thus by 1860, 11 percent of the Irish household sample involved families where children were without a father's presence when the census was taken. Although in absolute terms the 49 such families among the Germans outnumbered the 41 sample fatherless Irish families, they only constituted four percent of all the German households. The social impact of these statistics is difficult to assess. The

Table 8   Female heads of household

Female heads of household	Year	Native	British	Irish	German	Total[a]
N	1850	13	9	11	16	51
	1860	32	13	50	63	176
As percent of	1850	6	9	6	4	5
all heads of household	1860	9	9	14	5	8
Percent living with	1850	69	56	91	56	67
children	1860	66	69	82	77	76

[a]Includes other heads of household not tabulated.

fatherless family pattern may well have reflected not so much widow-hood or desertion as the common practice of leaving wife and children in the city while the husband sought work elsewhere. The increasing proportion of fatherless households among the Germans may signal the appearance of a larger group of men dependent like many of the Irish upon casual labor wherever it could be found. On the other hand, the aging of early settlers of itself must have created proportionately more widows as time passed.

That the vast majority of adult women of all nativities, however, were securely ensconced within the marriage relationship is suggested by the results of the special sample of all women 15 and over in the 1860 manuscript census (Table 9). There was variation in female marriage patterns by nativity, however. While a greater proportion of native adolescent women were married, after the age of 20 proportionately fewer were married than among their immigrant sisters. German women in every adult age category were living with spouses in greater proportions than the other groups. Children were a normal part of the married life of most of these women; only 18 percent of all married women in the sample had no children living with them, a percentage which dropped to 11 for those in their thirties and forties (Table 10). Again, however, patterns varied by nativity. Irish women had lower proportions of childless marriages and larger families, while native women had fewer children and more households without children. Figures for German women fell between the extremes but were closer to

Table 9   Females in each age group by nativity and marital status

Age group	Native N	Native Percent married	Irish N	Irish Percent married	German N	German Percent married	Other N	Other Percent married	Total N	Total Percent married
15-20	35	26	17	12	68	12	22	4	142	14
21-30	48	56	48	65	106	81	38	74	240	72
31-40	29	83	24	88	86	97	26	81	165	90
41-50	19	74	5	80	31	90	9	89	64	84
51-60	3	67	3	67	18	100	3	67	27	89
61+	6	17	4	-	10	40	6	50	26	31
Total[a]	140	77	104	60	320	71	107	62	671	64

[a]Includes females of unknown nativity.

Table 10   Childrearing patterns of married women 15 and over, 1860

Category	Native	Irish	German	Other	Total
Modal number of children	1	3	2	1	2
Percent childless	23	16	18	14	18
Percent aged 21-40 with children	66	84	75	74	74
Mean number of children per woman 15-20	.4	2.0	.6	0	.7
Mean number of children per woman 21-30	1.4	2.2	1.8	1.8	1.8
Mean number of children per woman 31-40	2.5	3.5	3.2	3.1	3.1
Mean number of children per woman 41-50	2.4	2.3	2.5	2.7	2.5
Mean number of children per woman 51-60	1.5	.5	2.2	2.5	2.0
Mean number of children per woman 61+	-	-	-	1.0	.4
Mean number of children per married woman	1.8	2.5	2.4	2.3	2.3
N	77	62	227	66	432

the Irish than the native pattern. Some of these differences reflect the greater concentration of married Irish women in the prime child-bearing years between 21 and 41, but even within these years Irish women tended to have larger families than their contemporaries while the families of native women were smaller. Irish patterns also apparently reflected a tendency for children to leave home earlier in their mothers' life cycles than was the case among Germans and natives, a tendency which was related to the younger age at which they seemed to have their families: the ratio of number of children of Irish mothers aged

15-30 to number of children of Irish mothers 31-40 was .99, while it was only .48 for the Germans and .72 for the natives.[18]

It is, of course, possible that these ethnic variations in childbearing patterns simply mirrored socioeconomic differences among the ethnic groups, with higher status associated with fewer children. In fact, however, among the natives and the Irish there was some indication that the reverse was the case, although this relationship did not hold either among the Germans or for the sample of wives as a whole.[19] There is no indication that immigrant women of higher status had adopted a lower "native" fertility by 1860. Whatever the cause, it seems clear that Irish women who married had more children earlier than other women; that fewer native women married and that those who married had fewer children; and that marriage was most common among German women, whose favorable sex ratio meant that "young girls here go like lager beer."[20]

Differences in the experiences of the unmarried women of each group suggest factors that may have influenced some of the variation in marriage patterns (Table 11). A far larger proportion of native females of undefined status resided in the households of others than among the immigrants; likewise, twice as large a proportion of native as of Irish

Table 11   Status of females 15 and older by nativity, 1860

Status	Native		Irish		German		Other		Total	
	N	Percent	N	Percent	N	Percent	N	Percent	N	Percent
Married	77	55	62	60	227	71	68	64	434	65
Widowed head, no occupation	1	1	1	1	3	1	2	2	7	1
Head, employed	6	4	5	5	3	1	1	1	15	2
Daughter, employed	10	7	3	3	3	1	4	4	20	3
Daughter, no occup.	16	11	6	6	29	9	9	8	60	9
Live-in servant	4	3	18	17	36	11	15	14	73	11
Elderly relative	5	4	2	2	6	2	4	4	17	3
Position unclear, no occupation	13	9	2	2	9	3	3	3	27	4
Position unclear, employed	4	3	4	4	2	1	1	1	11	2
Other	4	3	1	1	2	1	-	-	7	1
Total	140		104		320		107		671	

women were daughters resident in their parents' home. The proportion of live-in servants among the immigrants on the other hand, was far greater than among the native women (some of whom themselves must have been the daughters of immigrants). The ratio of employed to dependent unmarried nonhousehold heads varied from .53 for native women to .93 for Germans and 2.5 for Irish. Thus marriage—and no married women in the census sample indicated other employment— freed many immigrant women from the necessity of working to support themselves, but many native women were under no such compulsion in the first place.

These data on the lives of Milwaukee's women thus begin to suggest not only the degree to which family life was a prop to individual immigrants in adapting to Milwaukee and the personal circumstances within which women faced their new lives, but also the relative success of different groups in that adaptation by 1860. The natives could afford to support unmarried women; most unmarried Irish women had to work, as did many of their German counterparts, but they were more successful in finding, or arriving with, husbands. Household size can serve as a similar indicator of both adjustment prospects and accomplishments (Table 12). The household includes not only husband, wife, and children, but any parents, brothers and sisters, unattached children, boarders, or servants who may have lived with a family. While the modal household unit was small—four members or less—in both census years, there was a clear increase in the percentage of households in the next largest category by 1860. Native households tended to be larger than those of other groups, German households smaller. Given the fewer children in native families, it is the presence of servants and boarders, including the unattached females noted earlier, which accounts for the larger size of native households. In fact, the percentage of households consisting of family members declined among the native born by 1860 but increased among immigrant households. The proportion of households with boarders declined among all groups.

By and large, therefore, German and Irish householders and their wives and children made their adjustment to American life within a nuclear family setting. Relatively few shared the family hearth either with other newcomers from the old country or with noncompatriots who could have extended family horizons beyond their ethnic bounds.

Boarding was nevertheless an important feature of life in Milwaukee as in other nineteenth century American cities and served to incor-

Table 12 Size and composition of sample households (by percent of total group in each category)

Category	Native	British	Irish	German	Total
			1850		
	(N=226)	(N=102)	(N=192)	(N=414)	(N=1,020)
Household size					
1-4	45	56	47	64	56
5-9	48	39	48	33	40
10-19	6	5	4	3	4
20+	1	-	1	-	-
Composition[a]					
Family only	44	68	76	77	-
Boarders present	33	22	17	20	-
Servants present	42	18	13	10	-
			1860		
	(N=359)	(N=147)	(N=361)	(N=1,178)	(N=2,266)
Household size					
1-4	36	43	48	53	49
5-9	55	53	49	45	48
10-19	8	4	3	2	3
20+	1	-	-	-	-
Composition[a]					
Family only	40	71	86	85	-
Boarders present	25	16	8	10	-
Servants present	49	17	7	8	-

[a]The percentages do not total 100, since there is overlap between households with boarders and with servants.

porate most single persons and many young couples into the fabric of a society structured around family units.[21] In 1850, where a pilot study of all males aged 15 and over made possible a closer analysis of living patterns, 447 men with last names different from the head of the household in which they resided were found within the sample households (Table 13).[22] Almost two fifths of these boarders had occupations either the same as the head of the household or so closely related as to suggest that these were households of master, journeymen, and apprentices, or merchant and clerks, on the familiar model found both in American and European preindustrial urban settings. More than two fifths of the households which took in boarders included boarders of this type. Such households constituted more than a majority of all the German and other immigrant households with boarders; there were notably few among the Irish, and Irish boarders also showed little propensity to live in a work-related situation.

Table 13 Boarding in Milwaukee, 1850: males 15 and over (by nativity of head of household)

Category	Native	British	Irish	German	Other	Total
Number of households with boarders	79	24	35	86	21	245
Households with boarders as percent of all households	35	24	18	21	25	24
Number of boarders in all households with boarders	150	35	57	173	32	447
Ratio of boarders to heads of household in total sample	.66	.34	.30	.41	.38	.44
Mean number of boarders per household with boarders	1.9	1.5	1.6	2.0	1.5	1.8
Percent of boarders of same nativity as head of household in which they reside	79	53	42	78	35	70
Percent of all boarders in households of this nativity with same nativity as head	50	62	62	83	44	65
Percent of all boarders with occupation similar to head	44	31	12	41	34	37
Households with boarders with occupation similar to head as percent of all households with boarders	42	33	14	51	52	41
Households with boarders with occupation similar to head as percent of all sample households	15	8	3	11	13	10
Households with males aged 15 + with same last name as head, as percent of all households	17	18	14	7	14	12

Even among those boarders not tied to the householder through employment, only 38 percent—or a quarter of all boarders—lived in what could be termed a true boardinghouse situation, where three or more men lived in a household with no apparent blood or occupational relationship to the head. Furthermore, 45 percent of these lived in the four sample boardinghouses which had more than five boarders. Thus even boardinghouse living provided a relatively intimate setting for most Milwaukeeans who experienced it, and 70 percent of these boardinghouse residents in 1850 selected a boardinghouse run by a person of their own nativity. This was particularly true for Germans and natives, whose larger numbers presumably permitted them a greater selectivity. Among all boarders, including employment-related boarders, 65 percent resided in households headed by persons from the same country of birth. Again, natives and Germans were most apt to enjoy such common bonds with their landlords, and German landlords in particular tended to recruit mainly German boarders.

Most nonhousehold heads in 1850 were young, unmarried, and propertyless, though there were variations by nativity (Table 14). Native men showed a greater propensity than other groups to board even after marriage (which was also true for native women), and native and British nonheads of household were more frequently property owners. The Irish included more older men who did not head their own household, while the Germans were particularly young, single, and propertyless. It is also worth noting that fewer of the nonheads in German households were sons, brothers, or other relatives than was the

Table 14   Characteristics of all male nonheads of household in 1850 (by nativity)

Nativity	N	Percent of all nonheads	Percent aged 15-30	Percent married	Percent owning property
Native	771	28	80	14	11
British	282	10	75	9	12
Irish	482	18	77	9	6
German	897	33	85	6	5
Other and unknown	299	11	79	7	7
Total	2731	100	80	9	8

case especially among the natives and the British (Table 13).

This combination of small numbers of boarders in any one household, frequent work relationships between landlords and boarders, even more frequent ethnic ties, and the age-related character of boarding must have helped both to integrate such outsiders into family and community and to prevent the presence of strangers from impinging upon the intimacies of family life in a fashion noted by later critics.[23] Ernst Frank, for example, a young German mechanic, grew so intimate with the family of the newspaper editor from Berlin with whom he boarded that his brother complained of the amount of money Ernst was forced to spend on the "theater, excursions, concerts, circuses etc." which he attended with them.[24] The relationship could be a natural one; it also seems to have been temporary. It appears that the evolution of their life cycles ultimately led most Milwaukee males to head their own households. Relatively few married men failed to form their own households (somewhat less true for the native born); relatively few older men were not householders (with some exceptions among the Irish and the British). Even for those who did not head their own households, however, life within a family context was the norm. Milwaukee, despite its frontier status and large immigrant population, was little different in this respect from the more carefully studied situation elsewhere,[25] and there is no reason to expect any real change by 1860. The success of the German, particularly, in attaining the status of householder and in integrating nonhouseholders in family living situations must have augured well for both personal adjustment and community formation, while Irish patterns may have been both cause and consequence of somewhat greater personal and community disorganization.

Literacy

The greater handicap under which Milwaukee's Irish labored is also suggested by the heavier incidence of illiteracy in this group. The federal census query concerning literacy is the only available measure of the prior education of Milwaukee's householders; literacy was defined very loosely by the census, but there is little reason to assume that the same criteria were not applied regardless of nativity of respondent. On this assumption, illiteracy among Milwaukeeans was virtually confined to the Irish; over a quarter of all Irish household heads were illiterate in 1850, a fifth in 1860.[26]

Some of the Irish illiteracy is accounted for by their greater propor-tion of female heads of household, who particularly by 1860 included a disporportionate share of the illiterate household heads in their ranks. Age also played some role; in 1850 Irish heads of household under 30 exhibited a disporportionate tendency to illiteracy; by 1860 it was the 31-40 year olds who were more apt to be illiterate.[27] The implication is that the handicap of illiteracy fell more heavily upon the famine immigrants of the 1840s than upon either the better-endowed immigrants of the older generation or the more recent arrivals. These illiteracy rates meant that a fifth to a quarter of Irish heads of household arrived without a fundamental prerequisite for real economic mobility or much effective community participation in Milwaukee as it emerged from its frontier condition. By contrast, even the inability of most Germans to speak English upon arrival was probably less crucial in the long run, as their numbers made English initially less necessary while their literate orientation aided its ultimate acquisition.

Demography and Accommodation

The migrations that peopled early Milwaukee thus bequeathed to the city a distinctive frontier urban population pattern, whose ethnic components were differentiated in certain important ways. While age and sex distributions, family structures, household size and compositions, and educational backgrounds all reflected the selectivity of these migrations, they inevitably influenced and to some extent also mirrored the accommodations of the newcomers in Milwaukee. The socioeconomic edge of the native born and the burdens under which the Irish labored seem to have been evident early and will be examined more carefully in the following chapters. But how can one measure the effect of such factors as household composition and marital status upon the psychology of adjustment, crucially important though they must have been? The inner dynamics of family life, as members reacted to the situations which they encountered in the first days and months and years of Milwaukee, must likewise remain largely unrecorded.

Only for the Frank and Kerler families, products of middle-class small town German backgrounds who arrived around 1850, does an extensive correspondence permit some insight into the role of the family for one immigrant group. "I have many acquaintances in the city," wrote Veronica Frank, the young wife of an aspiring merchant, "but they do not mean as much to me as my relatives."[28] Her life and the lives of her relatives bore out the truth of her statement. Both she and her husband-to-be had emigrated in family groups, and the rhythm of their private lives and those of their siblings was dominated by family celebrations, family visits, family gossip. Nieces and nephews came to live with the Franks for the sake of the education and business training available in Milwaukee, while they and their children spent lengthy holidays at the farms of Veronica's family outside the city. Parents and grandparents were intensely involved in the health and well-being of the children, taking delight in the development of their individual personalities. Parents continued the financial support of grown children when possible and necessary, and adult children in turn felt that their parents were owed respect and obedience, even if they did not always receive it. The arrangement of marriages remained a family affair, and while the preference of the young couple for one another was the final factor, family satisfaction and financial considerations were carefully taken into account and spelled out in a marriage contract. Only in the case of Ernst, the youngest Frank brother, who married after several years in America, do these formalities seem to have been slighted to some extent, but even in his case, the rapidity of his courting and its coincidence with family pressures upon him to settle down and become a sober businessman suggest the practical side of the affair.

If calculation underlay courtship and marriage, however, the wedded life itself was viewed through an almost impenetrable haze of sentiment. Love came quickly and endured, though companionship between husband and wife seemed more evident in the rural branch of the family than in Milwaukee, where Veronica and her sister-in-law Emma had fewer claims upon the time of the aspiring businessmen they had married. Perhaps it was the tension of this situation which finally led Ernst and Emma to leave Milwaukee for small town life and the closer companionship of her family. Marriage brought the two sets of parents-in-law into contact with one another and was a way of extending the family relationship rather than forming a new family cell. Throughout the correspondence, the psychological and practical support which the network of relatives provided for all its members is evident; they did not face the new world alone.

Taken as a whole, then, the Kerler and Frank families seem to have successfully translated to America the German family patterns of their class and time,[29] and there can be little doubt of the vital importance of family life in structuring and cushioning their American transition. How typical they were in this respect is a question which deserves more careful exploration. Within two weeks of stepping off the pier in Milwaukee, August Frank arranged both a business partnership and a marriage for himself. The close relationship between securing family ties and economic establishment must have been equally self-evident to large numbers of other immigrants who flooded into Milwaukee in its first quarter century.

A Better Livelihood

3 The most pressing task of the immigrant newly arrived in Milwaukee was to find employment. Since most immigrants moved to America in search of economic security, they themselves must have defined the success or failure of their venture largely in economic terms. "Of the emigrants from Arendal, I think," wrote a Norwegian woman from Milwaukee in 1850, "probably none went on board with a heavier heart than I, and thanks be to the Lord who gave me strength to carry out this step, which I hope will be for my own and my children's best in the future . . . When I think, however, that there will be a better livelihood for us here than in poor Norway, I reconcile myself to it and thank God."[1] Like a Milwaukee butcher who had been prepared to return to Germany because he did not like his job, the average immigrant could not have fully justified his move to himself until he was satisfied with his economic position, or at least with future prospects for himself or his children, nor would he have had the time or the ability to attempt further integration into American society. The employment patterns of Milwaukee's immigrants and the economic rewards they reaped from their employment thus represent fundamental measures of how well immigrants fared in early Milwaukee.

Economic achievement also inevitably conditiond the terms upon which the native born received their immigrant neighbors. Individual social status in American society was in part a function of earning ability; moreover, the concentration of immigrants in particular occupations encouraged the development of group stereotypes in the light of which individual members were often judged.[2] His job also often represented the immigrant's first extended set of relations with the society within which he had settled, his main chance to interact with persons of other nativities and to establish natural relationships as a first step to broader social interaction.

The probable influence of employment patterns on social integration can, of course, be overstated. For a group as populous as Milwaukee's Germans, even on-the-job contacts with non-Germans may have been limited and seldom may have extended beyond a formal basis in any case; the transition from business to social relationships may have been difficult for many. Moreover, while the urge to succeed economically may have led the immigrant to adopt some American ways more readily—business methods, craft techniques, knowledge of English, the American business ethic—simply because such ways were necessary to fulfill the goal he had set himself upon emigration, that very goal may have blinded him to other facets of his adaptation. Provided that he were able to succeed economically, he may have had little desire to acquire much further acquaintance with American life, given a strictly economic basis of dissatisfaction with the old country.

Finally, employment and wealth patterns must have played a role in community formation as well as individual adjustment. Scholars have noted that successful individuals often tend to remove themselves from ethnic community life, that once class divisions appear as a consequence of selective "successful" economic adjustment, internal unity is undermined and, by implication, more rapid individual assimilation follows upon such community disintegration. By this reasoning, an ethnic group containing persons potentially successful on American terms enjoyed lesser chances of achieving a strong and lasting community than did one economically homogeneous.[3]

Yet economic adjustment may have cut two ways in this context. The more heterogeneous a group, presumably the more self-sufficient and sustaining it could become, producing its own leaders, generating its own employment, turning itself into a miniature society independent of the host community—assuming, of course, that there was little desire for closer contact with American society.[4] Conversely, a homogeneous group whose members were of low economic status would in effect expel successful countrymen, who would be forced to dissociate themselves from the defining stereotype of the group if they wished to achieve status. The leaderless mass in such a situation would be without cultural reinforcement of non-American traditions, would have few internal economic or social bonds, and could easily subsume ethnic in economic identity. Whether differences in ethnic employment and wealth patterns in Milwaukee were sufficiently great to encourage such divergence in community structure is worth exploration.

Employment Patterns

"Nowhere but in the West," promised an 1856 German guide-book, "can the immigrant so quickly find employment and abundant sources of income, which, with hard work, sobriety, and thrift, will secure independence for him in so short a period of time, even if he arrives penniless."[5] By and large Milwaukee lived up to that promise although, in expected fashion, the opportunities which it offered were circumscribed by the differential abilities of the various nativity groups to take advantage of them. During the antebellum period the Irish were never to overcome their initial handicaps, nor were the somewhat more favorably situated Germans and British able to overcome the prior advantages of the native born.

The federal manuscript censuses of 1850 and 1860, with their questions concerning occupation, tell the story. Care, however, is required in its interpretation. When job titles are grouped into an approximate status hierarchy, census information can be used to derive essentially static reproductions of the distribution of occupational status among the nativity groups in the population, manifesting both the opportunity offered to each by the city's economy and the abilities of each ethnic component upon arrival. So used, the censuses identify sources of income but say little about either relative chances of advancement or individual achievement of success. However, comparison of the static picture over time does permit an approximation of net shifts in employment patterns if allowance is made for changing internal composition of ethnic group membership. Thus the censuses delineate the framework within which the individual immigrants functioned in their quest for security, while providing benchmarks against which to measure the aggregate achievements of the various nativities. Furthermore, they permit comparison with similar "snap-shots" of the occupational hierarchy of other cities at the same time period.[6]

Manual labor occupied over two thirds of the Milwaukee heads of household in both 1850 and 1860 (Table 15). Within this group, skilled laborers formed the single most numerous category, although they were outnumbered by the combined weight of the semiskilled and the unskilled. The occupational pyramid narrowed further toward the top; clerks and petty proprietors clearly outnumbered the professional and mercantile elite. There was little change in the pattern during the decade separating the two censuses, but in neither year was the overall pattern

Table 15   Occupational status of Milwaukee household heads by nativity

Occupational category[a]	Native		British		Irish		German		Total
	Percent	Index[b]	Percent	Index[b]	Percent	Index[b]	Percent	Index[b]	Percent
					1850				
	(N=226)		(N=102)		(N=192)		(N=414)		(N=1,020)
1	13	2.6	1	.2	2	.4	3	.6	5
2	11	2.7	6	1.5	2	.5	2	.5	4
3c	-	-	2	-	-	-	-	-	-
4	6	2.0	1	.3	1	.3	3	1.0	3
5	16	1.3	12	1.0	7	.6	10	.8	12
6	32	.9	54	1.5	17	.5	41	1.1	36
7	9	.9	12	1.2	10	1.0	10	1.0	10
8	3	.1	2	.1	55	2.4	26	1.1	23
0	10	1.4	10	1.4	6	.9	5	.7	7
Total	100		100		100		100		100
					1860				
	(N=359)		(N=147)		(N=361)		(N=1,178)		(N=2,266)
1	11	3.7	1	.3	1	.3	2	.7	3
2	·21	4.2	3	.6	2	.4	2	.4	5
3c	-	-	3	-	1	-	1	-	1
4	10	2.5	9	2.2	2	.5	2	.5	4
5	16	1.4	14	1.2	7	.6	10	.9	11
6	26	.8	46	1.3	19	.6	38	1.1	34
7	7	.6	10	.8	15	1.3	12	1.0	12
8	4	.2	9	.4	43	1.8	28	1.2	24
0	5	.8·	5	.8	10	1.7	5	.8	6
Total	100		100		100		100		100

[a]Occupational categories: 1. professional; 2. proprietors, managers, and officials; 3. semi-professional; 4. clerical and sales; 5. petty proprietors, managers, and officials; 6. skilled; 7. semiskilled and service; 8. unskilled.

[b]The index measures the degree to which a particular nativity group is over or under represented in a particular category in relation to the proportion of the total group of heads of household in that category. To compute it, divide the percentage of the nativity group in any given category by the percentage of the total population.

[c]Indices were not computed for 3, since the category was so small.

reflected within the occupational structures of the individual nativity groups. The Yankees dominated the upper ranks, the British and Germans congregated in the middle, while the ranks of the Irish were bottom-heavy.

Specifically, the Irish in 1850 clustered to a greater extent than any other group in a single category, that of unskilled labor, where their concentration was two and a half times that of all heads of household. The Irish were underrepresented in every other category; only in the semiskilled trades did they come close to proportions commensurate with the larger workforce as defined by the sample. The second most numerous category for the Irish was skilled labor, but within that category they had a smaller proportion than any other major nativity group in Milwaukee. In 1850, therefore, the Irish were firmly at the bottom of the occupational ladder, and there, despite some improvements, they remained in 1860. Their concentration in unskilled labor declined at a time when the proportion of such labor within the city as a whole increased. Their share of skilled craftsmen rose to some degree but more important was their disproportionate employment in semiskilled work. Thus, the Irish demonstrated some gradual improvement in status as the migrants of the 1840s accumulated years of residence in the city without significant numbers of newcomers, but the dwindling proportions of the old "middle-class" Irish were also evident.

The British in both years formed the second most concentrated group, notably within skilled occupations. They were also overrepresented in clerical work, shopkeeping, and semiskilled trades. While they had relatively few persons at the top of the occupational ladder, they also had few laborers. Concentration decreased by 1860, but most changes were minor.

Like the British, though not as disproportionately, Germans tended to cluster in the skilled crafts. However, the Germans were also overrepresented among laborers in both census years, and in 1860 among the semiskilled as well. There were few major shifts between 1850 and 1860. The slight decrease in their proportions of professionals could be accounted for by the same reasoning as in the case of the Irish: in relative terms, the earlier professional immigration was diluted by that of the rural proletariat of the 1850s. Professionals were in fact slightly less dominant within the city as a whole, as the frontier tendency to attract a disproportionate number of native lawyers abated.

It was the native born who not unexpectedly occupied the highest niches in the city's economy. In both years, they were overrepresented among professionals, merchants both large-scale and small, and clerical workers. While artisans were most numerous in both years, they still were proportionately fewer than in the city as a whole and declined relatively from 1850 to 1860. Natives were also underrepresented among the semiskilled and especially the unskilled.

Measures of ethnic domination within occupational status groups, reflecting also, of course, the relative sizes of the different nativity groups, clarify the occupational patterns (Table 16). Thus, Yankees dominated the professions in both years, but the more numerous Germans also contributed a good share; Irish and British professionals made little statistical impression on the city. The city's leading business-men were also predominantly Yankee, especially by 1860. In the ten years between censuses, the German share of this class increased but that of the British and Irish each declined as their population growth fell behind. It is clear that in both census years, the native born in absolute as well as proportionate terms controlled the leading sectors of the city's business and professional life.

Table 16　Ethnic representation within occupational status categories

Occupational category[a]	N	Native		British		Irish		German	
		Percent	Index[b]	Percent	Index	Percent	Index	Percent	Index
				1850					
1	49	57	2.6	2	.2	6	.3	29	.7
2	45	56	2.5	13	1.3	11	.6	16	.4
3	3	-	-	68	6.8	-	-	33	.8
4	31	45	2.0	3	.3	7	.4	36	.9
5	118	31	1.4	10	1.0	12	.6	35	.9
6	362	20	.9	15	1.5	9	.5	46	1.1
7	107	20	.9	11	1.1	18	.9	38	.9
8	233	3	.1	1	.1	45	2.4	46	1.1
				1860					
1	78	51	3.2	3	.5	4	.2	31	.6
2	114	65	4.1	4	.7	6	.3	21	.4
3	16	6	.4	25	4.2	13	.7	56	1.1
4	89	40	2.5	15	2.5	8	.4	30	.6
5	254	23	1.4	8	1.3	9	.5	45	.9
6	767	12	.8	9	1.5	9	.5	58	1.1
7	271	10	.6	6	1.0	20	1.1	54	1.0
8	545	2	.1	2	.3	29	1.5	60	1.2

[a]Occupational categories: 1. professional; 2. proprietors, managers, and officials; 3. semi-professional; 4. clerical and sales; 5. petty proprietors, managers, and officials; 6. skilled; 7. semiskilled and service; 8. unskilled. The rows do not add up to 100, since other smaller nationalities are not included.

[b]The index measures the extent to which any nativity group is concentrated in an occupational category in relation to that group's proportion in the sample as a whole. To compute it, divide the percentage which any group comprises of the total number within an occupational category by that group's percentage within the entire sample (Table 2).

In the middling ranks, the Americans and the Germans in 1850 had approximately equal numbers of petty proprietors, managers, and officials with the Irish, British, and other nationalities splitting the remaining business evenly. The number of small German shopkeepers kept pace with the growing German population in the following decade, however, so that by 1860 Germans controlled almost half of this category. The other three major nationalities fell behind. Yankees were the most numerous group among the clerical workers in both years, but their share and that of the Germans declined by 1860, while the English and Irish increased. Since such positions were often held by young men, this suggests the potential upward mobility of the maturing foreign-born children of early British and Irish immigrants.

Chances were good that the antebellum Milwaukeean seeking the services of a craftsman would have found himself employing a German. Irish artisans were proportionately unimportant; even the natives and British retained only about a fifth of the jobs by 1860. However, since this category does not distinguish between employers and employees, it is impossible to judge status differences within the artisan category. The Germans were also the most numerous component in the semiskilled and service category, although the Irish increased their proportionate share by 1860 as their concentration in labor decreased—again, a step upwards. The Irish and the Germans divided the market for day labor almost evenly in 1850, but ten years later it was the Germans and other continental Europeans who were performing two thirds of the common labor in Milwaukee. The average Milwaukee ditchdigger was "Dutchman" and not "Paddy."

One consequence of the German occupational distribution in a Milwaukee which they dominated numerically was, therefore, high visibility at all levels of the city's economic ladder. While German numbers were heaviest in the middle occupations, the Germans also had large shares of the city's professionals and a majority of its laborers. As a result, it would have been difficult to type the Germans according to any economic class. The deviant groups from the German "norm" were the Yankees in high status occupations, the Irish with lower status profiles, and to a certain extent the British with concentration exclusively in the middle.

The derivation of these employment patterns from data for heads of household introduces a possible bias; underestimation could be anticipated at the lower end of the scale where dependent sons and other single males could be expected to cluster. A "trial run" for the present study, involving occupational data for the entire employed or adult (defined as 15 and over) male population, retabulated to conform to the categories used in the sample analysis, makes it possible to control for such differences for 1850 (Table 17).[7] Comparison of the two tabulations suggests that the sample underestimated native participation in the work force and overestimated that of the Germans, who, as noted in the previous chapter, included proportionately fewer nonheads of household. When the occupational distribution of the entire labor force is considered, the sample is found to have underestimated clerical and particularly craft sectors and clearly overestimated the proportion of petty proprietors. Some of the differences reflect definitional problems in collapsing the total work force tabulation particularly in the case of the major and petty proprietors. Others, however, reflect actual differences between the employment patterns of household heads and nonheads.

As expected, nonheads were relatively less numerous at the upper end of the employment spectrum than their more settled compatriots, but this did not involve concentration in the ranks of the unskilled. Nonheads moved in greater proportions than heads of households into the ranks of semiskilled and clerical workers; also evident was a marked tendency for immigrant—but not native—nonheads to concentrate more strongly in the skilled trades than was true for the heads. Thus, while the overall age difference between heads and nonheads inevitably kept a greater proportion of nonheads from appearing on the top rungs of the employment ladder, their numbers at the middle levels suggest the potential for intergenerational mobility displayed by Milwaukee's immigrants. Also notable, however, is that despite the varying ratios of heads to nonheads from group to group and despite the differing overall employment trends of heads and nonheads, the trend of ethnic differences remained fairly constant. Thus the heads of household sample remains a fair predictor of general employment patterns as they differed among nativity groups in 1850, and there is little reason to suspect that the 1860 sample is any less satisfactory.

The relationship of the ethnic hierarchy of employment in Milwaukee to the differing European backgrounds of its immigrant settlers is evident, as is the advantage which cultural familiarity, access to capital, and the selectivity of the westward movement conferred upon the native born. But there were additional factors at work, as

Table 17 Percentage distribution of 1850 total male work force and all nonheads of household among occupational status categories

Occupational status[a]	Native		British		Irish		German		Total	
	Work force	Nonheads	Work force	Nonheads	Work force	Nonheads	Work force	Nonheads	Work force	Nonheads
	(N=1,619)	(N=771)	(N=676)	(N=282)	(N=1,185)	(N=482)	(N=2,430)	(N=897)	(N=6,462)	(N=2,731)
1	9	7	1	1	1	1	2	2	4	3
2	10	1	1	-	1	-	2	-	4	1
3	1	1	-	-	-	-	1	1	-	1
4	14	20	3	4	2	3	4	7	6	10
5	16	14	10	2	7	1	8	5	10	7
6	34	28	68	61	23	19	51	45	43	37
7	6	12	8	20	9	16	5	19	7	16
8	5	6	7	6	51	51	22	16	21	18
9	5	11	2	6	6	9	5	5	5	7
Total	100	100	100	100	100	100	100	100	100	100

aOccupational categories: 1. professional; 2. proprietors, managers, and officials; 3. semi-professional; 4. clerical and sales; 5. petty proprietors, managers, and officials; 6. skilled; 7. semiskilled and service; 8. unskilled; 9. other and unknown.

comparison of Milwaukee employment patterns with those found in several other American cities makes clear (Figure 7).[8] While the ethnic hierarchy of employment in all these cities was strikingly similar to Milwaukee's despite their differences in size, age, economic functions, regional location, and ethnic composition, there is some variation in pattern which cannot be explained merely by differences in the occupational categories utilized in the different studies. When the ambiguity in classification of skilled and semiskilled occupations is taken into account, there seems little major variation in the Irish trend; Milwaukee's British seemed somewhat more concentrated in the skilled ranks than elsewhere, and the natives generally more predominant in the top two categories. The main differences lay in the German occupational patterns. In comparison with the entire work force, Germans were less overrepresented in skilled crafts in the midwestern cities where their share of the total work force was greater, and a smaller proportion of the employed Germans were found in nonmanual positions as more appeared in the ranks of the common laborers.[9]

Selective migration from ports of entry, differential opportunities dependent upon varying urban economies, and the limitations on employment choice set by the ethnic composition of each city can help explain these differing tendencies. Contrasts in the economies of the three eastern cities clearly exerted selective attractions, but an east-west selectivity could also be anticipated. Contemporaries advised immigrants to "Lose no time . . . in working your way out of New York and directing your steps westward, where labor is plentiful and sure to meet with its reward" and noted that it was the poor who could afford to travel no further who were bound to their port of entry. Only those with trades requiring large urban markets were advised to remain behind in the port cities.[10] Such selectivity implies that Milwaukee may have seen disproportionately fewer of either the poorest or the most highly trained. Its attraction was exerted for those either working to earn money for a farm or those lacking the highly specialized skills and knowledge which promised success in the East yet with the means and foresight to move west and take advantage of the economy of a frontier city. There the demand for labor in construction and transportation-related areas was high. On the other hand, Milwaukee's workshops supplied only a local, at most regional, market limiting the amount of skilled labor required and providing little factory employment. A city like Milwaukee could thus fulfill the employment requirements of the less skilled but not penniless among the Germans and the British—the British overconcentration in the ranks of the craftsmen is explained by

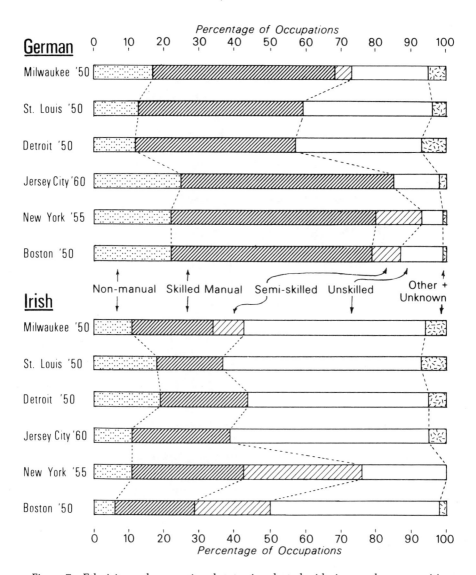

Figure 7   Ethnicity and occupational status in selected mid-nineteenth century cities

Source: Milwaukee: Table 15; St. Louis: Frederick Anthony Hodes, "The Urbanization of St. Louis," Ph.D. diss., St. Louis University, 1973, 72-73; Detroit: JoEllen McNerg-ney Vinyard, "The Irish on the Urban Frontier: Detroit, 1850-1880," Ph.D. diss., University of Michigan, 1972, 49; Jersey City: Douglas V. Shaw, "The Making of an Immigrant City: Ethnic and Cultural Conflict in Jersey City, New Jersey, 1850-1877," Ph.D. diss., University of Rochester, 1972, 21; New York: Robert Ernst, *Immigrant Life in New York City, 1825-1863* (New York: King's Crown Press, 1949), 214-217; Boston: Oscar Handlin, *Boston's Immigrants: A Study in Acculturation* (New York: Atheneum, 1968), 250-252.

large numbers in the building trades, as the following chapter will demonstrate—and may have attracted greater proportions from that sector of the emigration than did the eastern cities.

However, ethnic composition also played an inevitable role in employment patterns. In Milwaukee in 1850, where the Germans accounted for 38 percent of the entire work force and the Irish only 18 percent and where 21 percent of all employment was unskilled, no group the size of the Germans had the luxury of refusing such employment. Only a minority among the Irish emigrated to the frontier of the 1830s and 1840s, yet frontier towns had a demand for common labor relatively as great as the eastern ports. The Germans, as the most numerous relatively unskilled group present (regardless of selectivity operating within the German emigration) had to fill such jobs or go unemployed. There were not enough Irish to do the dirty work. Knowledge of this fact, however, may also have been an attraction— work was theirs for the asking with little competition, and so they came, those unskilled among the Germans to whom the ports had little opportunity to offer.

The lesser numbers of the Irish, in turn, can be attributed to greater inability to afford the westward trek. As a result, one could anticipate that the Irish who made their way to Milwaukee were those better endowed, more capable, more venturesome. If so, however, as a whole they did no better and perhaps less well, at least initially, than their brethren who remained in the east, and the stage migration paths noted earlier suggest that Milwaukee may have drawn those unable to find work in the ports who used the construction gang as a ticket west. While it is thus difficult to sort out the relative influence of selective migration and opportunity at the destination on the ethnic occupational structure in Milwaukee, it is at least clear that for Milwaukee's Irish as for the Germans and perhaps the British, frontier settlement did not necessarily mean greater economic advantage in the simple Turnerian sense, although the frontier situation at least initially seemed to play into Yankee hands. How far it did so, as well as the significance of occupational patterns for immigrant well-being, can be assessed by turning to the rewards of those occupations.

The Rewards of Employment

Ideally, in order to investigate the levels of living which their occupations permitted Milwaukee's immigrants to enjoy and the amounts of wealth which they were able to accumulate, information on income, savings, investment, and expenditures would be required, but such information is hard to come by. The closest approximation to a measure of the rewards of employment is the information on real property ownership in the manuscript censuses for 1850 and 1860.[11] Ability to employ servants provides a supplemental measure.

As one could anticipate from the structure of employment, there was little equity in the distribution of real property in antebellum Milwaukee (Figure 8). In 1850 the wealthiest 10 percent of the heads of household owned 88 percent of the real property valued in the census, 90 percent ten years later, while the concentration of landed wealth within the top 1 percent increased from 44 to 47 percent. Property distribution widened among the bottom ranks of the property holders over the ten year period, but the fact remains that three fifths of all Milwaukee householders were still propertyless in 1860. Only a minority were able to grasp the opportunity of a frontier city in its infancy; if anything, concentration of property holding was greater in Milwaukee than in older sister cities.[12]

Not all nativity groups fared equally ill, however. The British had the most equitable distribution of property in both census years, followed by the natives and the Germans, with the Irish exhibiting the greatest internal inequality in 1850. Ten years later the markedly more even property distribution among the Irish contrasted with the general trend toward greater inequality evident among the other groups and for the city as a whole.

Even more important, if absolute value as well as proportionate distribution of property is considered (Table 18), the dominant position of the native born is indisputable. The improved property-holding status of the Irish by 1860 remains evident, however. They ranked lowest in 1850; almost three fifths held no real property, and a smaller portion owned property valued at more than $1,000 than among any other group. A decade later, however, the proportion of propertyless Irish householders was much closer to the city norm, and those owning more than $1,000 in property had risen by more than 12 percent. The British, in a far less disadvantaged position to begin with, exhibited even more impressive movement out of the ranks of the propertyless in 1860, as well as an increase in larger property holders almost comparable to that of the Irish. While the Germans showed somewhat similar

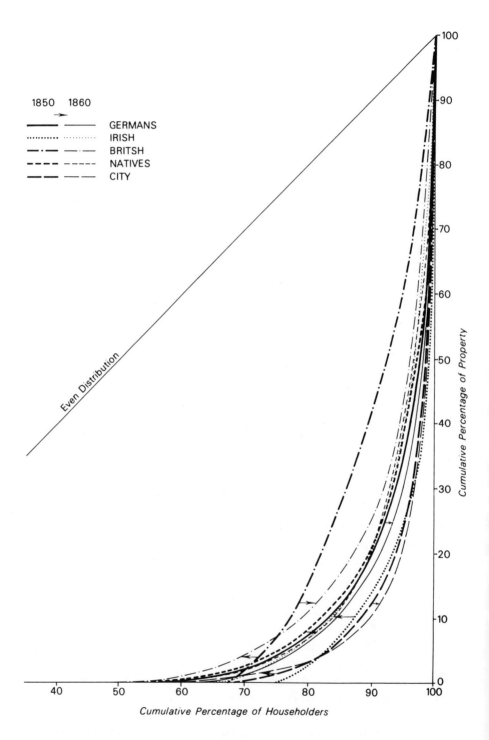

Figure 8   Real property distribution, Milwaukee 1850 and 1860

Table 18　Real property ownership by ethnicity and age (percentage of heads of household of each ethnic group)

Age	Native		British		Irish		German		Total	
	1850	1860	1850	1860	1850	1860	1850	1860	1850	1860
21-30										
No property	57	64	61	76	78	77	75	77	70	75
$1-999	12	17	21	20	21	11	20	15	19	15
$1,000-9,999	27	19	18	4	1	12	5	6	10	9
$10,000+	4							2	1	1
N	69	90	32	25	68	93	147	250	316	458
31-40										
No property	54	51	61	40	74	64	59	61	61	59
$1-999	13	9	14	19	19	20	28	20	21	18
$1,000-9,999	25	25	25	33	6	15	11	17	15	19
$10,000+	8	15		8	1	1	2	2	3	4
N	85	131	43	67	85	135	168	556	381	889
41-50										
No Property	37	41	82	59	58	53	60	59	56	54
$1-999	7	5		7	25	14	20	20	15	15
$1,000-9,999	37	25	18	24	17	25	20	18	24	21
$10,000+	19	29		10		8		3	5	10
N	42	94	19	41	24	87	65	241	150	463
51+										
No Property	52	32	86	54	73	72	45	60	57	7
$1-999	8	10	14	15	20	12	38	19	22	16
$1,000-9,999	32	22		31	7	16	17	19	18	20
$10,000+	8	36						2	3	7
N	25	41	7	13	15	43	29	126	76	223
Total										
No Property	52	49	67	53	73	66	64	63	64	61
$1-999	11	10	14	16	20	15	25	20	19	17
$1,000-9,999	28	23	18	25	6	17	10	15	14	17
$10,000+	9	18	1	6	1	2	1	2	3	5
N	226	359	102	147	192	361	414	1178	1020	2266

gains in the upper ranks, the continuing arrival of new immigrants undoubtedly accounted for the almost unchanging proportion of propertyless Germans. By 1860 German ownership patterns were much more like those of the Irish than the British. Even the British, however, remained well behind the natives in the race to control the real estate of the city. Property holdings thus mirrored the occupational ranking of Milwaukee's nativity groups and confirmed the improving status of the Irish contrasted with the more static structure of the still growing German colony.

Ethnic differences in property holding did not result from age differences between nativity groups. In almost all age groups in both years, natives held more property and with greater frequency than persons born abroad. Likewise, natives showed a tendency to own increasing amounts of property with greater age in both census years (except for the older men in 1850) and for each age group (except for the youngest) to improve its property holding over time. For all groups, in fact, property holding among the 20 year olds failed to increase by 1860—perhaps reflecting lessening economic opportunity for the young as the city matured—but, with the exception of the Germans in 1850, all the foreign born exhibited greater proportions of propertyless householders than the natives in the oldest age category as well. It was generally the 40-year-olds who did best among the Irish and Germans, while the British pattern was erratic.[13]

Variations in property holding were most clearly a function of the occupations to which the different nativity groups had access; the native born advantage tends to decline when occupational variation is controlled. The hierarchy of property ownership by occupational status is evident in Table 19. Unskilled labor was as closely associated

Table 19   Milwaukee real property ownership by occupational status (percent)[a]

Amount	1	2	3	4	5	6	7	8	Total
				1850					
No property	49	18	100	65	60	64	57	79	64
$1-999	58	24	-	81	76	85	88	98	83
$1,000-9,999	84	67	-	100	100	99	100	99	98
$10,000+	100	100	-	-	-	100	-	100	100
				1860					
No property	46	5	69	64	55	57	63	78	61
$1-999	53	6	75	75	67	81	83	93	78
$1,000-9,999	77	35	100	100	98	99	99	100	95
— $10,000+	100	100	-	-	100	100	100	-	100

[a]Occupational categories: 1. professional; 2. proprietors, managers, and officials; 3. semiprofessional; 4. clerical and sales; 5. petty proprietors, managers, and officials; 6. skilled; 7. semiskilled; 8. unskilled.

with nonownership of property as it was with significant numbers of Irish and Germans, while the nonmanual occupations dominated by the Yankees included the more sizable proportions of propertied house-holders. However, Table 20 indicates that by 1860 the native born maintained a better record of property holding than their immigrant peers only within the professional category, and even there they were closely challenged by the Irish. Within the manual occupations and shopkeeping, in fact, the native born were less apt to own property than the immigrants. By 1860 it was Irish clerks, shopkeepers, and semiskilled laborers, German laborers, and British artisans who led their occupational categories in home ownership propensity. Irish and British laborers were even able to increase their proportion of property owners by 1860, in the face of the overall decline of property holding in this category. Persistence evidently paid off in terms of property holding; continuing German in-migration probably mitigated against

Table 20   Nonproperty ownership by nativity and occupational status (percent)[a]

Occupational category[a]	Native	British	Irish	German	Total
			1850		
1	36	100	67	64	49
2	8	50	20	14	18
3	-	100	-	100	100
4	71	-	50	55	65
5	58	58	64	59	60
6	63	66	59	65	64
7	48	75	47	49	57
8	83	100	85	71	72
			1860		
1	32	50	33	63	46
2	7	-	-	4	5
3	100	75	50	67	69
4	56	54	29	85	65
5	62	62	42	52	58
6	62	42	61	56	57
7	69	60	55	64	63
8	85	77	79	78	78

[a]Occupational categories: 1. professional; 2. proprietors, managers, and officials; 3. semi-professional; 4. clerical and sales; 5. petty proprietors, managers, and officials; 6. skilled; 7. semiskilled and service; 8. unskilled.

similar improvement in the German record. Thus, property ownership was more widespread among the native born, and the average size of their property holdings was far greater than among the city's foreign born, but much of the difference was a consequence of native dominance of the more lucrative occupations. In the middle and lower ranges of the occupational scale, the immigrant could and especially by 1860 did compete successfully for property, the tangible sign of success, to assuage the "longing for the little bit of land, all their own" noted by a later nineteenth century observer as characteristic of the Germans of Milwaukee.[14]

The implication is that differences in values spurred Milwaukee's immigrant heads of household to more frequent home ownership than similarly circumstanced native counterparts.[15] Ethnic variations in dwelling types and in the tendency to take in boarders lend some support to such an interpretation. By 1860, nativity had a significant bearing upon the type of dwelling of a household.[16] German families were more apt than others to live in two or multi-family units. Not quite a third of all households in each ethnic group which lived in such multiple units reported property ownership; this represents a lower than average ownership rate than among the natives and British as a whole, about average for the Irish and the Germans.[17] Among the Germans, where the number dwelling in non-single-family units (208) was sufficiently large to permit occupational classification, clerks and petty shopkeepers constituted a proportion larger than their share in the entire sample would suggest, while unskilled workers were under-represented. Thus Germans whose occupations required expensive central locations were most frequently found in non-single-family dwellings, and their numbers included owners as well as renters.[18] There were undoubtedly many who like August Frank, were glad to convert parts of their new homes into separate apartments to help pay the mortgage, many who were willing to rent such apartments until they too could afford their own homes.[19]

Only the natives and the Germans shared their homes with boarders with sufficient frequency to permit an assessment of possible relationships with home ownership. As noted in the preceding chapter, natives exhibited a much greater propensity to welcome boarders; the native households doing so tended to be of the same middle and upper class background as the native sample as a whole. However, only slightly over a third of all native householders with boarders reported property holding, at a time when about half of the native household heads owned property. Over 44 percent of the German householders with boarders were property owners, about seven percentage points more than in the German sample as a whole. Among the Germans, the practice of taking in boarders was found disproportionately among small shopkeepers, the skilled and the semiskilled, and was notably absent among the unskilled.[20] While many of the boarders in both German and native households were probably employees of the household head, data on boarders when combined with the information concerning dwelling units suggest some willingness on the part of middle-class Germans to share their quarters and thereby enhance their capacity to acquire property in a fashion not so current among the native born.

In addition to property ownership, the ability to employ household help was an important fruit of occupational success and a sign of middle-class status in the mid-nineteenth century. By that measure (Table 21) the wives of the native-born householders were far more likely to enjoy the comforts of economic success than were their immigrant sisters, even when their husbands were of the same occupational status. The proportion of native employers increased by 1860, while the proportion of Irish and German employers declined—another

Table 21 Percent of all households employing servants, by nativity group and occupational status

| | Nativity group | | | |
Year	Native	British	Irish	German
1850	42	18	13	10
1860	49	18	7	8

| | | | | | Occupational status[a] | | | | |
1860	N	1	2	4	5	6	7	8	9
Native	174	88	85	53	57	16	8	8	35
German	96	46	63	22	20	5	9	-	5

[a]Occupational categories: 1. professional; 2. proprietors, managers, and officials; 3. no significant data; 4. clerical and sales; 5. petty proprietors, managers, and officials; 6. skilled; 7. semiskilled; 8. unskilled; 9. other and unknown.

indication of the dwindling representation of earlier middle-class emigrants by that year.[21] Though significant numbers of Germans were able to acquire property, and an even larger proportion were in occupations which could aspire to property ownership, after twenty-five years of German settlement in Milwaukee, not even a tenth had achieved sufficient economic security to provide their wives with household help. For most, what funds they had were probably devoted to purchasing homes, establishing businesses, perhaps also to bringing over relatives from Germany.

While the general emphasis is thus upon the slow consolidation of immigrant socioeconomic positions in the antebellum years—consolidation threatened in the case of the Germans taken as a whole by continuing lower-class immigration through the mid-1850s—some immigrants were able to make places for themselves among the ranks of the well-to-do Milwaukeeans. Ten percent of the Germans, after all, could afford servants. While natives constituted four fifths of the householders owning property valued at over $10,000 in 1850, that percentage declined to slightly over half by 1860. And while in 1860 the top tenth of 1 percent of Milwaukee's population, which controlled 14 percent of the city's combined real and personal wealth, included only two foreign born among the 16, and while only 17 percent of the top 46 property holders in the city were foreign born compared to their 80 percent proportion in the adult population, emphasis can be placed on the fact that five Germans, two Scots, and an Irishman were able to make it into that select group. The average wealth of the foreign born lagged 30 years behind that of the native born in Milwaukee by one measure, yet individual immigrants could at least expect yearly increases, even if at a rate slower than for the natives.[22] That fact, plus demonstrable immigrant success in some occupational categories and in acquiring property, must have supported immigrant hopes for economic security in Milwaukee.

Implications

The integration of Milwaukee's immigrants into its growing economy proceeded along lines which differed for each major nationality. In general, the participation of the several groupings followed familiar stereotypical patterns, albeit with certain differences. The British held the most favorable position among antebellum Milwaukee

immigrants, both in terms of occupational status and property ownership, yet they had not "merged imperceptibly" into the native population. They moved mainly in the middle circles, as artisans, while the
Yankees more readily climbed the heights. There were exceptions, of
course, to be noted in the following chapter, but the British retained a
clear economic pattern distinguishable from that of the natives.

The Irish of Milwaukee likewise conformed to their accepted status
as an urban proletariat. Yet Milwaukee did well by many of them,
judging by their persistence and their improving posture with regard to
occupations and property ownership by 1860. They appeared to have
found in the semiskilled occupations a particular route to security.
They must have benefited also from the large numbers of Germans who
were obliged to share with them the city's menial tasks. There was
probably little hope that "Paddy" could change his image in a Milwaukee settled by those who had known him in the East, but at least he
was not exclusively associated with the city's dirty work.

Milwaukee's German population contained an extensive proletariat
of its own, along with its more stereotypical artisan community and its
professionals and businessmen. As could be expected, given its relative
size, it had the widest range of internal differences and the least
economic homogeneity of any nationality group in the city, including
the native born. As a local chronicler noted in 1861:

> The sturdy thrift of Germany is conspicuous over all . . . Although the
> majority of the Germans are of the middle and lower classes, still the profes-
> sions, the arts, manufactures, and commercial as well as political positions
> have been entered by cultivated and highly educated Germans, and today we
> cannot enter any of the higher branches of business without encountering
> them. German, perhaps, in manner and accent, but American at heart . . . In
> the political field, at the bar, and with the baton and pencil, our German fel-
> low citizens have helped to confer honor and beauty upon Milwaukee, and in
> manufacturing they have done more than any other, in developing the re-
> sources of the State and in accumulating capital at home.[23]

It was high praise indeed and demands further exploration. Perhaps the
very heterogeneity of the Germans ensured that the achievements of
those prominent few at the top would cover the menial labors of the
many on the bottom with the mantle of vicarious respectability and
leave to the Irish alone the proletarian opprobrium.

These patterns of socioeconomic achievement suggest that only the

Germans had the size and range of occupations and achievement within their numbers to support a potential community in the full sense of the word, one performing community supportive functions largely independent of the wider Milwaukee society. While the Irish were far more homogeneous and hence undoubtedly quickly acquired a community image, they constituted in effect a socioeconomic class united by a common economic predicament, and of course by background and religion, but dependent upon the larger society for employment, services, and leadership, as well as for status recognition for those who made good; whether they could have supported anything like a full Irish community capable of enduring over time is questionable. Further exploration of such implications of the varying immigrant socio-economic patterns for their adjustment and community formation, however, should be linked to more careful consideration of their specific paths through the different branches of the Milwaukee economy. The problem of economic adjustment was a human one, and the immigrants' judgments of their success and failures, and the larger community's judgments of them, cannot be inferred from statistics alone.

The Industrious Worker

4 Census statistics have suggested the substance behind the Milwaukee immigrants' hopes that "there will be a better livelihood for us here," a substance tempered, of course, by the high mobility of the immigrants into and out from the city. While twenty years or less was too short a time for many of those who remained in the city to make a fortune—the few fortunes of the pioneer period generally went to the native born with their better connections and familiarity with American business ways—it was long enough for a sizable proportion of newcomers to attain the comfortable lot that was the traditional desire of the immigrant. But the significance of such economic achievement for either individual adjustment to Milwaukee life or community formation defies statistical expression. Only through a more detailed examination of the immigrants' career paths and employment conditions as laborers, craftsmen, merchants, and professionals can the broader implications of their participation in the city's economic life be assessed. While the general design of this study precludes estimation of occupational mobility rates, insights derived from the experiences of immigrants who prospered during the period and from the opportunities offered by the various sectors of the Milwaukee economy can illuminate the nature of the opportunity which the new city offered to its foreign-born residents and hence the outlines of probable mobility.

The Laborers

Daniel Kennedy was only eleven when he arrived in Boston from Ireland with his father; his mother died before their emigration. His father soon went "into the Country" seeking work, leaving the boy with a friend. On that day, Kennedy later recalled, "I began life on my own account." He found a job and worked for three years until he moved west with his newly remarried father. The Kennedy family arrived in Milwaukee in May 1844, and in rapid order young Daniel worked in a hotel, split rails for a farmer near the city, and then joined his father in a dairy business selling milk to lake steamers. He had left the hotel after a month when refused his pay; he had left the farmer because he served too many prayers and not enough food. Dairying proved a more profitable venture: "We made money and when I pulled out from home I left him very comfortable."

I went to Chicago bought a horse, got trusted for a dray and harness and started out draying and in those days draying was very good. Easily made from $15.00 to $20.00 per week in summer. In the winter I graded up the third ward marsh. Afterwards I started teaming in the summer season and grading and hauling wood I had a whack at almost every thing that was going those times. I always had something to do. In '53 there was quite a panic and things were very dull. When the old Watertown R.R. started I went to work on the road until the company bursted I graded the road at Pewaukee, filled across the lake and graded over a mile at Pine Lake. When the company broke up they were owing me about $300.00 which I lost. This amount may not seem large now but it was a whole lot them times. In '58 H. L. Page was elected mayor and he appointed me a member of the force.

Kennedy remained with the force, and by 1878 was Milwaukee's chief of police; four years later he left for Kansas City and a very successful real estate business.[1]

Kennedy's is a Milwaukee immigrant success story. Native wit and willingness to work undoubtedly made up for lack of education, but success also involved credit and political pull. The political element, the difficulties with payment for work, as well as the reliance on small-scale agriculture, teaming, and construction jobs, made his an almost stereotypical career.[2] Yet how many unskilled laborers were able to match that stereotype? Could many expect to use casual labor as a stepping-stone to upward mobility and did those who advanced possess any special advantages? Answers can be suggested by looking at the conditions of laboring in early Milwaukee, as well as at the career paths of others who, like Kennedy, made it up from the bottom.

In finding a job, the unskilled laborer in Milwaukee was dependent for the most part upon personal inquiry or the good offices of his friends; he was advised to visit construction sites, markets, brickyards, the docks, wherever large numbers of laborers might be required. The landlords and bartenders of boardinghouses, saloons, and hotels patronized by the newcomers undoubtedly functioned as informal recruiting agents; the emigration agencies which specialized in passage arrangements and land sales also promised free information concerning employment to the immigrants who visited their offices.[3] Occasionally, local immigrant societies attempted to match immigrants and employers in a more systematic fashion. In 1852, for instance, a Milwaukee German workers' educational society opened employment bureaus in the various wards of the city, where volunteers gave free advice and recommended workers to inquiring employers.[4] Three years later, the German Society of Milwaukee, an immigrant protection association, included job referrals among the services offered to newly arrived immigrants.[5]

Such organized efforts functioned only sporadically, however, and relatively few could benefit from them. Help-wanted advertisements appeared occasionally in the press, although usually for jobs requiring large numbers of hands.[6] These large-scale employers provided many immigrants with their first jobs, mainly construction work, where personal recruiting by agents supplemented press advertisements. As an incentive to attract labor for Milwaukee canal construction in 1840, for example, contractors advertized "good board and lodging" and "cash payments made at the end of each month," and many of Milwaukee's earliest foreign born undoubtedly put in their first hours of American labor on that canal. Contractors for public works projects continued to recruit in Milwaukee throughout the antebellum period, and although an 1851 guide may have exaggerated the promise of such labor—"But few of these who are moderately temperate, and commonly careful, will, at the expiration of their engagements, leave without considerable sums of money in their possession"—such projects outside the city were one important source of employment for the unskilled immigrant, and for some, a way of accumulating capital for future businesses.[7]

Unskilled labor within Milwaukee itself was also plentiful. The massive leveling and filling operations required to make the site habitable proceeded on and off for years. Some of the projects may have been a form of make-work. A citizen complained in 1848 that the grading of the first ward bluff to provide fill for the third ward marsh was carried out solely for the purpose of providing Democrats (that is, immigrants) with jobs at the expense of the property holders, and in fact an 1857 visitor noted that such work had been responsible for providing employment for large numbers of laborers during periods of job scarcity when many could not otherwise have remained in the city.[8] Immigrants were linked with construction labor within Milwaukee almost from the first; Jeremiah Coffee, his two yoke of oxen, and his old horse trained to pull a driverless cart of earth were familiar sights at filling operations during the 1840s. Coffee, despite his reputation for great industry, probably never made more than a living from his work, but other Irishmen like John Furlong and Peter O'Donnel, and Germans like George Abert, eventually moved up to more profitable contracting ventures of their own. More common, probably, were the modest "successes" of men like James Fox, whose two years of construction labor earned him a permanent post as section foreman for the Milwaukee and Mississippi Railroad, or William Gray, who for many years found it "a hard struggle to support his family with the low rate of wages for labor," until construction work at the city gas works led to a steady job there "at fair wages."[9]

Closely linked with construction work and representing a step up from common labor was draying of all kinds. Not only earth but a variety of other freight had to be moved in a port city like Milwaukee, and immigrants generally did the moving. Just over two fifths of the 34 teamsters, cabmen, and carriers in the 1850 heads of household sample were Irish, just under two fifths German, while ten years later Germans constituted slightly over half of the 72 drivers, the Irish less than two fifths. Within the entire work force in 1850, 41 percent of the drivers were already German, 37 percent Irish. As a German traveler in 1854 discovered, competition in the business was intense; his boat was met by one German and four Irish drivers, and it seemed to him that:

The Irish want to claim this trade for themselves exclusively, and begrudge the Germans their small earnings. When, despite their importunities, we hired the only German cart that had come out from town, the Irish followed us a good distance with abuses and insults against the "Dutchman" and finally even with stones. Our German carter was rather fearful and timid in the face of these insolent Irish.[10]

Such intense competition probably resulted from the relative ease of entry into the hauling business. It was said that a man could buy a horse and cart cheaply, perhaps half on credit, feed his family with the income from hauling—"with the large amount of business being done, this is a hard, but also lucrative occupation"—buy further horses and wagons, employ them on public works, and with luck, either move into larger scale contracting or use the nest egg as capital for a farm or other business. In the meantime, horse and family could share the same shanty and further save on expenses.[11] By 1860, 52 percent of the 29 Irish teamsters in the manuscript census sample owned property averaging $1,560 in value, compared with 43 percent of the 35 German teamsters in the sample, who held an average of $1,000 worth of property. For both groups, teaming and draying thus constituted a better than average route to property ownership for the unskilled immigrant.

The railroads, docks, and warehouses which were the physical signs of Milwaukee's commercial functions were another major source of jobs for the unskilled, and a limited amount of casual labor found employment in Milwaukee's factories, although not on the scale of eastern cities. But most of the casual labor of any kind available to Milwaukee's immigrants had its drawbacks for the person in search of economic security. For one thing, it tended to be seasonal. Winter brought with it a slack season not only in construction and closely linked trades but also in the movement of goods on the Great Lakes, which meant a lessened demand for longshoremen and draymen. All too often, winter meant an often fruitless search for work chopping wood or cutting ice or reliance upon charity of one sort or another. Employment opportunities also fluctuated from one year to the next: a business recession could cut back employment, while a building boom or a new railroad could suddenly create a labor shortage. Not only was casual labor irregular, but wages were relatively low. While an 1846 newcomer felt that day laborers received good wages, an immigrant two years earlier had probably described the situation more realistically when he wrote home: "If anyone wants to support himself by day labor he seizes every opportunity for work." Daily wages for skilled craftsmen could be twice those of the day laborer.[12]

There was always the additional problem—especially serious for construction workers—that pay might not be forthcoming. Even if the employer did not default entirely, there were frequent shortages of cash; payment might be in the form of orders on a local store with inflated prices.[13] Such difficulties led, in one notable instance, to a riot in Milwaukee in 1853, when over 300 Germans who had been employed in constructing the LaCrosse and Milwaukee Railroad complained that the contractor had not paid them as promised and rallied at the company's Milwaukee office to demand their wages. Told that the company could not be held responsible for the contractor's fraud, they vented their frustration by breaking into a dry goods and grocery store beneath the company offices. Several arrests followed, and the entire group of Germans surged to the jail to rescue the prisoners, a red flag waving in the van. When the mayor attempted to confiscate the flag, he was hit on the head with a shovel and a full-scale riot broke out; "rowdies" yelling, "the damned Dutch," attacked the workers, who attacked the officials, and several persons were injured before firemen and police drove away the mob. When the company finally promised to pay the workers from the funds due the contractor, the prisoners were released, sparking a jubilant victory parade.[14] Few incidents were quite so dramatic, but frequent labor demands for "just pay," in cash, and at proper time, indicated the gravity of pay problems, undoubtedly exacerbated for the immigrants by language difficulties in communication with their employers.

Casual labor was also dangerous. Frequent accidents on the job meant, if not death, then considerable pain and injury for the hapless laborer and further problems of convalescence. The young workman without a family could find himself evicted from his boardinghouse by a landlord who appreciated neither the extra care he required nor his inability to pay the rent, while an accident to a family man could often leave his dependents in direst straits. Sickness, injury, and death, as well as the need for relief resulting from fluctuations in employment demand, were important stimuli for the emergence of immigrant benefit associations and protective societies.[15]

While the difficulties of casual labor were not experienced exclusively by the foreign born, their numerical preponderance in such work made its hazards an everday fact of immigrant life. Nevertheless, some were able to use it as a stepping-stone to more ample security, while others were able to earn at least enough to purchase property on a limited scale.[16] Such security, of course, often involved the labor of an entire family. The Kroegers, for example, arrived in Milwaukee penniless in 1844. The crippled father took whatever odd jobs his condition permitted, the mother did laundry, the young boys sawed wood, and the sister entered domestic service.[17] Other families even more desperate set their younger children to begging or raiding backyard swill barrels for garbage and grease to feed the hogs.[18]

For every young Kroeger or Daniel Kennedy who helped support his family through casual labor as a youth, there were also boys like John Massini, who was apprenticed to a machinist after leaving school at age 12, Henry Riemenschneider, apprenticed to a machinist at 14 after three years work in tobacco and pail factories, or the young Kieckhefers, who were put to carpentering and masonry at 13 and 14 respectively.[19] For families who could do without immediate income from their sons, such apprenticeships were a means of ensuring a more secure future for their children. "In the settlement of them to their trade," a Wisconsin guidebook promised, the immigrant would find "none of the difficulties so common in his own country to contend with, from the fact that it is not necessary to provide premiums for them before they will be taken as apprentices, for none are here required. The boy is in himself considered a premium, because from the very commencement of his servitude he is put to ready and profitable use."[20]

School attendance provides one measure of the extent to which families made use of the labor of their children. The federal census noted all children between the ages of five and 17 who had attended school at some time during the previous year. In both 1850 and 1860 (Table 22), children of native-born fathers had the best school attendance record, followed, in order, by British, Irish, and Germans in both

Table 22 Percentage of children 5-17 years old in sample households attending school

Attendance	Native[a] All children	British[a] All children	Irish All children	Irish Laborers' children	German All children	German Laborers' children
			1850			
	(N=241)	(N=109)	(N=237)	(N=113)	(N=331)	(N=106)
Boys	83	63	68	57	56	65
Girls	69	67	54	58	57	48
Total	76	65	62	58	57	58
Ratio of boys to girls	.91	1.22	1.21	1.17	1.40	1.65
			1860			
	(N=429)	(N=215)	(N=490)	(N=165)	(N=1,276)	(N=376)
Boys	76	72	66	71	65	58
Girls	72	67	65	73	61	55
Total	74	70	66	72	63	57
Ratio of boys to girls	.95	1.13	1.02	1.32	1.04	1.16

[a]Since there were so few native and British laborers, their children are not included here.

years, all three immigrant groups improving their records by 1860.
Boys generally had a greater likelihood of school attendance than girls.
Such figures suggest the extent to which their poorer economic position
led immigrant parents to substitute either employment or job training
for formal schooling; they also suggest the frequency with which
immigrant girls left home, probably for employment as live-in
servants.[21]

But the difference in Irish and German patterns implies that something beyond mere economic necessity influenced school attendance
rates. This becomes particularly evident when the attendance of
laborers' children is isolated. Proportionately fewer sons and more
daughters of Irish laborers attended school in 1850 than among the Irish
sample as a whole; ten years later both sexes recorded better school
attendance than did the total Irish sample, perhaps reflecting a faith in
schooling as a means to acquire the greater security which the group as
a whole demonstrated that year. By contrast, the children of German
laborers were less apt to attend school by 1860 than were either the
children of Germans in general, or of Irish laborers. The diverging
paths of the two groups suggest once again the aggregate consequences
of the continued in-migration of lower-class Germans during the fifties.

While women could take in sewing and washing and a limited
amount of work was available from Milwaukee clothiers, domestic
service was the best alternative for many girls who had to work to help
support themselves and their families.[22] There is "a prejudice in favor of
'Old Country' children, especially females," noted an 1851 Wisconsin
immigrant guidebook. "Girls from the age of 11 and 12 are sought after
as day-helps, either to nurse children or attend about house, getting
from half a dollar to six shillings per week, and board, while the adult
female help or servants get from four to six dollars per month and
board." Parents were assured that domestic service involved no loss of
status, that it meant training for the household the girl would hope to
run after her own marriage, and a chance to earn a nest egg in the
meantime. "The German girls who have been here for some time, have
mostly been in service in Yankee households; this is quite usual here
and even well-to-do girls do not scorn to do so."[23] Veronica Frank, for
example, was able to recruit as her maids the daughter of a farmer who
lived near her brothers and the daughter of a butcher whose shop was
across the street from her husband's business. "It is a real problem with

the girls here," she complained. "They want high wages [she paid 75¢ a week] and want to do but little."[24]

A British visitor as early as 1841 observed that "all the drudgery and heavy work at our hotel is performed by the poor German girls, who are actually obliged to carry heavy logs of fire-wood, wash the house linen, and scrub away from morning till night," but Irish girls proved the most numerous among servants (Table 23).[25] They did not, however, enjoy an unchallenged near monopoly of domestic positions. Their numbers were too small, those of the Germans too large. Germans, in fact, constituted almost half of the 73 servants found in the 1860 sample of adult women, the Irish a quarter, and the natives only a twentieth; this of course, includes servants in immigrant as well as native households. Domestic service may have played a different role among the Irish; the average Irish domestic tended to be older than her German or native-born counterpart, suggesting that service for them was less frequently a phase in the life cycle, more often a permanent occupation—and indeed domestics of all nationalities were more frequently mature women by 1860.

But in the first generation at least, domestic service not only augmented family incomes and provided nest eggs, but it brought an

Table 23   Female servants in native households in Ward 1, 1850, and Ward 7, 1860 (percent)

Servants	Native	British	Irish	German	Other
		1850 (N=280)			
Aged 10-19	70	40	44	63	-a
Aged 20-29	20	60	48	34	-a
Aged 30+	10	-	8	3	-a
		1860 (N=489)			
Aged 10-19	56	42	31	54	-a
Aged 20-29	37	31	57	42	-a
Aged 30+	7	27	12	4	-a
Ethnic distribution, 1850	7	4	47	35	6
Ethnic distribution, 1860	12	6	43	32	7

aNot tabulated.

important segment of the immigrant population—the future mothers of second and third generations—into intimate contact with middle-class American homelife. They quickly learned English, adopted American dress, and with it, undoubtedly, American attitudes. The young German serving girls were fixtures at the casual balls and *Biergarten* dances of the Germans, and through them the young laborers and journeymen, who became first dance partners, then marriage partners, were brought into closer contact with native ways than they ever may have achieved in their own working spheres. "Those who find a suitable German wife here are best off," Carl de Haas wrote from Milwaukee in 1849, since girls who have been in service in Yankee households "understand better, then, the language and customs of the Americans, with whom the Germans must assimilate nolens volens as soon as possible; they can be very useful by their knowledge of American conditions."[26] In another respect, however, the presence of the foreign "hired girl" must have colored native attitudes toward others of her nativity, and in Milwaukee this meant that both Germans and Irish would be associated with servant status. Finally, domestic service represented a limited close contact between members of various immigrant groups probably otherwise rare in Milwaukee. While many households employed either all Irish or all German girls, others mixed foreign-born servants in varying combinations. The influence of such contacts, along with those with the native employer, cannot be measured precisely, yet domestic service was undoubtedly one of the few ways in which Milwaukee's immigrant groups breached the barriers erected by segregating forces of background and occupation, to interact as individuals.

Market gardening provided a final economic path which could be taken by the unskilled immigrant and his family. In a city such as Milwaukee, rife with property speculation and development, there were at any given time numerous small tracts of land near to, even intermixed with, built-up areas, which the immigrant could rent.[27] Intensive family labor on such plots produced vegetables and fruits for the city markets or door-to-door peddling, or provided pasture for a few cows. The 1850 census sample included five small "farmers" (three German, one Irish, one British) and four greenhouse operators (two British, one native, one German). By 1860, three of the six farmers and nine of the 13 greenhouse operators were German, while all four dairymen were Irish. A better inventory of the direct urban-fringe market gardening of the city, however, is found in the 1860 agricultural manuscript census for Milwaukee, which listed 113 units with an annual product in excess of $50, specializing in vegetables, fruit, cows, and swine. Three of the four such units in the second ward, and eight of the ten in the sixth ward, were run by Germans. Germans and some Dutch farmed the 42 ninth ward units, while the 57 small farms of the south side were fairly evenly divided among the Germans, Irish, and Yankees. Even smaller backyard gardens within the built-up German areas housed chicken coops and a cow or pig, and produced vegetables, eggs, and milk, which were brought by the wagonload each morning to the Green Market in the east side German neighborhood, where Milwaukee housewives did their daily shopping.[28]

That such small-scale agriculture could provide a laborer with a toehold in the city's business life is shown by the experience of John T. Kopmeier, as well as the cases of the Kennedys and Kroegers discussed earlier. Kopmeier arrived in Milwaukee with only a farming background and worked several years as a laborer before he found a steady job loading ice for another immigrant whose business career had begun with food speculation and a dairy. Kopmeier married, invested his earnings in a few cows, and then with the profits began his own ice business. While he peddled milk in the morning and ice in the afternoon, his wife tended the cows until ice proved so profitable that he could give up the dairy.[29] Thus market gardening, or even the pig or two left to root under the house and the cow in the shed behind, supplemented the laborer's income and for at least a few became both a full-time operation and a path to middle-class status.

The Craftsmen and Manufacturers

"May we remark," boasted Milwaukee's 1851 directory, "that Milwaukee is favored with a very superior class of mechanics, who finish their jobs in a manner unsurpassed by any elsewhere." The majority of those superior mechanics, as earlier indicated, were German. By and large they brought their skills with them from Germany; could they but apply those skills in Milwaukee, they would stand from the outset several rungs above the bottom of the economic ladder, with the opportunity of climbing higher before them. For many a journeyman the goal was to establish himself as an independent master craftsman with his own shop, in a country where he was promised there were neither guilds to closely regulate trade nor rank among artisans. Yet, in America as in Europe, the old craft system was breaking apart, soon to be displaced by factories largely dependent upon unskilled labor. Milwaukee lagged behind more eastern American cities in this process, yet even in Milwaukee certain journeymen would soon find themselves faced with the alternatives of eking out a living in a small repair and custom shop incapable of competing with local or eastern factories, accepting factory employment, or attempting to move into retailing, which demanded a whole new range of skills.[30]

Other adjustment problems unrelated to the changing American manufacturing system affected the immigrant artisan's dream. His small capital was often insufficient to compete against the Yankees, whose greater initial means and better access to credit enabled them to buy the best machines and tools, to purchase raw materials cheaply in large quantities, and to keep a wider selection of wares in their work-shops. Lack of English could lead to serious misunderstandings with customers, while differences in method between America and the old country also presented problems. In America, for example, workers were usually paid by the piece or by contract, so that speed yielded greater profit. The German artisan, accustomed to a slower pace, could often do a better job, but his frontier customers were seldom willing to pay a premium for excellence. The result was that until the German learned more slap-dash methods—and until he stopped taking such frequent breaks to puff on his pipe—he might find it difficult to compete with native workmen in such fields as building, woodworking, tailoring, and printing.[31]

Moreover, crafts were often defined differently in America—the West loved the jack-of-all trades. The house carpenter was expected to draw up plans and make cost estimates; the confectioner manufactured soda water as well as pastry; the distiller turned out whiskey as well as brandy; painters were also varnishers; glaziers made window frames; carpentry was closer to joining, but joining included chairmaking as well. Sometimes the redefinition completely eliminated certain trades—glaziers, joiners, locksmiths, paperhangers often found themselves put out of work by amiably adaptable carpenters.[32] Thus the highly specialized European workman frequently had to learn what from his point of view was an entirely new trade in order to earn a living with his old training or rest content with a helper's job.

Other trades were affected by American reliance on imported goods or on factory production elsewhere in the country; local craftsmen might find it impossible to compete with such items as shoes, chairs, brushes, and needles produced by eastern American factories. A German, for example, reported that a shoemaker "would have poor business because every shopkeeper in Milwaukee sells boots and shoes." Another commented, "I would not recommend to all trades-people that they come here to settle, inasmuch as everything is done differently and for the most part in factories, and until one is ac-quainted with the local conditions, many sacrifices must be made." Where such factory production operated on a local basis, the Yankee's greater access to capital again gave him the edge. Moreover, the increasing use of machinery in American production penalized the German craftsman unfamiliar with it, while rewarding the Briton used to the more advanced methods of his own country. Even in 1860 Mil-waukee had comparatively few factories, relatively little complex machinery, yet a German in 1846 reported a general impression of machinery and engine plants lining the river and marveled that "here almost everything is run by machine."[33]

Foreign artisans also had to accustom themselves to producing a dif-ferent finished product. American styles in tailoring, for example, took time for the German to learn. Silversmiths, coppersmiths, and others whose product depended on stye likewise required time to adjust their skill. The American do-it-yourself habit caused additional trouble for the immigrant craftsman—even in the city, for example, American women often baked their own bread. Americans used no salad oil, so the oil miller was out of luck; they were unwilling to pay for fine turned woodwork, often forcing the skilled turner into the factory; they pre-ferred to buy their books already bound, so the German binder had little hope of supporting his own establishment unless he could set up a larger factory bindery on the American model.[34]

Some problems of style and even method could be solved if the immi-grant craftsman catered exclusively to his fellow countrymen. In New York, for example, German builders confined their operations to German residential areas where employers and employees alike spoke the same language and were accustomed to similar production methods. Milwaukee's large German population could likewise support the oil millers, bakers, and brewers who permitted them to maintain old habits of eating and drinking. But how many immigrants wished to continue wearing clothes whose style would immediately brand them as foreign? How many Germans would continue to pay extra for careful workmanship when they were continually confronted by cheaper and perhaps more showy American goods? The major advantage enjoyed by the German workman in Milwaukee, a visitor from Germany found, was the moderation and thrift of his life style—but that was a distinct disadvantage for those forced to rely upon him as a consumer.[35]

With so much against him, the newcomer was advised to work for a time in the shop of another before setting up business on his own, and most probably did so. Many never became independent craftsmen, while many, learning the ways of the frontier city market, switched trades several times before settling down in the one they found most profitable.[36] A closer look at the artisans in the two census samples suggests which trades those were and how effectively the artisans met the challenges of adjustment.

Given the numerical dominance of the Germans among the skilled workmen of Milwaukee, it was almost inevitable that the census noted their presence in most trades (Table 24). The size of the German population meant not only that they created a market for their own skills, but also that other groups were almost forced to patronize them. With only limited competition from craftsmen of other nationalities, the German artisan of Milwaukee probably suffered fewer handicaps than his *Landsmann* elsewhere. The restricted frontier economy set the greatest limitation on the numbers and kinds of skilled crafts entered by the Germans. Milwaukee's occupational needs were relatively simple. Only about 185 distinct occupations appeared in the city's 1850 census, compared with 992 in Boston in the same year.[37] Only a few of those occupations involved large numbers of mechanics. Nevertheless, despite the large numbers of German craftsmen and the limited variety of trades found in the city, rudimentary ethnic specializations were evident.[38]

Carpentering, reflecting the demand created by the rapid physical growth of the city, was the field which generally attracted the largest number of skilled workmen within each nationality. The proportion of carpenters who were natives dropped an estimated 40 percent in 1850 to only 12 percent by 1860, while the German share rose from 28 to 54 percent.[39] Carpenters constituted only about 15 percent of the German skilled workmen in both years but included relatively greater proportions of the craftsmen of other nationalities: in 1850, 47 percent of the native craftsmen were carpenters, 31 percent of the British, and 25 per-

Table 24 Numbers of sample artisans in selected trades, by nativity

Trade	Native 1850	Native 1860	British 1850	British 1860	Irish 1850	Irish 1860	German 1850	German 1860
Carpenter	34	17	17	15	8	15	24	73
Mason	4	7	2	4	1	7	13	25
Painter	3	2	3	3	1	2	5	13
Cabinetmaker	2	-	2	1	1	-	13	25
Coachmaker	-	3	-	-	-	3	4	10
Brewer	1	1	1	-	-	-	12	9
Blacksmith	4	4	5	2	4	5	10	22
Baker	-	2	-	-	-	-	7	13
Shoemaker	5	2	7	5	6	11	17	71
Tailor	2	1	4	3	6	4	26	52
Tanner	1	2	-	1	-	-	6	17
Butcher	1	3	4	5	-	-	7	23
Cooper	2	1	1	-	-	4	8	34
Machinist, etc.	5	7	2	5	1	2	2	10
Total skilled[a]	73	104	55	67	32	68	163	445
Percent of group who are skilled	32	26	54	46	16	19	41	38
Percent of skilled who are in group	20	12	15	9	9	9	46	58

[a]Includes miscellaneous other occupations not specifically listed in this table. Derived from Tables 15 and 16.

cent of the Irish, concentrations which dropped by 1860 to 16, 22, and 22 percent respectively.

While carpentry was therefore the most important trade for non-German skilled workmen, it was a trade in which the Germans were dominant by 1860. As practiced in the West, carpentry was crude but often profitable. The Roman Catholic bishop, a native of Switzerland, reported that building was done hurriedly in Milwaukee, neither beautifully nor solidly. A two story frame house was erected in three weeks, a larger brick house in six. Such carpentry required a good deal less of both skill and labor than the European was accustomed to: "From base to ridgepole everything comes finished from the factory . . . and only a few laborers are needed to erect a complete building out of the several parts."[40] Many of the carpenters on such projects probably worked as journeymen for native master builders, although approximately half of the 241 carpenters and builders listed in the 1860-61 directory—presumably men who accepted contracts on their own account—had German names, suggesting that the Germans included a share of masters proportionate to carpenters as a whole.[41] Since most of Milwaukee's physical expansion during the 1850s was in German areas, a large number of German carpenters may well have worked for German masters on houses built for their fellow countrymen. Of the six house builders listed in the 1860 manufacturing census, two of the three largest, as well as the two smallest, were German.

It was probably not coincidence that the immigrants who were able to establish large-scale construction firms in Milwaukee were either American-trained or spent time familiarizing themselves with American ways before striking out on their own. John Rugee, for example, ran one of the large German firms. In his teens he had come to America with his middle-class family but soon tired of their farming experiment and apprenticed himself to a Poughkeepsie carpenter and joiner. After several years as a journeyman carpenter he came to Milwaukee in 1851 and found a job as construction superintendent in the firm of a prominent native-born builder, who made him a partner two years later. Other prominent builders were British. Like Rugee, Charles James acquired his knowledge of carpentry in New York, while James Douglas picked up his skill in Canada.[42]

Despite the small-scale operations of most German carpenters, carpentry nevertheless provided greater security in terms of property ownership than several other trades (Table 25). A majority of all German carpenters owned some real estate by 1860, with an average value of about $1,050. Thus while the building industry attracted native and British craftsmen in greater than average numbers, sufficient work remained to provide at least a living for a good number of Germans. Germans were also numerically predominant in masonry and painting, although these trades were important for other immigrant groups as well.

Blacksmithing too occupied members of all the major groups, although in this trade the German percentage rose from 40 to 65 percent by 1860, with German names constituting about 61 percent of the 109 blacksmiths listed in the 1860-61 directory. The average blacksmith's shop was a small affair, even the larger ones averaging only two to three employees.[43] The limited sample of German blacksmiths for 1860

Table 25   Real property holdings of Germans in selected trades, 1860

Trade	Percent holding property	Mean value of property (dollars)	Median value of property (dollars)	N
Carpenter	51	1,050	500	74
Mason	56	820	600	25
Cabinetmaker	39	1,120	1,000	23
Shoemaker	38	910	800	71
Tailor	38	710	450	53
Cooper	35	1,140	900	34
Butcher	33	3,110	1,500	24
Blacksmith	38	1,325	1,000	21

suggests that while most did not own property, those who did had been able to amass above-average holdings.

Shoemaking and tailoring shared the distinction of being trades dominated numerically by Germans but from which most reaped little reward. They constituted 45 percent of all shoemakers and 63 percent of all tailors in 1850, and 74 and 70 percent respectively by 1860; of the 281 shoemakers listed in the 1860 city directory, about 70 percent had German names. But most of the German shoemakers probably worked in small repair shops. Census statistics tell the story: in 1860, the manufacuring census listed only 51 establishments with an annual value of product over $500; their mean value of product was $7,302, with an average employment of 6.4 hands. However, all but three of those shoemaking establishments employed fewer than fifteen hands each and altogether accounted for only 31 percent of the output listed in the census. Two large firms produced 65 percent of Milwaukee shoes by value of product. By 1860 those two firms each employed over 60 hands and used rudimentary factory techniques, while the largest of the remainder employed only 11 persons.[44] Both of those large firms were American-owned. The average firm among the 24 recognizably German establishments employed only 3.5 hands and produced a total value of product of $2,224; only one German firm was above the mean for all shoemakers in terms of employees and value of product. Most of Milwaukee's shoe production came from two local factories, leaving the average immigrant shoemaker either an operative in one of them, or the owner or one of the few employees in a small custom and repairing business.

Some of the 150 or more shoemakers working in the larger factories may, like Vincenz Schoenecker, have been able eventually to set up their own firms. But others undoubtedly saw the arrival of the factory preempting the artisan shoemakers' dream of comfortable independence in America. John Fischback, for example, deserted the craft almost as soon as he mastered it, for the grocery business, while the police and fire departments provided escape routes for Jerry O'Connor and Patrick J. Duffy. The one German who operated an above-average sized manufactory began with a retail shoe store and ended up running a tannery—far more an entrepreneur than a mechanic. Most immigrant shoemakers could look forward only to wages of about $7.00 a week and a lesser chance of property owning than fellow craftsmen in trades not suffering from factory competition.[45]

The immigrants who prospered through tailoring were likewise not the artisans but the merchant capitalists. Tailoring in Milwaukee had begun as a craft industry in which most articles were custom produced to individual order. Major competition came from ready-made clothing imported from the East, until large-scale production began in Milwaukee as well. By 1850, 69 percent of the value added by clothing manufacture in firms with an annual value of product of over $500 came from six Milwaukeee establishments; by 1860, eight to ten large firms generated about two thirds of the value added in clothing, although the number of small firms had more than doubled. The 20 clothing firms listed in 1850 averaged 12.6 employees, the 43 firms in 1860 averaged 13.4. Rather than set up their own businesses, many of the immigrant tailors found work in such large shops. The average tailor reportedly earned about $7.50 a week in 1856 but faced increasing competition from female labor.[46] German tailors were less likely to own property, or owned property less valuable, than most German artisans.

But a few immigrants were able to turn the clothing business to profitable account. Three of the six leading clothiers in 1850 were immigrants, as were four of the eight top firms in 1860. The owners of these immigrant firms were Jewish; their access to savings through close networks of relatives and friends apparently gave them an advantage enjoyed by few other immigrants. The firms were family affairs with often changing partnerships—the vicissitudes of involvement in such firms as those of the Shoyers, Adlers, Friends, and Macks, for instance, can be followed through the city directories from year to year. Usually these men were not themselves tailors. David Adler was trained as a baker, Solomon Adler as a glazier, Elias Friend as a clerk, Leopold Newbouer as a school teacher. But experience in the United States had convinced them of the profits to be made in the retail clothing trade, from which they moved first into wholesaling, then manufacturing. David Adler, for instance, ran a bakery in New York for three years before deciding that retail clothing was a likely business and Milwaukee a good location; his brother Soloman first went into general retailing in Montgomery, Alabama, and then opened a retail clothing store in New York before engaging in a series of similar Milwaukee ventures, while Friend founded his Milwaukee clothing store with earnings from clerking in Greensboro, Alabama.[47] The profits from tailoring thus went to immigrant entrepreneurs with access to capital and previous mercantile experience, not to the trained tailors themselves. Tailoring, in fact, came as close as any occupation in Milwaukee to fulfilling the stereotype of the immigrant "sweatshop"—complete with immigrant boss—despite the continued survival of many small independent shops.

In addition to tailoring, where special entrepreneurial connections were important, some German immigrants achieved success above the level of the small craft shop in two other fields—brewing and tanning. The notoriously unquenchable German thirst for beer provided Milwaukee's brewers with a market which they could enter on relatively favorable terms, and their industry came to achieve popular identification with the city itself. Alas for legend, however—Milwaukee's first brewery, the Lake Brewery dating from 1840, was founded by Welshmen and not Germans, and as late as 1860 the single most popular brew in Milwaukee measured in the census terms of value of product and, number of men employed in producing it, was the Pale Cream Ale of the Sands brewery, whose origins can be traced back to 1841.[48]

The ale produced by these pioneer establishments was not to German taste, however, and within a year after the opening of the Lake Brewery, a Württemberger, Hermann Reutelshofer, set up a German-style lager beer operation with the financial backing of the pioneer baker, Johann Meyer. The brewery managed to survive an early period of financial insecurity, and the continual flow of German settlement in the following decades was sufficient to support at least seven German breweries by 1850, 19 in 1860. The foundations of most of the large German breweries were laid in the 1840s. It was in 1844, for example, that Jacob Best and his sons transferred their brewing operations from the Rhineland to Milwaukee to establish the city's second German brewery. Two of the sons withdrew from the parent firm and established their own brewery in 1850; after lying idle for a year, it was purchased in 1855 by Frederick Miller, "fresh from managing a brewery in Württemberg," who had "migrated to America with $10,000 in gold," while the parent company—ultimately renamed the Pabst Brewing Company—went on to become the largest of the German breweries by 1860.[49]

The leading German brewery ten years earlier had been the City Brewery, founded in 1846 by John Braun. When he died in 1851, his former braumeister and boarder, Valentine Blatz, bought the brewery and married the widow. Blatz had arrived in 1848 with three years of apprenticeship and four years of employment in major German breweries behind him and by 1860 was running the city's third largest brewery in terms of value of product.[50] The second largest German firm in 1860 rested on similar foundations. Joseph Schlitz, the son of a well-to-do wine speculator, put his bookkeeper's training to use after his 1855 arrival in August Krug's brewery, which had been established six years earlier. When Krug died in 1856, Schlitz took over the brewery and married Krug's widow in 1858.[51]

Not all breweries established during the 1840s grew, of course, and even the larger establishments experienced initial difficulties in finding secure footing, but by the late 1840s an assured local market existed and in the 1850s export to neighboring areas began on a limited scale.[52] While the earliest breweries were sponsored by men who probably had a greater thirst for than knowledge of beer—Meyer's father-in-law, a farmer, took over the Reutelshofer operation, for example—most of the major breweries were soon run by men trained in the craft in Germany. The older breweries themselves provided experience for some of the later entrepreneurs, while those who entered the trade from other backgrounds generally had some direct or indirect association with the production or marketing of beer.

Capital seemed to present a major problem for the pioneeer immigrant brewers. The Bests and Miller were able to bring funds with them from Germany. Others evidently invested profits earned from other Milwaukee ventures when brewing appeared more profitable, as the case of Meyer suggests; breweries also attracted a certain amount of local investment. Fred Goes, the proprietor of a downtown peddlers' goods and variety store, for example, seems to have provided the capital for his joint venture with Falk, while Joseph Gerstner, partner in a moderate-sized firm of merchant tailors, may have played a similar role for Peter Gerstner's brewery. Several brewers built beer halls to distribute their products, and most entered retailing at least to the extent of operating beer gardens on their premises. For most of the smaller brewers, brewing was probably only a sideline to a saloon operation.

Thus, with an assured market that eventually attracted investment, and with skills imported from Germany, brewing became one of the few trades in which Milwaukee Germans were spectacularly successful by 1860. Nevertheless, only 11 German firms produced over $10,000 worth of beer in 1860, while the 13 remaining German brewers operated on a very small scale. Moreover, in both census years, the largest single brewery was owned by an American; Yankee competition in this field was limited by German taste alone. German brewers could live off *Landsmänner* with profit but profit only for a limited number. Those who attained this kind of success, however, provided community leadership and the example that some German artisans, given the right combination of skill, backing, and market conditions, could make the move from small-scale artisan to manufacturer. Moreover, for their employees, the average wages of $8.00 a week by 1856 meant a somewhat higher level of living than that of many Milwaukee mechanics.[53]

Tanning, although not dependent upon the special demand of the immigrant consumer, was another trade where some Milwaukee Germans found spectacular success. The tanner, noted one immigrant guidebook, was at the top of the artisan's ladder in the West, and certainly in Milwaukee by 1860 it was a tannery which produced the highest value added by manufacture of any trade followed by Germans. Milwaukee's first tannery was opened by a Yankee in 1842, but he was soon followed by a German, Christian Doerfler, for whom tanning was apparently subsidiary to glove-making.[54] Then in 1848, Frederick Vogel, a 25-year-old German-trained tanner with two years of experience buying hides and selling leather for a cousin's Buffalo tannery, persuaded his cousin to invest $12,000 to help him set up a tannery in Milwaukee. A year earlier Guido Pfister, a coworker of Vogel's in Buffalo, had opened the Buffalo Leather Store in Milwaukee, and Vogel marketed his leather through Pfister's store. In 1849 the two bought into each other's businesses and became full partners four years later. Vogel's cousin sold his interest in 1857 for $45,000. As early as 1850 the firm was more than seven times larger than any of the other three tanneries (all American-owned) listed in the manufacturing census, in terms of both number of employees (35) and the value of product ($45,000), and by 1860 was far in the forefront with an employee roster of 60 men and a production worth $120,000.[55]

Others followed in the path blazed by Pfister and Vogel, and by 1860 eight of the nine tanneries listed in the manufacturing census were German. Several were founded by former employees of earlier tanneries. Among them, for example, R. Suhm's firm represented a particularly striking cooperation of entrepreneur, retailer, and mechanic—a former Pfister and Vogel clerk, he was a shoe store owner at the time of its founding, one of his partners was a tanner, and the other a leading German businessman and politician; like Pfister and Vogel, this firm combined both tanning and retailing. The third ranking firm in 1860 was evidently a similar combination of tanner and retailer, the latter in this instance a Yankee wool dresser and dealer; while another German tanner evidently attracted capital from a leading grocer.[56] The average German tannery, however, remained a small operation, doing a local business like many other Milwaukee German craft shops. Milwaukee was advantageously located for tanning, and it has been suggested that German tanning methods were superior to American at the time. But the second-ranking firm was American and few of the German firms were as successful as Pfister and Vogel, with their access to capital and their business experience.

Cooperage, by contrast, offered employment but few entrepreneurial opportunities to German mechanics. The growth of Milwaukee's breweries, flour mills, and packing plants produced an ever-increasing demand for barrels, so that the seven coopers who appeared in the 1850 manufacturing census had grown to 55 by 1860. Only three of the 1850 coopers were German—three of the four smallest, although 56 percent of all coopers in the 1850 census were German. By 1860, when the largest cooperage was Yankee-owned and employed 27 men to produce a product valued at $34,000, the largest German firms employed only three or four mechanics and produced values in the $2,000 to $2,499 range.

At a time when the 1860 sample suggested that over 80 percent of the city's coopers were German, therefore, most were either employees of American entrepreneurs or masters and journeymen in small shops. But jobs were available, livings could be made, the average German cooper certainly held more real estate than his tailoring or shoemaking brethren, and perhaps these were the reasons behind Wagner and Scherzer's observation that coopers, along with tanners, carpenters, masons, and shoemakers, all did well in Milwaukee.[57] Furthermore, a cooperage required little initial capital, and 1860 in any case was still early days for the German cooper, as Charles Stolper illustrated. He arrived in 1854 at the age of 20, learned the trade by working for a German cooper, and six months later found employment in Layton and Plankinton's packing plant. Within a year he opened his own cooperage with very little capital and experienced initial difficulty even in paying the rent, but by 1857 was able to buy a lot and build his own shop, and soon had the business on a paying basis. He acquired an interest in several small cooperages around the city, and by 1868 was doing "big business." One secret of his success may have been the fact that John Plankinton was "always a good friend" to him.[58]

Milwaukee's German butchers were in a similar position. They provided the majority of the manpower and ran the small shops, while the few fortunes were made by Yankees and, in this case, Englishmen. Meat packing on a commercial basis began about mid-century as a sideline among butchers supplying the local Milwaukee market, and by 1860 Milwaukee was packing for a national market. One firm alone, Layton and Plankinton, accounted for about half the total output and a second, run by Edward Roddis, another quarter, employing 25 to 30 men each. Layton, "a fine looking representative of the English agricultural class," arrived with his son in the mid-forties and began small-scale butchering for local hotels and boardinghouses. In 1852 he formed a partnership with John Plankinton, a Yankee butcher, for beef and pork packing with capital borrowed from the local banking firm of Marshall and Illsley. By 1860 they had about $60,000 invested in the business, the Roddises $20,000 to $25,000.[59]

Without access to the capital necessary for this sort of operation, most of the Germans remained butchers with small meat markets. Many, like Charles Munkwitz, began with the savings of two or three years' labor in a local meat market or packing plant, where the pay was fair, $1.50 a day in 1856, but the work seasonal. Some, like the English George Munn, moved back and forth from their own shop to employment with the large firms before achieving final independence. At least 35 of the 46 butchers in the 1860 manufacturing census were German, yet only four had an annual value of product of over $10,000, only one employed more than three persons. At least one of the somewhat larger operations was operated by an Irishman, John Furlong, probably in conjunction with his wholesale grocery.[60] Few of the German butchers in the 1860 sample were able to achieve property ownership, yet those who did all held above-average amounts of property.

Furniture making presents a final example of the sort of craft dominated numerically by Germans but financially by natives. Of the 11 furniture makers in the 1850 manufacturing census, only four were German, yet 63 percent of the cabinet and chair makers of Milwaukee in that year were German. In 1860, the same pattern persisted; the four largest shops were Yankee.

One German who attempted operations on a large scale was August Flerzheim; his problems were perhaps indicative of the obstacles in the way of the German artisan. A cabinetmaker who arrived in Milwaukee in the late forties, Flerzheim entered into a partnership in 1854 with William Noyes, a Massachusetts native and also an experienced mechanic. Capital resources were supplied by a third partner, Henry Brugman. By 1857 the firm was doing a large business but apparently generated neither the business acumen nor capital reserves to withstand the depression of the late 1850s. In 1860 Flerzheim was running a furniture store on salary, leaving Noyes alone in the business to settle up its liabilities. Success in cabinetmaking apparently depended on the combination of capital, skill, and an early start, or capital alone with a retail trade to establish close customer connections; few Germans had the requisite resources, nor could they compete effectively with large-scale manufacturers either in Milwaukee or the East.[61] Some sample members were able to do moderately well in the way of property accumulation, but many more German cabinetmakers were probably employees in the large 20-30 man shops of the Yankee entrepreneurs.

In a growing city where most areas of production were divided between a few large producers on the one hand and many small craft shops on the other, the average foreign-born mechanic, if not an employee in a large shop run by an American entrepreneur, was thus either a master or journeyman in a small craft shop. Some trades, such as carpentry, cabinetmaking, cooperage, and butchering, provided a better living for the artisan than others like shoemaking and tailoring where factory production was becoming dominant. But only in brewing, where Germans formed their own market, tanning, where one

firm was able to link capital and special skills, and the clothing business, where the family connections of a special group of entrepreneurs
apparently aided in capital provision, were a few Germans able to enter
the ranks of large-scale producers.

A closer look at all German firms producing products valued at over
$10,000 in the manufacturing censuses suggests that, with few excep-
tions, even the larger German firms produced for a local and in many
instances a German market. Only eight German firms were among the
38 which fell into this category in Milwaukee in 1850. Of these, two
were brewers, one a tanner, and two were clothiers. The remaining
identifiably German firms included a soap and candle factory, a blacksmith, and a founder. By 1860 the situation was somewhat improved;
35 of the 109 firms with a product valued at $10,000 or over were Ger-
man—32 percent as compared with 21 percent ten years earlier.
Brewers were most numerous (eight), followed by clothing manufacturers (six), liquor dealers and distillers (four), millers (four), and tanners,
butchers, and tobacco manufacturers (three each). The largest value
added by manufacture was produced by the Pfister and Vogel tannery.

Cigar manufacturing and liquor distilling were both trades catering
to local tastes, as was the one German confectionery in the listing. The
entrance of Germans into milling brought them into one of Milwaukee's
high-growth industries. Jacob Bertschy, an innkeeper and public figure
in the German community, bought the Eagle Mill, the city's oldest, in
1846, and 12 years later brought his son-in-law J.B.A. Kern into partnership. Real expansion apparently occurred when Adolph Kern
(possibly J.B.A.'s father) invested in the mill the "comfortable fortune"
he had earned in over 25 years of business in Philadelphia. In this
case, then, it was probably Kern's capital which provided entree into
heights of production usually not scaled by Milwaukee Germans.
Another firm on the list, John Eigner's flour bag factory, may well have
developed as a sideline to his father's grocery business, perhaps supported from the savings it generated, while Henry Niedecken's book
bindery provided an important service for his friends in Milwaukee's
leading German cultural and business circles. The chandlery was the
sole survivor of the vogue for soap, starch, and vinegar manufacture
among young German immigrants in the forties.[62]

The activities of Milwaukee's Irish and British artisans were less
easily traced. Carpentering and meat packing attracted the British, and
some were able to establish large-scale firms; several also were notably

successful as machinists and founders.[63] The Irish left little record of any but small-scale craft production.

In summary, while many artisans arrived with skills which gave them important economic advantages over their unskilled fellow countrymen, there were major reasons, most notably lack of access to capital, which blocked attempts to translate those skills into comfortable business independence before 1860. Milwaukee's pioneer situation exacerbated normal problems of capital accumulation for persons unfamiliar with the counry. Even native-born manufacturers found that:

All new enterprises were supposed to have their own capital, for if they had not the chances were small for accommodation at the banks, because all the capital the banks had was required by those handling the products of the counntry at large. The commercial interests were the paramount objects in view by the banks then in existence, and anyone having sufficient "nerve" to go into manufacturing must do it on his own resources or bust.[64]

Although German banks began aiding German craftsmen in the later fifties, most craft shops rested on capital brought over from Germany or accumulated slowly through employment in the shops of others, and then only gradually augmented through small-scale custom manufacture. Few made fortunes thereby, and the 1860 census sample seems to suggest that for most trades even property ownership among artisans was the exception rather than the rule.

This realization undoubtedly underlay much of the trade union activity which periodically manifested itself in antebellum Milwaukee, particularly within crafts where the chances of advancement were smallest—tailoring, shoemaking, cabinetmaking, printing. While there were some faint signs of labor organization among the natives in the early and middle forties, the first major strike activity occurred in 1847 and 1848 among masons and bricklayers, journeymen coopers, journeymen shoemakers, and ship carpenters and caulkers. The issues were wages and hours, and in the case of the ship carpenters, limitation on the employment of unskilled apprentices. Given their numerical predominance in most trades by 1850, most of the strikers must have been immigrants—indeed their employer claimed that the striking shoemakers (whom he had imported from Boston) were "humbugged and intimidated by foreigners and their blustering was the result of alcohol"—but the only clearly successful strike was that of the ship carpenters who may well have been Yankees and Canadians protesting the hiring of increasing numbers of unskilled immigrants.[65]

The strike in 1848 among journeymen cabinetmakers and joiners, most of them German, crystallized the issue for immigrant mechanics. The journeymen had formed a union to work for improved pay in the face of a threatened wage cut. Price agreements with employers were signed, but soon broken. In the process, Milwaukee's largest employer of cabinetmakers, A. D. Seaman, insulted his workers "by saying to us scornfully that he can get on well without us, but that we subsist only in his pity (he meant that he only gives us work out of pity). His expressions were coarse and vulgar, saying that he didn't give a damn for us and that we should all go to hell." The workers in turn demanded what they felt were their rights as citizens:

Although most of us are German, we are nevertheless free and have no wish to be simply vassals of such a wordbreaker. We are upright mechanics and want to earn our livings in an honest way. We do not want to be submissive to such a man and do not want to put up with donating our labor free, thereby robbing our families of the necessary means to live.[66]

Such words proclaim not only the desperation of workmen with families to feed during hard times, but also all the disillusionment of men who had been promised that there was no shame in being a mechanic in America, no rank among artisans who has served their time. To look forward to a society of equals and then to find that money apparently gave a man a right to tell his workers to go to hell— that, perhaps, rankled more than anything.

Seaman, in his fight against the strikers, advertised in the Milwaukee newspapers for sixteen cabinetmaker's apprentices. The union countered with letters which they sent as far away as Detroit and Cincinnati, urging out-of-town cabinetmakers not to break the strike. When a second employer joined Seaman in refusing to pay union prices, however, about half of the original union decided to erect a cooperative workshop and warehouse on a "socialist" basis in the hope of creating more work and better wages. Beginning "during the worst business period that Milwaukee has ever experienced," the group was able to raise $1,200 and hang out its sign for business in March 1849, soon obtaining a state charter and expanding its premises. But internal dissension arising from the mistrust of the Catholic clergy for its socialist aims as well as a dishonest secretary led to its rapid demise.[67]

The cabinetmakers' venture set the mold for workingmen's activities during the following depression years, when pragmatic unionism was replaced by the quest for a panacea for general social ills and when intellectual reformers captured the German workers' movement.[68] Their efforts had few economic consequences, nor were attempts by groups like the tailors to set up cooperative purchasing and marketing organizations any more successful, and strike activity became evident again by 1852. Fear of competition from women was probably the driving force behind the organization of the typographical union by German printers in May 1852, who demanded the firing of "unauthorized interlopers"—women hired to set the type for Mathilde Franziska Anneke's suffragist *Die Frauenzeitung* at the printshop of the city's leading German daily. The printers were successful, the union met sporadically thereafter and achieved permanent status in 1859, becoming at once the first Milwaukee union with a national affiliation and the oldest surviving union in the city. Cigarmakers also included a demand for the restriction of female workers in their unsuccessful 1852 action. Carpenters, shoemakers, cabinetmakers, and girthmakers and saddlers were others who contributed to the "lively" union activity between 1852 and 1855 hailed by Milwaukee's liberal German press, but the continued efforts of the journeymen tailors to improve their lot attested to the difficult position of many of the city's artisans.[69]

The tailors' union was founded August 30, 1853; master craftsmen and factory owners were specifically excluded from membership. The union drew up the customary bill of prices, but the employers, while agreeing to increases of 25-30 percent on many pieces of clothing, refused to accept the entire bill. So the tailors went on strike, some 120 parading through the streets September 2 to musical accompaniment in protest against the employers' stand. A "Committee of 18" was appointed to bargain with the employers; the tailors wanted a minimum wage of $7.50 a week, while the employers maintained that many hired during the busy season were worth only $5.00. The committee countered that foreigners were often hired for less than their worth because they knew no English and, amid reports of hunger, resolved to continue the strike until two thirds of the employers agreed to the prices. Many of the leading German firms agreed to the union price list, but several Yankee firms attempted to bypass the strikers by sending material to nearby Watertown tailors for manufacture. Tailors there, however, agreed not to accept such scab work and offered financial support to

the Milwaukee tailors if needed. Attempts to get the work done elsewhere, however, may have succeeded, for the strike ultimately failed
and by the following spring internal disputes, possibly between English-
and German-speaking factions, had split the union in two. By 1860 a
reorganized union, with leadership carefully balanced between its German and Irish elements, was successful in convincing all but one of the
large clothing manufacturers to raise their rates and rewarded each
cooperative employer with an open-air musical serenade and loud
hurrahs in a public demonstration of union strength. They defended
their organization in the following terms: "The social position of the
great mass of the people—the workers—in our present political organization is such that the future will bring us poverty for ever-increasing
numbers through more widespread lower pay."[70]

They, and the cigarmakers and printers who joined them in union
activity at the end of the antebellum period,[71] thus bore witness to the
limits of achievement among Milwaukee's immigrant craftsmen in the
first generation of the city's history. Those trades most active were precisely those in which journeymen had fewer chances of becoming
master craftsmen or even homeowners. While their activities were not
without German precedent and followed the rhythms of the labor
movement in America in general,[72] they also can be interpreted as specific responses to the contrast between the dream of independence
achieved by some and the reality of working class status for the many
in Milwaukee.

The Merchants

The lines separating mechanic from merchant among Milwaukee's immigrants were fine ones, often crossed and often blurred both
by censuses and city directories. Many merchants did a certain amount
of manufacturing, while many independent craftsmen provided their
own retail outlets. For the Germans in both 1850 and 1860, and particularly for the Irish in 1860, however, mercantile pursuits offered a surer
road to property than the traditional artisans' trades. In merchandising,
as in the trades, immigrants met the same difficulties of capital acquisition and exhibited a similar tendency to use employment in older firms
to achieve the necessary experience and savings to augment those
brought from abroad. They likewise concentrated in fields patronized
by the local immigrant populations.

Lacking an equivalent to the manufacturing census for retail firms, there is no precise way to measure either relative commercial success or division of business between large and small firms.[73] Property ownership represents a certain measure of savings, however, and therefore, a list of Milwaukeeans who paid over $100 in city taxes in 1858 presents some general indication of the most successful sorts of German businesses. German merchants on the list included five grocers, four dry goods dealers, two dealers in wines and liquors, two real estate brokers, a commission merchant, a druggist, a lumber dealer, and a bank president.[74] The wealthier, more propertied German merchants thus concentrated in consumer goods businesses where they could cater to the everyday needs of the local population in much the same way as the smaller scale shopkeepers. They ran many of the grocery stores, drapers and clothiers, tobacconists, liquor stores, general stores, and fancy goods stores, leaving American merchants to handle heavier tools and hardware, building materials, machinery, metal goods, to take care of the city's commission business, the exporting, importing, and wholesaling.[75] The grocery business was the one type of merchandising which attracted the Irish in any numbers—about 16 percent of Milwaukee's retail grocers in 1860 were Irish—but in the heads of household samples they concentrated in no other trade, nor were the British sufficiently numerous among Milwaukee's sample merchants to demonstrate any such concentration.

Thus the business pattern in 1860 was one of general immigrant concentration in local retailing, while the native born dominated regional commerce and wholesaling. This pattern was undoubtedly responsible for the low ratio of affluent German mercantile firms to American ones noted in Milwaukee in 1854 by Dr. Wagner—about one to 20 in his estimate. Most German houses had not yet reached the scale where they could command large returns, nor could one expect otherwise. Trade in Milwaukee, Wagner found, demanded exact knowledge of business conditions, a good deal of adroitness, a practiced eye, and a capital from 5,000 to 6,000 dollars. Moreover, he volunteered, it was difficult for any German to compete with the sharp trading habits of the Yankees.[76]

The immigrant merchant needed more funds than most were able to bring if he wished to operate on a large scale. He also needed time to learn English, to acquire a knowledge of American tastes and products, to establish business connections and learn new methods of selecting, pricing, and selling goods—a whole new "tone" of bargaining and selling was required. The nuances of the frontier habit of dealing in exchanges of goods rather than in cash were initially perplexing, cautioned a German businessman in Milwaukee, who advised the potential merchant to plan to spend several years first as a clerk in a retail store, then as a bookkeeper in a wholesale firm or commission house before attempting to set up on his own. Henry Frank, who became a farmer, confessed that he had sometimes thought of returning to the pharmaceutical trade for which he had been trained, "but I would be inexperienced in the merchandising end of it. If I were to get a good partner who knows the Yankee tricks it would be good." The need to learn Yankee business methods meant that even the experienced immigrant merchant, with capital, was well advised to postpone investment and preferably to begin his American career as a partner in an existing business.[77]

Like their native counterparts, Milwaukee's pioneer immigrant merchants brought to the city business experience and capital generally acquired elsewhere in the United States. Many of them, products of the fitful emigration of the twenties and thirties, had little specific training in any one line and so switched businesses often, while shops changed hands frequently as new fields of endeavor appeared to promise a better return. They turned particularly to businesses which catered to the growing immigrant population, advertising themselves as "German establishments" and appealing to the German public "to always support *our own* countrymen by preference as far as possible." From such a basis they could slowly expand, learn American methods, and themselves train newcomers, for whom some adjustment problems were thus mitigated. However, even though Milwaukee by 1851 was a city where "the German language is almost a *sine qua non* for a business or professional man," as a British immigrant found, it was still necessary to learn English if custom was not to be confined to the German community, or contacts with wholesalers limited only to the German houses of the East. The careers of many young clerks with years of careful training in leading mercantile firms of Germany behind them, their hopes buoyed by excellent letters of recommendation, often involved a spell of peddling as a way to learn English, American business habits, and trade goods. From peddling the newcomers could turn to clerking, saving money perhaps by sleeping under the store counter each night, with the eventual hope of partnership with employers, using savings to join a friend in business, or finding someone willing to contribute capital to match their labor.[78]

The career paths of successful immigrant merchants in Milwaukee illustrate the means by which American experience and capital could be accumulated. Henry Stern's memoir recounted an almost prototypical case. His German training included a classical secondary education, commercial college, and apprenticeship in a Carlsruhe mercantile firm. When he arrived in America at 23, his letters of recommendation brought him a position with a German merchant in Boston, but he found the place so filthy that he left two days later, turning to peddling to learn the language and business methods. After a few months a position with a New York importer took him to New Orleans for a time. On his return, he reencountered Julius Goll, a traveling companion from his trip to America, whose talk of the west decided the two to set up their own business in Milwaukee. They carefully chose that city because the German immigrants would provide the market they sought. With capital of $800 which Stern had brought from Germany, $800 from Goll, and slightly over $1,000 lent by Stern's father, a German yarn merchant, they purchased $5,000 worth of dry goods, clocks, and so forth, in New York for $1,200 down, apparently with the backing of Stern's former employer, and also agreed to sell $3,000 worth of watches on commission from another German immigrant. With this stock they arrived in Milwaukee in August 1850 and rented the first story of a building on one of the main business streets for their shop, living in a small side room. Since customers came slowly, they also took their goods around the countryside in a wagon, selling to small town merchants.

The young men had promised one another not to marry until the business brought in enough for two families, but Goll married within a year and Stern, lonely, soon followed suit. When , in July 1852, Stern sold out his share—in order, as he told it, to go into business with a newly arrived brother—he obtained $2,671 on his original investment. His father gave him the loaned money as a wedding present, and he was able to increase his capital from $4,009 in June 1853 when he took his brother into partnership to $31,168 by 1860, $70,000 two years later.[79]

Goll, in the meantime, had been joined by August Frank. According to Frank's correspondence, it was in fact Goll's discontent with Stern which led him to search for a new partner. Knowing this, a mutual friend, John Kerler, Jr., invited Frank to abandon his Michigan farm and return to the mercantile career for which he had been trained, offering the dowries of his marriageable sisters as potential capital. Frank came to Milwaukee, chose the prettier though less well endowed sister, and joined Goll with a stake of $1,400 from her dowry, $500 from his farm, and a $1,000 loan from his father-in-law; by 1860 the partners were netting a profit of $6,000 on annual sales of $80,000.[80]

The elements of their successes—good training, peddling to gain initial familiarity with language and business, clerking with an established firm, support from that firm or loans from elsewhere in the formation of the new business—were repeated in various combinations in other Milwaukee mercantile success stories. The case of John Pritzlaff, however, demonstrates that a middle-class background was not absolutely essential. A Pommeranian of "plain but much respected" parentage and only an "ordinary education," Pritzlaff arrived in the United States in 1839 with neither funds nor skill, and found his way to Milwaukee after two years of canal labor. Working first as a teamster for a local newspaper publisher, then as a cook on a lake schooner, cutting timber on Milwaukee lots during the winter of 1845, he became a porter in a Yankee-owned hardware store at the salary of $200 a year. He slept in the store to save money and by the following year felt sufficiently secure to marry. When the firm was sold, he remained with the new owners, undoubtedly learning much of the business, and in 1850 opened a small retail hardware store with a partner, August Suelflohn. Neither had any money; Pritzlaff's American employer furnished the captial at 7½ percent interest, and they agreed to buy all stock from him at 7 percent over cost. Their initial stock was valued at $4,000 to $5,000; sales in the first year amounted to only $12,000, but in 1853 Suelflohn received $3,300 from Pritzlaff for his share of the business, good return for no initial capital investment. Pritzlaff built up a "large trade with all classes, but more particularly with his countrymen"; after 1855 further expansion was assisted by the German Second Ward Savings Bank, and he eventually became one of the largest hardware wholesalers in the Midwest.[81]

As such careers suggest, capital was a major problem for the immigrant merchant, whether self-made or trained in the field. Some built their firms on careful savings, often as little as $500 to $1,000, or the investments of relatives; others were lucky enough to find backers in established firms, who were perhaps attracted by the prospect of investment in retailing to immigrant customers. The existence of this loan market, as well as the prospect of tapping the savings of immigrants who often banked with trusted shopkeepers or invested surplus funds in land speculation, must have been important stimuli to the founding of German banks in Milwaukee after the passage of Wisconsin's free banking act in 1852.[82]

The first of these banks, the Germania, was capitalized at the legal minimum of $25,000 when it opened in August 1854, and by January 1, 1855, had deposits of slightly over $50,000. It apparently grew out of the exchange business which its officers and sole shareholders, G. and C. H. H. Papendieck, had conducted for several years. It was forced to "wind up" in the bank panic in the spring of 1855.[83] Its immediate successor was no more successful. The People's Bank opened in November 1854. Hermann Haertel, who had placed fingers in many Milwaukee pies since his arrival in 1843, was president and chief shareholder; a local Yankee lumber dealer and his New York relative were the other shareholders. Demand deposits grew to $86,281 by July 1857; in April of that year, the bank announced that since it enjoyed the general support of "our" people, it was desirable to enlarge its stock fund. Nevertheless, by September a general banking crisis forced it to suspend specie payments. The bank's resources were assigned to trustees, with the stipulations that German bills of exchange and receipts for trans-Atlantic fares be paid immediately, as well as all deposits made the day of closing, thus protecting its immigrant customers.[84]

The third attempt to establish a German bank succeeded. This was the Second Ward Bank, organized in 1856 by A. C. Wilmanns, a grocer and dry goods dealer, resident since at least 1846; William H. Jacobs, a former employee of the Marshall and Illsley Bank in Milwaukee; and Jacob Bertschy, the pioneer innkeeper and miller; like the earlier German banks, it was capitalized at the legal minimum. Several months after formation, a "savings bank" was associated with the new venture, which accepted deposits of as little as $1.00 at a semiannual interest rate of 7 percent "to fulfill the long-felt need to provide industrious and thrifty people with an opportunity to invest and increase their savings with security, to minimize unnecessary expenses, and to set aside a small amount for a later period in their lives when they will be less able to earn their livings." This appeal for the funds of many small depositors apparently made the bank a community institution—it was described in 1860 as the "popular German Bank" and Jacobs, the one banker with the proper training, as a man "who understands how to

make a German bank prosper, even in the present difficult conditions."
While the shareholders changed and deposits declined sharply during
the troubled years of the late 1850s the bank's survival was demonstrated by 1860 and the German community now presumably had a
means of harnessing its savings to finance its own expansion.[85] German
businessmen were also able to support a mutual fire insurance company, established in January 1852 and on a very sound footing by the
end of the decade.[86]

At the other end of the business spectrum were the city's saloon
keepers and grocers. The heads of household sample in both years
indicated German predominance in saloonkeeping, and at least 67
percent of the 105 saloons listed in the 1859 city directory were run by
persons with German names, 13 percent by Irishmen. Most of the
immigrant-owned taverns were probably small affairs—among 1860
sample members, the saloon keepers included a greater proportion of
nonproperty owners (58 percent) than among German shopkeepers in
general, and the average property holding of $1,375 was considerably
less than the $3,500 average of all shopkeepers in the sample.[87]

Yet such property holding still formed a respectable record compared
with that of most artisans, let alone laborers—and may explain one of
the attractions of saloon keeping. The saloon held out the promise of
upward mobility for laborers and artisans. A common pattern involved
some form of labor, the proceeds of which were invested in a small
grocery which the wife could run on the side, then the addition of a
saloon, which would eventually yield sufficient profits for the laborer
to quit his job and tend bar full time if he were lucky; often even the
grocery could be dropped. John Dusold, for example, went from teaming to a grocery and then to a saloon, and the labors of Henry Kauf-
mann as a bricklayer within seven years augmented the three cents in
his pocket on arrival in Milwaukee into a stake large enough to begin
saloon keeping. George Schuster went from laboring to a grocery and
then to a saloon; Joseph Gleisner from laboring to brewery labor to
saloon keeping and then to teaming.[88]

As Gleisner's case suggests, saloon keeping probably involved high
turnover, given the marginal nature of many of the ventures. In a group
of 152 immigrant saloon keepers in 1859 city directory, most of whom
were probably German, 47 percent could not be located in the directory
three years earlier. Of the remainder, 28 (or 18 percent of the original
group) had been tending bar in 1856, but only three in 1852. Ten

percent of the entire group had been grocers before turning to saloon keeping, while 19 percent were formerly mechanics (including four tailors, four butchers, three shoemakers, three cabinetmakers, and a variety of other trades). In addition, saloon keeping in 1859 attracted three former laborers, three clerks, three shopkeepers, two teamsters, a musician, a hostler, a sailor, and several other miscellaneous occupations. Among a similar group of 26 Irish, only 28 percent could not be located three years earlier; previous occupations included four grocers, two laborers, two clerks, a sailor, a porter, a mason, a carpenter, a foundry foreman, a lime merchant, and a salesman.

Grocers were less likely than saloon keepers to have a nonmercantile background, but even so a survey of some 160 Irish and German grocers in the 1859 directory yielded Irishmen whose previous occupations included laboring, draying, carpentry, street inspectors, and milkmen, while Germans went into the grocery business from barbering, basketmaking, machinist's work, teaming, tailoring, millinery, pottery, dry goods sales, shoemaking, cooperage, clerking, blacksmithing, and laboring.[89] Thus salon keeping and, to a lesser extent, the grocery business, represented for many immigrants a way of investing savings in a chance for independence. Most such businesses were located away from the downtown area; probably few reached any great size, since the "success stories" generally suggest a more careful training for most who made good. Nevertheless, the corner grocery or tavern remained important, not only as a focus for local sociability but also as a focus for the immigrant's economic ambitions.

The Professionals

The smallest class within any group of immigrants were the educated professionals. Certain types of education were much in demand in a frontier city like Milwaukee—that of a lawyer or the doctor, for example. As the city matured, the minister, the editor, the teacher, the architect would all find need for their services. But the Greek scholar, the highly specialized physician, the academic theologian, or the lecture-circuit intellectual would not find an early market for his wares. For the foreign-born professional, the situation in a town like Milwaukee was even more complex. On the one hand, the German-trained lawyer or public official would face the problem of relearning his profession, and even if he were able to learn a law different in both theory and practice, he would always be faced with a language handicap because of the American emphasis on oral argument. On the other hand, the increasing size of the German population itself created a demand for doctors and teachers who spoke a familiar language, and also, to fulfill special German cultural needs, such persons as musicians not generally in great demand on the frontier.[90] Professionals among the Irish and British might also have adjustments to make but the absence of language barriers, and their proportionately small numbers of culture consumers meant that pressures against serving the outside society or in favor of retaining an ethnic orientation were absent, and they probably mingled more freely with the native-born professionals. In addition, of course, the contrasting character of British-Irish and German emigrations by the 1840s meant that there was a larger pool of potential professional settlers for Milwaukee among the Germans.

Lawyers were the most numerous professionals in both census years, but only one Irish and two German lawyers appeared in the 1850 sample; in 1860 two Irish and two German. The 1860 city directory listed at least 11 German lawyers. The Irish lawyers were generally Irish by birth, but often American by training if not also by early rearing— Hans Crocker grew up in New York and received his legal training there, as did Nelson Graham in Ohio, while Edward G. Ryan and Thomas Knox, both of whom had some Irish legal education, completed their studies for the bar in Chicago and New York respectively. All four gentlemen had legal experience elsewhere in the Midwest before coming to Milwaukee.[91]

Most of the German lawyers, however, received their legal training as young men in Milwaukee, following the precedent of Friedrich W. Horn, who began "reading law" under Eduard Wiesner, the pioneer German justice of the peace, and then himself became a justice in Mequon before undertaking more formal legal training. Charles Bode too began his legal career as a justice of the peace, later studying for the bar examination, while the elected office of registrar of deeds and service as notary public provided Karl Julius Kern with a back door to the legal profession. Others began to read law immediately in local Yankee firms. For Edward Salomon, who had studied mathematics and science at the University of Berlin, a job as clerk in a rural Wisconsin district court aroused an interest in law, which brought him to Milwaukee to read law under Ryan. Nathan Pereles had a more involved career. The poor son of Hungarian village teachers, he used his European training to operate a retail grocery store in Milwaukee until he was sufficiently successful after six years to "abandon a trade never congenial to his tastes" and read law in a Yankee office.[92] By 1860, therefore, these men and several others, all apparently American-trained, were in a position to provide their countrymen with legal advice if required. Since most were in partnership with American lawyers, they could also serve as bridgeheads between the two nationalities.

Immigrant physicians were more numerous than lawyers—while the 1850 census sample included one Irish and two German doctors in a total of seven, six of the 16 in 1860 were German, one Irish. Eighteen of the 50 doctors in the 1860 directory had German names. All of Milwaukee's German doctors for whom information is available were trained in the universities of Germany, even Henry Harpke, who after three years of Wisconsin farming returned to Germany for his medical degree and then set up practice in Milwaukee. Some, like Francis Huebschmann, Milwaukee's first German physician, soon followed the practice of many pioneer American doctors of abandoning medicine for other fields, in Huebschmann's case, politics.[93] The remainder probably provided a good deal of the health care of Milwaukee's German population—although the ratio of doctors to potential patients was far greater among the native born—but the extent of their practice among Americans is uncertain. A friend wrote Huebschmann from Chicago in 1843 that "two well-educated and well-behaved German physicians have been living here for years, without still associating or holding any intercourse with a single yankey-family of what they call, standing . . . they among the yankeys, pass by the common nickname of 'Dutch doctors' always expressed sneeringly and contemptuously."[94] Huebschmann, however, was one of ten doctors who formed the Milwaukee Medical Association in 1845, while two other Germans were among those who revived it in 1855. Nevertheless, when another German doctor, Joseph Stadler, whose medical training was obtained at Pavia in Italy, applied for admission, he was told that his papers did not constitute proper credentials. The Medico-Chirurgical Club of 1851 also admitted at least six German members.[95] There were no instances of medical partnership with Yankees, but partnership was not common among doctors in any case. German doctors were the most numerous class of educated Germans in Milwaukee, and the frequent occurence of their names in the political and social movements of early Milwaukee suggests the leadership they assumed.

At least two British doctors, trained at the Royal College of Surgeons, established themselves in Milwaukee in the early fifties, gaining "large and remunerative" practices. The one Irish doctor recorded, James Johnson, received his training in Massachusetts. He arrived in 1844 and became wealthy through land investment but remained active both politically (within reform movements) and within the Catholic church, perhaps filling for the Irish the role played by the German doctors.[96]

For other educated immigrants, positions in Milwaukee society were not so well assured. The various immigrant churches, about twenty by 1860, required ministerial services, several apothecaries were established by German doctors and university-trained pharmacists, and several architects also put down roots in Milwaukee. Others, however, found themselves in the position of Christopher Schmidt, a graduate of the University of Würtzburg, who upon arrival in 1853, "being unable to find other employment . . . commenced by shoveling on the streets," and then tried in turn painting, clerking, and farming. The educated "Latin farmers" in the countryside surrounding Milwaukee were also notorious. Language teaching was a favorite occupation, while Fritz Anneke, former officer and revolutionary refugee, tried a variety of schemes to support his family, from typesetting, riding and swimming instruction, to railroad work and finally a state librarianship.[97] As the Germans increased in numbers and prospered, however, they were able to support not only doctors, lawyers, ministers, and an occasional architect, but generated also a demand for editors, teachers, and musicians, persons who could transplant to new soil what Milwaukee Germans considered the best of the old culture. Thus a former law student like Hans Balatka was able to find a permanent position as director of Milwaukee's Musical Society, while others found employment teaching first in private schools, then in public schools and subscription schools supported by the German community.[98] The other immigrant communities lacked either the size or the self-consciousness to support this type of educated leadership.

Conclusion

From the day laborer at the bottom to the educated professional at the top, Milwaukee thus offered varied paths to security. If the laborer was young and amibitious, he could try to learn a trade and

work to strike it rich—a few succeeded. For others a steady job, perhaps a foreman's position, or the advance to teaming and even contracting, meant the opportunity to buy property, perhaps invest in a
farm, grocery, or saloon, with the hope of greater security for the children through education and apprenticeship to an established trade.
Lack of capital and connections largely confined the immigrant artisan
to either a journeyman's job or a small-scale shop; in some trades,
where mechanization was becoming important, he had little chance of
changing his lot. In other fields, however, the early decades of the city
were a time when the immigrant craftsman, serving a local market of
his fellow countrymen, could acquire the knowledge and resources for
later expansion. The same held true for the immigrant shopkeeper. In a
city like Milwaukee, where most Germans were newcomers to America, time was needed before they would have the financial resources to
challenge Yankee dominance. By the late fifties a few had made it. For
the rest, while continual new immigration meant less statistical
improvement of the aggregate German position when compared with
that of the Irish, it also meant a continual expansion of the local market
upon which many of them depended, and the basis for future improvement.

In terms of the adjustment of the German immigrants, their occupational patterns meant that despite the large numbers of laborers, their
public image was generally one of industry and thrift, tempered with an
intellectual and cultural aura that was the marvel of the city's native
born.[99] By 1860 some Germans had acquired prominent places in the
city's economic life, while others enjoyed the solid feeling that they
were already on the way up. Many Germans were employed by fellow
countrymen, and others could find the beginnings of intergroup contact
in working for Americans. Indeed, it was said that Germans preferred
Yankee bosses,[100] perhaps because they, as Pritzlaff found, could
provide the best initiation into American business life. Milwaukee's
streets were not paved with gold for the average German immigrant,
but the evidence of opportunity was there, and there were fellow
countrymen who had begun to seize it by adapting German training
and experience to the American scene. This is not to discount the
amount of real poverty and suffering to which the charitable institutions of the immigrants bore witness, but rather to stress that unre-
lieved misery was not the sole lot of the immigrant. The Germans, in
sum, were an occupationally stratified group fitting in, to a greater or

lesser degree, at all levels of the city's economy, able to provide much of their own employment and most of the necessary internal services, while still relying on the native born for the economic ties to the world beyond the city. They thus seem to have possessed the type of socio-economic base that would permit the development of a full "community"; it remains to determine whether they developed a corresponding territorial base, equally necessary for ease of community interaction in the midnineteenth century.

The Private Residences
of Our Citizens

5   To the Milwaukeean of the antebellum period, his city's social ecology was as varied and easily identifiable as its topography. "An especially noteworthy feature," remarked a German resident of several months in 1853, "is the separation of the various nationalities into different quarters of the city, although the immigration of Americans, Germans, and Irish has been in fairly even numbers ever since the founding of the city."[1] Recent scholarship has questioned the incidence and intensity of immigrant urban residential concentration, particularly given the relative lack of spatial differentiation of any sort in cities of the early industrial period,[2] but popular neighborhood nomenclature in frontier Milwaukee insisted otherwise. "Yankee Hill" and "Tory Hill," "German Town" and the Irish "Bloody Third," "Nauvoo" and "the wooden shoe district" or "Hollandsche-Berg"—the very names suggest the variety of neighborhoods in antebellum Milwaukee characterized by ethnicity, wealth, or even morality.[3] The extent to which contemporaries were correct in their insistence upon the residential segregation of the city's nationalities from one another warrants closer investigation.

What was there about Milwaukee or its population groups which encouraged the development of distinctive residential areas? To what extent did residential concentration reflect the socioeconomic variations within and between groups noted earlier? Was concentration, in fact, equally characteristic of all groups and for the whole period? And what influence did such concentration exert upon organized community life or even individual immigrant adjustment? If some or all of Milwaukee's immigrants created a special kind of residential environment for themselves, distinct from the pathological ghetto of classic theory, that achievement forms an essential element in the analysis of their adaptation.

Concentration and Congregation

Linkage of census and city directory information makes it possible to assess residential concentration at any level from the lot to the block to the city as a whole. But it is worth analyzing residential patterns at the ward level initially in order to provide comparability with patterns elsewhere and to establish a basis for political analysis later in the study. Such ward level data confirm the extent of segregation by nativity observed by residents in frontier Milwaukee (Figure 9). The Irish in 1850 congregated in the third and fourth wards, the Germans in the second ward, the natives in the first and fifth wards in proportions greater than their respective shares of the city's population as a whole. Equally notable is the way in which the natives avoided the German second ward, the Germans shunned the Irish third and fourth, and the Irish kept clear of the first and second wards. Ten years later, the dominance of the leading nativity group had increased in the areas of all but one of the old wards. Statistics for the new ward divisions underline the almost exclusively German character of wards two, six, eight, and nine by that date, the Hibernian cast of ward three, and the Yankee aversion to all but wards four, five, and seven. Despite a population proportion so large that their predominance in all neighborhoods would be anticipated, the slight presence of Germans in several wards is striking.

Clearly, settlement patterns were not random. The Germans avoided the Irish, almost everyone avoided the Germans, and the Yankees and the British sought out one another. In fact (Table 26), 47 percent of the sample Irish households, 43 percent of native households, and 42 percent of German households were clustered in single wards in 1850. While native and Irish householders were scattered somewhat more evenly throughout the city ten years later, the Germans clung even more tenaciously to their own neighborhoods, and among all three groups, a greater proportion than before were living in wards more exclusively of their own nativity (Table 27).

The commonly used "index of dissimilarity" provides a way to compare more precisely the patterns of residential concentration of the different groups over time, and likewise permits comparison with the experiences of immigrants in other American cities (Table 28).[4] When the index is calculated to measure the segregation of each major group from the remainder of the population, the relatively high and increasing values highlight the clearly segregated nature of the city by 1860. The

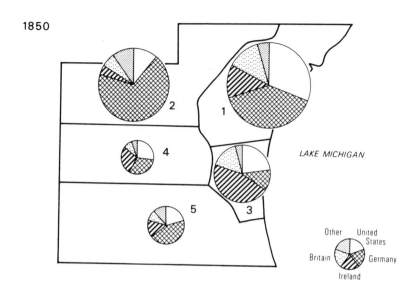

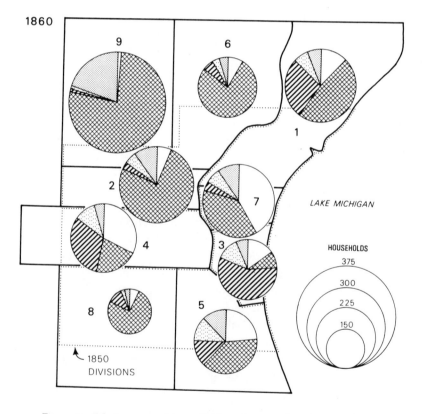

Figure 9   Ethnic composition of Milwaukee wards, 1850 and 1860

Table 26 Percentage distribution of Milwaukee nativity groups among wards

Nationality	Wards					Total
	1	2	3	4	5	

Total population, 1850 (comp. E. Prieger in *WB*, April 2, 1851)

Nationality	1	2	3	4	5	Total
Native	34	19	20	14	13	100
British	34	11	36	10	9	100
Irish	25	5	45	16	9	100
German	28	44	6	9	13	100
Other	25	27	15	9	24	100
Total	30	24	21	12	13	100

Heads of household, 1850 (sample data)

	1	2	3	4	5	Total
Native	43	12	20	13	12	100
British	32	23	26	11	8	100
Irish	15	6	47	19	13	100
German	30	42	6	9	13	100
Other	23	34	15	6	22	100
Total	24	26	20	11	13	100

Heads of household, 1860 (sample data using 1850 ward boundaries)

	1	2	3	4	5	Total
Native	40	11	9	22	18	100
British	25	18	18	16	23	100
Irish	23	7	35	22	13	100
German	21	54	2	4	19	100
Other	16	60	5	5	14	100
Total	24	38	10	11	17	100

Heads of household, 1860 (sample data using 1860 ward boundaries)

	1	2	3	4	5	6	7	8	9	Total
Native	9	5	9	22	15	5	31	3	1	100
British	12	10	18	16	19	6	13	3	3	100
Irish	20	2	35	22	8	4	3	5	1	100
German	11	19	2	4	8	15	9	11	24	100
Other	8	13	6	6	14	5	12	3	33	100
Total	12	12	10	11	10	10	12	7	16	100

Table 27   Population concentration in wards of ethnic dominance

Ethnic group	Percentage resident in wards containing[a]							
	75 percent dominance		50 percent dominance		32 percent dominance		25 percent dominance	
1850 (5 wards)								
Native	-	-	-	-	(1)	43	(2)	56
Irish	-	-	-	-	(1)	47	(2)	66
German	-	-	(1)	42	(3)	85	(4)	94
1860 (9 wards)								
Native	-	-	-	-	(2)	53	(2)	53
Irish	-	-	(1)	35	(2)	57	(3)	77
German	(4)	69	(4)	69	(7)	97	(7)	97

[a]Number of wards in each category is noted in parentheses.

Table 28   Indices of residential segregation and dissimilarity among Milwaukee nativity groups, 1850 and 1860

Nativity group	Indices		
	Of segregation		
	1850 (5 wards)		*1860 (9 wards)*
Native	18.8		33.2
Irish	42.9		52.7
German	27.8		44.1
	Of dissimilarity		
	1850 (5 wards)	*1860 (1850 wards)*	*1860 (9 wards)*
Native and Irish	33.1	26.0	38.4
Native and German	30.8	44.4	53.6
Native and British	17.2	21.0	23.4
Native and Other	38.1	53.6	53.7
Irish and German	51.2	53.2	59.4
Irish and British	33.5	22.7	32.4
Irish and Other	47.0	58.4	67.3
German and British	24.7	35.9	43.4
German and Other	15.4	11.3	26.8
British and Other	32.0	45.8	56.0

Irish were segregated earliest and most strongly, but all three groups exhibited strong clustering tendencies. The nature of the process can be illuminated by using the index to measure the dissimilarity of the residential patterns of the groups from one another.[5] The highest indices in both census years document the Irish tendency to avoid residence among Germans and other foreign born, in the face of the weakening momentum of Irish dissimilarity from the natives and the British, and the Germans and others—mainly Dutch, Scandinavians, and central Europeans, who were groups with much cultural similarity to one another.

By this gross measure, it thus appears that antebellum Milwaukee families tended to sort themselves spatially on the basis of national background to a greater degree than anticipated by current scholarship, exhibiting indices of dissimilarity approaching and even exceeding those of urban residents of the classic ghetto period of the late nineteenth and early twentieth century.[6] Nor, indeed, was Milwaukee alone in this regard, judging by information available for several other cities in the same period (Figure 10).[7] While Sam Bass Warner, Jr., and Colin B. Burke rejected both city size and ethnic mix as explanations for variation in patterns of segregation over space and time and suggested the influence of a slow growth rate in confining immigrants to segregated neighborhoods,[8] these scattered data suggest that in the mid-nineteenth century at least, segregation patterns may have been more clearly associated with cities of relative youth experiencing rapid growth, particularly but not solely of their foreign-born populations. It will require more extensive, careful, and comparable analyses of residential patterns in other mid-nineteenth century cities to sort out fully the factors promoting or discouraging segregation in different cities and for different nativity groups, but this initial comparison suggests the utility of looking more closely at Milwaukee residence patterns in order to account for this ward level clustering and assess its implications for community life.

Ethnic Areas

Wards are relatively large areal units for the measurement of residential concentration, especially when contemporaries emphasized the existence of boundaries within wards dividing one group from another. One could, of course, map the exact location of each residence

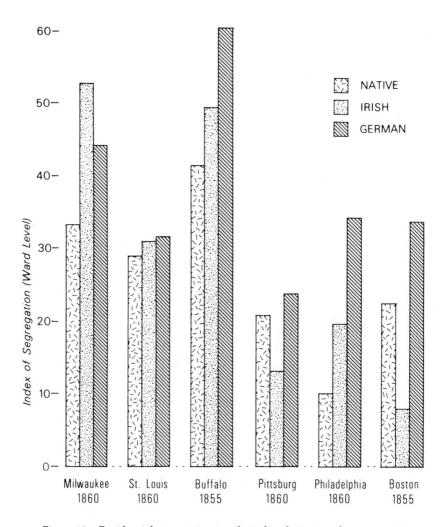

Figure 10   Residential segregation in selected mid-nineteenth century cities

Source: Milwaukee: Table 28; St. Louis: author's calculations from Frederick Anthony Hodes, "The Urbanization of St. Louis," Ph.D. diss., St. Louis University, 1973, 72-79; Detroit: author's calculations from JoEllen McNergney Vinyard, "The Irish on the Urban Frontier: Detroit, 1850-1880," Ph.D. diss., University of Michigan, 79-80; Buffalo: Lawrence A. Glasco, "Ethnicity and Social Structure: Irish, Germans and Native-Born of Buffalo, N.Y., 1850-1860," Ph.D. diss., State University of New York at Buffalo, 1973, 66, and author's calculations, 60, 66; Pittsburgh: author's calculations from Michael F. Holt, *Forging a Majority* (New Haven: Yale University Press, 1969), 319, 343; Boston (natives): Leo F. Schnore and Peter R. Knights, "Residence and Social Structure: Boston in the Ante-Bellum Period," in Stephan Thernstrom and Richard Sennett, eds., *Nineteenth Century Cities* (New Haven: Yale University Press, 1969), 253-254; remaining Boston and Philadelphia: Sam Bass Warner, Jr., and Colin B. Burke, "Cultural Change and the Ghetto," *Journal of Contemporary History*, 4 (1969), 179.

according to the nativity of its owner,[9] but further analysis would still demand some measure of reaggregation. As a compromise, the creation of artificial subunits within the city—in this case, a grid of cells roughly four city blocks in area—provides a way to measure with greater precision the proportions of different groups clustering spatially as well as the areal extent and character of such clusters. Contiguous cells dominated by households of the same nationality were grouped into what were termed ethnic areas; ethnic dominance was somewhat arbitrarily defined as occurring when 60 percent of the heads of household in a cell reported the same country of birth.[10]

These ethnic areas, neighborhood units based only on the two variables of ethnic dominance and contiguity, are mapped in Figure 11. The 1850 pattern was skeletal, as the ward data suggested, but east and west side German neighborhoods were evident, as was the beginning of a south side German concentration, while strong east side intraward concentrations of natives and Irish also emerged. By 1860 the major German, native, and Irish areas had all grown and were joined by west side native and Irish areas, outgrowths of embryonic secondary 1850 clusters. The south side retained an areally extensive mixed area, and another emerged to the northeast, but the older east and west side mixed areas gave way to clearer ethnic definition. None of the other nativity groups was sufficiently numerous, given the criteria used, to establish its own area, though there was a definite tendency for Scandinavian settlement on the south side and Dutch concentration to the northwest.

But how large a proportion of their respective groups did such areas contain? A look at their populations suggests the extent of the ethnic segregation which they represent (Table 29). Almost three quarters of all German households in 1850 resided in areas of German dominance, over four fifths by 1860. The Germans were followed in their tendency to congregate first by the Irish, then by the natives in 1850, although a decade later the natives were more apt to reside within their own areas than the Irish. German and native concentration in their ethnic areas increased over the ten-year period, that of the Irish declined. When members of these groups did not reside within their own areas, they tended to favor mixed areas over those dominated by other groups; when they did reside in other ethnic areas, natives generally preferred German over Irish neighborhoods, while Irish favored German over native. The British shifted their favor from mixed to native areas by

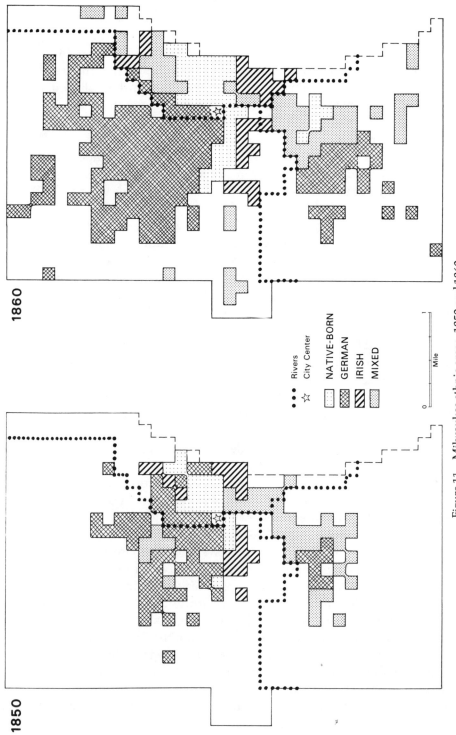

Figure 11 Milwaukee ethnic areas, 1850 and 1860

1860

1850

Rivers
City Center
NATIVE-BORN
GERMAN
IRISH
MIXED

0   Mile

Table 29 Nativity distribution summarized for all areas of each ethnic group

Area type	Native		British		Irish		German		Other		Total	
	1850	1860	1850	1860	1850	1860	1850	1860	1850	1860	1850	1860
	Percent of each nativity within area											
German	17	16	25	23	10	16	73	83	54	74	42	57
Native	41	53	23	37	4	9	5	4	8	6	15	15
Irish	8	7	19	11	50	47	3	2	5	5	15	10
Mixed	34	24	33	29	36	28	19	11	33	15	28	18
Total	100	100	100	100	100	100	100	100	100	100	100	100
	Percent of area residents of each nativity											
German	9	4	6	3	4	4	71	73	10	16	100	100
Native	61	57	15	16	5	10	15	12	4	5	100	100
Irish	11	10	13	7	64	71	9	7	3	5	100	100
Mixed	27	21	11	11	24	25	26	33	12	10	100	100
Total	22	16	10	6	19	16	41	52	8	10	100	100

1860, while other nationality groups increasingly shifted from mixed to German areas.[11]

There were variations in pattern among different areas of the same ethnicity.[12] Especially by 1860, west side Germans shared their area with other groups to a greater extent than did their more intensely segregated east and south side fellows, but in both years all three German areas were more exclusively of one nativity then any native and most Irish areas. Among natives and Irish also, the earlier east side areas were the ones of greatest dominance. Despite their widened boundaries, German and Irish areas in general became more ethnically homogeneous between 1850 and 1860; this was not true of the native areas.

The measurement of group concentration in ethnic areas thus underlines the significance of ethnic origins in determining residence in Milwaukee. Segregation—or perhaps voluntary congregation—occurred to a far greater extent than indicated by ward-level statistics. A large and increasing majority of Germans by 1860 lived in areas becoming ever more intensely German. Although the proportion of the total Irish population who lived within Irish areas was declining, those areas themselves were also becoming more intensely Irish. The natives too sought the residential propinquity of their own kind, despite the growing proportions of foreign born living in their neighborhoods.

Although the indices of dissimilarity did not so indicate, it was the largest of these groups, the Germans, who achieved the greatest congregation. In fact by 1860 the proportion of German households resident in cells at least 80 percent German had increased from 19 to 54 percent. This compares with an increase for natives in 80 percent native cells from 11 to 14 percent and from 11 to 18 percent among the Irish.

Such intensification of German residential concentration was occurring in a decade when Germans were pouring into the city at a much faster pace than were new Irish or native residents, as noted earlier. The rapid turnover of the city's German population (Table 30) and the areal extent of the expanding German areas suggest a congregation achieved through the accretion of new housing for the newcomers arriving and passing through the city at a great rate. The diminishing concentration of the Irish in the face of their relatively greater crude persistence and residential immobility, in turn may indicate the beginnings of group assimilation, the gradual absorption of some at least of the Irish into non-Irish areas as they achieved the sort of satisfaction which made Milwaukee the journey's end for many.

Neighborhood Evolution

How were the peoples of early Milwaukee able to achieve territoriality on such a scale? It could be argued that ethnic congregation was a simple byproduct of the socioeconomic differences among Milwaukee's ethnic components. Native dominance of the upper occupational categories, after all, meant that any upper class neighborhood would inevitably take on a Yankee cast. But ethnic congregation was

Table 30   Persistence of household heads within Milwaukee 1850 to 1860 by nativity (percent)

Nativity group	In same house	Elsewhere in same ward	Elsewhere in city	Leaving
Native	12	20	12	56
British	7	20	13	60
Irish	15	24	10	51
German	7	17	9	67
Other	2	9	15	74
Total	9	20	10	61

more than just class segregation in respectable guise. Economic distinctions, for example, are insufficient to explain the segregation of Germans and Irish of similar socioeconomic status from one another. Moreover, indices of dissimilarity for occupational categories exhibited values generally lower than for nativity categories with the exception of the sharp dissimilarity between the residential patterns of laborers as opposed to those of professionals and clerks (Table 31).

The close relationship between nativity and socioeconomic status, however, did result in contrasting characters for the ethnic areas of different groups and for different areas dominated by the same group— characters which begin to suggest how Milwaukee's neighborhoods emerged. The west side German area in 1850, for example, had a more distinctive working class orientation than did the east side area,[13] and the latter's proximity to the central business district attracted a greater proportion of young men and small households. The east side remained younger and more middle class in its occupational patterns by 1860, and the more peripheral south side German area became clearly working class; the west side included a significantly greater proportion of homeowners than the other two German areas. Paralleling the German trend, the west side Irish area in both years seemed somewhat lower in status than the east side Irish area. On the other hand, both native areas were apparent havens for the economically secure.

The differing characters of these areas can be understood as the pro-

Table 31   Indices of dissimilarity for occupational status groups by ward

	1850 above diagonal, 1860 below						
Occupational status[a]	1	2	4	5	6	7	8
1	-	17.5	43.8	23.8	23.8	30.6	36.6
2	16.8	-	28.4	27.5	20.8	22.9	28.2
4	17.8	30.5	-	23.2	38.0	38.1	44.1
5	22.8	35.9	16.0	-	15.2	15.4	21.6
6	31.2	44.9	28.1	16.1	-	18.4	12.8
7	44.5	57.6	34.4	24.9	24.1	-	17.3
8	40.5	54.5	36.2	28.3	14.3	43.8	-

[a]Occupational categories: 1. professionals; 2. proprietors, managers, and officials; 3. no significant data; 4. clerical and sales; 5. petty proprietors, managers, and officials; 6. skilled; 7. semiskilled; 8. unskilled.

duct of their residents' rent-paying ability and need for easy access to different types of employment, interacting with neighborhood accessibility, employment location, and physical environment, but influenced also, undoubtedly, by a desire to live near others sharing the same culture, status considerations, stage in the family cycle, by the decisions of developers, and the simple inertia of early precedent. It was the evolution of Milwaukee's central business district that provided the focus for this process. The town's center had been established by the location of Juneau's trading post, near the first site suitable for a ferry landing on the east side above the mouth of the river. The first stores and warehouses were erected nearby, and East Water Street became the city's major business axis (Figure 12). The center of Kilbourn's west side development, at what would become the corner of Chestnut and Third Streets, remained a secondary node throughout the antebellum period. When Kilbourn in the early 1840s began grading the west side bluff to permit the westward extension of Spring Street from the ferry and then improved its West Water Street connection up to Chestnut, he simply was recognizing the commercial dominance of the East Water-Wisconsin Street area.[14]

Grading northward on the east side after 1839 eased the extension of East Water to the site of a spring, where the market place was established. Bridges began to link the two sides of the river after 1841, and massive earth-moving operations soon smoothed the bluffs to provide access to airy homesites and filled the low-lying swamps to permit commercial expansion north and south along East Water. In the meantime, the 1842 completion of the water power canal attracted industry to the west side, while clearance of land titles on the south side sparked a mixed commercial-manufacturing boom there as well.[15]

By the early 1850s, as a result, East Water's "few frame stores . . . built on posts above the water, as there were no docks to confine the river," had given way to "two proud rows of buildings with many shops, tastefully built of solid brick," and the initial intermixture of stores, warehouses, workshops, and residences was yielding to an emerging functional differentiation of the city's space. The basic division, as contemporaries noted, was between work and residence, according to topography: "While the low and level lands on either side of the river offer excellent localities for business streets, stores, warehouses, mills and founderies, the higher grounds on the bluff, extending northwardly along the Lake shore, or rising from the valley of the

Figure 12 Milwaukee, 1855. Increase A. Lapham, "Map of the City of Milwaukee"
(New York: George Harrison, 1855); copy in the State Historical Society of Wisconsin,
Madison.

river, present delightful sites for residence." But internal divisions had also emerged within the low-lying business district. As a booster of the Civil War period noted, in Milwaukee "the warehouses and lumber yards fringe the docks; the foundries and machine shops occupy the level ground a block or two back; while the heavy wholesale and retail houses line the main business streets, which run next to and parallel with the rivers."[16] City directories make it clear that such internal differentiation was well underway by the end of the 1840s when two thirds of the city's general retail shops, seven tenths of the offices of its professionals, eleven twelfths of its banking and insurance firms, and one third of its food markets, but only about 6 percent of its dwellings, were located within the eight-block area roughly bounded by Huron and Market Square, Main and the river. By 1860 the expanding retail area had clearly pushed commission merchants and warehouses downriver, additional commercial nodes were appearing across the bridge to the south side and along West Water Street, while grocers and other businesses dealing in such daily necessities as bread and beer began to abandon central locations for residential neighborhoods. In general, however, the central district remained the city's commercial node, an important location of employment and an attraction for businessmen and shoppers alike, with the warehouses, docks, and—after 1851—railroad terminals providing further bustle and jobs on its fringes.[17]

Manufacturing was somewhat less concentrated (Table 32). In 1850 major manufacturing concerns were almost equally divided among the central business district, the west side canal area, and the area south of the Menomonee Valley. These locational patterns were generally maintained through 1860, except among brewers, who scattered especially throughout the northwestern quadrant of the city, and the brickmakers of the southwest. The small workshops which carried on much of the city's production concentrated along or near the river which formed the main axis of the city's life. Woodworking shops and the needle trades, for example, clustered within and slightly to the north of the retail area, and only shoemaking establishments appeared widely dispersed. These manufacturing districts also included the city's heaviest population concentration, but other large sections of the city apparently contained few workshops, and growing numbers of Milwaukeeans had to commute to work.

Radiating outward from the central core of the city were the neighborhoods, mixed commercial-residential close to the center, almost

Table 32 Location of manufacturing employment, by number of hands employed by ward

Industry	1850					1860						
	1	2	3	4	5	1-7	2	3	4	5-8	6	9
Agricultural implements	-	4	4	-	-	-	-	-	11	51	-	-
Blacksmiths	12	-	20	-	-	-	27	11	-	-	-	-
Boots and shoes	7	15	106	16	-	41	50	199	28	16	4	-
Clothing	1	10	276	-	4	-	84	483	-	9	-	-
Confectioneries	2	7	18	6	-	8	4	20	13	10	3	-
Cooperages	-	43	2	6	-	-	59	1	1	30	43	53
Flour and grist mills	-	27	-	-	8	2	30	-	20	15	17	-
Furniture	2	16	75	30	3	41	25	54	36	3	-	-
Gas	-	-	-	-	-	-	-	30	-	6	-	-
House construction material	12	10	29	21	79	23	38	18	125	215	-	-
Iron manufacture	9	53	-	9	33	5	51	-	65	84	-	-
Leather and tanning	16	4	46	7	-	7	15	12	10	77	17	-
Liquors and beer	14	21	15	-	-	20	49	23	2	10	11	5
Mineral products processing	4	-	1	20	-	8	-	2	34	-	-	-
Paper and printing	-	2	5	11	-	35	-	37	20	-	-	-
Provisions	-	-	-	-	-	-	17	13	59	30	3	16
Soap and candles	6	5	1	7	-	-	-	9	6	14	-	-
Tin, copper, sheet iron	1	10	25	-	-	4	10	24	10	28	-	-
Tobacco	9	15	4	14	-	-	49	57	30	-	-	-
Wagons and carriages	14	21	36	25	3	3	25	16	25	28	-	-
Miscellaneous	18	25	36	9	2	26	43	49	44	150	32	1
Total 1850 1,427	127	288	699	181	132							
1860 3,377						223	576	1058	539	776	130	75
Percent of total	8.9	20.2	48.9	12.7	9.3	6.6	17.1	31.3	16.0	23.0	3.8	2.2

Source: Data provided by Margaret Walsh, from U.S. Census of Manufactures, mss. schedules, 1850, 1860.

purely residential toward the fringes. While the demands of business users stimulated land values and led to an absolute decrease in residence at the center, block after block of new plats were added to the periphery. An "addition, division, and subdivision" mania in the late 1850s accounted for an estimated 35 percent of the city's total platted area by 1860. Even such peripheral areas, however, remained tied to the city center by foot traffic. The farthest boundary was only three miles from the center of the business area, and 92 percent of the population in 1860 lived within two miles of downtown, 58 percent within one mile. The first horsecar service was not introduced until May 1860—over the opposition of some of the city's businessmen who predicted dire consequences for the commercial vitality of the downtown area once the streets were thus blocked to traffic—and although omnibuses ran regular routes between piers and hotels, and out to the cemeteries, they were apparently unimportant for commuter carriage.[18]

Uninfluenced by changes in transportation technology, the new subdivisions were essentially extensions of the class and ethnic neighborhoods established almost as early as the city itself. If a visitor to Milwaukee in 1860, for example, left his downtown hotel and walked east and slightly south toward the lake, he would soon have found himself in a "monotonous and uninteresting" section of "modest and unpretending frame buildings" chaotically grouped and interspersed with reed-covered remants of the area's partially drained swamp. Few of the early "straggling cheap-built houses erected on posts above the marsh water" probably remained, but as the visitor neared the lakeshore, he could not help but note the colonies of squatters' shanties, flimsy, easily moved, vulnerable to cold and flood, and crowded with large families. This "somewhat disreputable" neighborhood was the Bloody Third, home of the largest single concentration of Milwaukee's Irish. There was no church, and its fringes contained the largest single aggregation of saloons in the city; newspapers reported its drunken brawls with a resigned frequency.[19]

The choice of site had been a natural one for the Irish, who came to the city with little in the way of skills or money. Their labor was initially needed for nearby filling and grading operations, and the harbor offered continuous employment opportunities, as did the neighboring business district as it developed. Since business expanded along the river rather than eastward, the area was generally safe from commercial intrusion, and the unhealthy swamp on which it rested caused more prosperous members of other groups to abandon it as soon as possible. The location was sufficiently central that land values, while far lower than for other areas of equal distance from the center, nevertheless remained higher than on the city fringes, and so the Third Ward Irish paid for their ease of access to day labor and such semiskilled jobs as teaming with relatively high density living.[20]

The east side Irish area thus had many of the characteristics of the classic immigrant reception ghetto, and by the time of the Civil War Milwaukee landowners, realizing the profits which immigrant housing in such an otherwise unattractive locality could yield, began moving frame buildings, "being sold cheap when the property was wanted for other structures," from other parts of the city "into the Third Ward for rental to families of immigrants." Yankee ingenuity thereby provided the new city with the substandard central housing for conversion to immigrant tenements that was influencing residence patterns in older cities. The Third Ward remained the "spiritual home" for Milwaukee's Irish until the 1890s when improved living standards and a disastrous fire would lead to the inheritance of the area by a more recent group, the Italians.[21]

North of the city center was an even more foreign environment. Stretching along the river under the shadow of the first ward bluff was the strip of filled bayou and swamp and cut-down hillside that, with the vast expanse of platted blocks climbing up from the river on the opposite bank, had become the city's German Town, the east and west side German areas.

The earliest German settlement was the east side one, just north of the central business crossroads. The site was as physically undesirable as that to the south and was not as close to major sources of casual employment. However, most of the early German settlers were reportedly craftsmen, not dependent upon day labor, and could benefit sufficiently from a location near the market and the business district to bear with the poor site. Fortuitous factors undoubtedly played an initial role. One of Milwaukee's first German settlers, Matthias Stein, located his gunsmith's shop on the hillside near the spring to enjoy the area's good hunting. He was soon joined by Louis Trayser, who established the first German tavern nearby, while a German baker, and Eduard Wiesner, the unofficial adviser of the city's first German settlers, located not far away near Juneau's cabin. Around this nucleus of conviviality, mutual aid, and perhaps somewhat inexpensive lots, German settlement converged. The area filled with small workshops and became the first focus of Milwaukee's German culture.[22]

The first sign of German settlement on the west side occurred in 1839, when the colony of Old Lutherans arrived in Milwaukee. The city was in the depths of depression and Kilbourn and Juneau were engaged in bitter competition for settlers. Kilbourn therefore gave one of the Germans a piece of land near the center of his plat, on which the colonist built a half-timbered German-style house. Such promotion evidently encouraged further Old Lutheran settlement in the area, and Kilbourn's embryo town center filled quickly with small frame houses. Further Germans were undoubtedly attracted to the area after 1842 when the construction of the water power canal not only provided jobs for laborers, but attracted factories and mills, and bridges to connect it to the older east side settlement. There is little doubt that the higher land on the west side made living more pleasant, and for those Germans whose work did not require immediately central locations, or who could not afford even unhealthy and crowded central quarters, the west side offered an alternative. Soon the "almost purely American settlement" of the area in the 1840s "dissolved like a mist" before the newcomers. German settlement was able to expand freely in this sector, while extension of the east side German area was blocked for the moment by topography and the east side Yankee neighborhood. By the 1850s, when new German arrivals were the main factor in swelling the city's population, most of the new subdivision took place in the north-western sector. The new lots were smaller than the city average, and many of the small-scale developers were themselves German.[23]

German visitors to Milwaukee were quick to point out that the Germans of the central area were confined to the unhealthy swampland while the natives fled to the bluffs. German residents themselves referred to their neighborhood as the Swamp, complaining of the standing water which plagued most lots, the noxious pond ringed with privies which stretched in the late 1840s along East Water Street, and the pollution from the area's factories. On the fringes were hastily erected shanties similar to those of the Irish, and living density was the highest in the city in the east side German area.[24]

But it was not those pathological aspects of German Town that struck most observers. Rather, they commented upon the area's "German houses, German inscriptions over the doors or signs, German physiognomies . . . Many Germans live here who never learn English, and seldom go beyond the German town." The houses were one and two story "cozy cottages," complete with vegetable and flower gardens, woodsheds, chicken coops, and smokehouses; the area itself was seen as:

a hive of industry throughout, and the aggregate of manufacture annually thrown into market by these humble mechanics and artizans would astonish the reader. Cigars, boots and shoes, furniture, baskets, toys, jewelry, wearing apparel, and innumerable articles of every day use and consumption are here fabricated in small factories, and either sold to larger houses or peddled through the city.[25]

East Water Street as it ran through the area "was like the main street of a country town," while the market place was "a unique social center of German life in the community." Beer halls and saloons, boarding-houses and meeting halls clustered among the shops near the market and spilled across the river into the Chestnut Street area, which was the center of west side German life. The closely packed rows of buildings which lined the central streets of the neighborhood, each with its own wooden sidewalk at the level of its door connecting the neighbor's by a flight of steps up or down, gave way further out to separate houses and shops interspersed with empty lots and gardens. Winnebago Street, heading diagonally up the hill to the northwest past the brewery, was developing as a new business axis for the more recent subdivisions, while the Galena Street hill reportedly housed the "aristocracy of the older German families" in substantial residences, "most of them set in considerable grounds." Perhaps they, like August Frank, had left behind homes over their downtown shops once they could afford the luxury of "a nice walk when going home to eat" and quiet streets where their wives would no longer need to fear for the safety of the children.[26]

German Town was thus not so much a single neighborhood as a microcosm of the city as a whole, with its downtown, its central area of mixed shops and residences, its exclusive sections, and its extensive suburbs of small wooden homes and shanties. Its social ecology like-wise mirrored the city: its shopkeepers, merchants, and professionals resided near the center, its laborers fanned out toward the fringes, sandwiching the craftsmen roughly in between. This occupational vari-ation, linked with differences in timing of arrival, probably produced the slight pattern of segregation by province of origin within the area as well, as recently arrived unskilled Mecklenburgers and Pommeranians congregated on the periphery.[27] This in turn confirmed the undocumented contemporary sense of residential variation by religion—Catholics reputedly lived on the east side, Protestants to the west.[28] While socioeconomic as well as chance factors help explain the first German settlement in this sector, the increasing German population made it almost inevitable that congregation would increase. The newcomer welcomed the chance to live close to fellow countrymen; he found little in the way of cheap vacant downtown housing, and so he went to the fringes, where a place was prepared for him. The almost purely German neighborhoods thus seem the result not so much of exclusion from other parts of the city, or even impersonal economic segregation, but simply of the great numbers of the Germans and the ability of the frontier city to satisfy spatially their congregational instincts.

The major alternative area of housing for the immigrant was the south side. This area grew more slowly than the east and west sides, partly because of the extensive marshes, partly because of the contested title which was not cleared until the early 1840s. The construction of plank roads and the coming of the railroad opened the area and provided employment; several brickyards, a tannery, and an engine works gradually attracted more laborers, and the industrial future of the area became evident by 1860. The Catholic bishop chose a south side site for the city's second Catholic church in the mid 1850s "for the reason that the settlements here were, as yet, quite rare, and the grounds for the errection of a church, as well as for purchase by every immigrant, were still tolerably cheap. The result was that here also a considerable number of the faithful very soon settled, and affiliated themselves with the new parish." Thus the " 'don't care' kind of an individual" who made up the original south side population was gradually replaced by a mixed German and Irish settlement, which grew more strongly German toward the western fringes by 1860. Both densities and land values remained relatively low, and in the popular mind as well as statistically, the area was characterized more by its employment than by its ethnic status. After the Civil War, that industrial employment was to attract the new Polish immigration, who would claim the south side for their own.[29] In the meantime, a Scandinavian settlement also developed in the area, including a large number of persons "identified with marine activities," who had concentrated for a time after landing in the early forties on the lower east side.[30] The Dutch, later comers, settled in the newer west side neighborhood among their German neighbors, on a hillside which became known as the Hollandsche Berg.[31]

If few persons without business there found their way to the south side, that was not the case for Yankee Hill, Milwaukee's showplace. Originally an area of "stunted oak trees and primitive cliffs, ravines and knolls," streets were graded up the bluffs in the early 1840s and lined with "sundry gay white cottages." The bluffs provided "airy and healthy residences," which were "more attractive for residential purposes than the lowlands chosen by the immigrants. Thus the Anglo-Americans who became the town builders sold the land to the immigrants and became sufficiently prosperous to preempt the choice lands for their own homes."[32] While the Germans inhabited the lower, more unhealthy part of the city, German visitors noted,

nine-tenths of the merchants of East Water Street, which borders the unhealthy quarter, are Americans, but almost all of the wealthier among them have only their stores and offices there, while they live on the gentle slopes of the northern heights in a more healthy atmosphere. Mixed among them are several Irish men, who have become wealthy and who "Yankeefy" much more quickly than the Germans because of the similarity of the speech.[33]

The Milwaukee visitor could admire the beautiful and costly residences, the pretty gardens surrounded by wrought iron fences, the balconies, which offered fresh air and pleasant views. No taverns or stores invaded the residential area, although it sheltered the court house, lawyers' and doctors' offices, and several churches and schools, including the imposing Gothic of the Roman Catholic cathedral, with its neighboring "bishop's palace." The lakefront bluffs, despite the interesting views they afforded, were generally avoided because of the difficulty in getting fresh water from the lake (there were springs on the river side), and so they were preempted by a small Irish colony, living in a row of small and mean houses near the steep lakeshore. "The air there is gentler and cooler and epidemics of fever occur less often" than in the lower parts of town where immigrants more customarily lived. A few families of French-Canadians and half breeds also reportedly made homes for themselves in the upper part of the east side.[34]

Topography thus encouraged the creation of a prosperous American neighborhood within short walking distance of the business district, yet physically removed from it. For any services required, its residents could draw on the German quarter to the west or the Irish area to the south, while those Irish who took advantage of the empty lakeshore bluffs undoubtedly provided the Americans with servants as well. As a consequence, while some visitors would note that "the outskirts of the town are filled with pleasant residences displaying a fair amount of architectural taste," others observed the "side hills terraced for gardens of country seats overlooking the town, surrounded by paddies-huts, and uncultivated barren land."[35]

The same juxtaposition was evident in the fourth ward, across the river to the west. Here, in the swamp below Spring Street, the Irish settled early, probably attracted by Kilbourn's need for their labor in preparing his site. Then, when Spring Street was graded west up the bluff, one of Milwaukee's leading bankers, Alexander Mitchell, chose the site, with its "fine view of the city" for his "plain brick house which was then considered a splendid affair" and other "wealthy citizens" followed suit.[36] The result was undoubtedly a symbiotic relationship between immigrant shanty and Yankee mansion similar to that on the east side.

Such were the neighborhoods of antebellum Milwaukee. If the city was originally the undifferentiated "rummage" of occupations and ethnicities beloved of students of the preindustrial city,[37] it quickly left this stage behind as its virgin space was molded to fit the needs of its developing economy and the specialized roles of its different ethnic components. It must have been this malleability, combined with the massive German demand for housing in the 1850s, which led to the patterns of segregation the city exhibited.[38]

Implications of Congregation

What difference did the achievement of such segregated neighborhoods make for the immigrants of Milwaukee? Although it is difficult to demonstrate with the data available, it is easy to join other students of immigrant adjustment in arguing that residence near others of the same background must have eased the difficulties of initial adaptation to American life. Language problems particularly would diminish in importance, familiar patterns of neighboring could be reknit, informal social gatherings made possible, with lessened pressure to abandon quickly old cultural habits. Propinquity would ease the formation of formal community organizations as well, providing the threshold population necessary to support a wide range of services and activities which would further ensure the newcomer against the insecurity of his new environment.[39] While it can be argued that the combination of their massive influx in the 1850s and their occupational specialization would have made it difficult for the Germans to find others with whom to intergrate in any case, nevertheless, the fact that it was the very Germanness of Milwaukee that attracted so many of its German settlers, the fact that so many must have consciously chosen to live among other Germans, suggests that they were alive to these advantages.

This then raises a question about those who lived outside their own ethnic areas. Can such residence be taken as an index of assimilation, as often hypothesized?[40] A tentative approach to this issue is to examine the occupational status differences between persons who lived within and outside their own ethnic areas (Tables 33 and 34). By 1860, native-born professionals and businessmen were overwhelmingly concentrated in native areas; other white-collar workers were also shifting their preference from mixed to native areas, while native manual workers were moving from German areas, where they demonstrated some tendency to reside, into mixed and native areas as well. If their patterns can be regarded as standards for the assimilation-minded among the immigrants, it becomes evident that by 1860 some upper-status Irish and Germans were achieving at least residential assimilation. While the small number of upper-status Irish makes interpretation difficult, the movement of Irish and German professionals and businessmen into native areas by 1860 is clear.

There were differences in Irish and German patterns, however. In general, upwardly mobile Irish showed a greater tendency to select mixed areas, while similar Germans remained in German areas to a greater proportion. Germans in the remaining occupational categories were less likely to reside anywhere but in German areas by 1860; by contrast, there were signs of shifting concentrations of other white-collar Irish from Irish to mixed areas, and of Irish manual laborers from Irish to German areas. Germans in native areas exhibited occupational distributions much more similar to the native residents than did the Irish in such areas, although fewer lower-status Irish were living in Yankee neighborhoods by 1860 than ten years earlier. The occupational profiles of the Irish in native and mixed areas were more middle-class by 1860 than those of Irish resident in Irish and German areas; Germans in mixed areas were similar to those in German areas

Table 33 Percentage distribution of residents of ethnic area types by occupation and nativity

Area type	Professional and Major proprietors			Other Nonmanual			Skilled manual			Semiskilled and unskilled		
	Nat.	Ir.	Ger.	Nat.	Ir.	Ger.	Nat.	Ir.	Ger.	Nat.	Ir.	Ger.
1850												
	(N=53)	(N=8)	(N=21)	(N=50)	(N=16)	(N=53)	(N=73)	(N=32)	(N=168)	(N=27)	(N=124)	(N=149)
German	8	-	71	6	19	41	27	13	83	33	8	75
Native	62	-	5	42	-	15	32	3	4	26	4	4
Irish	8	12	-	6	44	4	9	53	2	4	54	3
Mixed	22	88	24	46	37	40	32	31	11	37	34	18
Total	100	100	100	100	100	100	100	100	100	100	100	100
1860												
	(N=114)	(N=10)	(N=48)	(N=95)	(N=33)	(N=150)	(N=94)	(N=69)	(N=434)	(N=39)	(N=212)	(N=448)
German	11	10	63	13	15	76	22	16	85	18	17	84
Native	78	30	27	56	6	5	33	12	3	31	7	1
Irish	3	10	-	9	33	2	7	42	1	10	52	2
Mixed	8	50	10	22	46	17	38	30	11	41	24	13
Total	100	100	100	100	100	100	100	100	100	100	100	100

Table 34 Percentage distribution of occupations by nativity group and ethnic area type

Occupation	Ethnic area type, 1850				Ethnic area type, 1860			
	German	Native	Irish	Mixed	German	Native	Irish	Mixed
	(N=37)	(N=92)	(N=17)	(N=80)	(N=56)	(N=192)	(N=24)	(N=87)
Natives								
Professional and major proprietors	11	36	24	15	22	46	17	10
Other nonmanual	8	23	18	29	22	28	37	24
Skilled manual	54	25	41	29	37	16	25	41
Semiskilled and unskilled	24	8	6	13	12	6	17	18
Not in work force	3	8	11	14	7	4	4	7
Total	100	100	100	100	100	100	100	100
	(N=19)	(N=7)	(N=96)	(N=70)	(N=58)	(N=34)	(N=169)	(N=100)
Irish								
Professional and major proprietors	-	-	1	10	2	9	1	5
Other nonmanual	16	-	7	9	9	6	7	15
Skilled manual	21	14	18	14	9	24	17	21
Semiskilled and unskilled	53	68	70	60	64	44	65	50
Not in work force	10	18	4	7	16	17	10	9
Total	100	100	100	100	100	100	100	100
	(N=302)	(N=22)	(N=13)	(N=77)	(N=937)	(N=41)	(N=17)	(N=135)
Germans								
Professional and major proprietors	5	5	-	7	3	32	-	4
Other nonmanual	7	36	15	27	12	19	18	18
Skilled manual	46	27	31	25	40	37	18	34
Semiskilled and unskilled	37	27	32	35	40	12	53	42
Not in work force	5	5	22	6	5	-	11	2
Total	100	100	100	100	100	100	100	100

but German residence in Irish areas more clearly involved the lower classes.

That residence was some sort of index to assimilation, therefore, is implied by the fact that those Germans who resided among the wealthy natives tended to be successful on what were essentially native terms; also worth noting, however, is the relatively small proportion of Germans who chose that route. The Irish path, moreover, involved the intermediate stage of residential assimilation to German or mixed areas. This further clarifies the differences in German and Irish residential behavior noted earlier in the chapter, differences which may in part have reflected the continuing in-migration of the Germans and the different sizes of the two groups. For both, separate ethnic areas had significantly different and changing occupational spectra. For both, the more central and older areas seemingly improved in status over the ten-year period, while more heavily laboring class areas—somewhat more recent concentrations—developed farther toward the city fringes. The older areas apparently filled with persons who did not move on at a rate fast enough to make room for the newcomers who had to leapfrog older settlements and move to the fringes. Given the flimsy methods of house construction, it was a simple matter for older settlers, as their status improved, to tear down and rebuild while retaining the accessibility advantages of their central locations. While some older settlers forsook centrally located residence for suburban living by 1860, particularly among the Irish and natives, it seems clear that such movement was insufficient to people the expanding fringe, and that many newcomers must have settled immediately in the suburbs.[41]

The pattern of immigrant settlement in Milwaukee thus implies a new twist to the conventional ghetto hypothesis. Milwaukee's two main immigrant groups were certainly segregated. For the great majority of Germans, particularly, residence involved minimal neighborhood contact with either natives or Irish. The new city permitted its major immigrant group to carve out an entire sector for itself, large enough to provide for internal variations in residential status. There was little sign among either Germans or Irish of the type of movement predicted by the classic ghetto hypothesis—movement from central receiving ghetto to more middle-class but still ethnically-defined fringe neighborhoods. In a city like Milwaukee, where primitive transportation placed a premium on central location, the newer immigrants developed the outer areas while the areas of first settlement improved in status as their residents gained greater security.[42]

Moreover, while both Germans and Irish demonstrated movement toward residence outside areas of their own concentration as a step in the direction of broader interaction with persons of different backgrounds, the two followed different paths. German businessmen by 1860 tended to move into Yankee areas, and Germans who lived in such areas had occupations similar to those of the native residents—class rather than ethnicity had guided their residential decisions. However, except for the central business area and the south side where occupation probably influenced residence, few middle-class Germans took the step into mixed areas, which was common among the Irish, for whom German areas also provided entree into a more middle-class environment. Irish areas thus were generally unable to retain the full spectrum of occupations exhibited by the German areas. Native areas probably also demonstrated the operation of class as much as ethnic factors: middle and especially lower-class natives did not form native residential areas but rather lived in ethnically mixed neighborhoods. The Germans thus came as close as possible for any subgroup within a city to developing both the socioeconomic heterogeneity and locational concentration required to meet the ecological criteria for an independent community, while the residential as well as the occupational patterns of the natives and the Irish suggest that they were both becoming class-defined rather than true ethnic communities. But to what extent were the Germans actually able to generate from their ecological base an interactional community as well? That is the next issue to be explored.

Vereinswesen

6 Adam Ernst was a busy man in 1860. One night a week he
attended the meeting of Armenia Lodge Number 94 of the Odd Fellows,
where he was an officer. Another night the hardware factory foreman
made his way to the Sons of Hermann Lodge where he again joined
brother officers in leading the proceedings. A third evening found him
in the regalia of an officer of the German Druids.[1] If his lodge duties
left him any time to spare, Milwaukee's German community had a host
of other activities to offer. There were music groups and drama societies, mutual benefit associations, debating clubs and educational groups
and gymnastic organizations, shooting clubs and carnival clubs, church
societies, old fraternity assemblies, political pressure groups, tavern circles, chess clubs, professional organizations, and for his wife, sewing
circles, benevolent associations, and parties and balls of all sorts.
During the 1840s and 1850s the Germans of Milwaukee had developed
a wide range of organizations and institutions to meet the social needs
of almost any group member; no other immigrant group in the city
could match their record.

Such associational activity among immigrants is often interpreted as
a way of coping with the trauma of adjustment in the face of exclusion
from native American society. New forms of organized activity were
created or adapted in an attempt to fulfill the old supportive functions
of the close-knit village community. There was no possibility of complete transfer, of course; thus such artificial community formation represents a stage along the path of acculturation.[2] But it is difficult to view
the rich associational life of Milwaukee's *Deutschtum* as an innovative
response to the immigrant situation. Many of the city's Germans had
never been peasants. Theirs was not the culture of the village. They
counted in their ranks representatives of Germany's urbanized and educated "general estate"; their numbers encompassed also the lower

middle class world of the urban artisan and shopkeeper and the petty bourgeoisie of the communities which Mack Walker has termed the home towns of Germany.[3] Whether bourgeois or *kleinbürgerlich*, the divorce of their kind from the traditional life of the countryside had occurred before their move to America.

The middle class associational life which had flowered in the German cities of the Enlightenment was filtering farther down the urban social ladder by the middle of the nineteenth century, and in the home towns could rest on the older associational tradition of the declining guilds. When such Germans came to America, they brought their *Vereinswesen* with them. Their origins in Milwaukee were essentially middle class and built on German precedent, and it would be the middle classes—the professionals, the shopkeepers, the artisans—who would dominate most of Milwaukee's organized community life.[4]

To stress the transference of urban Germany's *Vereinswesen* to the American urban frontier is not, however, to deny the role of associational life in the process of immigrant adjustment in Milwaukee. By preserving familiar forms of social interaction and reinforcing the independence from broader Milwaukee society which German economic and residential adjustments encouraged, such associations helped ease the immediate problems of adjustment.[5] Furthermore, even when organizations were dedicated to the preservation of non-American values and activities, their proliferation can be interpreted as a step in the direction of group assimilation. A similar process had, after all, made America, too, a "nation of joiners,"[6] and thus to create, to join a German *Verein* was also to act as an American.

The role of organized social life for an immigrant group is easily exaggerated, however. Too often, a mere listing of associations and meetings can create an impression of seething community spirit when in fact joiners like Adam Ernst may have constituted only a minute proportion of the group. Lacking membership lists, the extent of participation is difficult to gauge. Moreover, while recent research had demonstrated the crucial importance of formal associations in binding an ethnic community together, there appears in general to be little correlation between numbers and different types of associations and the strength of community identity.[7] In fact, it has been argued that diversity of associations and viewpoints hastens the process of community disruption by inhibiting its ability to present a united front in defense of its interests.[8]

If those interests are defined in essentially political terms as the preservation of a single sense of identity on all fronts, such may be the case. A closer examination of Milwaukee associational life will indeed demonstrate progressive internal differentiation within the German community from the easy informal unity of the pioneer years through religious and cultural diversification and conflict to a multiplicity of subcommunities and organizations reflecting the needs and interests of a heterogeneous people. But it will be argued that precisely because the Germans were so numerous and various, "community," to be effective, required definition in terms sufficiently broad and vague as to encompass and even draw strength from a diversity which permitted it to perform for Germans of all lifestyles its critical cushioning functions. The Irish, in contrast, were restricted by their numbers and narrow socioeconomic base to a limited sphere of activity in which they functioned as Irishmen, and no community developed able to contain broader differences of interest.

Informal Socializing

In Milwaukee as elsewhere, informal socializing lay at the base of the social structure. For the earliest east side German settlers, Matthias Stein's gunshop and Eduard Wiesner's liquor store were leading "resorts" among the men, while the women must have met casually as they collected their water from the town pump at the future site of the market near Stein's shop. Trayser's inn was probably the location of the nightly German rendez-vous noted by an English visitor in 1841; it was the prototype of the boardinghouse with bar that served as headquarters for newly arrived immigrants and that gradually evolved into the *Bierstube* or tavern familiar to Germans from the homeland. With the increasing immigration of the 1840s, taverns "sprang up like mushrooms," following settlers out into the newer German areas of the city to serve as focal points for the social life of the neighborhoods.[9]

These German taverns, reported a contemporary, "were more like social clubs, where neighbors met in friendly converse, discussing around tables the questions of the day, or playing cards, each partaking of refreshments according to his individual desire, and each settling his own score."[10] Like clubs, different taverns catered to different clientele. Most, apparently, had a rather raw and uncouth atmosphere, dominated as they were by newly prosperous tavern keepers:

The publican was almost the only man who took in cash. Since he was thoroughly familiar with all local and personal conditions, he could pose as a disinterested counsellor. He arranged land sales, and let himself be well-paid by both parties; he located jobs; he became the spokesman of his countrymen in all public matters; and whoever sought any major public office of necessity had to remain on friendly terms with him. In such circumstances, a man who had little education at home easily acquired a swollen head, while the steady enjoyment of alcoholic drinks contributed to his brutalization. The invective "Geschwollener" ("swell") which he applied to every respectable-looking or even well-dressed man, fit the publican himself in the most insolent sense of the term.[11]

But the familiar atmosphere and the services provided by the tavern keeper were essential for the new German immigrant. He felt uncomfortable in taverns run by Yankees, who did their drinking quickly standing up—"You can't stand around, you get neither bench nor chair, just drink your schnaps and then go"—and disliked the ready drunkenness induced by the American habit of "treating," or buying drinks by the round.[12]

For those annoyed by the "raw arrogance and vulgar conduct" of the average tavern keeper, there were other taverns whose hosts, "often men of consequence, perhaps prominent political refugees, or scholars unable to capitalize their German learning, jealously guarded the reputation of their places." In such taverns the leading men among Milwaukee's early Germans clustered around their reserved tables and over long evenings fostered the acquaintances which would result in the first community organizations. Even after the construction of halls devoted solely to such purposes, taverns continued to provide meeting rooms for social and political events, and a convivial atmosphere for turning strangers into friends. If the clientele of the various taverns could be reconstructed, the resulting distribution would undoubtedly reflect one of the fundamental sets of cells on which patterns of social interaction were based. By 1860 the best of Milwaukee's taverns offered beer that was both good and cheap, food which was often free, stimulating conversation, music, perhaps a singing host; it was little wonder that a visitor reported that "he who has a thirsty throat and an even moderately well-filled purse, will find an earthly paradise in Milwaukee."[13]

Although the tavern was chiefly a men's resort, women were welcome at dinners, parties, and dances, while in its summertime guise— the beer garden—the tavern became a social center for the whole family. The first of Milwaukee's many outdoor beer gardens opened on the northeast side near the river in the summer of 1843. It offered "well-cultivated flowers, extensive promenades, rustic bowers, and a beautiful view from Tivoli Hill," as well as a German brass band providing music one afternoon and evening a week, all for a 25¢ admission fee. Other German beer gardens followed, perhaps the best known being the Milwaukee Garden, established on the western outskirts of the city in 1850 and covering the better part of a city block, which was said to accommodate over 12,000 persons. Such private gardens took the place of the nonexistent public parks; they provided recreation opportunities, a goal for family walks, a chance for acquaintances to form among families whose paths would not normally cross.[14]

Impromptu balls were another form of early community activity. The first one was held in 1841 in a west side shack to accommodate a young Chicago German in search of a wife. The organizers, including Trayser and Stein, located a fiddler and a clarinetist in nearby communities and concocted a "wine" out of whiskey, sugar, and vinegar. The young man selected his bride but there was no happy ending: by the time she prepared her trousseau, or so the story goes, she found her intended already married. German musicians soon played regularly at Milwaukee gatherings, and by 1844 frequent German "balls" were regarded as permanent institutions.[15] Such informal socializing culminated in the first public appearance of Milwaukee's German residents as a unit in 1843, but by that time institutional forces were also at work binding individual migrants into social groups. The most important of the early institutions in this respect were undoubtedly the religious denominations.

The Social Influence of Religion

Religion, which created one of the deepest divisions among Milwaukee's Germans, was indirectly responsible for the first coalescence of a sense of German unity and remained the basis of much organized community life. For many though by no means all Germans, religion was a fundamental part of life which, it must have seemed, provided spiritual continuity in a world otherwise disrupted. Some immigrant denominations, particularly the Roman Catholics, incurred a certain amount of hostility from Milwaukee's native settlers, but in general church going was an activity sanctioned by Americans and hence a way for the immigrants to behave in an American manner while retaining a familiar ritual. Moreover, while some feared that the transplantation of established European churches would encourage antidemocratic dependence upon pastors among immigrant congregations, the multifarious organizations which emerged in the average parish served rather to encourage voluntary participation among a wide segment of the immigrant population while disguising its novelty with essentially conservative goals.[16] Thus the immigrant churches of Milwaukee were not only places of spiritual refuge for the individual but progenitors of wider community activity.

This was particularly the case with the Roman Catholic church, which may have numbered about a third of Milwaukee's Germans and most of its Irish among its members by 1850.[17] Its episcopal organization, combined with a missionary system accustomed to serving frontier areas, international ties which guaranteed at least some European financing, and a fairly steady stream of educated immigrant clergy, all meant that church organization proceeded quickly with little effort on the part of its Milwaukee communicants. The first organization, the first leaders, the initial funds, were provided from outside. Given the haphazard nature of early migration to Milwaukee, both German and Irish, and the generally unskilled character of those migrants, such outside educated leadership was of great advantage in the first formation of community-serving associations.

Milwaukee's earliest Catholics were its French-Canadians. They received their first visit from a priest sometime before the end of 1835, and regular missionary visits to the city's approximately 20 Catholic families began a year later. Milwaukee's first permanent priest was Patrick O'Kelley, a native of Kilkenny, sent by the bishop of Detroit in 1839, who erected a small church on two east side lots donated by Solomon Juneau. With the express hope of improving the Irish public image, he fostered a total abstinence society, which gained as many as 250 members but soon collapsed. He evidently proved incapable of adequately ministering to the growing German element in his congregation and retired to Michigan with ill health as his excuse in 1842.[18]

His replacement was Martin Kundig, Swiss-born, ordained in Cincinnati, and formerly pastor of an Irish parish in Detroit. Kundig found a parish of about one hundred families, a $200 debt on an unfinished church, no rectory, "spasmodic and meagre" church attendance, and "Catholic affairs not a little neglected." With the assistance of Thomas Morrissey, an Irish priest from Ann Arbor, he molded a parish community—or better, two communities—from this sorry state of affairs. He changed the church name to St. Peter's, enlarged the building, and by providing separate services for the German and English-speaking sections of his flock, could soon report that "the triple parish has become nicely united." He went on to establish a range of organizations to draw every class of parishioner into close contact with the church and with one another. They included a girls' school taught by two Irish women he had known in Detroit, and a boys' school which opened in the fall of 1842 with 25 pupils under the tutelage of a "scholarly Irish gentleman." His Irish successor the following year was joined by a German teacher. The parish roster also included a church building society to occupy the men with fund raising, and an association for women to encourage care for the church, sewing for the poor, helping poor girls and other "works of mercy." Sunday schools providing religious instruction in English, German, and French appeared by the end of the year.[19]

Kundig also revived and extended the moribund temperance movement, founding the Wisconsin Catholic Total Abstinence Society in 1842, which soon reported a membership of 600-700. The temperance movement, widespread elsewhere in the United States and Ireland as well, had spawned Yankee temperance societies (and a "cold water" hotel) in Milwaukee, and the Catholic move won the approbation of the city's native society. Both Catholics and non-Catholics probably saw it as a way of weaning Milwaukee's Irish to sober respectability; despite the multinational character of the society's officers, it is questionable how much support it drew among the Germans.[20]

The temperance society provided Kundig with the basis for a double coup, achieving both the appointment of a bishop for Milwaukee and the first organized German community activity. On the society's first anniversary, St. Patrick's Day 1843, he brought together an estimated 3,000 Catholics from 24 southeastern Wisconsin congregations to march in a temperance parade which attracted the participation of leading non-Catholics of Milwaukee. The day culminated in the foundation of a Repeal Association to support Irish home rule and a decision that the Total Abstinence Society would participate as a unit in the city's forthcoming celebration of the passage of federal legislation authorizing Milwaukee harbor improvements. Kundig then apparently acted to attract German participation. The city's Germans held a special meeting at the Catholic school three days later, with Stein presiding and Kundig as vice president. The result has already been described: Milwaukeeans were treated to what would be the first of many German public spectacles at the Harbor Parade.[21] If St. Patrick's Day 1843 marked the coming out of Milwaukee's Irish, then the harbor procession five days later equally signaled the German debut. Kundig had pulled together old settlers and educated new arrivals, Catholics, Lutherans, and freethinkers in a public appearance as a community, an impression that all groups would continue to foster, despite internal differences, as Germans took an increasingly active public role.

Kundig also achieved his other goal. He saw to it that copies of newspaper reports of the St. Patrick's Day demonstration were sent to every bishop, vicar-general, and superior in the United States, and when the provincial council of American bishops met in Baltimore in May, Milwaukee received its see. The new bishop was John Martin Henni, Swiss-born, 39 years old, who had spent 16 years in Cincinnati, serving as vicar-general of the diocese and pastor of a German parish, editing the first German Catholic newspaper in America.[22]

Henni was to concern himself with the construction of a cathedral and the formation of further parishes, the encouragement of Catholic education, and the preservation of the Catholicism of the city's Germans from erosion by actively opposing German anti-clericalism.[23] He completed the division within St. Peter's congregation in 1847 by establishing St. Mary's only two blocks away for an exclusively German congregation, and remained wedded thereafter to the concept of separate national parishes. With the growth of Bavarian, Austrian, and other south German settlement on the relatively isolated south side, a second German church, Holy Trinity, was dedicated in 1850, followed by St. Joseph's on the west side in 1855, after German Catholics there objected to the long walk to St. Mary's and pointed out the sense of separate community generated by that hardship. The old St. Peter's itself was replaced by a new cathedral, St. John's, in 1853, which remained an English-speaking parish staffed by a series of often cultivated Irish and American-born pastors, while a second English parish, St. Gall's, was organized in 1847 to serve the south and west sides. It was entrusted to the Jesuits in 1855 with the hope that they would establish an institution of higher learning in Milwaukee.[24]

The German parishes quickly developed the complement of associations which Kundig had inaugurated at St. Peter's. They ranged from mutual benefit associations to women's altar and rosary societies; from sodalities for young men and women, fund-raising building societies, and associations to foster social contact, to drama and debating societies, accompanying parishioners through all phases of their lives. It was hoped that this range of activity would encourage a sense of community and, in the words of one pastor, "rescue wandering sheep and protect the remainder from the rapacious wolves of worldliness and modernity"; men's activities generally received more emphasis than women's since women, it was felt, should not be encouraged to leave the home.[25]

Schools were quickly established in all parishes, even in impoverished Holy Trinity where a Catholic Free School was governed by a committee of five lay trustees and supported by a 75-member men's society. The mutual benefit associations were another important part of parish life for small shopkeepers, artisans, laborers, and their families, and as such were the first men's societies to be organized at St. Mary's and St. Joseph's; only at Holy Trinity was there evidently a several years' delay. The founding members of St. Joseph's initial association complained of the difficulties attendant upon their efforts; they lacked a tested model, they said, and were unknown to one another, coming from all areas of Germany and having little or no experience of *Vereinswesen*. But the second association, founded the following year, quickly acquired a reputation as one of the strongest in the country, and the other two parishes soon also felt the push for additional societies. Parish priests provided leadership in such activities, but strong lay initiative was also evident, particularly at St. Joseph's where, for all their low occupational status and self-confessed organizational inexperience, founding parish members successfully challenged the bishop over the location of the church and arranged their own finances.[26]

Irish parishes seemingly failed to develop similar associational variety. St. John's, for example, apparently limited itself to the original women's poor relief society, a total abstinence society founded in 1857, and an 1858 young women's sodality; the first mutual benefit association appeared only in 1871.[27] There were, however, other Irish associations enjoying church support though lacking clear parish ties. Kundig's Repeal Association functioned through 1843, and a Hibernian Benevolent Society was formed in 1847 which claimed 100 members in 1854 and was still going strong in 1856 under the presidency of the assistant pastor of St. John's, with middle-class merchants and craftsmen as other officers.[28] Two priests and a group of laymen at St. Peter's in late 1849 organized a conference of the St. Vincent de Paul Society dedicated to aiding the poor, which was reorganized with 42 members at St. John's and 51 at St. Gall's in 1859. It was thus only late in the period that its effects were felt; members were mainly Irish shopkeepers and craftsmen, with a sprinkling of laborers. The mid-fifties also saw the appearance of the Milwaukee Catholic Institute, a literary association which three years later numbered 100 members and a library of 300 volumes. It was led by cathedral assistant pastors; other 1854 officers included a portrait painter, a druggist, a public school principal, a merchant tailor, and a bank bookkeeper.[29] Admittedly impressionistic evidence thus suggests a more middle-class orientation among Irish church associations, with less concern for direct involvement of the average parishioner in communal activity. Perhaps the lack of other institutions competing for Irish allegiance meant that Irish priests had fewer fears than their German counterparts that their flocks would stray if complete services were not provided, or perhaps the laboring Irishman simply was not a joiner.

The "institutional" church thus appeared at an early date among the German Catholics of Milwaukee and played an important role in stimulating communal action among Germans and Irish alike, as parishes became fundamental cells of community life reflecting the geographical and ethnic divisions of the city. Under Henni, the church also developed citywide institutions, including not only schools and a seminary but a hospital and orphanages. Sickness, both the usual malaria and lesser maladies and also periodic smallpox and cholera epidemics, was a particular scourge for immigrants without relatives to care for them, and the growing public concern for this problem was met in 1848 when the Sisters of Charity, who had come from Baltimore in 1846 at Henni's request to teach the Catholic girls of the city, opened Milwaukee's first hospital. Its patients in the first year were mainly Irish and German; it was supported by public subscription, supplemented by various kinds of government aid and the volunteered services of doctors of all creeds and nativities. Henni also founded orphanages for boys and girls after the cholera epidemic of 1850 left many children of immigrant parents homeless, in his unwillingness to "expose these little ones to the danger of being drawn away by Protestants."[30]

Regardless of motive underlying their foundation, these institutions were important not only for those they helped but for those who

supported them: when unaccustomed German women forced themselves to the unpleasant task of door-to-door soliciting and learned how
to organize a fund-raising fair for the orphanages, an important kind of
acculturation was occurring.[31] The funds for Henni's projects came not
only from such local ventures and Sunday contributions but also from
his fund-raising trips throughout the United States and Europe and
from the profits of his "uncanny sense of real estate appraisal." These
activities generally won him the support of the natives, despite occasional opposition to Catholicism, most notably in 1844 when the pastor
of the First Congregational Church, J. J. Miter, preached a sermon on
the "Patriot's Duty," in which he denounced Catholics as "the passive
subjects of a foreign hierarchy" who should be deprived of civil and
political rights. More critical opposition came from anticlericalism
within the German community itself, but Milwaukee's priests generally
retained the respect of their congregations and continued to play a
major role in the public life of the community.[32]

The role of the Protestant churches in molding Milwaukee's immigrant community differed from that of Roman Catholicism in several
respects. In general, there was no institution ready to form churches for
the immigrants. The native congregations which gathered in the first
years of settlement had little initial interest in proselytizing among the
foreigners and differed doctrinally from the German Protestants, most
of whom were Lutheran. The polity of most Protestant churches made
the organization of a congregation dependent upon the gathering together of a group of like-minded persons who sought out a pastor. Missionary societies sent preachers to the west, and ordained ministers
immigrated as individuals in the hope of attracting the nucleus of a congregation, but the democratic form of organization meant that a
minimal sense of community interest, which fine doctrinal distinctions
often obscured, had to precede the appearance of a church. While the
shared soul-seaching involved in forming a congregation undoubtedly
created a strong communal identity—stronger perhaps than among
Catholics—the struggles also delayed Protestant church organization
and left large numbers of Germans outside organized religion for
years.[33]

The experiences of Milwaukee's first German Protestant congregation illustrate these difficulties. The Old Lutherans were already a
community upon arrival but could not afford to support a pastor. One
of their number, a former teacher, held services, until the head of the

Buffalo synod forced upon them the pastoral attentions of L. F. E. Krause, minister of the far larger rural Old Lutheran settlement. When Krause demanded a horse and buggy for his periodic trips to Milwaukee, the poverty-stricken congregation rebelled; Krause retaliated by excommunicating the congregation and not even the visit of the head of the synod was able to effect a reconciliation. In June 1846 the majority formally separated from Krause, soon joining the new Missouri Synod which accepted congregational self-government, and called a new pastor from Saxon settlers in Missouri. The months of contention had undoubtedly moulded the congregation, called Holy Trinity, into a strong community. Members met frequently in one another's homes for services and socializing; not until 1850 were they able to build a fitting place of worship. The minority of the original congregation survived as St. Paul's, and a third Old Lutheran congregation formed under the Calvinist-leaning Gottlieb Kluegel. [34]

Thus, by 1847, when the Catholics were already well organized, German Protestantism numbered only a small membership organized in the three congregations of the splintered Old Lutheran community, and a Lutheran missionary could report that many of the city's Germans were "rationalistic infidels." Many were ready to form congregations, however, if the right minister appeared. The contempory German movement for "free congregations" independent in polity and rational in dogma found adherents among Milwaukee settlers, and as early as the mid-forties a certain Pastor Schmitz attracted many of the young, free-thinking, up-and-coming Germans who formed a "pure evangelical congregation." When the group divided over the cost of church construction, many then transferred their loyalty to Heinrich Ginal, a rationalist from Philadelphia who founded a short-lived "free Christian" congregation around 1845. [35]

Schmitz himself shortly lost his pulpit to Asmus Diedrichsen, who had accepted a country post and supplemented his salary with biweekly sermons in Milwaukee halls and taverns until he received the call from Schmitz' congregation. Soon, however, Diedrichsen abandoned his liberalism to take over the pulpit of L. Dulitz, who had originally been invited by a group of 13 families to form a congregation on the model of the Prussian state church. Dulitz made way for Diedrichsen when he led part of his congregation into the newly formed Wisconsin Synod, while Diedrichsen's old congregation, in turn, joined with former Ginal followers in forming a German Lutheran Reformed United congregation under Pastor Helfer, who soon converted it into Milwaukee's first free-thinking (that is, completely rationalist) congregation, of which he became the speaker. Finally, in 1848, John Muehlhaeuser, a colporteur for the American Tract Society who had served a 10-year pastorate in Rochester, arrived in Milwaukee. He preached in leading Presbyterian and Congregational churches, and when ill health forced him to give up his book agency, a number of Germans requested him to gather a congregation. From his Grace Church pulpit he took a leading role in establishing the Wisconsin Synod in 1849.[36]

By 1850, therefore, a confused series of maneuvers had resulted in at least five German Lutheran congregations, all but Grace located on the west side, all quite recently formed, with small and shifting memberships divided on issues of theology or polity, in addition to an ultra-liberal congregation which had left Lutheranism behind. They were joined by several other denominations, including Zion congregation of the Evangelical Association (a form of German Methodism founded in Pennsylvania at the turn of the century) established in late 1846; German Methodist Episcopal and Baptist churches by 1850; another German Baptist congregation in 1855; and a German Old School Presbyterian congregation. One of the native Episcopal churches also began missionary work among the Germans in the northwestern part of the city.[37] Census statistics on church buildings and funds suggest that even by 1860 most of the German Protestant congregations remained relatively small and poor. There is no evidence that they developed the associational structure of the Catholic parishes, though the Lutheran churches quickly established schools and Holy Trinity had even founded a small teachers' seminary in 1855. However, the laborious process of gathering congregations of like-minded persons, selecting pastors, and overseeing church construction must have welded together strong community cores, which could provide havens for the immigration of the 1850s, when Holy Trinity, for example, opened a branch school among the Pommeranians in the northwest part of the city.[38]

The Welsh, Dutch, and Scandinavians were also able to establish congregations of their own, all of which followed a pattern of initial union, then separatism and the formation of new congregations once the immigrant settlement was large enough to afford to institutionalize its doctrinal and liturgical differences.[39] Milwaukee's Jewish settlers took a similar path. The earliest Jewish immigrants arrived in 1844, and by 1847 the first group of 12 met in the home of Isaac Neustadl for the

Yom Kippur feast. The formation of a Jewish cemetery association the
following year led to the establishment of Imanu-Al congregation in
1849, when the Jewish population numbered about 70 families. Dissension arose ostensibly over the issue of liturgical customs in 1854, however; the majority separated to form a second congregation following
Polish customs. They in turn divided, with those favoring a German
liturgy forming a third congregation in 1855. Thus about 200 families
supported three congregations; many switched back and forth, until the
visit of Isaac Mayer Wise in 1856 convinced them that only a "rational"
and "attractive" moderate unified congregation could hope to prosper.
The three consolidated as the B'ne Jeshuran congregation and three
years later numbered slightly over half of the city's Jewish families
among its members. While Jews continued to figure prominently in the
social life of Milwaukee's educated German society, a specific Jewish set
of associations then developed on this religious base, which included
benevolent societies, benefit balls, and in 1859, united protest when a
local Yankee lawyer made a derogatory reference to Jews in the course
of a circuit court trial.[40] Only the English and the Scots failed to seek
expression of ethnic identity in religious separatism once sufficiently
numerous to do so, participating instead in the active congregations of
the native born. For the other immigrants of Milwaukee, the desire to
worship in familiar forms proved the beginning of emerging ethnic
awareness and fostered some of the basic cells of organized life.

The First Associations

While religion thus divided the Germans into diverse smaller
communities, it also accustomed many to working together for a
common cause with persons originally strangers and provided local
bases for wider community activity. At an even earlier date, however,
the informal socializing of the first settlers began to coalesce into a
series of secular associations, some for mutual benefit, some to perform
needed services, some in reflection of old world patriotism, others for
simple enjoyment. The initial organizational consequence of the
German public life which had begun with the Harbor Parade surfaced a
year later when Germans established first a fire company, then a militia
unit in response to similar activity among the native born. The same
men, young merchants who were to play important political and
economic roles in the growing settlement, were behind both ventures,

and such companies remained important foci of German social life throughout the antebellum period. Membership in a militia unit was almost requisite for a young businessman: "That is the way to become known here, and one can do business only by being known." The blue and scarlet uniforms and brisk marching of the pioneer Washington Guards epitomized the new pride of the developing German community; their Military Hall, near the market, served for 10 years as the center of German communal life. German militia companies came and went, but the city could generally boast at least one and usually two or three, while new fire companies formed as German areas of residence expanded, each acquiring a reputation of its own, whether "swell" or "sporty" or "rough and ready."[41]

That same year, 1844, also saw the formation of the German Democratic Association, to which most German men reportedly belonged. The group combined political debate with defense of German community interests and played a major role in the political fights of the mid-1840s. Perhaps to carry its intellectual excitement over to other spheres, perhaps simply to formalize a *Stammtisch* group, many of the same men organized a German Association for Entertainment and Education the following year. It soon evolved into a mutual benefit association, directed by the same officers—in the main, relatively mature storekeepers and craftsmen; by 1849 it had survived initial vicissitudes to report a membership of over 100 and a treasury of almost $200.[42]

It was during the same period that the first of the Catholic mutual benefit associations was organized, but the Protestant churches apparently left such concerns to secular organizations. Unlike the pioneer German Association, most benefit societies took the form of fraternal orders. The natives had earlier established Masonic and Odd Fellows lodges; the Germans followed, beginning in 1848 with the formation of the seventh American branch of the Sons of Hermann and including, by 1860, a Masonic lodge, three Druidic lodges, two Odd Fellows lodges, two lodges of the Sons of Liberty, and one each of the Harugari and the Seven Wise Men. While the Masons and Odd Fellows, judging by their officers, attracted leading German businessmen, many of the others were led by lesser known shopkeepers and craftsmen, for whom the mutual benefit aspects must have been an important part of their appeal. The ritual which surrounded their activities, however, led a German visitor to speculate that they provided a surrogate religion for those who had abandoned churchgoing upon emigration but lacked the education to fill the resulting emotional void with higher learning or culture. Both their rationalism and the secrecy of their ritual brought the wrath of the Catholic clergy down upon them—Catholic members of the Sons of Hermann were refused church burial—but to those whose very decision to emigrate meant a rejection of the old community life to which religion was bound lodges provided a substitute companionship.[43]

Independent mutual benefit societies like the German Association were not entirely supplanted by fraternal lodges, however, and continued to appear throughout the period. As older societies matured, their dues may well have become too steep for newcomers, their members may have grown reluctant to admit newcomers to the fellowship, or the younger men may have been reluctant to accept the burdens of an aging membership. Thus, just as most Catholic parishes added a second society in the 1850s, new ones were also formed by various special interest groups—members of specific occupations, or neighborhoods, or even those from the same locality in the homeland.[44]

Special interest groups also began to appear among the German settlers in the mid-40s. Some sort of informal music corps was in existence even before the marching bands of the militia companies, and in 1846 hunting and shooting clubs were organized, followed by the first singing societies the next year.[45] It was in 1846 as well that the emerging sense of common concern led to an important community-wide venture, the formation of the Deutsche Unterstützungs-Verein, or Relief Society. Destitution among newcomers in winter was frequent, as they faced the harsh climate and seasonal unemployment, and in December Milwaukee's Germans adopted the by then familiar device of a public meeting to organize a society to collect donations and distribute relief to the destitute, thereby also, it was hoped, ending the professional begging which plagued the city. Succeeding winters saw the sporadic revival of the organization until the German Society, founded in 1855 to aid and protect arriving immigrants, took over many of its functions. The harsh winters of 1856-57 and 1857-58 led to the reappearance of the Relief Society itself, and by December 1858 its executives included prominent natives as well as Germans and its name was changed to the Union Relief Society.[46] What began as a purely German responsibility culminated in citywide acceptance of organized charity among the city's poor regardless of nativity.

Concern for affairs in the homeland seemingly played a lesser role in community organization. There were collections for revolutionary exiles, and a Three Cents Club whose members pledged three cents a week to support the revolutions of 1848; news of the revolutions provoked a mass parade in which Milwaukeeans of all nativities marched under the revolutionary banners of the European republics to the strains of the "Marseillaise."[47] But European concerns seemed largely peripheral to developing community life. It was local needs which generated most of the German community-wide mobilization and the smaller societies of the early years. But those same needs were creating not only a German community but also a set of viable subcommunities, potentially disruptive of any sense of unified *Deutschtum* within Milwaukee, that could be expected to multiply with the increasing size and heterogeneity of German settlement in the 50s.

With the exception of the native Americans, no other nativity group developed such a varied set of associations. Most lacked sufficient numbers, while the low-class status of many Irish and later Dutch undoubtedly inhibited much socializing beyond that of the church or the tavern. The Scots, despite their lack of an ethnic church, grouped together to raise money for victims of the 1847 famine in Scotland, for curling, and for celebration of the birthday of Robert Burns, activity that culminated in the organization of a St. Andrew's Society in 1859 "to aid natives of Scotland, and their wives, children, and grandchildren, when in destitute circumstances."[48] But such activities in general represented the charitable, social, and sporting concerns of men for whom ethnic origins represented an embellishment to daily activities, rather in the same fashion as the kilts they wore at their meetings— periodic moments of *auld lang syne* for men well integrated into wider Milwaukee society, rather than the very stuff of which their "society" was made, as was the case among the Germans.

Only the Irish to some extent echoed the German experience. The temperance movement sponsored by the church first brought them together; its concern for temperance as a means of improving the reputation of the Irish, however, evidences a class split which would characterize Irish associational life. The story of Irish community development was seemingly one of gradual separation of the Protestants from the remainder of the Irish with the brief appearance of organized Orangemen in the mid-forties,[49] the development of middle-class associations both within and outside the church for the upwardly mobile, and the abandonment of the rest to the politicians. Despite the greater stability of the Irish neighborhoods, much of the sense of grass roots community action that emerges from the German experience seems absent.

The Repeal Association continued the work of community coalescence begun by the Total Abstinence movement. But the membership fees and dues probably priced the association beyond the Irish laborer, and leaders included not only Irish businessmen, but important Americans as well. It demonstrated its strength with Fourth of July and St. Patrick's Day celebrations but then apparently dissolved later in 1844, a probable victim of the year's more immediate concern with American politics. Irish famine relief committees appeared in 1846 and 1847, but while the city was generous—$630 was collected at one meeting alone in 1847—the Irish as a group appeared to have little involvement, and in terms of reputation were once more in the position of charity recipients. Irish militia and fire companies appeared at about the same time as the native and German ones. The militia's checkered career resembled those of the German companies, but there was at least one company throughout most of the period to afford status and recognition to aspiring Irishmen. The fire company was perhaps less well-equipped than most other companies, with a less constant cadre of officers, but it too attracted the services of numerous young Irishmen. There was no evidence of other secular organizations. Because of their religion, fraternal orders were barred to the Irish, and it was not until after the Civil War that Catholic lodges developed.[50]

It was within this context that the sinking of the *Lady Elgin* in 1860 was so disastrous to the Irish, since it left them largely bereft of even this small organized and effective component. As a consequence of a Milwaukee incident which had involved Wisconsin abolitionists in a conflict with the federal government, the state governor seized the arms of the Irish militia, the Milwaukee Guards, when its captain indicated that in future similar incidents he would uphold the authority of the national rather than the state government. To raise money for new arms, the group sponsored a steamboat excursion to Chicago in September 1860 to hear Stephen Douglas speak. On the return trip the *Lady Elgin* was rammed by a schooner and sank; about three quarters of her 400 passengers died with her. They included not only the Guards but members of other militia companies, firemen, the German City Band, and many other Milwaukeeans. It was estimated that one out of every three Irish homes in the Third Ward lost a relative. The city responded with a massive collection for dependents of the victims, but the loss of many of the most active Irish helped further dissipate an organized Irish community.[51]

The German Athens

By the early 1850s, critical German visitors noted that Milwaukee seemed to possess more genuine German spirit and unity then any other American city. "This *gemütlich* atmosphere shines everywhere, lends the physiognomy of the city itself a friendly and comfortable air, and has even infected American society, whose stiff and icy tone has thawed to a limited extent under the influence of German customs."[52] Cultural and intellectual as well as political and social associations had begun to appear in the late 1840s, and the resulting texture of its life earned for the city the title of the German Athens. In the process, however, the introduction of classical music and drama, liberal reform groups and educational associations, underlined the divisions within the German settlement which had been obscured by the need for cooperation in the pioneer period. Cultural amenities for the few were earned at the price of greater divorce from the interests of the many, so that class and educational differences as well as religious distinctions engulfed Milwaukee's *Deutschtum* in the last decade before the Civil War.

The social divergence and cultural florescence that marked German life in Milwaukee and in other American cities at mid-century, have often been attributed to the influence of political refugees from the European revolutions of 1848. Even without their presence, however, the maturing of the pioneer settlement ensured the wealth to support cultural activities and attracted the services of professional men who had the interest and ability to patronize them. Such men found their way to Milwaukee well before 1848, members of the same classes, equipped with comparable educations, possessed of similar ideals, as the better-known Forty-Eighters. Moreover, because their exit from Europe was voluntary, they were perhaps more prepared to regard America as a permanent *Heimat*, worth the investment of their lives. They helped found the first political and social associations because the community required them, but once they were numerous enough to support the cultural amenities as well, their attention turned in that direction.[53]

Foremost among this group of early leaders was Dr. Franz Huebsch-mann, who arrived in Milwaukee at the age of 25 in 1842, a year after receiving a medical degree from Jena University. He was "a man of culture, fine intellect, and good abilities, but unfortunately," according to an American contemporary, "all these qualities were rendered nuga-tory by his irascible temper. He would rule, or he would ruin." His German friends, however, found that "his passion gentled itself, as soon as the memory of his old fraternity days was awakened" and relived in song.[54] The circle of friends also included Moritz Schoeffler, the son of a well-to-do family who provided him with a good education and apprenticed him to a printer. He emigrated at 29, and published (and wrote, set, printed, and delivered) a German newspaper in Jeffer-son City, Missouri, before coming to Milwaukee in 1844 to found the city's first German newspaper.[55] The young poet and school teacher, Alexander Conze, was another, a Jena and Leipzig student whose ro-mantic nature led him to service and death in the Mexican War.[56]

Karl Julius Kern's Latin Grocery was the meeting place of this circle. Kern, an aristocrat whose schemes for a fortune from land speculation ran afoul of his lust for gambling, offered tavern service in German, English, French, Latin, or Greek, and later became a prominent lawyer. The group of educated early settlers further included men like Karl Winkler, a young Bremen pharmacist, and Ferdinand Kuehn, trained in a Swiss banking house; doctors like Stadler, Luening, and Wunderly; Henry Niedecken, a university-trained blank book maker; Frederick Fratny, a Jesuit-educated Austrian political refugee who arrived in 1847 to edit Milwaukee's second German paper; August Greulich, a local Democratic politician, whose years of wandering around the United States had been preceded by university training for the priesthood; and A. Henry Bielfeld, poet, land agent, and German postmaster.[57] It was this circle, in conjuction with the city's German "founding fathers" of less cultured background—men like Wiesner, Stein, and Trayser—who set the cultural as well as the political and social mold of the German community.

The Americans had a Beethoven Society devoted to choral music for a brief period in 1843, and there was, of course, the German Band so prominent in early parades, but a serious German musical tradition began only in 1847, when Huebschmann, Niedecken, and two others formed the first male quartet. Soon after, the 16-member Sociale Män-nergesangverein began its nightly music making in the city's taverns, and by Christmas the Deutscher Manner-Gesang-Verein, dedicated to the appreciation of "fine singing" and to providing "a focal point for the social life of Milwaukee's Germans" made its appearance. Concerts, informal songfests, and social excursions followed, there was an abortive attempt to found a theatrical society, and by the following autumn a third singing society, for "workers," was lifting its voice.[58]

The growing social divisions which these activities suggest came into the open with amusing consequences in early 1849 when Theodore Wettstein, a newly arrived merchant, decided to hold a subscription ball to bring together the more cultured German families. With the help of two other businessmen, he drew up a list of 60 families to receive invitations. Among those accustomed to the extreme informality of the German balls which had been the rule, the news of the undemocratic and formal "closed" ball created a furor. The "swells" were accused of trying to import European class differences, and to counter them, a People's Ball was held the same evening, open to everyone who could pay 50¢, no formal dress required, and "with no distinction between working and non-working girls." Wettstein's ball was nevertheless such a success that he organized a series of three the following autumn, and the delicate strains of the polonaise and the waltz attracted even old timers like Eduard Wiesner to learn finer ways, while luring farmers and their wives from the countryside, driving their oxcarts in tie and tails, with bare feet to save their dancing shoes. However, the contention aroused by the original ball continued for several weeks in the press and in the streets (where Wettstein was burned in effigy), and "swell" was to remain a favorite epithet to describe the "greens," the newer group of better educated Germans, as opposed to the "grays," or the older settlers.[59]

The arrival of the Forty-Eighters, therefore, only intensified a process of cultural organization and social differentiation already underway. At first there were attempts at cooperation among all groups, spurred by the reformist enthusiasm of the newcomers, to raise the level of all areas of the city's German life. They foundered on the often bitter anticlericalism of many of the newcomers and the sense of social distinctions which, for all their political egalitarianism, they brought with them. The old days when a worker could address an educated man by the familiar *du* were passing.[60] When Mathias Stein washed his hands of the debacle of the second abortive drama society and sailed off to London to visit the Crystal Palace Exhibition, he symbolized the end of the old era of easy camaraderie; Henni's flirtation with the Whigs, to be discussed in the next chapter, equally signaled the consequences of the new era for the coalition Kundig had worked so hard to encourage. At a later stage, rifts would open within the elite group itself, as common cultural interests proved insufficient to maintain unity between old settlers and young turks, liberals and political radicals. These trends can be seen in music and drama as in the city's free-thinking societies and German reform groups.

A casual visit on a bitter winter afternoon in November of 1849 produced the best known of the cultural groups, when Theodore Wettstein joined with Jacob Mahler and his talented wife to produce a list of Milwaukeens with musical talent, whom they invited to form a Musical Society. Mahler, a wine merchant whose stock had not yet arrived from New York, handled the organizational chores. It was the presence of Hans Balatka which encouraged them to attempt a more professional group than had hitherto been the case. Balatka, a former law student and political refugee from Austria, had briefly tried "Latin farming" with his wife in rural Wisconsin but soon moved to Milwaukee, where his musical talent attracted notice. A later generation would judge him a dilettante in terms of musical accomplishment, but his gift lay in his tact and energy as director of the society and his ambition to make it the best in the northwest. Founding members included the old quartet and also newcomers who were only beginning to make names for themselves in the city. When the society was formally organized in April 1850, it chose an English name to attract American participation, and elected Rufus King, editor of the *Sentinel,* as one of its first officers.

Society membership soon grew to well over 100 and its annual concert series became increasingly ambitious. One of its greatest successes was its 1853 performance of Lörtzing's opera *Czar und Zimmermann* before an opening night audience of 800, an estimated two fifths of them American. Its popularity and membership fluctuated from year to year, and a rival society flourished briefly in 1860, but when Balatka left in late 1860 to found the Philharmonic Society in Chicago, the Milwaukee Musical Society had become a community institution. Its concerts and balls were highlights of the Milwaukee season, a symbol of the German culture for which the city had become renowned and a bridge of sorts between Germans and natives.[61]

Drama too benefited from the changing character of German settlement. An amateur group founded in 1849 and including a fair number of early settlers foundered after a spring and fall season in the wake of a benefit performance scandal but had at least survived longer than the abortive attempt of the previous year. The revival of German amateur theater came in early 1852 with a benefit play for the injured owner of a popular German tavern. Its success led to further performances and an expanded company, a gradually more serious repertoire, and finally a permanent stage in the Market Hall. When its founder, a tavern keeper and pioneer cultural enthusiast named Joseph Kurz, left in late 1853 to establish a German theater in Chicago, his legacy also included the company's first professional, a young German actress whom he found starving, not in a garret but in a log cabin where she supported herself and her sick mother with her sewing.

After Kurz' departure, the society kept at constant loggerheads with the series of directors whom it hired. Physical violence broke out at least once at rehearsal, and in 1858 the Drama Society finally split in two over the hiring of actors. Political rivalry and tension between grays and greens as well as artistic questions were evidently involved; it was Schoeffler, Kern, Wettstein, Kuehn, and other pre-1850 settlers, staunch Democrats all, who withdrew to form the amateur 81-member German City Theater Society, while the Republican Forty-Eighters led by Bernhard Domschke, spokesman "for the local 'Kultur' and 'Intelligenz' " supported the existing professional company.[62]

Concerns for self-education and social reform also bore associational fruit in the early 1850s. Their origins can be seen in the ephemeral Association for Entertainment and Education of 1845. Many of those involved in that venture participated with educated newcomers in the formation of a German debating society in 1849. By the following year their concerns began to intersect with those of craftsmen whose economic frustrations were leading them from strikes and wage negotiation to schemes for cooperative workshops and general social reform. The emigration of the late 1840s had not only strengthened Milwaukee's German intelligentsia but had brought to the city "educated mechanics" who were "enthusiastic partisans of the new communist and socialist doctrines" which were exciting workers in Germany. The consequence was a "workers' meeting" in August 1850 to explore the possibility of forming a Milwaukee industrial congress similar to efforts in eastern cities. "To make the worker independent of capital or money and to secure for him the exercise of his natural right to life and to the necessities and comforts of life—that is the task of social reform," the

workers proclaimed, a task to be achieved through producers' and consumers' cooperatives. The sponsors of the manifesto included both artisans and intellectuals; although they saw themselves as radical and
almost all had records of involvement in rationalist groups, the debating society, revolutionary fund raising, or opposition to Wettstein's
brand of elitism, by and large they were established figures in the
German community.[63]

Their call resulted in the creation of a Northwestern Association of
Workers whose purpose was "to free ourselves from the ever-increasing
bonds of the Money Power." Its momentum quickly dissipated, however, and the following spring a new Workers Union was formed,
which promised to combine mutual benefit features with long-range
social reform. Most of its leaders appeared to be actual workers, some
with previous trade union experience. Between its first announcement
and its final organization, however, the character of the Workers Union
changed. Perhaps its leaders had listened to the tailors, whose recent
attempts at cooperative production had taught them that the worker
should first "learn what socialism is, instead of immediately just
jumping into it without any theory"; perhaps the model of workers'
educational societies in Germany was too familiar to resist; or perhaps
nonlaboring intellectuals moved in and changed its direction. At any
rate, what finally emerged in July 1851 was a Workers' Reading and
Educational Society. Its first president was a woodworker, its secretary
a master bookbinder.[64]

The society met twice a week for debates and lectures on such topics
as socialism and land reform, as well as on more general political concerns and even natural science. Favored speakers included local newspaper editors, newly arrived political refugees, and familiar fixtures of
the local scene like Huebschmann. It soon shed the last remnants of a
workers' movement and by early 1852 had become "the main association of the free thinking and radical Germans." Its 1852 officers
included Dr. Aigner and August Kruer, both local newspaper editors;
Hans Balatka of the Musical Society; a free-thinking watchmaker and
gunsmith named Emmanuel Kraatz; and the master bookbinder Otto
Laverrenz. These were men by occupation and outlook far removed
from the almost anonymous founders of the original 1851 labor movement. Women were admitted to meetings and administration. The
association attempted to recapture some of its purpose in the fall of
1852 with its sponsorship of ward employment bureaus and a mutual

benefit society, but as a contemporary noted, the intellectuals "did not succeed in forming a friendly, brotherly bond between the educated Germans and the German worker, nor in arousing in the workers an enthusiasm for higher learning. Not even the most popular format was able to attract interest in the lectures. The listeners' benches grew ever emptier," and by 1853 the workers were back forming labor unions and the intellectuals had merged the society with the rationalist Union of Free Men.[65]

The rationalist movement constituted another facet of the German reformist attack on Milwaukee life in the early 1850s. Like the workers' movement, it had its roots in the intellectual currents of pre-revolutionary Germany and had surfaced in Milwaukee in the mid-1840s.[66] In its search for an acceptable mode of worship, it sought to provide an association which would bring together the liberal German settlers; in its attacks on organized religion, it deepened the fissures in the wider German community.

The earlier rationalist congregation broke up after Pastor Helfer's free-living as well as free-thinking private life forced his flight to St. Louis. With the arrival of Eduard Schroeter in 1851, the Freie Gemeinde was reorganized and he became its first speaker. He was a 39-year-old political refugee whose conversion to the movement to reform German Protestantism from within occurred shortly after he completed his training for the ministry; a western speaking tour undertaken after a fruitless attempt to found a congregation in New York brought him to Milwaukee, where he also edited a journal, *Der Humanist*.

His congregation espoused the equality of all, men and women alike, under the rule of "reason, and the great teachings of nature and history." Neither belief nor disbelief in a divinity was maintained; the congregation sought the mental and moral freedom of its members through song, speech, and the mutual exchange of opinion. The atmosphere at their services struck an outsider as cold and bare, and many of the artisans' wives who attended with their husbands seemed to miss the comforting ceremonies of the old religions. Perhaps for this reason, a special "humanistic" association was formed among the women in the spring of 1852, along with a singing society. Membership appeared equally divided between grays and greens and included many who were active in other liberal and cultural causes.[67]

The congregation was not without internal dissension, particularly over the delicate philosophical and financial issue of whether the speaker of a free congregation should be paid. By May 1853 Schroeter was happy to accept the speaker's post in a rural congregation and was succeeded by another refugee theologian, Heinrich Loose. In the meantime, a second free-thinking group had appeared, the Verein Freier-Männer, founded in June 1852 to support rationalist causes. It was not a real congregation, had no paid speaker, and remained relatively unimportant until its union with the Workers' Reading and Educational Society, when it quickly "took first place among the societies of the city." Its leaders included guiding lights from both the Workers' Society and the Freie Gemeinde; its goals were "the mutual enlightenment of members in the fields of religion, politics, and socialism, influencing popular education, striving for the political realization of socialistic ideas, and brotherhood within the association." Membership grew to several hundred, with Sunday morning lectures and debates providing intellectual stimulation and members of the former workers' group adding a mutual benefit association.[68]

Soon a third rationalist society appeared, which was to work with the other two for a union of all Milwaukee free-thinking Germans. This was the Sociale Turnverein, founded in 1853 following two unsuccessful earlier attempts to transplant the German Turner movement for physical and political regeneration to Milwaukee soil. Its 21 charter members seem to have been mainly young men not yet active in other groups, but prominent Forty-Eighters and older German businessmen and community leaders soon joined. By its second year, it had constructed a permanent Turn-Halle on the west side and was offering a gymnastic school for boys, a rifle squad, singing and dramatic sections, sports competitions and exhibitions, lectures and debates, and occasional balls.[69]

There was probably a good deal of overlapping membership among the three free-thinking organizations, and in the fall of 1853 they united to call for a convention of all Wisconsin free-thinking groups as a prelude to the formation of a national association of radical Germans. The 63 delegates representing 23 groups included members of the various Milwaukee German fraternal lodges, the Theater Society, and the city's three liberal German school associations. The result was the formation of a Bund Freier Menschen, or union of free people, with a central committee divided into five sections to deal with the press, schools, gymnastics, art, and mutual benefit. It was not, however, the powerful union of liberal Germans for which many, led by Schroeter, had hoped;

Schoeffler, whose opposition to Schroeter dated from squabbles within the Freie Gemeinde over the use of his printing press, used the 15 fraternal lodge delegates whom he had brought into the convention to defeat any plan for closer union, and the Bund disappeared apparently unmourned sometime during the winter of 1854-55.[70]

The two original free-thinking societies finally merged into a Verein der Freien in May 1854, after Loose agreed that a paid speaker was a final remnant of priestly rule, but by that time its intellectual tone had declined, and it was losing members to the Turners. The Verein finally dissolved in 1855 as many of its remaining members were caught up in Republican politics (the Sociale Turnverein inherited its library and treasury), only to be resurrected again in 1858 under the guidance of one of its former leaders.[71]

One of the lasting beneficiaries of the intellectual excitement of the period was thus the Turnverein, which by the mid-fifties had inherited the mantle of its predecessors and became "the center of the intellectual life of the German citizens." The key to its success probably lay in the widening scope of its activities—gymnastics classes for girls were formed in 1855, for example—and in its introduction of a mutual benefit fund in anticipation of the need which would result from the panic of 1857. The high point of antebellum Milwaukee Turnerism came in 1857, when over 7,000 Turners from all over the midwest poured into Milwaukee for the annual Turnfest of the western branch of the national Turner-Bund. Milwaukee's Turners also continued the practice begun earlier by the city's free thinkers, both German and English-speaking, of holding annual celebrations of Thomas Paine's birthday, and their outdoor celebrations took on the "true character" of old country folk festivals, or so it seemed to the participants. The growing involvement of the group in Republican politics, however, ultimately led to a schism in 1860 and the formation of the Independent Turnverein.[72]

The other lasting product of those years of excitement was educational. Throughout much of the antebellum period, from a third to over half of all children attending school in Milwaukee were not in the public school system. Partly this was because public school facilities were always inadequate, especially in the newly developed parts of the city which tended to be heavily immigrant, partly because parents distrusted the public schools. For some, it was an issue of language. German parents preferred that instruction at least begin in German before children faced the extra difficulty of English, or desired schools which provided instruction in both languages. While bilingual instruction was permissible under local law, it was not until 1857 that one German ward received the first German instruction in a Milwaukee public school, and even that was discontinued in the austerity drive of the early 1860s. Germans were never able to achieve the control over the education of their children for which they agitated and which they felt their numbers warranted.[73]

The solution for Lutherans and Catholics was parochial schools, which ensured religious orthodoxy as well as cultural and linguistic continuity. As a Milwaukee priest explained, "German children, if Anglicized, by some strange fate generally become alienated from Catholic life. On the other hand, Irish children, if well instructed by their priest in any English Catechism, generally are saved to the Catholic faith."[74] To prevent such alienation, schools were quickly established in all Catholic parishes (only in St. Gall's was there evidently some delay), and the Lutherans did likewise. The first Lutheran teacher appeared by 1846, and in 1847 Holy Trinity was operating a regular school, Grace Church by 1848. The Catholics also opened German and English convent schools for girls, and the Jesuits briefly attempted to offer instruction in "all branches of a commercial, classical, scientific, and philosophical education" to boys between the ages of 6 and 25 but soon found that their students were completely unprepared for an academic education and gave up the project as a "humbug" in 1859. Church-sponsored education thus remained essentially at the elementary level. While the exact proportions educated in such schools is uncertain, the extent of the effort which their support involved for a relatively poor segment of the population should not be underestimated.[75]

But public school education was equally unacceptable to many of the city's free-thinking Germans. While they approved of it on philosophical grounds, from a practical viewpoint they objected to its failure to include German instruction, the lack of secondary education before 1858, the minimum number of subjects taught, and what they felt to be the mindless and mechanical cramming which passed for instruction in the public schools. They did not want to accept for their children lesser standards than they had known at home. Thus, encouraged by the success of the cooperative Music Society, a group of parents—generally free-thinking and representative of both older and newer settlers—met in the spring of 1851 to form the Milwaukee Schul-Verein and incorporate the German and English Academy. Peter Engelmann, teaching at the time in his own private school, was selected as director, while a free-thinking former Lutheran teacher was hired for the elementary instruction.[76]

The *Verein* was to congratulate itself for the selection of Engelmann. He was 28 at the time, the son of a Rhenish farmer. He had studied botany and mathematics at German universities and taught in a *Gymnasium* before his revolutionary activities forced him to emigrate in 1849. In America he had tried farming and farm labor as well as private tutoring and village school teaching; his appointment to the academy finally enabled him to marry an American woman whom he had met in Michigan. Engelmann's aim at the academy was always "more to educate and train the young for self-instruction, than to cram with undigested knowledge," and many of his educational innovations were to influence Milwaukee's public schools.[77]

The academy's 40 original pupils grew to 250, including some sons of native parents, and by late 1853 it occupied its own building on the upper east side. Elementary subjects included not only reading, writing, arithmetic, and grammar, but also geography, history, nature studies, drawing, English, and exercises in visual comprehension and memory, while older students added natural science, penmanship, mathematics, and principles of construction. The success of the school led to imitators, beginning with the West Side German and English High School, whose origins lay in 1853, when west side parents decided to save their children the walk to the Engelmann school and provide a post for Loose after the dissolution of the Freie Gemeinde. It was followed that same year by the South Side German and English Academy, although within four years internal dissension led to its six-year suspension. Not until 1859 did the Engelmann school announce the foundation of a secondary school for girls, offering instruction in hand work, drawing, and singing as well as penmanship, geography, arithmetic, history, natural history, French, English, and German; until that time, parents unwilling to send their daughters to the convent schools patronized a series of private "institutes."[78]

The liberal academies were supported by tuition payments and the fund-raising efforts of a Frauen-Verein, whose balls and other benefits also provided scholarship support. Originally associated with the Engelmann school, it expanded its activities to support all the "free schools" of Milwaukee and merged with the women's association of the old Freie Gemeinde. The Frauen-Verein ensured the survival of the schools during the difficult financial period of the late 1850s, and served as an important umbrella organization for the activities of the more leisured and cultured among the German women.[79]

The schools, the music and drama groups, and the leisure-time activities of the Turners were the most lasting legacies of the post-1848 period. A more bitter heritage was the anticlericalism which wracked Milwaukee's *Deutschtum* during the period. It paralleled the home-grown nativism of those years but, like so much else, had German roots. Liberals and radicals were fearful of church influence on politics in their new homeland; the churches feared for their membership and property in the face of secret and socialist organizations; the enmities of each side fed on the fears of the other and inflamed the pages of the local German press. Church objection to Catholic membership in fraternal lodges was a bone of contention by the late 1840s. The bishop's refusal to allow the Musical Society to perform Haydn's *Creation* oratorio in the cathedral in 1851, since one of the ticketsellers was a notorious anticlerical agitator, stirred up further controversy, which culminated when the visit of the papal legate to Milwaukee in 1853 aroused the same radical German objections there as it did in other cities of America. There were threats of church burnings, priests and nuns were abused on the streets, and the German quarrel entered Milwaukee politics.[80]

Symbolic of its virulence were the *Flug-Blätter* of Vojta Naprstek, a Czech whose combination bookstore, art gallery, lending library, reading room, and music library was a focal point of German cultural life. In an attempt to advertise new rationalist literature in 1850, he ordered a recent article on Galileo reprinted on long strips of paper, along with a list of the books which he had for sale, which friends pasted before dawn on prominent Milwaukee walls and fences. The successful advertising device was repeated a second time, with a parody of a sermon advising the faithful *not* to buy his books. The response so delighted Naprstek that the third handbill was twice the size, and with number five the joke became a weekly publication, "in jest and in earnest, dedicated to the enlightenment and elevation of the depressed state of the clergy." The popularly written and grossly illustrated anticlerical tracts were purchased "in the thousands" every week at a penny each, and except for a brief break in 1853, continued to appear until November

1854 when Naprstek left for New York once the political controversy between Republicans and Democrats overshadowed the anticlerical cause.[81]

By 1860 a pious Lutheran who had earlier bemoaned the unbelief of the Forty-Eighters was able to report that "a few years ago one could not drink a glass of beer in the saloons without being angered by anti-Christian remarks or raillery against preachers. These blasphemers are now silent and their blasphemous anti-Christian publications have ceased . . . of the blasphemers I have known most of them have come down and are impoverished and other unbelievers no longer raise their heads with the same boldness as formerly." The passage of time led to acculturation of a kind or to the failure that meant withdrawal from public life for the German newcomer, and old German causes gave way to the newer excitements of American politics or business. Joseph Weydemeyer pronounced a general obituary on German reform in Milwaukee by the end of the decade when he wrote to Karl Marx that "The German newly rich—and society here is in the main composed of them —are much too conceited. In general, life among these pretenders is dull."[82]

The German Press

The press played a crucial role in German community formation, helping to arouse a sense of united *Deutschtum* and reflecting and fomenting its divisions.[83] The pioneer German journal, the *Wisconsin Banner*, was a byproduct of the 1844 campaign to grant liberal suffrage to the foreign born in the question of a state constitution. Feeling that the city's Democratic organ was an insufficient spokesman for the German viewpoint in the face of Whig attacks, Franz Huebschmann assembled $170 from among the German settlers to finance Moritz Schoeffler's announced project of founding a German Democratic newspaper; Schoeffler had recently arrived in Milwaukee from his Jefferson City, Missouri, endeavor. The *Banner* first appeared in September 1844 and by 1850 its 4,000 weekly and 1,400 daily subscribers reportedly made it second only to the *Sentinel* among Milwaukee newspapers. Like the English language papers of the day, it was a four-page sheet, devoted largely to advertisements and reprinted stories from other European and American papers; but it provided space as well for extensive notices of meetings, entertainments, and other local events, contentious editorials, lengthy letters to the editor, and an ever-increasing coverage of local news. It thus served as a community bulletin board and as a vehicle for consciously molding German political opinion and must have helped form a sense of social as well as political community.

Schoeffler quickly became an influential, fairly liberal leader in the Democratic party and married the daughter of one of Milwaukee's pioneer brewers. According to later German opinion, his main virtue as an editor lay in his ability to speak clearly on public issues while not completely descending to vulgar name-calling. When the revolutions of 1848 brought men of greater education and literary ability to Milwaukee and elected office took more of his time, Schoeffler relinquished the editorial side of the paper but retained control of its business and technical operations. Under a succession of educated and able editors, the *Banner* retained its liberal Democratic orientation, with a mild dose of anticlericalism for spice.[84]

As the political infighting of the 1840s continued, Rufus King, the editor of the Whiggish *Sentinel*, decided that a second German paper was required to counter the influence of the *Banner*. The project, long in incubation, finally resulted in the appearance of the *Volksfreund* in early 1847. King supplied both funds and copy, while the nominal publisher, a former *Banner* worker named Friedrich Rauch, simply handled typesetting and proofreading. King soon brought Frederick Fratny, an Austrian political refugee, from New York as permanent editor. Fratny, however, found the paper's attempts to make Whiggery palatable to the Germans not to his liking and raised funds to purchase the paper himself before the end of 1847. Under Fratny, the *Volksfreund* turned Democratic, while remaining at odds with the *Banner*. While Schoeffler long viewed him as a Whig in radical's clothing, Fratny considered Schoeffler a hidebound conservative and used his paper to support what were considered radical social causes such as land reform and a biting anticlericalism, although his politics followed the straight Democratic party line on most issues. Their printed barbs against one another provided constant gossip for their readers and led to a certain split in what until then had been a more or less united German political front. The more "progressive" and perhaps better educated tended to take Fratny's side, while his support of workers' causes assured their readership as well. Matters improved over time, however; both editors frequently appeared on the same platform and in the same organizations, and Fratny himself grew less vitriolic over the years as his health worsened, until on his deathbed in 1855 he transferred his paper to Schoeffler. The combined sheet was then known as the *Banner und Volksfreund.*[85]

Factionalism and perhaps dissatisfaction with the anticlerical stance of the other two papers may have led to the publication of the third German newspaper, the *Volkshalle*, in May 1851. Its backers were rumored to be August Greulich and Hermann Haertel, partners in a mercantile firm, both early settlers and prominent political figures; Greulich, at least, had close connections with the Catholic clergy. *Volkshalle* announced an independent political position but apparently won its good-sized following largely on the basis of rather crude personal polemic and scandal mongering. By autumn, ownership of the paper passed to a new group whose editor was a colorful newcomer, Gustaf Adolf Roesler von Oels, a Silesian schoolteacher and leftist member of the Frankfort Parliament, whose fiery red beard and bright yellow suits had won him the soubriquet of *Reichskanarienvogel.* He promised his readers a paper independent of either party, supporting land reform, free trade, and a sound banking system, opposing slavery, forceful territorial acquisition, and liquor laws. He quickly inherited Fratny's vituperative opposition to his predecessor and had a difficult time attracting subscribers. Roesler's position became more precarious after he became sole owner of the *Volkshalle*, and he finally abandoned it in early 1852.[86]

The paper's plant was purchased by a Catholic joint stock company headed by Joseph Salzmann, pastor of St. Mary's parish, and financially supported by Greulich. The anticlerical attacks of Fratny and others had become sufficiently strong that the church decided to counter them with its own organ, thereby also assuring a paper which its flock could read in safety. The editor of the new journal, the *Seebote*, was Armand de St. Vincent, an elderly Frenchman who had served first in the Prussian army, then in the papal curia, and in America had helped edit the Cincinnati journal founded by Henni. Recommended from pulpits in the German parishes, the *Seebote* proclaimed itself Catholic and democratic but was pronounced reactionary by its rivals and became a sitting duck for Fratny's scorn. Publication expenses prompted its outright sale to Greulich and two others, who retained its Catholic orientation. When blindness forced St. Vincent to retire from the editorship in late 1853, he was ultimately replaced by

Christian Ott, a university-educated Bavarian who had been running a bookstore in Milwaukee for several years. In 1856 Greulich's partners were bought out by Peter V. Deuster, who had begun his career as a printer's devil in the early days of the *Banner*. He and Greulich continued as partners until the latter retired in 1860; the *Seebote*, its political stand now regularized but still Catholic in orientation, became one of Wisconsin's leading Democratic journals.[87]

A final choice of political stance was the product of Bernhard Domschke's perseverance. Domschke, a Saxon, had become a free thinker while a university student; he took part in the 1848 revolution and spent a precarious four years after his arrival in America in 1851 teaching school, serving as speaker of a Boston free congregation, and working on Karl Heinzen's radical paper in Louisville. When Heinzen could not pay his staff, Domschke and a friend made their way, penniless, to Milwaukee. His Sunday morning address in the Market Hall on "The Democratic Church" so angered the Democrats that Fratny challenged Domschke to a debate, which brought him to the attention of Milwaukee's Republicans. With Rufus King once more in the lead, they provided Domschke with press and quarters, and in October 1854 the *Corsar*, Milwaukee's first German Republican paper, appeared. Fratny rose to the challenge of a new opponent, but the harsh attack with which Domschke responded in print to the sick man reportedly alienated many who might otherwise have responded favorably to his newer brand of radicalism. Most Milwaukeeans, despite his excellent theater and musical reviews, remained wedded to their older sheets, and after two years of privation, Domschke had to give up the paper. A few days later, however, he recruited new supporters and issued the *Milwaukee Journal*, which lasted ten weeks. It was followed in turn by the *Atlas*, supported by Carl Schurz and the editorial aid of several other prominent newcomers. After Domschke subjected the fragile new publication to the financial strain of daily publication in late 1858, however, it gradually collapsed, only to be replaced by the *Herold*. Domschke finally found a good business partner in W. W. Coleman and the *Herold* during the Civil War became one of the most important German papers in the northwest.[88]

Despite the frequent name changes, Domschke's publications remained Republican, and while his difficulties demonstrated the lack of response to that party among Milwaukee's Germans, his efforts meant that the views of the new party received full airing on a fairly regular basis. They also meant that from 1851 on, Milwaukee's Germans generally had at least three papers to choose from: one addressing itself to a fairly conservative Catholic readership; one liberal-middle-of-the-road; and one appealing to radicals (although Fratny's radicalism was more of a grass-roots variety, Domschke's the middle-class version which included abolitionism). While the early *Banner* was an important instrument in creating a sense of unity among Milwaukee's Germans, the appearance of journalistic diversification was a measure of the development of even more important subcommunities.

There were other journalistic endeavors among the Germans, of course. According to one listing, 31 new journals appeared in Milwaukee in the ten years after 1851, 15 of them German. One was a newspaper, *Grad'Aus*, established around 1856 and published regularly in the latter part of the decade, which was edited for a time by Otto Ruppius, a German novelist who came to Milwaukee after his escape from German imprisonment for his revolutionary activities. Its precise politics are unclear, although sufficiently irregular to earn the scorn of the *Banner und Volksfreund*. The paper changed hands several times; Ruppius retired to publish a literary journal, *Westliche Blätter für Unterhaltung, Kunst, Deutsches Leben* and soon moved with it to St. Louis; and the old *Grad'Aus* became the independent Democratic *Volksblatt*. Then there was Schroeter's shortlived *Humanist*, whose demise in early 1854 was succeeded by the appearance of the *Arbeiter*, an advocate of "radical socialism" edited by a group of Forty-Eighters. Mathilde Franziska Anneke's *Frauenzeitung*, a feminist monthly, similarly reflected the ideals of the revolution, as did *Atlantis*, a literary and scientific monthly brought to Milwaukee for a time in 1854 by Christian Esselen. Other, even shorter-lived German publications included the *Stimme der Wahrheit*, an organ of the Whig Club headed by Roesler von Oels which was published daily during the 1852 campaign from the *Seebote* presses, and the *Hausfreund*, an "entertainment" paper edited by Peter V. Deuster, also printed by the *Seebote* for a few months in 1852. The fates of most publications suggest that while the German community was sufficiently diverse to support several newspapers (even if rather precariously), it was still too small to support even more specialized endeavors.[89]

The Irish were never able to support their own newspaper. The *Courier*, under the editorship of American-born John A. Brown between 1843 and 1847, served as both Democratic spokesman and Irish advocate, and for a brief span in 1844, also published the biweekly *Immigrant and Irish Repealer*, but its rapid demise suggests the small demand for an exclusively Irish journal.[90]

Conclusion

The sense of German common purpose forged in the mid-forties thus effectively diversified into a series of more specialized subsocieties.[91] For Catholics, numerous parish organizations provided outlets for all ages, while schools and press consciously defined community interests. The educated, often areligious Germans created their own set of institutions. Their views were echoed in most of the German dailies; they created their own schools, cultural societies, and religio-political associations to provide the cultural and intellectual stimulation to which they were accustomed. The less well-educated developed a social life centered in the lodges, and to a certain extent, the various workers' organizations. The Protestants found a common focus in the running of their churches, and if church societies were not as all-inclusive as among their Catholic brethren, they could be supplemented with lodges, theater groups, and singing societies for those who needed a richer social life. It was the upper classes who left the clearest account of their community, whose special interest community was in fact often defined as Milwaukee *Deutschtum*, but the subsocieties of church and lodge were probably far larger. Perhaps larger still was the mass of those who never became active joiners, those who remained in Milwaukee only briefly and who found what local community they possessed in neighbors, fellow workers, the group at the corner saloon, the women who shopped on the same street.

Certain common interests, however, did continue to support an umbrella sense of German unity throughout the fifties. The anticlericalism of the early part of the decade died down once the issues which would ultimately lead to civil war appeared on the horizon, drawing together the older educated group of Democratic leaders and the conservative churchgoers in an uneasy alliance against the "greener" radicals. The Fourth of July festivities which had begun in 1843 continued to bring out all elements of the Germans in a common celebration of their loyalty to their adopted country, in the early years often in the face of Yankee indifference or even hostility. In 1852, under the stimulus of one of the socialist workers' organizations, the Germans attempted a May Festival to bring together all Milwaukeeans in a day of celebration which proved notably successful, although its reprise the following year, in the height of the anticlerical uproar, was a disaster. Catholics boycotted it because of the presence of too many atheists and Jews, and the Democrats were suspicious of Whigs and Freesoilers; among the natives only the Cricket Club showed its colors, and the day ended in a brawl between celebrating Germans and Irish policemen.[92]

The nostalgia for the old country community demonstrated by the attempt to import the May Festival did not disappear, resulting in 1857 in the full-fledged appearance of the German *Carneval* in Milwaukee. The balls and other private carnival celebrations which marked the onset of Lent during the forties and early fifties finally led to the forma- tion of a Carnevals-Gesellschaft to support a public *Volksfest* on the German order. Prince Carneval and his court reigned from Burg Nar- halla for two winter days, gracing masked balls, theatrical perform- ances, and a grand Shrove Tuesday parade complete with decorated wagons, bands, costumed attendants, and satirical tableaux. Prince Carneval returned the following year to further bemuse the Americans and divert the Germans in the middle of the hard depression winter, and by 1860 a workers' group formed a second Carneval Association to drown their troubles in merriment.[93]

Various sporting events also brought Germans together, while neigh- bors continued to join for common action on such issues as schools, neighborhood markets, street improvements, and tax assessments. But as the city grew, further special interest groups continued to proliferate, and the first *Landsmänner* societies of persons from the same areas in Europe appeared. South side youths formed their own Lyceum because they felt remote from other organizations; a group of downtown clerks and students formed a Junta with similar goals of self-improvement. Former university students held nostalgic reunions, leading older Ger- mans formed a Natural History Society, further singing societies added their voices to the city's choruses.[94]

Women too were drawn into association, first through the churches, then through the free thinking groups which led to the important Frauen-Verein. Not only did women associate on their own, but they also played important roles in the various musical, dramatic, and free- thinking groups. For some, mainly the wives and daughters of the more active professional men and merchants, life was a full round of benefit balls, concerts, amateur theatricals, and tea dances. For others, it re- volved around church choirs, ladies' sewing circles, altar and rosary societies, and family visits. Others, of course, worked. Milwaukee's women were brought out of the house and into cooperation but were also separated by class through the development of social organizations.

The development of associations also reinforced the process of ethnic differentiation encouraged and reflected by residential patterns. Tentative cooperation of Americans, Germans, and Irish within women's groups, young men's associations, and special interest organizations like horticultural and musical societies tended to dissolve by the early fifties, as it became clear that the Germans had evolved a satisfying alternative society of their own. Henni's decision to form separate Irish and German parishes furthered the isolation of those two groups, while the church's establishment of a variety of associations for the educated Irish helped keep them apart from their fellow English speakers. It also meant that the Irish themselves were probably divided (like the Germans) between the middle-class "visible" community and the amorphous group life of the lower class.

In the case of the Germans of Milwaukee, the assertion that immigrant associations were responses to exclusion from native society thus becomes meaningless. To many outsiders, of course, all Germans remained "Dutchmen," and this realization may have contributed in a negative sense to community solidarity. But more important, not only could Yankee institutions do little to satisfy adjustment needs which the natives did not share; most members of the two groups lacked the common tastes and common experiences which form the basis for social interaction. Only time could alter that situation, in a process to which both groups would contribute.[95]

The Germans had managed to create a community on the basis of similar language, residential propinquity, and common attitudes toward the enjoyment of life, as a look at their patterns of political participation will confirm.[96] That minimal sense of common concern was probably broad enough to encompass most Germans who settled in the city. Their numbers and backgrounds ensured the cultural security and institutional variety which meant that few would feel it either necessary or satisfying to leave the community completely. It was an ethnic and not a class community, one which owing to its very heterogeneity could function all the more effectively to ease and perhaps protract the transition from German to American for its members. Its rich associational variety, even the excitement of its internal disagreements, was a crucial part of its attraction.

To Stand Firm
in the Ranks of the Democracy

7
It was in their political accommodation to urban American life that Milwaukee's Germans developed and maintained a public image of common action. "Nowhere else [in American cities] do the Germans count for so much in political affairs," noted Franz Löher in 1847.[1] In a city where the wards possessed a good deal of autonomous authority, German residential patterns gave them political power if they chose to organize it, while their range of socioeconomic characteristics was narrow enough in the early years to minimize internal political conflict, yet broad enough to permit the emergence of leadership. Furthermore, both the local and the national scene in the 1840s and early 1850s generated the types of political issues that encouraged the development of a sense of ethnic unity and common peoplehood. But the same forces which disrupted the unity of that community in other spheres likewise revealed the political limits of German ethnicity when issues arose on which the community divided. The political arena molded and reflected immigrant community consciousness and charted the acculturation of community members; they in turn helped cast it in forms which for better or ill were permanently shaped by the struggles of their accommodation process.

Origins of Immigrant Political Activity

Theoretically, at least, to participate in politics was for the immigrant a conscious and deliberate decision, in contrast, for example, to his economic adjustment. He had to find a job, but there was nothing which required him to vote. While the attraction of the American political system may have influenced his move to America, yet language difficulties, unfamiliarity with a strange political system, the natural shyness of the outsider, even restraints placed on his political activity by the native born may have tended to hinder his immediate participation. If this was the case, political participation marked a relatively late stage in the accommodation process and was the product of compelling personal reasons—perhaps a need for the rough sort of job security and social welfare temptingly proffered by the political boss, or, more abstractly, a nationalistic urge to influence American policy toward the mother country. Entering the political system on such grounds, immigrants would presumably vote en bloc until upward mobility and assimilation destroyed their unity of purpose and introduced new demands upon the political system.[2]

Certainly Milwaukee was too new, at least in the 1840s when Löher exclaimed over the political role of its German citizens, to have a political system sufficiently well developed to fuel a classic machine. This model of political participation likewise assumes a lower-class homogeneity which Milwaukee's Germans never exhibited. However, as Raymond E. Wolfinger has pointed out, the appearance of a middle-class element may have been a necessary prerequisite for the ethnic candidacies which alone could interpret politics to the masses with sufficient ethnic saliency to ensure bloc voting. Prior development of ethnic organizations to provide immigrant experience in public affairs may have constituted another necessary precondition for immigrant political participation.[3]

Given the middle class backgrounds of some pioneer European-born settlers and the associational activity of the mid-forties, such reasoning would suggest the relatively early entry of Milwaukee's immigrants into its political life. In fact, many had presumably completed a tutelage in American life elsewhere in the United States and could be expected to respond immediately to Milwaukee issues of personal relevance to them.[4] The very newness of the city must have created many such issues, while the still malleable nature of its politics may have encouraged newcomers to believe that they could help solve them. Decisions concerning which hills to grade, which streets to surface, what kinds of sidewalks to require, where to erect bridges, when to construct a new school, what types of public works contracts to let, and whether pigs should roam freely in the streets—all affected the well-being of Milwaukee's early foreign-born residents as well as native interests and could be expected to further stimulate the rapid politicization of Milwaukee immigrants.[5]

Immigrant politicization was indeed quickly manifest, though not precisely for the hypothesized reasons, as the record of politics in the village years shows. Under the 1839 village charter, suffrage was extended to all free white males, 21 years of age and over, who had lived in Milwaukee for at least six months and who were residents of the ward in which they voted. There were thus no formal bars to immigrant participation in village elections, although territorial and national participation was open only to citizens.[6] The Irish, many of whom must have been eligible for citizenship, took rapid advantage of the situation. By 1843 it was claimed with evident exaggeration that over 400 Irishmen were voting in Milwaukee, not always legally; the size of the Irish electorate is perhaps better suggested by the great Democratic indignation over Whig claims to "control" 13 east side Irish votes. Ties developed elsewhere in the United States, and local rhetoric linking the Whigs with aristocracy and nativism placed the Irish squarely in the Democratic column as early as 1841. By 1843 ethnicity had become an issue in local politics. Not only were there charges and countercharges over the control of the Irish vote; property owners frustrated in their attempts to gain village approval for grading East Water Street north toward Yankee Hill noted the improvements along Michigan Street in the Irish area and blamed their problems on the influence of Solomon Juneau, prominent in Democratic circles, and his friendship for his fellow Catholics. "The little difficulty in regard to the grading" played an important role in ousting Juneau from his postmastership, an early *cause célèbre* with ethnic overtones.[7]

Germans were prominent among those who attended the assembly to protest this affront to the city's founding father, and in the elections that spring, his ethnicity apparently defeated a German nominated for justice of the peace, notwithstanding that "as there are many of his countrymen in this neighborhood who are but little acquainted with our language, it was the wish of a large majority of the Democrats that he should be elected to that office." Germans had identified with the local Democracy by the 1841 territorial election. Even earlier, Germans had responded with a storm of protest to the "gross insult" tendered them by Frederick W. Horn, Eduard Wiesner's Whiggish protege, in a toast at the 1841 Washington's Birthday celebration, in which he implied it was ignorance which led his fellow countrymen into the arms of the Democrats. But when Dr. Franz Huebschmann, shortly after his arrival in 1842, joined with Wiesner and Mathias Stein to count all Germans eligible to vote in national elections, he arrived at a grand total of seven; a second survey in the winter of 1843-44 found only 13.[8]

Thus the Irish, undoubtedly bolstered by numbers, previous political experience, and a sense of solidarity and determined respectability engendered by the temperance societies of O'Kelley and Kundig, probably preceded the Germans into Milwaukee politics. While some Germans, at least, were politically responsive at an early date, it was in late 1843 that the issue appeared which infused Milwaukee politics with such ethnic overtones that it provoked the first consciously ethnic political activity of the Germans and perhaps of the Irish as well.

The catalyst was not a matter of immediate welfare but rather the question of suffrage qualifications for voting on a constitution for the proposed new state. At a heavily attended meeting in the Milwaukee court house in December 1843, Germans and Irish joined to petition the territorial legislature for the right of noncitizens to vote for delegates to the proposed state constitutional convention as well as to vote on the constitution itself, a right already granted in Indiana, Illinois, and Michigan. They argued that a law less liberal than in the neighboring states was not only undemocratic but poor policy, as it would "retard Emigration." The essentially nativist character of their opposition was evident in the *Sentinel's* comment on their petition: "Is it not going a little too far, to make a law that will enable such individuals as have loaded down many a scow during the past summer [individuals described as 'dem'd ungenteel'] to vote the moment they land upon our shores?"[9]

In January 1844 the territorial legislature extended the suffrage on the statehood question to all free white males 21 or older who had lived three months in the territory,[10] but the struggle over immigrant political participation was by no means ended in Milwaukee. Whig demands for revocation of the suffrage provision led to another public meeting of Milwaukee's immigrants in defense of their right to vote. They also helped form a "Milwaukee Democratic Association," held numerous neighborhood discussion sessions, and united to elect German and Irish village trustees, cementing the alliance with a joint St. Patrick's Day celebration and participation in the city's Fourth of July festivities.[11] By late summer, the bitter nativism which was clouding the campaign for the territorial legislature led Germans to take the next step in community mobilization: led by Huebschmann, they collected funds to establish a German newspaper to present their point of view. The first issue of the *Wisconsin Banner* under the editorship of Moritz Schoeffler appeared September 7, 1844. That same month, the Germans treated Nathaniel P. Talmadge, the new territorial governor and an advocate of immigrant suffrage, to the city's first *Fackelzug,* or torchlight parade.[12]

Such activity culminated in late autumn in the formation of a German Democratic Association whose purpose was "to awaken single-mindedness among the Germans, and for instruction in and dissemination of the principles upon which the edifice of the United States rests, and for the creation of unity and harmony in the political activity of the Germans." Huebschmann presided over the organization, which re-reportedly most Milwaukee Germans joined. It interested itself not only in the statehood question but also in the projected city charter, in such local issues as the demand for a German postal clerk who could read German names, and in the defense of Germans slandered in the American press. Its encouragement led numerous Germans to take an active interest in the presidential election that year; quite a number joined the Hickory Club, erected a "freedom tree" of hickory on the west side that remained a local landmark for years, and poured into the streets by the "thousands" to celebrate Polk's victory. Other gains of the association included the appointment of a German, A. Henry Bielfeld, as postal clerk the following year.[13]

The year 1844—the year which saw the maturation of German social life—was thus also a crucial year for German political participation. This was doubtless in part a function of increased numbers. The individual was bolstered by enough of his fellow countrymen to feel no longer strange or alien, and both his political and his social life can be viewed as a result of new self-confidence drawn from numbers. But major credit for this political emergence is owed to a few leaders, notably Wiesner, Stein, Huebschmann, and Schoeffler—the "oldest settlers" and the liberal intellectuals. Huebschmann appears to have been the guiding light behind most of the steps toward political involvement. It seems evident that the initial politicization of the Milwaukee immigrants did not occur because their votes were sought by native politicians, but for some because they voted as a matter of course from the start, for others because the better educated and more aware within their own ranks aroused them to action.

However, Huebschmann's two-year search for a catalytic issue should also be noted. It was the combination of numerical strength and an issue which involved their dignity that aroused the Germans. Local town problems were not the politically galvanizing issues in Milwaukee; rather German group entry into the political system of the frontier town was part of a nationwide reaction to a national nativism.[14] Once aroused, however, political awareness was soon transferred to local town-forming issues, as the activity of the German Democratic Association indicated. It is also worth noting that one of the first associations which the Germans formed was a political one. Up to that point they had little organizational practice to ease their transition into politics. Rather, common political action apparently stimulated organization on other fronts as well.

Local nativism continued to play a prominent role in sustaining immigrant participation. In the fall 1844 election for county sheriff, John White's candidacy was opposed because he was a foreigner and a Catholic; he was the only member of the Democratic ticket not elected and it was charged that Protestant clergymen had campaigned against him at the polls. Furthermore, the Reverend J. J. Miter's infamous Thanksgiving sermon was apparently aimed against the candidacy of another Irishman for city constable in the 1845 spring elections. An attempt to impose restrictive suffrage provisions in a proposed city charter aroused immigrant opposition which was instrumental in its defeat in early 1845. When the Democrats that spring named a slate of town officers pointedly omitting anyone who had opposed White's candidacy, party nativists bolted and named their own candidates; the Whigs supported the rebel ticket, which proved victorious. The *Banner* had urged Germans to vote for the regular ticket and claimed that the victory of the "irregulars" was due to the desertion of the Democracy by the nativists within the party; the election strengthened the saliency of nativism as an election issue in Milwaukee.[15]

The *Banner*, itself a product of growing German political awareness, was becoming a factor in further stimulating German political participation. It directed at the Germans a barrage of propaganda, urging them to become citizens, to inform themselves on political issues, to attend nominating caucuses, to vote, and to vote a straight Democratic ticket.[16] Germans were apparently reluctant to attend the nominating assemblies, however, and despite their growing numbers in the city, remained relatively underrepresented. The spring regular Democratic slate of nominees, for example, apparently included only one German to three Irishmen; although the nine Milwaukee delegates to the county nominating convention for territorial delegate included August Greulich and an Irishman, the German attempt to push John Helfenstein, an American of German parentage, as delegate failed. By fall of 1845, however, two Germans and two Irishmen were among the nine delegates to the county convention. The city charter, finally acquired in January 1845 in the face of east side opposition, sanctioned the political participation of the immigrants, despite suffrage requirements somewhat less liberal than those of the village period.[17]

Patterns of Immigrant Voting

The incorporation of the city not only marked the beginning of a new phase in Milwaukee politics but it also permits a more precise investigation of immigrant voting behavior after 1846. Under the charter, the city was divided into five wards, whose boundaries remained stable through 1856. In early 1856 the city was divided into seven wards, later that same year into nine (Figure 9). Election returns for the years 1846 to 1856 thus form a consistent series. While the small number of wards does not lend itself to correlation analysis, nevertheless the German predominance among second ward heads of household in 1850, as well as the Irish plurality in the third ward provide grounds for using the voting record of those wards to shed light on immigrant behavior at the polls. Changed ward boundaries and a confused political situation complicate analysis after 1856, but the 1860 census suggests that for voting purposes wards two, six, eight, nine, and to a lesser extent one can be considered German, with the third ward remaining Irish.

Milwaukee politics in the years between 1856 and 1860 could be expected to reflect the changing concerns of a maturing city as well as the broader issues stirring a nation undergoing rapid economic and social change. The period saw the political shifts which brought the nation from the aftermath of Jacksonian reform to the brink of Civil War, destroying one party sytem and creating another in the process. In this shifting political universe, the voting patterns of Milwaukee's immigrants suggest that the ethnic concerns which accompanied their local political initiation continued to shape further participation and conditioned the politicization of each year's crop of new immigrants. However, the character and consequences of that ethnic orientation underwent considerable modulation.

Voter turnout in Milwaukee remained at a relatively constant 50 to 60 percent of the estimated electorate throughout the period (Figure 13), with some variation from election to election as presidential contests and controversial issues drew out larger numbers of voters.[18] The natives, as indexed by the fourth ward, demonstrated the steadiest voting habits, with the highest estimated turnout and fewest fluctuations. Turnout in the German second ward, on the other hand, fluctuated more with the election issues and levels and increased over time in comparison with other wards as the heavy immigration of the early fifties was drawn into the electorate. In contrast, participation in the Irish third ward evidently fell off for a time and was never so abnormally high as to reflect efficient machine "control"; it did not seem as issue-oriented as that of the second ward and after 1850 followed the city pattern rather closely. The foreign born were thus assimilated rather easily to the voting habits of the city, if these estimates are any indication.

They also tended to maintain their Democratic affiliation (Figure 14). Historians have documented the close relationship between ethno-religious differences and political affiliation in the nation as a whole at the time, and Milwaukee was no exception.[19] Milwaukee's settlers, native and immigrant alike, brought with them to the new city political perceptions linking immigrants and Democrats which were only reinforced by the nativism that greeted the entrance of the immigrants into Milwaukee public life. In general, the Democrats managed to maintain or recapture immigrant loyalty through the political shifts of the early to mid-fifties; the late fifties brought clear signs of erosion but not enough to destroy the tie between the foreign born and the Democracy which generally kept Milwaukee a Democratic city throughout the antebellum period.

In the eight gubernatorial elections, the city abandoned the party only once, in an election where the personal character of the Democratic candidate was a major issue. With that exception, the overall pattern was one of growing Democratic strength to 1853, followed by gradual decline. The fourth ward, with its relatively large native proportion, showed the least Democratic recovery and lowest Democratic percentages. The fifth and eighth wards, with growing German proportions, demonstrated the most precipitous decline between 1857 and 1859, but it was the German west side and Irish third ward which consistently polled the greatest Democratic margins.

Presidential elections produced similar Democratic growth through

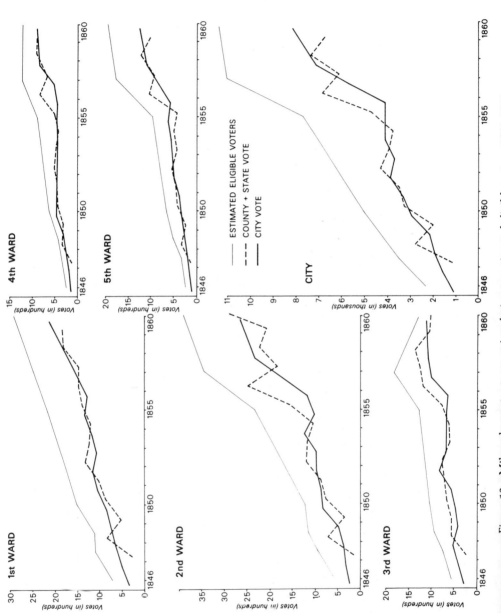

Figure 12. Milwaukee voter turnout in relation to estimated eligible voters, 1846–1860

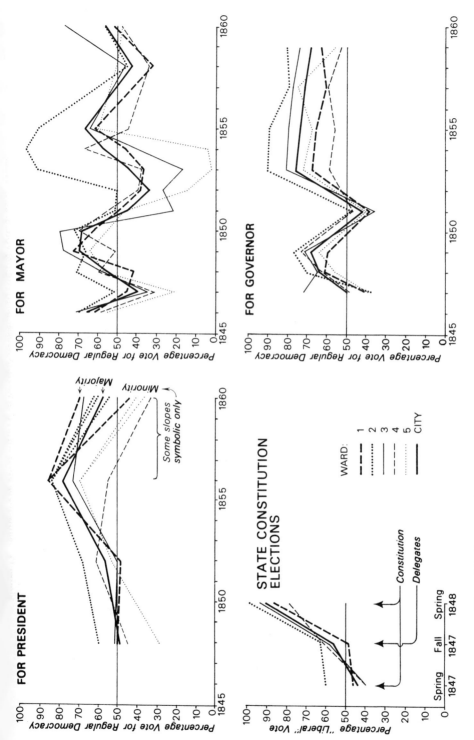

Figure 14   Democratic party vote as percentage of total votes cast in Milwaukee, 1846–1860

1856, with the immigrant wards generally leading the trend as the fourth ward began to fall away toward the Republican column by 1856. In 1860 the Douglas Democrats lost proportionate strength but retained a clear majority in five heavily immigrant wards, particularly the Irish third, but lost the German eighth as well as the more mixed and native wards. The second ward was also the most determinedly pro-immigrant suffrage in the early contests fought over the state constitution proposals.

The mayoral elections, however, defy attempts to find a common pattern, reflecting as they did the chaotic state of local politics where personalities, issues, and ward jealousies became more important than party labels. The one constant was the loyalty of the second ward to the Democracy through 1855. There was no real contest in the city elections in 1856 and 1857, as Democrats gained office unopposed; 1858, 1859, and 1860 saw Germans give increasing support to "reform Democratic" and even, by 1860, local Republican candidates, in opposition to the regular Democratic Party candidates. The growing divergence of the eighth ward from the other German wards is evident on the city level as well. The wild fluctuations of the third ward in city elections belied the operation of a smoothly functioning Democratic machine there, but it is nevertheless evident that the Irish remained more faithful during the troublesome years of the late 1850s than did the Germans.

The structural shifts of the early fifties mirrored in low turnouts and uncertain party majorities were also reflected in increased ticket splitting in those years, as measured by an "index of deviation" (Figure 15),[20] but by the end of the decade a stabilizing trend was evident. Ticket splitting tended to be more common in local elections, where voters were presumably more familiar with personalities and issues and the party system itself periodically broke down; widely deviant elections were sometimes explained by ethnic backgrounds of particular candidates which fostered ticket splitting or highly issue-oriented contests which minimized it. Ticket splitting was no less common in heavily immigrant wards than in other parts of the city; the foreign born were not automatically the "voting cattle" of their opponents' charges.

Political Leadership and Office Holding

Voting returns provide a measure of minimal participation only. For the Milwaukeean truly involved in the political life of his city,

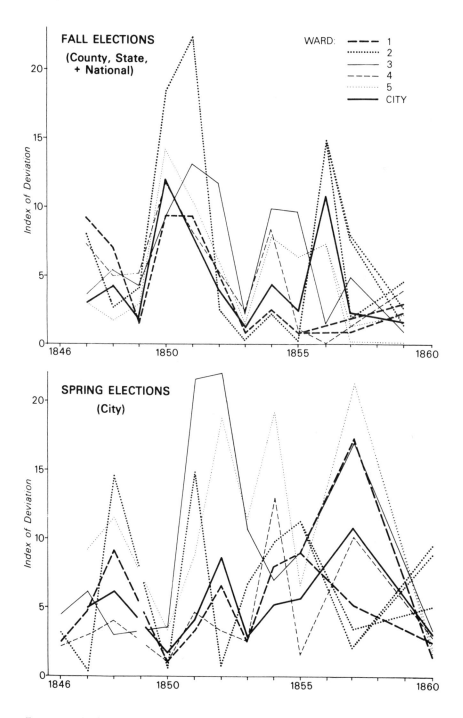

Figure 15   Ticket splitting in Milwaukee elections: indices of deviation, 1846-1860

every spring and fall brought a busy round of rallies, conventions, and caucuses designed both to influence the voter and to permit him to influence his party. Such activities provided platforms for aspiring political speakers, chances to gain experience in conducting political meetings, for serving on committees, drafting resolutions, holding party offices, all preliminaries to elective office. How large a proportion of the Germans actually participated in politics in this more comprehensive manner? What kinds of persons were willing to put themselves forward into positions of leadership?

A listing of Germans whose names were published in conjunction with political activities during the first ten years of active German participation in Milwaukee politics (1843-52) yielded 79 persons engaged in 186 different leadership roles in connection with 32 separate events. If persons whose names appeared only once are eliminated, the leadership cadre shrinks to 40 persons in 146 roles, or an average of 3.65 each.[21] However, the roles were not evenly divided. The four most prominent leaders (Huebschmann, Schoeffler, Haertel, and Greulich) held from nine to fourteen roles each, while the names of the great majority appeared only two or three times. Thus a small group of persons took on the tasks of political leadership in the early years, and they came from a relatively narrow segment of the German male population. Nearly half of the leaders (19) were tavern keepers and grocers—persons in frequent daily contact both with their German customers and their native suppliers. They were followed by professionals such as editors and doctors (8), and various skilled craftsmen (7), with other nonmanual workers constituting the remainder.

The base of active participants in leadership roles probably expanded after 1852, although it is difficult to provide any real estimate, since the newspapers became less consistent in listing officers, speakers, and committee members as the novelty of participation wore off. Especially after the number of wards was enlarged in 1857, the Germans were forced to run party affairs in several different wards, the number of available leadership positions was greatly expanded, and a broader occupational base reflected the socioeconomic status of the population in the different wards.[22]

By the 1850s as well, Germans were holding ward and minor city offices as a matter of course. Office holding among the city's immigrants began in the village period. The first German official was Daniel Neimann, a tavern keeper, elected constable in 1840; within two years, he was followed by F. W. Schwartz as an elected fence-viewer, and Eduard Wiesner became justice of the peace, an office soon occupied by Mathias Stein. By 1844, Stein and Schwartz had been elected ward trustees. Although the Germans failed in their efforts to name J. P. Helfenstein the city's first mayor when he declined the nomination, nevertheless the first city government included two German aldermen and two German constables— one each in the first and second wards. A. H. Bielfeld, the former German postal clerk, was appointed city clerk in the new government, while Moritz Schoeffler became the city's first German school commissioner.[23] The Irish too began political office holding early. In 1844, an Irishman was president of the board of trustees. While several Irish candidates were included in the 1845 ticket reportedly defeated on nativist grounds, the Irish too were able to elect two aldermen and a constable in the first city government.[24]

The foreign born also elected delegates to represent Milwaukee on the state level, although not in proportion to their numbers in the city. Huebschmann and James Magone were two of the city's five delegates to the 1846 constitutional convention; when the proposed constitution was rejected largely because of its banking provisions, a new convention was held in late 1847 and early 1848, to which Milwaukee sent three foreign-born delegates out of seven—Schoeffler, Garrett Fitzgerald, and John L. Doran.[25] Beginning in the late 1840s, the second ward (and later the combined sixth and ninth) sent Germans to the state assembly with fair regularity, and two Germans served in the state senate—Huebschmann in 1850, August Greulich in 1856. The third ward during the 1850s was generally represented in the assembly by an Irishman.[26]

Although Doran served as city attorney in 1847, 1848 marked the real beginning of what was to become the accepted division of spoils in Milwaukee politics: while the native born continued to dominate the major offices, the victorious Democratic ticket included a German, Karl Geisberg, in the treasurer's post, with an Irishman, Timothy O'Brien, as marshall. The various reform tickets of the 1850s permitted other nationalities to occasionally take over these positions—Germans served as marshall in 1851, 1855, and 1856, for example—and the offices of city clerk in 1859 and comptroller in 1856 also went to Germans. Milwaukee's first Irish-born mayor, Hans Crocker, was elected in 1852, but in upbringing and outlook he was already a member of the city's American professional and business elite, and not until the 1860s did an Irishman more closely associated with the city's Irish residents become mayor. Irish and Germans also held a variety of lesser city offices as well as serving on the ward level. In the late 1840s and early 1850s, the three alderman in all wards except the third often included one German, while by the late fifties all aldermen in wards two, six, eight, and nine generally were German, as well as occasional aldermen in other wards. The third ward usually sent one or two Irishmen to the city council.[27]

Thus while the antebellum era saw only token representation of the foreign born in Milwaukee's major offices, the Germans relied increasingly on their *Landsmänner* to represent them, first on the city, then on the state level. At the outset, the tendency of Germans to support a person for office simply because of his ethnicity acted as a unifying force in creating a common political posture, and German candidates were careful not to run against other Germans.[28] The reform movements of the fifties, however, along with the rise of Republicanism toward the end of the decade, pitted German candidate against German candidate, while growing German dominance within various wards led inevitably to divisive contests among Germans on the ward level even within the Democratic Party. German patterns of voting, leadership, and office holding thus all suggest a breakdown of initial unity with developing political maturity, a suggestion which can be explored through a consideration from the immigrant perspective of some of the major issues in the city's first decade and a half as a municipality.

Issues and Campaigns

The history of immigrant and particularly German participation in antebellum Milwaukee political life is one of initial unity on the suffrage issue, which gradually broke down in the face of growing differences within the German community. The temperance question provided a new rallying point, disrupted in turn by German anticlericalism, which then faded as antislavery and the rise of the Republican party crystallized a new and more lasting opposition within German ranks. Yet despite shifting local issues, the emergence of a new national party system, and the changing composition of the immigrant population, Milwaukee's immigrants by and large remained faithful to the Democrats. Indeed, it was their bid for real power within the local Democratic party that left it in a seriously weakened condition by 1860.

By assiduously fanning the flames of immigrant resentment aroused in the constitution battle of 1844 and damning the Whigs as a "money aristocracy" determined to erect in America a privileged class, the Democrats consolidated their immigrant support in the following years. Old battles were refought in the first city election of the spring of 1846, as Whigs charged Democrats with "truckling to foreigners" and immigrant voters blacklisted those of both parties who had either petitioned against liberal suffrage or refused to sign petitions in its support. When all but one of the Whig candidates were defeated, a *Banner* correspondent hailed the election's "beneficial influence" in demonstrating to Germans "what they could accomplish when, true to their principles, they stand firm in the ranks of the Democracy." When statehood once more became a possibility in the autumn, vigorous German participation at all stages in the process of delegate-selection resulted in Huebschmann's election to the state constitutional convention. While his candidacy was enough to drive some nativists out of the party, all but one of the Milwaukee Democratic delegates were elected (the defeated Democrat was a nativist); Whigs, however, captured the major offices in the country election which was open only to citizens of six months' residence.[29]

As convention delegates deliberated over the new state constitution, Milwaukee Germans kept up their pressure for liberal suffrage with mass meetings, petitions, and parades. The proposed constitution with its liberal suffrage provisions won such support from the Germans that local Whigs sponsored the publication of the *Volksfreund* to provide anti-constitution propaganda. Opposition to the constitution was grounded not only in its suffrage clause, however—the *Sentinel*, spokesman for Milwaukee Whigs, indeed argued that it objected to the requirement that noncitizen voters take an oath to support the state "as unfair and as putting adopted citizens to extra expense"—but particularly because of bank prohibition, debtor homestead protection, and married women's property rights clauses. Such objections led many conservative and even immigrant voters out of the Democratic ranks, and into joint support with the Whigs of an anti-constitution ticket for city offices in the spring of 1847. Its opponents were able to defeat both the constitution (locally and statewide) and the Democratic city candidates in the April election. Only the second ward supported both, earning for this loyalty the nicknames of Iron Ward and Banner Ward; when the third ward voted against the constitution, Irish leaders were accused of having dismissed "Irishmen and Foreigners of all Nations" as "a lot of ignoramus dogans" who "did not know what they wanted themselves" and therefore "had no right to vote in any less then five years."[30]

The constitutional issue was never again to receive quite the same degree of attention from the Germans. Leaders had to resort to constant publicity to maintain any kind of interest in the German Democratic Association, which soon abandoned broader political issues for questions of immediate local concern.[31] While the second ward gave the Democratic slate of delegates for a new constitutional convention 63 percent of its vote in the fall 1847 election, its turnout was the lowest in the city, and its participation rate remained little higher than any other city ward in the lethargic election of March 1848, when acceptance of the new constitution was a foregone conclusion.[32]

With the suffrage issue settled, political strains surfaced within the German community. The *Volksfreund* had dropped its Whig affiliation to join the *Banner* in the ranks of the Democracy but carried on a hard-fought battle with its rival during the fall 1847 election for territorial delegate to Congress. Schoeffler and the *Banner* supported the scandal-tinged regular party candidate, Moses M. Strong, but German voters evidently agreed with the *Volksfreund* that virtue took precedence over party: the second ward gave Strong only 37 percent of its vote, compared with a city average of 48 percent, in one of the ward's rare desertions of the Democratic slate. He ran 20 percent behind his ticket in the second ward; the Irish third ward, in contrast, gave him 72 percent of its vote.[33]

By the spring of 1848, the "artisans and laborers" who attempted to revitalize the German Democratic Association, probably with the help of the *Volksfreund* editor, Frederick Fratny, charged that an older "dynasty" of leaders was working for its own political benefit against the true interests of the Germans. The established leaders, especially Huebschmann and Schoeffler, were branded as the "German regulators' clique"; it was claimed that "every association, in which these men are found, becomes unpopular among the core of the Germans, artisans and laborers, because of them." The *Volksfreund* shook its head over Huebschmann's dealings as broker for office nominations as well as Schoeffler's drunkenness during a public speech. The "dynasty," in turn, saw opponents as traitors to the party. The quarrel was more than a circulation fight between two rival newspapers. It had surfaced over an issue of morality versus party loyalty but it revealed tensions between "grays" and "greens," ins and outs, perhaps also between classes, which had remained submerged in the common campaign for the dignity of the suffrage. The *Volksfreund* revealingly complained that "Mr. Schoeffler moves in a learned society, to be sure, which strives to act as the guardian of the plain artisan and handworker, considering him to be less learned and incapable of comprehending on his own."[34]

On ground thus prepared, the 1848 presidential election proved a portent of future divisions. Land reform, which included both free-soil and anti-speculator principles, agitated Fratny's circle and aroused general German interest in 1848; more specifically abolitionist sentiment had surfaced within the German community at least as early as 1844. Thus, when Martin Van Buren ran for president as a Free Soil third-party candidate in 1848, he attracted a certain amount of support among prominent liberal Germans of Milwaukee. Only after a good deal of equivocation did Fratny finally throw his support to Lewis Cass, the Democratic candidate; he felt it necessary to insist editorially that a vote for Cass was not a vote for slavery but rather a vote for popular sovereignty and democratic principles, and that the aristocratic, slaveholding Whigs and their candidate, Zachary Taylor, remained the chief enemy. The German ranks held, but the Democratic vote in the second ward (the highest in the city) was down to 59 percent from its usual 70 percent level, and the city's German chronicler was later to claim that "it is not improbable that even at that time the party showings here might have been entirely different if Fratny, who had quickly won a large following and who had great influence upon the working class, had placed himself [squarely] upon the side of the Progressive Party."[35]

These stirrings of sentiment were as yet little more than straws in the wind, yet for Milwaukee's German leaders the need to unite Germans and once more arouse their political interest must have seemed all the more crucial in light of the potential German voters who were streaming into the city in ever greater numbers by the end of the decade. While most Germans continued to vote Democratic for want of a better alternative, party enthusiasm was generally low and local concerns such as aldermannic records, discriminatory street improvements, and charter reform dominated city election campaigns.[36] Germans were beginning to respond to the problems of the maturing city without reference to ethnicity, and when a new issue emerged that touched an ethnically sensitive nerve in most Germans, their leaders realized the full extent to

which they had failed to convert their unity during the years of the constitution struggle into permanent power in party and legislative councils.[37] That issue arose in 1848, when the state legislature passed a
Whiskey Law requiring every liquor dealer to post a $1,000 bond to
cover all possible damage done on the day or day after a person became
inebriated in his place of business.[38] An "extremely well attended" Milwaukee meeting was held to protest this law in May of 1849, and
another the following January, when appropriate steps for its repeal
were considered. It wasn't just that Germans liked their beer. As the
Banner put it,

> We are no defender of intemperateness, but we hold fast to the basic princi-
> ple that every person is independent and should be responsible for his own
> actions, and that those who arbitrarily transgress the laws of nature and
> damage their own bodies should alone bear the consequences. The trade in
> spirits is a legal one, permitted all over the world because experience has
> demonstrated that spirits in moderate quantities are no more damaging than
> our food, which itself sometimes disastrously undermines our health when it is
> enjoyed to excess. Besides, we are for free trade in all things.[39]

The spring city election was seen as a way to signify support for
repeal and to elect officials who would not enforce the law, although,
since there had been no attempt at enforcement, some temperance men
questioned whether the issue had not been consciously raised in the January meeting to arouse and unify German voters. Pre-election tension
was heightened when about 600 men, many of them German, mobbed
the home of Senator J. B. Smith, a leading temperance advocate. Native
reaction was strong, and thus when the Democratic mayor, who took
an anti-temperance stance, was reelected with 68 percent of the vote,
the election was interpreted by the Germans as a defeat for the "fanatic
nonsense of the temperance politicians."[40] The election itself was very
quiet, but a considerably increased turnout, especially in the second
ward, served notice that the Germans had found another unifying issue
capable of provoking participation.

The Whiskey Law remained in effect, still unenforced, until the following winter; attempts then and in subsequent legislative sessions to
pass a Maine Law prohibiting the sale of intoxicating beverages kept the
temperance issue alive, and it was soon linked to the question of
enforcement of the Sunday observance laws which Germans found
equally at odds with their accustomed life style. It was easy for Ger-

mans to interpret both as nativism in new guise and by October 1851 Germans had met first citywide and then in a state convention to petition against temperance and Sunday observance laws and form a German Central Committee to coordinate their efforts.[41]

Not all elections turned on the temperance question, of course. A growing taxpayers' revolt over heavy city expenditures and inequitable allocation of public improvements—Germans, for example, charged that the "nabobs" who objected to improving streets in "frog swamps" were forgetting that it was the poor workers who lived in the swamps whose taxes had helped pave the streets in the better residential areas— led to a charter reform movement and a reform-minded People's Ticket in 1851. While Germans were conspicuous in defeating the proposed charter because of its restrictive suffrage provisions, the Whigs and conservative Democrats who comprised the People's Ticket candidates were successful, and the elements of the old Whig party would continue to run under that banner in future local elections. Even the second ward gave the regular Democratic candidate for mayor only a slight edge. In the fall election, where temperance and Sunday observance were among the issues, other issues had greater salience, a confused variety of tickets made party-line voting difficult, and the Banner Ward slipped out of the Democratic column to the accompaniment of ticket splitting and little increase in turnout.[42]

Even more crucial in blunting the effect of a politically revivified *Deutschtum* in Milwaukee was the anticlericalism that was beginning to widen the fissures in the German community. As lines were drawn separating free thinkers particularly from Roman Catholics, their religious sentiments made many of the leaders of the old German Democracy, including Heubschmann, Schoeffler, and Fratny, suspect to Catholics. In the embittered atmosphere, German Catholics began to contemplate an alliance with the Whigs as the lesser of the two evils. In 1851 the conservative *Volkshalle* had supported the Whiggish People's Ticket against the regular Democracy; Greulich, a Catholic, ran for treasurer with the support of the Whigs, but was the only People's candidate to lose in that election.[43] By 1852, the conflict within the German community became an open political issue. The *Volkshalle's* successor, the openly Catholic *Seebote*, supported Greulich's candidacy for second ward alderman on the People's Ticket, and gave bitter opposition to Huebschmann, the free thinker, and Isaac Neustadl, a Jewish merchant resident in the city since 1844. Greulich was defeated, the latter two elected, and the *Banner* chose to interpret the outcome—victories by relatively narrow margins—as a blow struck for religious freedom. The second ward, however, gave its support to People's candidates for mayor and city attorney. The third ward also supported the victorious People's Ticket in the mayoral contest, undoubtedly in recognition of the Irish descent of its candidate, Hans Crocker, but otherwise remained faithful to the regular Democracy.[44]

Renewed efforts to present a united German front against Maine Law proposals in early 1852 foundered in the face of increasingly self-conscious German radicalism and a Yankee campaign (including a petition to the city council) against German habits of Sunday enjoyment. Natives were particularly annoyed by the Sunday concerts of the Milwaukee Musical Society during the summer of 1852, as well as by the Germans' Fourth of July celebration when that holiday happened to fall on a Sunday. Possibly because of the involvement of the free-thinking members of the Musical Society in the Sunday question, possibly to cement an alliance with the Whigs, the *Seebote* and the Catholic clergy apparently became temporary supporters of the Puritan Sunday.[45]

The alliance appeared to remain firm as the fall elections approached. Immediately following German participation in the formation of a Granite Club to support the presidential candidacy of Franklin Pierce, a German Scott Club under the chairmanship of Roesler von Oels appeared. Roesler, the former *Volkshalle* editor, put out a German Whig organ during the campaign. Although it was claimed that the Scott Club never exceeded "fourteen and a half members," and although Roesler told his friends openly that the suffering of his family alone had led him to accept Whig pay—"Friend, you don't know how much hunger hurts"—nevertheless the conservative Catholic group appeared to make a concerted effort to bring out the immigrant vote for Scott. Rumors were circulated concerning Pierce's reported involvement in a New Hampshire law prejudicial to Catholics (and countered with charges of Scott's nativism), and priests were accused of leading "many Irishmen of the lowest classes" up to the Whig meetings on Yankee Hill, there to mingle with the "richer capitalists and wholesalers" of that party. At least one of the city's priests reportedly maintained that the danger of foreign influence on American political life could be mitigated only by "baiting Irish against Germans" and turning Germans against one another. "You may wish to vote for this or that man, support this or that party," entoned the *Banner*, but Germans, don't do so because you belong to one or another church or because the priests lead and inflame you . . . Every honest Catholic is incensed by the boundless presumption with which several—only very few, we hope—Catholic priests ensnare the political freedom of their entire congregations and seek to use it for their own ends.[46]

Of greatest interest among the Germans was perhaps Greulich's race for the senate seat from the first and second wards. "True Democrats" were able to regard his loss and Pierce's majority in the city as signs that many Catholics had failed to fall victim to the blandishments of their pastors. In the first ward, which included not only Yankee Hill but also the reputedly more Catholic segment of the German settlement, both Greulich and Scott did better, however, than either the Whig ticket as a whole in that ward, or than they did in the second ward or citywide.[47]

The *Seebote* reportedly had withheld full support from the Whigs and by the spring of 1853 was again vigorously urging its readers to attend and participate in the regular Democratic caucuses, while continuing to carry on its editorial campaign against anticlericalism. When the People's coalition, with its emphasis upon conservative fiscal policy, retained office for another year, the *Seebote* pointed not to religious issues but to irregularities in the Democratic Party nominations and the use of rowdies by the party to break up peaceable meetings as reasons why many found themselves unable to support the Democracy. Only the second ward stood firm. The excitement of the anticlerical fight the previous year had stimulated second ward solidarity, and Byron Kilbourn of the Democrats, who was seeking city financial support for the Milwaukee and LaCrosse Railroad, reportedly bargained with a second ward "machine" headed by Heubschmann for its support. The "machine" delivered 92 percent of the ward's votes for the Democratic mayoral candidate, with somewhat smaller majorities for the other offices.[48] Every other ward, including the third (despite the candidacy of an Irishman for marshall on the Democratic ticket), threw its support to the People's Ticket.

By the fall of 1853, wounds were clearly healing and Germans of all persuasions found themselves once again shoulder to shoulder in the good cause of "personal freedom." After two abortive attempts to pass a Maine Law in the state legislature, the question of prohibition was put directly to the voters of Wisconsin, with the gubernatorial contest turning on the same issue. "No election had ever been so hotly contested, the liquor question overshadowing all others," recalled a pioneer Yankee resident.[49] Accusing the Whigs of using prohibition to attack the foreign born and split the Democrats, Milwaukee's Democratic leaders staged massive anti-temperance meetings of all nationalities and produced solid majorities against prohibition and for the anti-Maine Law state tickets in all wards. Germans were charged, probably correctly, with policing the polls to ensure that all German voters cast the proper "no" ballot, and high feelings between native temperance men and beer-drinking Germans spilled over into brawls, when the rainy election day produced the farcical scene of an umbrella battle in mud two inches thick at the second ward polling place. But, as the *Banner* tolerantly observed, "the sovereign people must have a bit of fun on such occasions"; the Germans had achieved a well-earned triumph, and the last of the prominent German Free Soilers were back in the fold. Although the majority of the state's voters favored a Maine Law, the *Banner* pointed out that

many Americans actually voted not for the law but against the foreigners. Others only voted against the little rum-hells. Many voted for the law in order to "kill" it. Many voted for it as a joke, or because they felt they would then get better liquor. But no one really knew what law he was voting for, since not a letter of a law had been submitted.[50]

When the legislature finally passed a Maine Law in 1855, the governor ended the issue with his veto.[51]

Anti-temperance unity did not carry over to the city election the following spring. The Regular Democracy finally defeated the People's Ticket in an election which demonstrated, according to the *Seebote*, that interest rather than party determined voting in city elections. The third ward, along with the first and fifth (whose "founding father," George Walker, was the People's candidate for mayor) remained to some extent faithful to the old alliance of church and reform. The election was also marred by a serious brawl between Irish and Germans in the first ward, where the Irish had become sufficiently numerous to rally behind their own aldermannic candidate and apparently attempted to challenge German voters at the poll. The incident suggests the function of residential separation in promoting the Irish-German alliance in the Democratic party.[52]

It was not the election, however, but the rescue by a Milwaukee mob

three days earlier of Joshua Glover, a black resident of Racine who had
been apprehended under the Fugitive Slave Law and imprisoned in Milwaukee, which captured public attention and by interjecting the slavery
issue into Milwaukee politics symbolized the new alliances which were
to emerge in local immigrant political circles. Although early German
Democratic leaders such as Heubschmann, Wiesner, Stein, and
Schwartz were outspoken opponents of slavery, racism was not
unknown in old line German Democratic circles, and during the late
forties and early fifties such spokesmen as Heubschmann, Schoeffler,
and Fratny were able to tie together the ideas of free homesteads, opposition to slavery and its expansion, states' rights, and opposition to
Negro suffrage, into a package bearing the label of the Democratic
Party.[53] They maintained that slavery was not a real party issue; when
abolition became a matter of increasing concern after the passage of the
Kansas-Nebraska Bill, the *Banner* was able to declare that "the language of Schiller and Goethe does not lend itself to the pronunciation of
the word slavery," while at the same time asserting that the new Republican abolitionists were simply nativists and temperance fanatics under
false colors, who were using the slavery issue to force the temperance
issue into the background and indirectly attack the foreign born. The
Banner warned that

as soon as the Germans desert the Democracy and go with the abolitionists,
they will elevate to power and prestige a sect which thinks to turn the entire
country into a "Water-Cure"; which wants to command what each citizen may
and may not drink; which seeks to prescribe the Bible to him as the highest and
only binding code of laws . . . which wants to suppress the Sunday relaxation
of the Germans for being a work of the Devil; which wants to snatch the
women away from their useful and influential sphere in the quiet domestic
circle of the family, in order to draw them into the stormy seas of never-ending
political agitation[54]

—a catalog of horrors for most Germans in contrast to which slavery as
an issue grew dim.

Germans who responded to the appeal of the newly formed Republican Party were castigated as "German nativists, radical and irretriev-
able egoists . . . they want to reform radically, but as in Germany they
stupidly want to plant the new tree without first preparing suitable
soil." To frighten conservative German voters fearful of revolution,
their revolutionary associations were stressed, their north German

accents were mocked, and the spectre of educated elitism was once more raised. "What good have their long years of sliding around on school and university benches—of which they are so dreadfully proud—done for the German 'official intelligentsia'? Here in America they make fools of themselves daily, hourly even, in the eyes of schoolboys, as soon as they begin to interfere in politics and other public affairs with their hothouse learning."[55]

It was, in fact, the free thinkers and former revolutionaries who found Republicanism most to their liking. The question of sending delegates to the 1854 organizing convention of the new Republican party was reportedly hotly debated in two meetings of the Verein-Freier-Männer but the Democrats led by Schoeffler and Fratny kept it from coming to a vote. They also refused to print notices of a public meeting to select delegates, and so three Germans attended on their own responsibility from Milwaukee—Christian Esselen, the free-thinking philosopher-publicist, and H. Henry Bielfeld and Dr. Wunderly, who had long been involved in local reform politics. The rise of the new party helped cement the reconciliation of the conservative Germans with their more liberal old-line political leaders, while dividing the old liberals from the newcomers, who were neither haunted by the fights against nativism of the 1840s nor already embarked upon promising careers within the Democratic party. Republican politics for them represented a natural extension of both their German struggle for freedom and the reformism of the associations they had already founded in Milwaukee.[56] Their relief at finding a more congenial political home than the old Democracy is evident; they had appreciated neither the old issues nor their Democratic bedfellows. As Esselen noted, "If we remind them of the connection of the Democracy with the Jesuits, we get for an answer the general horror of Knownothings, fearing whom seems to be the principal occupation of Germans even in Wisconsin."[57] Bernhard Domschke, to become the chief spokesman of Milwaukee German Republicans, spelled it out even more clearly:

The idea of forming a union of foreigners against nativism is wholly wrong, and destroys the possibility of any influence on our part; it would drive us into a union with Irishmen, those American Croats. In our struggle we are not concerned with nationality, but with principles; we are for liberty, and against union with Irishmen who stand nearer barbarism and brutality than civilization and humanity. The Irish are our natural enemies, not because they are Irishmen, but because they are the truest guards of Popery.[58]

Republicanism crystalized divisions of class, religion, and time of arrival within the German community.

In the fall elections of 1854, when a Republican ticket appeared for the first time, Bernhard Domschke arrived in Milwaukee to publish the first of his German Republican journals, and Isaac Neustadl, whose People's candidacy had attracted such opposition in 1852, presented himself as Republican candidate for county treasurer. The *Seebote* characterized the election as a contest to determine whether the United States would remain a free country in the face of the attack of Republican temperance men, abolitionists, nativists, church desecraters, and Catholic-murderers; Republican dominance would bring not the abolition of slavery but the inauguration of a new slavery of the foreign born, and a new martyrdom for Catholics.[59] The Democratic ticket won handily; only the fourth ward yielded to Republican appeals. The relatively smaller Democratic majorities in the first ward may suggest the potency of the new party's appeal among native voters similar in socioeconomic status to fourth ward voters, but the fact that Neustadl generally ran behind the ticket as a whole, particularly in the first ward, suggests native reluctance to vote for a foreigner even in Republican garb.

The mending of the split among German Democrats in the face of the new threat was completed in early 1855 when August Greulich presided over a meeting to form an anti-Know-Nothing Sag-Nichts ("say nothing") association to counter the Republicans; fellow committee members included other former German Catholic Whigs, as well as Huebschmann and guiding lights of the free-thinking and cultural associations. After a quiet spring election, when only the fourth ward remained completely out of the Democratic column and only one German ran (and lost) on other than the regular ticket, the anti-Know-Nothing movement widened its scope during the summer to include Irish and natives, and the fall elections were viewed in what were becoming the standard terms of "Know-Nothing nativistic temperance Republicans" against the true American Democracy. The "quiet election" produced Democratic majorities in all wards, and the party sent Greulich to the state assembly. The size of the majorities was down, however, and German Democrats worried about the need to create a tighter organization in the face of what they saw as a coming presidential campaign which would attempt to once more divide Protestants and Catholics and win on the issue of nativism.[60]

But such fears were premature. The spring elections of 1856 proved no contest, as the People's Party nominated the regular Democratic ticket. Nor were the fall elections much more exciting; while German Republicans attempted to stir up enthusiasm for their candidate, the Democrats swept every ward, with the Germans producing especially noteworthy majorities.[61]

The most important feature of this election, gathering momentum in the course of the campaign among all elements within the German wing of the party and soon spreading to natives and Irish as well, was the birth of a movement to replace what was viewed as a too easily maneuvered convention nominating system with the direct primary, a device recently introduced in St. Louis. This represented a revolt against "fixed" nominations which resulted in the corruption, graft, and taxes with which the Democrats were beginning to saddle the city and hence to some extent a revival of the concerns of the earlier People's Tickets. But it probably also involved German desires, buoyed by their strong election showings, to gain more than token power in Democratic councils, an interpretation suggested by the loss of native and Irish support for extensive reform several months later.[62]

The movement for party reform charts a growing maturity in German political participation; it suggests also the uneasiness of men trapped by quarrels of the past and dislike for Republican doctrines in a party whose local corruption was an embarrassment. The movement split not only the Democrats but German unity within the Democracy and left the party in a weakened position to face Republican onslaughts. On the other hand, it involved none of the old religious differences; Huebschmann and Greulich stood together on the reform issue. Despite fears among regular Democrats that German reformers were tools of the Republicans, it seems more likely that their moral stance gave potential Republicans a third local alternative untainted by nativism or temperance, and that by splitting the liberal ranks helped ensure continued Democratic dominance within the German community.

First victory for the reformers came in the 1857 city election. Major Democratic nominees were elected without opposition, but reform candidates won several offices, piling up impressive margins in German wards, while the other wards remained equally firm in their support of the regular Democratic ticket. New fuel was provided that fall when the Democratic convention nominated for governor former Milwaukee mayor J. B. Cross, implicated in the city's administrative problems,

over Huebschmann in what was considered a move redolent of bribery
and corruption. Second ward Democrats rejected the ticket, proposed a
series of specific party reforms, and ultimately sponsored a citywide
reform meeting. With the threat of bolt a reality, many German Democrats parted company with the reformers; Schoeffler abandoned his
friend Huebschmann and supported the regular ticket, while the
Grad'Aus, a newcomer in Milwaukee journalism, became the reform
spokesman. This internal struggle made Republican nativism, Carl
Schurz's Republican campaign for the lieutenant governorship, and
even revived Maine Law proposals, issues of secondary importance
among most of the city's Germans. The reformers were able to claim a
victory in the November elections on the basis of the smaller margin of
Democratic majority in the second ward, and that ward's election of
Alex von Cotzhausen, a prominent reformer, to the state assembly. The
remaining German wards and the third ward, however, rolled out their
customary massive Democratic majorities and even the fourth ward
found itself again in the Democratic column.[63]

But the revolt continued, fueled by an enormous city debt, heavy
taxes in a period when "hard times" were making themselves felt, and
ever more evident corruption. The German reformers were able to link
up with a "taxpayers' revolt" and obtain support from Democrats
throughout the city. Numerous ward meetings, particularly on the
northwest side, attested to grass roots support for reform. A reformed
nominating system was finally produced, but since the compromise still
retained delegate conventions, hard-line reformers among the Germans
in 1858 supported a People's Ticket of those resolved to clean up the
city government, which included German and native Republicans. The
reform ticket swept the city elections in 1858, and again in the fall;
while in the spring the heavily German eighth and ninth wards had
remained loyal to the regular party, with the sixth ward also somewhat
lukewarm in its support of reform, by the fall only the ninth among the
German wards remained firm in its support of the regular party. It was
not that the people had abandoned Democratic principles to support
the Republicans, the now united *Banner und Volksfreund* explained,
but only that they were upset with how they were being carried out.[64]

By the spring of 1859, the Democrats were functioning more accept-
ably and the People's Ticket, weakened by its inability to markedly
improve the city's financial situation, failed to maintain its momentum.
Some of the grass roots German reform enthusiasm was probably

drawn off by a new, depression-bred workers' movement, which utilized the ward level organization familiar from Milwaukee politics to agitate for improved conditions for the workingman; their political support tended to go to Republicans, who after the 1859 defeat of the People's Ticket ran under their own label. The Democrats too conducted a conscious campaign of revitalization, organizing Democratic Clubs in all wards for men of all ages. That autumn's Democratic victory, the *Banner und Volksfreund* could note, disposed of the last remains of "reform nonsense" at its source, the second ward.[65]

The burial proved somewhat premature. German discontent with their allotted place within the Democratic party remained close to the surface. Demands now centered particularly upon representation at party conventions proportional to Democratic votes polled in the previous election; to Milwaukee German party members, the spring campaign of 1860 demonstrated all the evils of the existing situation. A "managed" nominating convention, they charged, had refused to allow more than one German on the city ticket. The personal characters of some of the hastily named Democratic ward candidates, as well as the fact that two Democratic officials had been indicted for misuse of their offices, were also important in cutting the accustomed Democratic majority in the city by half. Only the fourth ward provided a clean Republican sweep, but the squabbles produced Republican ward representatives in all but the third and fifth wards, and John Tesch, a German running as Republican candidate for treasurer, carried all German wards except the eighth (where the Republican mayoral candidate had the lead).[66]

German Republicans, however, were not in the best position to capitalize on this discontent. Weak support for German Republican candidates by native-born Republicans periodically demonstrated the continuing nativism of the party, and their support for the People's Tickets had undoubtedly confused the ideological clarity of their appeal. Despite a strong start with the formation of German Republican Clubs in all Milwaukee wards in January 1859, by September the city's Germans were threatening to bolt because of what they considered the corrupt dismissal of the gubernatorial candidacy of Carl Schurz, Wisconsin's leading spokesman for German Republicans, at the party's state convention, and the nativist tendencies of some of the candidates. The *Banner und Volksfreund*, hardly an impartial judge, estimated that in that election, about sixty or seventy of the city's German "world improvers" voted the Democratic ticket, while another thirty or forty refused to vote at all.[67]

Milwaukee German Republicans were also reportedly unhappy with their party's nomination of Lincoln the following year but nevertheless put together a citywide German Republican organization and were especially sanguine about gathering support in the sixth and ninth wards, whose more recent settlers were presumably more immune to the appeal of the old Democratic rhetoric. Their hopes were bouyed by continued scandal among the city's Democrats. German Democrats, it was rumored, had difficulty whipping up their old enthusiasm—there were charges that the organizers of one south side rally found themselves reduced to hiring boys to carry torches, at the price of a dime each and a glass of beer. The transparencies which appeared at the Republican rallies suggested the basis on which they hoped to attract German voters from the "mighty fortress" of the Democracy: "Free labor, free homesteads, and free principles" and "the prosperity of the family through the protection of free labor" and (in English) "no niggers for the niggerless."[68] While Milwaukee ran counter to the statewide trend by giving its votes to the Democrats, Douglas polled a majority of only 901, in comparison with Buchanan's 3,267 majority four years earlier. The three most heavily German wards remained faithful to the Democrats, although not overwhelmingly so; the third ward provided the city's largest Democratic majority but the German eighth ward joined the more heavily native fourth, fifth, and seventh in the Republican column.

The myth would later develop that the Germans had elected Lincoln.[69] In Milwaukee, this was patently not the case. The Republicans had been unsuccessful in dissociating themselves from the nativism, temperance, and sabbatarianism whose opposition had become the raison d'être of political participation for large numbers of the city's Germans. German Republicans themselves further repelled many of their countrymen with their anticlericalism. Even many who resembled the German Republicans in background and outlook found themselves unable to reject the party which had given them political legitimacy in the early days of the community. Both Republican inroads and Democratic disagreements weakened the hold of the Democracy on Milwaukee's Germans, but tradition and "negative reference" voting were strong enough to ensure against its complete disintegration.

The role played by religion in the restructuring of antebellum Ger-

man party orientations is unclear. Their religion certainly kept many
Catholics out of a hostile Republican party, but when they perceived a
greater threat from German anticlericalism, Milwaukee Catholics—
Irish and German—had been willing to contemplate an alliance with
the similarly hostile Whigs. Many free thinkers found Republican mor-
alism as unacceptable as it was to their Catholic compatriots, but others
found that Republican anti-slavery covered a multitude of other sins.
And what of the Protestants, whose greater Republican proclivity has
been noted in other German settlements?[70] One local German historian
was to note that "when slavery became the all-absorbing issue, a large
majority of the Wisconsin German liberals, most Evangelicals, and a
considerable number of Lutherans and Reformed allied themselves with
the republican party, becoming strong factors therein," and indeed Milwaukee Lutherans reportedly slipped away from Democratic ranks in
increasing numbers after the Civil War.[71] Another German observer,
however, later recalled that in the politics of the antebellum period, the
"Lutheran element hardly appears as a distinct factor,"[72] and local
political infighting plus the identification of early "radical" leaders with
the Democratic Party may well have resulted in such a confusion of
"negative references" as to mute the appeal of Republicanism among
practicing German Protestants as well as Roman Catholics. Unfortunately, available data do not permit estimates of separate German
Catholic and Protestant voting behavior. It is always possible that the
conservatism of recently arrived Lutheran Pommeranian and Mecklenburger voters in the ninth ward helps account for the strongly Democratic cast of its voting; it is equally possible that the weak structure of
the isolated south side German community, with few social organizations or long established churches, may account for its otherwise inex-
plicable Republican drift.[73]

Conclusion

Milwaukee's antebellum political history suggests that with
the possible exception of the earliest years of the settlement, the Germans quickly entered the city's political arena, and generally participated *as voters* to the same extent as other nationalities. Their leaders
constantly complained, however, of their backwardness in speaking up
at citywide meetings, of their unwillingness to offer their services
beyond the ward level. By the late fifties, they showed considerable

sophistication within their ward caucuses—grilling candidates on issues, instructing their delegates, holding their elected officials to account, producing plans of action on specific ward issues.[74] But despite token office holding, the major segment of the city's Democratic voters was unable to bend the party to its will. Only by completely deserting the party could they force the native leaders to acknowledge their demands, yet German leaders had done such an excellent job of convincing the rank and file that salvation lay only within the regular Democracy that on the issue of "German power" Huebschmann was able to carry with him only his own second ward. Ethnic pride was a crucial factor in bringing the Germans into the Democratic Party, but it was not strong enough to break the habit of years and carry them out, particularly when Republicanism was the only real alternative.

The Germans, however, did not produce a "machine" vote even to the extent of the city's Irish.[75] They were willing to vote independently when issues of dollars and cents intervened, as in 1858, while internal religious differences also led some out of the arms of the Democrats in the early fifties. When the Germans supported a corrupt Democratic government in the later fifties, they did so not because of the personal services it provided them (the classic immigrant-machine relationship) but under protest because their negative image of its opponents left them nowhere else to go.

The importance of the nativism issue in provoking politicization also meant that European nationalism was a minor factor in immigrant participation in Milwaukee. While Germans took a keen interest in the revolutionary events of Europe in the late forties, this occurred only after the suffrage issue had coalesced the community politically, and the revolutionary societies were organized by men who had already acquired reputations in the constitution fight.[76] Similarly, political interest was aroused before the Germans had gained any real experience in running their own ethnic organizations. Rather, the feeling of unity gained in the constitution crusade spilled over and found expression in a proliferation of mutual benefit, volunteer, and social institutions in the following years, led by men well known for their political activities.

Finally, town-forming problems also took second place in provoking political participation. While the German newspapers expressed concern about such problems, public meetings on matters of local interest were not common until the late forties, when politics had already taught Germans how to come together to wield power. By 1849 such issues as swamp drainage, street grading, and cholera prevention had aroused German interest, and the following winter Germans partici- pated in the first of the charter reform movements. Maturing interest in urban affairs was more evident during the fifties, as the German inhab- itants of one second ward subdivision, for example, formed their own neighborhood organization to demand better streets in their part of the ward, and to work for aldermannic candidates sympathetic to their interest. Ward political clubs were gradually made instruments of ward betterment as well.[77]

In one sense, the vigorous German defense of their status as equal citizens which provoked their political participation was an effort at accommodation to American life. Yet that very desire for acceptance and equality led them to a distinctive pattern of political participation that set them apart from the native born of the city. It was in politics, above all—that most American of arts—where the German ethnic community counted; it was politics which, in effect, molded German ethnic consciousness. German social heterogeneity assured the leadership to make this possible, and German residential patterns ensured power at the polls. But in politics, as in other aspects of organ- ized community life, the frequent emergence of deep internal divisions also suggests the limitations of ethnic community for Milwaukee's Germans. Their community was a protective environment to facilitate their personal adjustments to American life, but both its diversity and their personal goals precluded the conscious marshaling of ethnic power for anything beyond the defense of their right to achieve that adjustment as painlessly as possible.

Conclusion

In April of 1858, Milwaukee's German Old Settlers—those who had arrived in the city before 1848—gathered to feast together and to reminisce. Already the early days of the city's German community had become the stuff of legend. As their speaker reminded them,

Who of all those here assembled would ever have let himself even dream, back in his fatherland, that he would help to found a state, a city? And yet, friends, is it not so? Have we not cleared the forest, drained the swamp, filled the hollow, leveled the hill, dragged the first log to the first cabin, carried the first stone to the first courthouse, set the first type, peddled the first wares? Have we not created a settlement from a log cabin, a village from a settlement, then a town, county, state, and finally, this city? . . . We are the founders of this beautiful queen of the west.[1]

The Germans were an essential part of Milwaukee, and they knew it. They were founders, not incidental late comers, and from the virgin land on the shore of Lake Michigan they not only helped build a city but created a community for themselves, one in its daily life perhaps as independent of the other elements of the city's population as any part of a larger whole could be.

The character and size of the German emigration played a role in the formation of that community. It was sufficiently diverse to include both employers and employees, skilled and unskilled, cultured and unlettered; it could therefore supply its own leaders, provide for most of the needs of its members—economic, social, cultural—within its own bounds, and contain the upwardly mobile. The successful were not forced to abandon their German way of life to enjoy the new status which they had earned. The city's frontier condition provided opportunities for German entrepreneurs and craftsmen as well as for the unskilled, and as the numbers of Germans grew, so did the opportunities to make a living without extensive contact with the non-German population. Their numbers permitted the Germans to turn an entire city quadrant into a "Little Germany"; in origin, the German neighborhoods were probably the product of socioeconomic differences, but it was the desire of Germans to live near others speaking the same tongue which alone can explain the degree of congregation that resulted, a congregation permitted and encouraged in the new city.

Thus the German emigration and the American frontier combined to facilitate in Milwaukee the creation of a German community in the ecological sense of the term. Most Germans lived together, many worked together, and on that basis they congregated socially as well. It was not so much that they were rebuffed by the native born as that they had little reason purposefully to seek out associations with others. The largely middle-class status of the city's natives militated against social contacts with the German worker, while middle-class Germans were often sufficiently scornful of the Yankee lack of culture to avoid seeking out contacts. When faced with a political challenge aimed at them as foreigners, they united for political action, a union sufficiently strong to endure in its basic outlines through a major shift in party systems. In the early years they united also in fire companies, military companies, benevolent and welfare groups as well as in more ad hoc parades and social festivities. Their common language, their common background in the eyes of the natives, were enough to bring them together despite differences of province, dialect, religion, and class brought from their still divided homeland.[2]

The forced unity of the early years soon wore off. Religious and class cleavages revealed themselves and a large variety of special interest groups appeared. But in that diversity lay the strength of the German community; it was not a community of like-thinkers and like-actors but a community within which a large number of persons sharing one essential characteristic, German birth, which marked them off from others in the same city, could strive to create satisfying lives for themselves. Even the thrust and parry of internecine argument was stimulating and accustomed. The existence of such a community undoubtedly eased the emotional adjustment of the newcomer by providing a relatively familiar range of services and by helping to ensure that many of his daily contacts would be with roughly the same types of persons he had encountered at home.

In satisfying his needs in such a manner, the community likewise unquestionably retarded any rapid acculturation to American styles of life. Intermarriage between Germans and other Milwaukee residents remained minimal.[3] A few businessmen, a few politicians began to interact with Americans as individuals on an equal level, but much of the contact between native born and immigrant remained on the same level of delegations treating with delegations that characterized political and civic affairs.[4] Children rapidly learned to speak English in the schools and the parents feared that they would lose the old tongue, yet playmates were persons raised within the same community, and the gulfs between the parents extended to the young.[5] As one German recalled of his arrival in Milwaukee in 1856, after ten years elsewhere in the United States:

What really made me feel at home was the fact that here was a place where the second generation was already growing up, a generation rooted in and maturing with the settlement, which could look back proudly on intellectual and cultural achievements; where the young men of my age were all school-mates and knew the histories of one another and of the older generation; and who through constant association and working together stood closer to one another than I had ever found to be the case elsewhere.[6]

"Ach, Heer Jeses," sighed a German woman in 1860 who had moved from Milwaukee to St. Louis, "so scheene is es doch nergends wie in Milwaukee"—nowhere is it as nice as Milwaukee.[7]

Ethnicity for Milwaukee's Germans was a language, a neighborhood, a set of associations within which friends were found, a way of enjoying life—to be defended politically if necessary. It accompanied rather than precluded Americanization. The *Banner* was never more vociferous in decrying German separatism than when it was defending German culture. The early years in America, John Kerler noted, were "apprentice and probation years" when "the German skin must be removed and American skin put on instead—then it will be fine"; his Milwaukee grandson was soon to bear an English name "to make a real American out of him" and his son-in-law would write of Germany, "We Americans do not fit there any more,"[8] yet their lives were lived within Milwaukee's *Deutschtum*. The German Athens in its own "apprentice years" looked forward to America rather than back to Germany and by its very diversity, by the superficiality of the common characteristics demanded of community members, ensured both its survival as long as newcomers required its services and its ultimate dissolution as its culture merged generation by generation with that of the larger society.

Milwaukee's Irish were more homogeneous, but they never created as comprehensive a community. The class identity of Irishness colored its relation to upward mobility, and assimilation became more a matter for the individual than the group. The ethnicity which has survived in modern America is probably of this kind, rather than that known by Milwaukee's Germans. To those who value the richness of cultural variety and political potential which ethnicity presents, the German-Americans may offer the paradoxical example of an ethnic culture whose own fullness and complexity encouraged its dissolution.[9] For that reason, if no other, the German experience demands closer comparative study and a chapter of its own in the annals of the urban immigrant experience alongside the assimilative success of the British at one extreme, and the saga of the "uprooted" at the other.

APPENDIX   NOTES   INDEX

Appendix

NOTE ON SOURCES AND METHODS

Federal census schedules, noted J. C. G. Kennedy in 1851, "comprise no insignificant portion of the history of every man, woman, and child living; and long after all those whose names they contain will have passed from earth, will they be appealed to in proof of our once having lived, for our place of residence, our children, and our property."[1] It is those schedules which made possible the statistical resurrection of Milwaukee's immigrant settlement, and although their use in historical research is now well past the pioneer stage, particular problems which arose in sampling, coding, and mapping census data for this study nevertheless require some review. A brief discussion of other major sources is also appended.

The Census Sample

Although Milwaukee between 1836 and 1860 was subjected to three federal censuses (1840, 1850, 1860), five territorial censuses (1836, 1842, 1845, 1846, 1847), a state census (1855), and a series of city school censuses in the 1840s and 1850s, only the 1850 and 1860 federal censuses provided the kinds of detailed information useful for this study.[2] The 1850 census listed, by dwelling and family numbered in the order of visitation, the names of all persons whose usual place of residence on June first was within that family; their age, sex, color, and place of birth; the value of real estate owned; the occupation of every male over fifteen, and whether or not he was married within the year, had attended school within the year, could read and write, and whether he was deaf and dumb, blind, insane, an idiot, a pauper, or a convict. To these questions, the 1860 census added a query concerning the value of personal property and requested information on the occupation of females as well as males.[3]

The value of such information, of course, depends on the reliability of the census itself, and the numerous problems which plagued the nineteenth century census taker inevitably led to errors and likely underenumeration.[4] One notable problem was the extended duration of the enumeration process; while the census theoretically listed every person present in the city on June 1, actual census taking in Milwaukee lasted from July 17 to September 5 in 1850, and from June 1 to August 16 in 1860. These were the summer months when new migrants passed through the port at a great rate and when seasonal employment must have attracted significant numbers of permanent residents away from the city, increasing the normal difficulties of accurate enumeration. One could thus anticipate a bias in coverage against the more unsettled foreign-born element of the city's population, a bias probably intensified by language problems, although it is worth noting that German papers were careful to publicize the nature and importance of the census,[5] and that German census takers were used in three of the most German wards—two, six, and nine—in 1860.

Several decisions were necessary before the wealth of information provided by the 1850 and 1860 manuscript census schedules could be used for this study. First, the size of Milwaukee's population—20,000 by 1850, over 45,000 ten years later—made some kind of sampling necessary to keep the project within reasonable time limits. Second, the population subject to inclusion in the sample was limited to heads of household, on the assumption that their ethnic background, socioeconomic status, and residential decisions governed the accommodation process for their families as well as for themselves; this decision obviously limited the later utilization of the sample in answering questions concerning other household members which had not been conceived as part of the original research design. An independent systematic sample of every fourth head of household was drawn from each of the two censuses; since the schedules were arranged by ward, the resulting samples were automatically stratified to include ward sample members proportionate to each ward's share of the entire city households. The result was a sample size of 1,020 households in 1850, 2,266 households in 1860, sufficiently large, it was hoped, to provide adequate representation of all important subgroups in the population of household heads. Chi-square tests were conducted to determine that this was indeed the case for the individual cross-tabulations derived from the sample data.

While such statistical techniques can be used to gauge the representativeness of the sample as a whole, it is more difficult to estimate the consequences of the decision to sample only heads of household. Few problems are involved for individuals resident in family units, but in the case of several unmarried persons living together, it meant that the first person listed was arbitrarily considered to be the "head of household." It also meant that boarders—the least stable element of the population—were left out of consideration, and that in general, young unmarried persons were less apt to be included in the analysis. If some ethnic groups contained a greater than average proportion of such persons, this could result in a bias against their full inclusion.

Such bias can be checked through the results of a pilot excursion into the 1850 manuscript census to collect selected information concerning all household heads and all males aged fifteen and over (Table A.1).[6] When males who are not heads of household are included, the native proportion is increased somewhat, the German decreased. But the differences are not so great as to suggest that major bias in gross ethnic patterns has been introduced by confining the sample to heads of household. Table A. 1 incidentally indicates that the 1850 sample is relatively accurate predictor of the ethnic composition of the total group of household heads.

Much of the coding of the census data was straightforward,[7] but the selection of an occupational code was a critical problem. The 1850 census contained some 188 different occupational designations; the 1860 census undoubtedly had far more. Occupation can be coded to indicate the precise nature of the work performed, the industry in which it was being performed, the status and living standard associated with it, or any combination of such criteria.[8] Since occupation in the

Table A-1   1850 Milwaukee nativity groups according to differing census samples (sample percentage by nativity)

1850 census samples	N	Native	British	Irish	German	Other	Total
All heads of household	4,101	22.7	10.5	19.0	40.4	7.4	100.0
25 percent sample	1,020	22.1	10.0	18.8	40.6	8.5	100.0
Males aged 15 and over	6,462	25.1	10.5	18.3	37.6	8.5	100.0

context of this study was to be used as a rough index of social status and standard of living as well as a description of what a man did, a variant of the occupational status hierarchy evolved by Stephan Thernstrom for his study of Boston's post-1880 population was adopted. This scheme has been utilized for a study of the population of antebellum Boston as well, and thus offers the advantage of comparability in its own time period as well as over time.[9] Adoption of an existing scheme simplified coding problems but its application in practice led to certain difficulties (for the classification, refer to Table A. 2).

First, the distinction between Class 2 and Class 5 is based upon a combination of property ownership and, in 1850, numbers of persons

Table A-2 Classification of occupations

1 Professionals

Architect	Physician
Civil engineer	Scientist
Clergyman	Pharmacist
Editor	Teacher
Lawyer	Veterinarian

2 Proprietors, managers, and officials (except petty)

Banker	Tavern proprietor
Broker	Boardinghouse proprietor
Financier	Barber shop proprietor
Public utility company official	Wholesale merchant
Insurance company official	Grocer
Pawnbroker	Bookseller
Land holder, speculator	Produce dealer
Land agent	Leather merchant
Farmer	Lumber and coal dealer
Contractor	Tobacco dealer
City official	Dry goods dealer
Military officer	Liquor dealer
U.S. government official	Hardware dealer
Ship's officer	Variety store proprietor
Stage proprietor	Merchant, unspecified
Livery proprietor	Factory owner
Hotel proprietor	

3 Semi-professionals

Actor	Fresco painter
Artist	Evangelist

Table A-2 Continued

Musician
Music teacher
Writer, journalist
Librarian
Photographer
Sculptor

Surveyor
Draftsman
Dentist
Nurse
Undertaker
Osteopath

4 Clerical and sales
Clerical public employee
Telegraph operator
Mail carrier
Accountant, bookkeeper
Office clerk
Auditor
Bank teller
Cashier
Messenger
Agent

Insurance broker
Bill collector
Solicitor, canvasser
Travelling salesman
Commercial reporter
Store clerk
Auctioneer
Clerk, unspecified
Hotel clerk

5 Petty proprietors, managers, and officials
Minor government official
Inspector
Railroad conductor
Foreman
Ship's mate
Farmer
Huckster, peddler
Petty merchant, unspecified
Tavern proprietor
Liquor dealer
Tobacconist
Brewery proprietor
Grocer
Produce dealer
Dry goods dealer
Merchant tailor
Shoestore proprietor
Hat and cap dealer
Milliner
Leather dealer
Crockery dealer
Cabinetware dealer
Hardware dealer

Music dealer
Bookseller
Horse dealer
Clothing dealer
Meat dealer
Lumber dealer
Greenhouse proprietor
Dealer in other foods
Cattle dealer
Second hand goods dealer
Marble monument dealer
Restaurant keeper
Hotel proprietor
Billiard saloon proprietor
Livery stable proprietor
Jobber
Contractor
Commission merchant
Factory owner
Private institution manager
Publisher
Dispenser

Table A-2 Continued

---

6 Skilled

Builder	Compositor
Carpenter	Engraver
Carver	Printer
Glazier	Lithographer
Mason	Bookbinder
Painter	Matchmaker
Paperhanger	Baker
Plasterer	Confectioner
Roofer	Food processor
Stonecutter	Soap maker
Sash, blindmaker	Potash maker
Lather	Chandler
Varnisher and finisher	Ropemaker
Joiner	Sailmaker
Turner	Shipbuilder, carpenter
Pipe fitter	Shoemaker, cordwainer
Cabinetmaker	Hatter
Chairmaker	Dressmaker
Trunkmaker	Milliner
Upholsterer	Tailor
Polisher, burnisher	Glovemaker
Coachmaker	Furrier
Wheelwright	Button, comb maker
Hamemaker	Umbrella maker
Coach trimmer	Bag maker
Brewer	Textile worker
Distiller	Spinner
Vinegarmaker	Weaver
Starchmaker	Dyer
Cigarmaker	Woolcomber
Gunsmith	Tanner
Musical instrument maker	Papermaker
Precision instrument maker	Potter
Locksmith	Straw worker
Blacksmith	Saddler
Boilermaker	Engineer
Brassworker	Machinist
Coppersmith	Millwright
Iron Molder	Mechanic
Iron Worker	Pattern maker
Silver, goldsmith	Toolmaker
Jeweller	Agricultural implement maker

Table A-2 Continued

Tinsmith
Other smiths

Locomotive worker
Factory worker

7 Semiskilled and service
Butcher, meat cutter
Cooper
Brickmaker
Shinglemaker
Sawyer, wood chopper
Miner
Welder
Whitewasher
Well digger
Barber
Bartender
Cook
Servant
Waiter
Watchman
Amusement worker
Scissors grinder

Clothes cleaner
Teamster, drayman
Driver, coachman, cabman
Carrier, mover
Milkman, iceman
Longshoreman
Seaman
Fisherman
Hunter
City employee, minor
Policeman
Fireman
Soldier
Sexton
Grader
Paver
Pile driver

8 Unskilled
Laborer, unspecified
Farm laborer
Factory laborer
Porter
Janitor
Hostler

Bill poster
Lumberman
Gardener
Drover
Washerwoman

9 Miscellaneous
Student
Widow
Almshouse, pauper

Jail
Male, no occupation
Female, no occupation

---

employed. The Thernstrom and original Knights demarcation between these two groups was the possession of at least $1,000 in personal property or $5,000 in real estate. Such criteria were difficult for anyone in the frontier city to meet, and it was clear in 1850 particularly that many of the city's largest businessmen were excluded from Class 2. Thus the 1850 criteria for Class 2 were set at the ownership of $5,000 in real property, or $1,000 in real property and ownership of a manufacturing firm employing five or more persons and with annual product valued at $5,000 or more in the manuscript census of manufacturers. This admittedly prejudiced the category against nonmanufacturers, but their central locations generally insured that most leading merchants were able to meet the property requirement. Since property values increased sufficiently to make the $5,000 threshold more realistic by 1860, the employment criterion was dropped, and criteria of $5,000 in real property or $10,000 in combined real and personal property were used for 1860. These manipulations were carried out to ensure comparability; Knights, however, changed his threshold to $1,000, for clearly similar reasons. The result is that the category of major proprietors, managers, and officials in the present study is probably unduly restrictive as a measure of status.

A further problem in adapting this status hierarchy arose from the nature of occupational designations in the census. Ideally, skilled craftsmen owning their own shops belonged in Class 5 or Class 2, depending on the size of their business. But the census made no consistent distinctions between such artisans and their employees or apprentices. Ownership of property was not sufficient to suggest that a person was self-employed, since he could have been both an employee and a homeowner. Nor was the manufacturing census a sufficient indicator of self-employment, since it only listed those firms with an annual value of product of over $500; city directories also failed to distinguish consistently employment status. Thus, unless a man's operations were sufficiently large-scale to push him into Class 2, all skilled workmen are found in Class 6, which as a result, includes both petty bourgeois master craftsmen and their lower status employees; consideration of those finer status differences was reserved for more impressionistic treatment in Chapter 4.

These difficulties arose from the attempt to code occupational status directly from occupational titles. A more effective alternative might have involved classification by industry and skill, to be used as one of a number of independent variables to generate a combined index of "social status" in the manner advocated by Eric E. Lampard.[10] Such an approach would still retain classification problems, however, since census titles were at times industrial (railroad) and at other times based on skill (smith) and only intermittently upon the combination of both (grocer's clerk). The occupational code used here was, incidentally, sufficiently detailed to permit both reclassification by trade where possible and the recovery of the original census job title.

A separate coding issue concerning household members should also be mentioned. Nonfamily members were isolated in the hope of determining the presence of boarders, employees, and others in the household, but it was often difficult to distinguish such persons from relatives. If age and birthplaces seemed to suggest that persons of different surnames could have been relatives, they were treated as such. The identification of servants presented a similar problem in 1850, since female occupations were not listed until the following census. Again, age, birthplace, and the order in which a person was listed within the household were all useful in determining servant status. Obviously, such procedures leave room for a good deal of error which probably resulted in greater under- than over-enumeration of both boarders and servants.

In order to map this census information, city directories had to be used, since neither census listed addresses or even page-by-page street designations. Nine directories covered the Milwaukee population at somewhat irregular intervals beginning in 1847 through 1860; they were the products of seven different companies, only one of which survived to produce a second and third volume.[11] The directories provided alphabetical listings of city residents and firms, giving home and occasionally business address, occupation, and whether or not the person was a boarder; beginning in 1858 they also provided a separate classified listing of businesses. Since no directory was compiled in 1850, the relatively comprehensive 1851 directory, which listed an estimated 25 percent of the total city population, was used to map the sample households. A sufficient proportion of names were found at addresses which coincided with a rational census taker's path to establish general locations. Names not found were checked in the 1848 directory (estimated coverage 17 percent) and if at the established location, the 1848 addresses were used. For 1860 the directory published in that year was used on its own, though its estimated coverage of 23 percent was not up to the standard set in preceding years.[12]

The proportions of each census sample located in the directories are presented in Table A. 3. Only 13 percent of the 1860 sample escaped the directory, compared with 42 percent in the combined 1848 and 1851 directories. Especially in 1850, coverage was far better for the natives than for the foreign born; the non-English-speaking Germans suffered particularly. By 1860 the Germans still received less than thorough coverage, but the gap had narrowed, doubtless in part owing to publishers' efforts to enlist German-speaking enumerators.[13] Likewise, there was a certain spatial variation in coverage, with core wards given more thorough treatment than the fringes. While peripheral location was highly correlated with foreign-born residents, mapping of the census samples made clear that among the foreign born it was residents on the fringe who were most often omitted from directory coverage.

Such biases in coverage were the result of problems inherent in making a directory canvass in the mid-nineteenth century. Other difficulties arise in attempting to subvert what was essentially a commercial tool to the needs of the modern researcher. Names are misspelled or misalphabetized, addresses are often only approximate locations, employment information is presented inconsistently. Thus, when a householder could not be identified in the directory, the addresses of sample members closest to him in the census were checked. If they were sufficiently close, he was assigned a location between them on the

Table A.3   City directory coverage for 1850 and 1860 census samples

Nativity group	Percent of sample located in directory for each ward									
	1	2	3	4	5	6	7	8	9	Total
1850										
Native	78	61	64	87	57	-	-	-	-	79
British	65	77	64	80	75	-	-	-	-	70
Irish	79	69	59	49	54	-	-	-	-	60
German	55	40	54	20	53	-	-	-	-	48
Total	65	51	58	60	51	-	-	-	-	58
1860										
Native	91	88	91	92	93	94	95	100	100	93
British	94	93	100	83	89	78	100	100	75	92
Irish	79	100	89	94	96	77	100	89	100	88
German	71	93	81	96	70	92	86	80	85	85
Total	78	93	90	93	82	90	90	84	86	87

assumption that the census taker followed a rational route. If one or more of his sample neighbors' addresses were missing or ambiguous, recourse was made to the addresses of his neighbors in the original census schedule.

Mapping was according to grid cell coordinates rather than pinpoint location to ease compilation and correlation of household character- istics by location. A square grid averaging four city blocks in size was laid over a map of the city and households were assigned to grid cells according to their addresses.[14] The four-city-block cell was selected as being a unit sufficiently small theoretically to constitute a homogeneous neighborhood yet large enough to include a representative group of residents. Given the vagueness of many addresses, it also forms ap- proximately the smallest unit within which accurate location was possi- ble for certain areas of the city; ideally, of course, it would require a floating grid to really average the error this involved. Cell boundaries were run along alleys wherever possible on the assumption that oppo- site sides of the street would have more in common than sides of a block facing different streets. Since Milwaukee's streets did not conform to a perfect grid, some of the cell sizes were adjusted to conform to topog- raphy and the vagaries of street lines. While an attempt was made to keep all cells equal in area, this was not always possible, particularly along the river. The grid as it was drawn could then be generalized to facilitate mapping of information, as presented in Chapter 5.[15]

In order to derive ethnic areas within the city based on these cells as building blocks, the percentage of each ethnic group resident in a given cell was mapped for 1850 and 1860. Then all cells with at least 60 percent of their population of the same ethnic group were defined as core concentrations of that group, and contiguous cells with concentra- tions of the same group were merged into an ethnic area. Any cell with a 50 percent concentration of one group which was completely sur- rounded by cells with 60 percent concentration of the same group was also included in the ethnic area of its neighbors; remaining cells with no clear concentration were assigned to mixed areas.[16] Small sample size particularly in peripheral cells created potential error but the pervasive- ness of the pattern when aggregated over large areas supports the gen- eral procedure.

Actual processing of the census data was performed using the DSTAT package of the STATJOB program library of the University of Wisconsin Computing Center.

Other Sources

A variety of other, less systematic sources supplemented the sample data in reconstructing the context of Milwaukee immigrant life. The Milwaukee press, for example, provided indispensable information on the associational and political lives of the city's immigrants. The newspaper collection of the State Historical Society of Wisconsin made it possible to follow the activities of the Germans through the files of the *Wisconsin Banner* (1845-47, 1849-55), *Der Volksfreund* (1847-50), *Wisconsin Banner und Volksfreund* (1855-60), and the *Atlas* (1860). The *Milwaukee Courier* (1841-47) and the *Milwaukee Advertiser* (1836-40 scattered) provided coverage for the years before the appearance of the German language press; the Democratic *Courier* was particularly good in its coverage of immigrant activities. The Salzmann Library of Milwaukee's St. Francis Seminary provided the only file of the *Seebote* for the antebellum period (1853-54), which was important for its presentation of the German Catholic point of view. The *Milwaukee Sentinel* (1844-60) was consulted for election results; the W.P.A. card index of local items in the *Sentinel* between 1837 and 1879, located in the Milwaukee Public Library, also made it possible to consult the *Sentinel* on specific issues of relevance to Milwaukee immigrant life. The 1854 volume of the *Atlantis*, a German literary journal published that year in Milwaukee, contained scattered items of local concern; Vojta Naprstek's *Flug-Blätter* (1852-54) are of interest only for their anticlerical polemic. Both may be found at the State Historical Society.

Local government documents were less helpful. Most early city records fell victim to the two fires which successively destroyed city offices during the antebellum period. Remaining early documents are deposited in the Milwaukee County Historical Center in Milwaukee. The earliest available tax roll listing more than delinquent taxpayers was the city's "Assessment Roll, and State, County and School Tax List" for 1861, whose use in this study, however, was limited by its failure to identify property holders by name. The Minutes of the Common Council, beginning 10 April 1846, were also consulted at the Center, although they were not utilized in any systematic fashion. While the center also possesses Probate Court records for the period, the unspecific nature of many of the documents conspired with the center's filing system to discourage their use. Records in the Wisconsin State Archives which proved most useful included the Executive Department file on immigration, 1852-1905, containing the manuscript reports and letters of the early state commissioners of immigration, and also the manuscript schedules of the 1854, 1846, 1847, and 1855 censuses, which were consulted for population totals.

The extensive map collection of the State Historical Society of Wisconsin was indispensable for the accurate mapping of census and directory data. Maps were also sources of information concerning topography, names of subdevelopers, and dates of plats, while a series of bird's-eye views in the collection encouraged the imagination to wander freely and familiarize itself with the street scenes of early Milwaukee.

Memoirs and letters provide another kind of direct link with the past. However, while they can add human interest and sometimes clarify contemporary attitudes, all too frequently they are both unrepresentative of the population as a whole and frustratingly silent on questions of vital interest. Relatively few letters of Milwaukee immigrants are available to the researcher. There is one superb collection, originally compiled by Dr. Louis F. Frank and recently published by the Milwaukee County Historical Center in an English translation edited by Harry H. Anderson.[17] The collections of the State Historical Society of Wisconsin both at Madison and at its Milwaukee Area Research Center at the University of Wisconsin-Milwaukee as well as the Milwaukee County Historical Center yielded the manuscript sources cited in the text; the files of the *Wisconsin Magazine of History* and the *Historical Messenger of the Milwaukee County Historical Center* proved to be rich mines of published letters and memoirs.

Travelers' accounts and immigrant guidebooks offered a different and extremely useful perspective on early Milwaukee. They proffered regulation doses of local color description, of course, as well as the usual tips on modes of travel and favorite hotels. But the best of them also acted as contemporary "participant-observers" of the local scene, and in their concern to explain America to the foreigner they touched upon topics such as the status of the different trades and the hierarchy of local organizations which the native born took for granted. Outstanding among the observations of the German travelers who visited Milwaukee in the antebellum period were those of Moritz Wagner and Carl Scherzer, veterans of seventeen years of travel and writing in the Orient before they transferred their techniques of analysis to the new world.[18] Their volumes, and those of other guidebook authors consulted for this study,[19] would well merit further attention for the German view of American life which they offer.

A final category of sources which requires specific mention is the local history compilation. The student of Milwaukee history begins with an enormous headstart, thanks to Bayrd Still's model urban biography, *Milwaukee: The History of a City*, which provides an excellent political and economic framework within which to set a more detailed case study but which also gives extended consideration to the experiences of the city's different ethnic groups.[20] Still's work caps a long tradition of Milwaukee historiography. Milwaukee's pioneer historians, Wheeler, Koss, and Buck, were in many instances witnesses of the events of which they wrote, and their works have the immediacy of primary sources, interspersing chronicle with personal commentary.[21] In comparison, it is tempting to dismiss the later works edited by Flower, Conrad, and Watrous as typical later nineteenth and earlier twentieth century compendia of reminiscence, topical history, and laudatory biography, of which Flower's is the most comprehensive.[22] But these works, along with the more recent Bruce and Gregory histories which follow somewhat the same pattern but attempt a greater unity, proved important sources for biographical information on Milwaukee immigrants, as did several of the blatantly "booster" publications of the period.[23] The biographies in these books have to be taken with a grain of salt. They were a form of self-advertisement, presenting the image desired by their subject, whose price of inclusion was often a subscription to the work in question; they were clearly biased toward the successful and the assimilated.[24] Yet they make it possible at least in some instances to modify the generalities of census trends with the detail of individual lives and were systematically analyzed both for this reason and specifically also for the light which they cast on the upwardly mobile and geographically stable segment of the immigrant community.

Notes

Abbreviations

AV	*Milwaukee Advertiser*
BV	*Banner und Volksfreund* (Milwaukee)
HMMC	*Historical Messenger of the Milwaukee County Historical Center*
MA	*Atlas* (Milwaukee)
MC	*Milwaukee Courier*
MCHS	Milwaukee County Historical Society
MWS	*Milwaukee Sentinel*
SB	*Seebote* (Milwaukee)
SHSW	State Historical Society of Wisconsin
VF	*Volksfreund* (Milwaukee)
WB	*Wisconsin Banner* (Milwaukee)
WMH	*Wisconsin Magazine of History*

Introduction

1. *MC*, March 29, 1843; Rudolf H. Koss, *Milwaukee* (Milwaukee: Herold, 1871), 135-137.

2. This interpretation is synthesized primarily from Milton M. Gordon, *Assimilation in American Life: The Role of Race, Religion, and National Origins* (New York: Oxford University Press, 1964), 63-80; S. N. Eisenstadt, *The Absorption of Immigrants: A Comparative Study Based Mainly on the Jewish Community in Palestine and The State of Israel* (London: Routledge and Kegan Paul, Ltd., 1954), 1-19; Lyle W. Shannon and Magdaline Shannon, "The Assimilation of Migrants to Cities: Anthropological and Sociological Contributions," in Leo F. Schnore, ed., *Social Science and the City: A Survey of Urban Research* (New York: Frederick A. Praeger, 1968), 52-55. See also George Eaton Simpson, "Assimilation," *International Encyclopedia of the Social Sciences* (1968), I, 438; Brewton Berry, *Race and Ethnic Relations* (Boston: Houghton Mifflin Co., 1965), 222-258; Charles Price, "The Study of Assimilation," in J. A. Jackson, ed., *Migration* (Cambridge: Cambridge University Press, 1969). It is generally recognized that complete assimilation, in America as elsewhere, should be viewed as the limiting and exceptional case, even over several generations, with some form of pluralism as a more likely outcome.

3. Simpson, "Assimilation," 439; Eisenstadt, *Absorption of Immigrants*, 241-258; Shannon and Shannon, "Assimilation of Migrants," 56-72; C. Bezalel Sherman, *The Jew Within American Society: A Study in Ethnic Individuality* (Detroit: Wayne University Press, 1961), 15-37; Caroline F. Ware, "Ethnic Communities," *Encyclopedia of the Social Sciences* (1930), V, 608-609; Berry, *Race and Ethnic Relations*, 236-270.

4. H. S. Morris, "Ethnic Group," *International Encyclopedia of the Social Sciences* (1968), V, 167-172; Ware, "Ethnic Communities," 607-612.

5. Gordon, *Assimilation*, 105.

6. For an extended discussion of the origins, functions, and consequences of such communities, see Judith R. Kramer, *The American Minority Community* (New York: Thomas Y. Crowell Company, 1970), 39-87. See also Eisenstadt, *Absorption of Immigrants*, 16-19, 241-255; Gordon, *Assimilation*, 242-245; Caroline F. Ware, "Cultural Groups in the United States," in Ware, ed., *The Cultural Approach to History* (Port Washington, N. Y.: Kennikat Press, Inc., 1940), 63-64, and in the same collection, Carlton C. Qualey, "The Transitional Character of Nationality Group Culture," 82-84; and Humbert Nelli's comments in *Italians in Chicago 1880-1930* (New York: Oxford University Press, 1970), 156-157.

7. Warren, *The Community in America*, 2nd ed. (New York: Rand McNally & Co., 1972), 6; Schnore, "Community," in Neil J. Smelser, ed., *Sociology: An Introduction* (New York: John Wiley and Sons, Inc., 1967), 95.

8. Schnore, "Community," 84-99; Amos Hawley, *Urban Society: An Ecological Approach* (New York: The Ronald Press Company, 1971), 10; Roland I. Warren, "Toward a Reformulation of Community Theory," *Human Organization*, 15 (1956), 8-11.

9. For the development of a related line of reasoning, see Kramer, *American Minority Community*, 39-87, esp. 44, and Raymond Breton, "Institutional Completeness of Ethnic Communities and the Personal Relations of Immigrants," *American Journal of Sociology*, 70 (1964), 193-205.

10. Frederick Jackson Turner, *Frontier and Section: Selected Essays* (Englewood Cliffs, N. J. : Prentice-Hall, Inc., 1961), 51; Stanley Elkins and Eric McKitrick, "A Meaning for Turner's Frontier," *Political Science Quarterly*, 69 (1954), 323-348. In an important criticism, however, Robert R. Dykstra has stressed that conflict as much as cooperation was the channel for community decision making, a process in which ethnic groups presumably found as legitimate a place as any other competing faction; see *The Cattle Towns* (New York: Alfred A. Knopf, 1968), 361-366. Moreover, Edward N. Saveth has noted that Turner himself, in writing about midwestern German immigrants for a Chicago newspaper, ignored the supposed frontier melting pot and stressed the cultural conflict arising on the frontier between German and Puritan; *American Historians and European Immigrants 1875-1925* (New York: Columbia University Press, 1948), 131-132.

11. Cf. Ray Allen Billington's introduction to Andrew F. Rolle, *The Immigrant Upraised: Italian Adventurers and Colonists in an Expanding America* (Norman: University of Oklahoma Press, 1968), *viii-x*, and Rolle's own thesis concerning frontier Italians, esp. 4-13, 122.

12. (New York: Grosset and Dunlap, 1951); see also Caroline F. Ware, "Immigration," *Encyclopedia of the Social Sciences* (1930), VII, 587-595; Louis Wirth, *The Ghetto* (Chicago: University of Chicago Press, 1928); Paul Frederick Cressey, "Population Succession in Chicago: 1898-1930," *American Journal of Sociology*, 44 (1938), 59-69, for earlier statements of the theme.

13. Sam Bass Warner, Jr., and Colin B. Burke, "Cultural Change and the Ghetto," *Journal of Contemporary History*, 4 (1969), 173-187; see also David Ward, "The Emergence of Central Immigrant Ghettoes in American Cities: 1840-1920," *Annals of the Association of American Geographers*, 58 (1968), 343-359, and "The Internal Spatial Differentiation of Immigrant Residential Districts," in "Special Publication No. 3: Interaction Patterns and the Spatial Form of the Ghetto," Department of Geography, Northwestern University, February 1970; Sam Bass Warner, Jr., "If All the World Were Philadelphia: A Scaffolding for Urban History, 1774-1930," *American Historical Review*, 74 (1968), 32-38; Howard P. Chudacoff, "A New Look at Ethnic Neighborhoods: Residential Dispersion and the Concept of Visibility in a Medium-Sized City," *Journal of American History*, 60 (1973), 76-93; Stephan Thernstrom, *The Other Bostonians: Poverty and Progress in the American Metropolis, 1880-1970* (Cambridge: Harvard University Press, 1973), 39-41.

14. Cf. Timothy L. Smith, "New Approaches to the History of Immigration in Twentieth-Century America," *American Historical Review*, 71 (1966), 1265-1279; Michael Parenti, "Ethnic Politics and the Persistence of Ethnic Identification," *American Political Science Review*, 61 (1967), 717-726; Robert P. Swierenga, "Ethnocultural Political Analysis: A New Approach to American Ethnic Studies," *Journal of American Studies*, 5 (1971), 59-79.

15. Max Hannemann, *Das Deutschtum in den Vereinigten Staaten: Seine Verbreitung und Entwicklung seit der Mitte des 19. Jahrhunderts.* Supplement 224, *Petermanns-Mitteilungen* (Gotha: Justus Perthes, 1936).

16. Carl Wittke, *We Who Built America: The Saga of the Immigrant* (New York: Prentice-Hall, Inc., 1940), 187-261; John A. Hawgood, *The Tragedy of German-America: The Germans in the United States of America during the Nineteenth Century—and After* (New York: G. P. Putnam's Sons, 1940); see also Joseph Schafer, "The Yankee and the Teuton in Wisconsin," *WMH*, 6(1922), 125-145, 261-279, 386-402; 7 (1922), 3-19. Albert Bernhardt Faust's *The German Element in the United States*, 2 vols. (Boston: Houghton Mifflin, 1909) is the most thorough and influential of the earlier works.

17. For examples, see Clyde Griffen, "Workers Divided: The Effect of Craft and Ethnic Differences in Poughkeepsie, New York, 1850-1880," in Stephan Thernstrom and Richard Sennett, eds., *Nineteenth-Century Cities: Essays in the New Urban History* (New Haven: Yale University Press, 1969), 49-97; Zane Miller, *Boss Cox's Cincinnati* (New York: Oxford University Press, 1968); Richard Jensen, *The Winning of the Midwest: Social and Political Conflict, 1888-1896* (Chicago: The University of Chicago Press, 1971); Paul Kleppner, *The Cross of Culture: A Social Analysis of Midwestern Politics 1850-1900* (New York: The Free Press, 1970).

18. Several studies have appeared recently which carry this process of reexamination past the initial phase. They include Philip Gleason, *The Conservative Reformers:*

German-American Catholics and the Social Order (Notre Dame: University of Notre Dame Press, 1968); Frederick C. Luebke's *Immigrants and Politics: The Germans of Nebraska, 1880-1900* (Lincoln: University of Nebraska Press, 1969) and *Bonds of Loyalty: German Americans and World War I* (DeKalb: Northern Illinois University Press, 1974); and Guido A. Dobbert, "German-Americans between New and Old Fatherland," *American Quarterly*, 19 (1967), 663-680.

19. Dayton was the smallest, with a population of 20,081. For the complete statistics, see Joseph C. G. Kennedy, *Population of the United States in 1860* (Washington, D. C.: Government Printing Office, 1864), *xxxi-xxxii*.

1. Milwauky Is All the Rage

1. Rudolf A. Koss, *Milwaukee* (Milwaukee: Herold, 1871), 49. Koss, a German-born doctor, merchant, and journalist, moved to Milwaukee in 1856 after five years' residence in a nearby town. His extremely detailed history of Milwaukee's Germans through 1854, which constitutes an important source for this study, was based in part upon his own experiences and the memories of persons whom he interviewed, and on "voluminous scrapbooks." Originally printed in German, his work was translated in part by Hans Ibsen for the Federal Writers' Project; the translation is available at the SHSW. The present study utilizes the German version except for lengthy direct quotations; in all instances, the original pagination is cited. For information on Koss, see *Dictionary of Wisconsin Biography* (Madison: SHSW, 1960), 212; Oscar Burckhardt, ed., *The Musical Society of Milwaukee 1850-1860 A Chronicle* (Milwaukee: Musical Society, 1900), 5.

2. Anthony Trollope, *North America*, ed. Donald Smalley and Bradford Allen Booth (New York: Alfred A. Knopf, 1951), 125; Frederika Bremer, *The Homes of the New World*, trans. Mary Howitt (New York: Harper and Brothers, 1853), 615; *An Exposition of the Business of Milwaukee* (Milwaukee: A. Baylies, 1863), 21, 13. See also James S. Buck, *Pioneer History of Milwaukee* (Milwaukee: Swain and Tate, 1890), I, 144; Wilhelm Hense- Jensen, *Wisconsin's Deutsch-Amerikaner bis zum Schluss des neunzehnten Jahrhunderts* (Milwaukee: Im Verlage der Deutschen Gesellschaft, 1900), I, 241; James S. Ritchie, *Wisconsin and its Resources* (Philadelphia: Charles Desilver, 1858), 85; James S. Buckingham, *The Eastern and Western States of America* (London: Fisher, Son, & Co., 1842), III, 293; Dr. Büchele, *Land und Volk der Vereinigten Staaten von Nord-Amerika* (Stuttgart: Hallberger'sche Verlagshandlung, 1855), 198.

3. Edward Hamming, *The Port of Milwaukee* (Rock Island, Ill.: Augustana College Library, 1953), 23-24; Lawrence Martin, *The Physical Geography of Wisconsin* (Madison: State of Wisconsin, 1932), 286-287; Joseph Schafer, *Four Wisconsin Counties: Prairie and Forest* (Madison: SHSW, 1927), 5-6.

4. Bayrd Still, *Milwaukee: The History of a City* (Madison: SHSW, 1948), 3-7.

5. Lawrence M. Larson, *A Financial and Administrative History of Milwaukee* (Madison: Bulletin of the University of Wisconsin no. 242, 1908), 10-11; Still, *Milwaukee*, 7-25. Walker's claims on the south side were not completely recognized until 1849, a factor which slowed settlement in this area. The first south side plat was received for record in August 1836, but not recorded until 1854. Still, *Milwaukee*, 12; Buck, *Pioneer History*, I, 112, 87.

6. A. C. Wheeler, *The Chronicles of Milwaukee: Being a Narrative History of the Town from Its Earliest Period to the Present* (Milwaukee: Jermain & Brightman, 1861), 31, 37; Enoch Chase, "Reminiscences," ms., SHSW, Milwaukee Area Research Center, University of Wisconsin-Milwaukee; Frank A. Flower, *History of Milwaukee, Wisconsin* (Chicago: The Western Historical Company, 1881), 142; Koss, *Milwaukee,* 50; Buck, *Pioneer History,* I, 106.

7. Lucius G. Fisher, "Pioneer Recollections of Beloit and Southern Wisconsin," *WMH,* 1 (1918), 270; see also Still, *Milwaukee,* 27; Wheeler, *Chronicles,* 73; Edward D. Holton, "Commercial History of Milwaukee," *Collections,* SHSW, 4 (1906), 254.

8. Still, *Milwaukee,* 28-29; Koss, *Milwaukee,* 93; Buck, *Pioneer History,* I, 81, 162.

9. Still, *Milwaukee,* 60, 168-199; William E. Derby, "A History of the Port of Milwaukee," Ph.D. diss., University of Wisconsin, 1963, esp. 168, 193-194, 212-216, 267-268; *BV,* June 9, 1859.

10. Still, *Milwaukee,* 42-47, 52-69, 268-299; City of Milwaukee, Department of City Development, *Milwaukee's Land Use Report* (1964), 23; Margaret Walsh, *The Manufacturing Frontier: Pioneer Industry in Antebellum Wisconsin 1830-1860* (Madison: SHSW, 1972), 171-209; James M. Edmunds, *Statistics of the United States (Including Mortality, Property, etc.) in 1860* (Washington, D.C.: Government Printing Office, 1866), viii; the percentages were computed from manuscript census of manufactures data made available by Margaret Walsh. For comparison, see similar computations for 1860 in Eric E. Lampard, "The History of Cities in the Economically Advanced Areas," *Economic Development and Cultural Change,* 3 (1955), 120: Lynn, 45 percent; Newark, 26.2 percent; Philadelphia, 17.5 percent; Cincinnati, 18.3 percent; Chicago, 4.9 percent.

11. Still, *Milwaukee,* 33-34; Koss, *Milwaukee,* 37; Larson, *Financial and Administrative History,* 11-18; the south side was unable to organize because of the disputed title claims. The ward separatism broke into open hostility over bridging the Milwaukee River, which lay within the province of neither ward; in the semi-farcical "Bridge War of 1845," mob action succeeded in closing the three bridges which had been built since 1840 for a short time. Vivid descriptions of the "Bridge War" can be found in all Milwaukee histories; see, for example, Wheeler, *Chronicles,* 114.

12. Larson, *Financial and Administrative History,* 23-27.

13. See the appendix for a discussion of the methods used in extracting, coding, and analyzing the heads of household samples; all census data not otherwise identified is derived from these samples. Unless otherwise specified, native refers to those born within the United States; German refers to those born in what would become the German Empire and excludes Austrians, Swiss, and so on; British includes the English, Scots, and Welsh. The Irish are treated separately; since available statistics fail to distinguish between them, the Scotch-Irish are included in the Irish category.

14. The percentages impute an unwarranted exactitude to the data. German names were more easily identified than Irish, but some German names may have reflected earlier immigrant generations while anglicization may have altered others beyond recognition. Irish names likewise could have been inherited from immigrant ancestors; many English-sounding Irish names were undoubtedly ignored. Later censuses also suggest that Irish were more likely than Germans to reside in households

headed by natives; such persons would not have appeared by name in the 1840 census which recorded only the names of household heads.

15. Howard Louis Conrad, ed., *History of Milwaukee from Its First Settlement to the Year 1895*, 3 vols. (Chicago: American Biographical Publishing Co., n.d.). See the appendix for a discussion of the use of such data.

16. Still, *Milwaukee*, 72.

17. *WB*, Dec. 26, 1846; Hense-Jensen, *Wisconsin's Deutsch-Amerikaner*, I, 20; Anton Eickhoff, *In der Neuen Heimath: Geschichtliche Mittheilungen über die deutschen Einwanderer in allen Theilen der Union* (New York: E. Steiger & Co., 1884), 365; Buck, *Pioneer History*, I, 70; II, 322; Koss, *Milwaukee*, 40, 45, 49-51; Flower, *History of Milwaukee*, 1570; Wheeler, *Chronicles*, 56; Conrad, *History of Milwaukee*, I, 364.

18. Koss, *Milwaukee*, 90-92; Hense-Jensen, *Wisconsin's Deutsch-Amerikaner*, I, 21; *MWS*, Oct. 16, 1895; *A Merry Briton in Pioneer Wisconsin* (Madison: SHSW, 1950), 30-31; *The City of Milwaukee Guide to the "Cream City"* (Milwaukee: Caspar & Zahn, 1886), 41.

19. *MWS*, Oct. 9, 1839; Koss, *Milwaukee*, 112; *MC*, May 24, Aug. 23, 1843.

20. Hense-Jensen, *Wisconsin's Deutsch-Amerikaner*, I, 22; Koss, *Milwaukee*, 155.

21. Kate Everest Levi, "Geographical Origins of German Immigration to Wisconsin," *Collections*, SHSW, 14 (1898), 343-350; Hense-Jensen, *Wisconsin's Deutsch-Amerikaner*, I, 26, 35-40; Schafer, *Four Wisconsin Counties*, 90, 94; Koss, *Milwaukee*, 103.

22. Excerpt from a paper by Christian Preusser published in the 1890's, reprinted in John G. Gregory, *History of Milwaukee, Wisconsin* (Chicago: S. J. Clarke, 1931), I, 622; see also Buck, *Pioneer History*, II, 81.

23. Preusser, in Gregory, *History of Milwaukee*, I, 622-623; see also Hense-Jensen, *Wisconsin's Deutsch-Amerikaner*, I, 118.

24. Buck, *Pioneer History*, I, 292; Walter Osten, "History of the Turner Movement," Turner Papers, MCHS.

25. Still, *Milwaukee*, 89; Humphrey J. Desmond, "Early Irish Settlers in Milwaukee," *WMH*, 13 (1930), 365-367; Koss, *Milwaukee*, 167.

26. See, for example, Robert G. Carroon, "Scotsmen in Old Milwaukee 1810-1860," *HMMC*, 25 (1969), 20-33.

27. Harry H. Anderson, "Early Scandinavian Settlement in Milwaukee County," *HMMC*, 25 (1969), 5-6.

28. Henry C. Lucas, "Reminiscences of Arend Jan Brusse on Early Dutch Settlement in Milwaukee," *WMH*, 30 (1946), 88.

29. William T. Green, "Negroes in Milwaukee," *MWS*, Oct. 16, 1895, reprinted in "The Negro in Milwaukee: A Historical Survey" (Milwaukee: MCHC, 1968), 7.

30. These figures comprise all blacks and mulattoes listed in the 1850 and 1860 censuses. Eight black households were drawn in the 1850 heads of household sample, five in the 1860 sample. Owing to the small size of the group, they are not included in the general statistical treatment of this study. For a thorough study of Milwaukee's early black community, see William J. Vollmar, "The Negro in a Midwest Frontier City, Milwaukee: 1835-1870," M.A. thesis, Marquette University, 1968.

31. While Indians were a visible element of Milwaukee's population in the early years of settlement, they were gradually removed from the area and, since they were specifically excluded from the census enumeration, elude detailed scrutiny.

32. Brinley Thomas, *Migration and Economic Growth: A Study of Great Britain and the Atlantic Economy* (Cambridge: Harvard University Press, 1954), 296; Marcus Lee Hansen, *The Atlantic Migration, 1607-1860* (New York: Harper and Brothers, 1940), 1-24, 146-198; Maldwyn Allen Jones, *American Immigration* (Chicago: University of Chicago Press, 1960), 94-105; Frank Thistlethwaite, "Migration from Europe Overseas in the Nineteenth and Twentieth Centuries," in Stanley N. Katz and Stanley I. Kutler, eds., *New Perspectives on the American Past* (Boston: Little, Brown, 1969), II, 52-81.

33. William Forbes Adams, *Ireland and the Irish Emigration to the New World from 1815 to the Famine* (New Haven: Yale University Press, 1932), 1-48, 160-165; Hansen, *Atlantic Migration*, 132-135; Arnold Schrier, *Ireland and the American Emigration 1850-1900* (Minneapolis: University of Minnesota Press, 1958), 11-13.

34. Adams, *Irish Emigration*, 160-222; Schrier, *Ireland and the American Emigration*, 3-16; Hansen, *Atlantic Migration*, 244-251; Oscar Handlin, *Boston's Immigrants: A Study in Acculturation* (New York: Atheneum, 1968), 38-47; Robert E. Kennedy, Jr., *The Irish: Emigration, Marriage, Fertility* (Berkeley: University of California Press, 1973).

35. Conrad, *History of Milwaukee County*, II, 439; Flower, *History of Milwaukee*, 1194, 394.

36. Seven percent failed to specify their county of birth. For pre-1836 emigration from Ireland, see Adams, *Irish Emigration*, 187-188; between 1831 and 1835, for example, Ulster provided an estimated 46 percent of the emigrants, Munster 27 percent, and Leinster 16 percent, with Connaught the most backward. The fourth ward may have contained a greater proportion of recent arrivals than other areas of Irish residence in Milwaukee. See Chapter 5.

37. Rowland T. Berthoff, *British Immigrants in Industrial America 1790-1950* (Cambridge: Harvard University Press, 1953), 107-108; Stanley C. Johnson, *A History of Emigration from the United Kingdom to North America, 1763-1912* (London: George Routledge and Sons, Ltd., 1913), 38-67; Maldwyn A. Jones, "The Background to Emigration from Great Britain in the Nineteenth Century," *Perspectives in American History*, 7 (1973), 37-52, 77-91; Charlotte Erickson, *Invisible Immigrants: The Adaptation of English and Scottish Immigrants in Nineteeth Century America* (Coral Gables, Fla.: University of Miami Press, 1972), 23-29, 232-237.

38. An example, perhaps, of the power of the "agrarian myth" discussed by Charlotte Erickson in "Agrarian Myths of English Immigrants," in O. Fritiof Ander, ed., *In the Trek of the Immigrants: Essays Presented to Carl Wittke* (Rock Island, Ill.: Augustana College Library, 1964), 64-79. For biographical information on these British immigrants, see Conrad, *History of Milwaukee County*, III, 174, 126, 175; II, 325; I, 320; II, 396, 457; I, 479; Carroon, "Scotsmen," 23, 27; Conrad, *History*, II, 318, 396, 406; III, 198, 149.

39. Ibid., I, 320; III, 175, 198; I, 479; Buck, *Pioneer History*, II, 93; Conrad, III, 111; II, 406.

40. Mack Walker, *Germany and the Emigration, 1816-1885* (Cambridge:

Harvard University Press, 1964), 1-9, 31-62; Hansen, *Atlantic Migration*, 85-89, 146-198, 211-220; Wolfgang Köllman and Peter Marschalck, "German Emigration to the United States," *Perspectives in American History*, 7 (1973), 512-531.

41. Reprinted in *WB*, March 21, 1846.

42. Walker, *Germany and the Emigration*, 70-78, 143-175; Köllman and Marschalck, "German Emigration," 523, 531-535; see also the discussion and scattered series of official data in Wilhelm Mönckmeier, *Die deutsche überseeische Auswanderung: Ein Beitrag zur deutschen Wanderungsgeschichte* (Jena: Gustav Fischer, 1912), 151-160.

43. Letter from Luther Whittlesey, Bremen, March 25, 1854; ms., SHSW. Whittlesey also assured his correspondent that the emigrating peasants were not revolutionaries; the late disturbances were caused by "idle students and professors" in a "'beer spree' dream of liberty."

44. Schafer, *Four Wisconsin Counties*, 94, 100; Hense-Jensen, *Wisconsin's Deutsch-Amerikaner*, I, 35-36; Levi, "Geographical Origins," 367-368. A Milwaukee priest in 1853 estimated that one third of the city's German community was Roman Catholic; he found persons from Westphalia, Rhenish Prussia, Baden, Rhenish Bavaria, Hesse, and Bavaria dominant in his flock. Anthony Urbanek to the Archbishop of Vienna, 1853, in "Letters of the Right Reverend John Martin Henni and the Reverend Anthony Urbanek," *WMH*, 10 (1926), 89.

45. The 1850 manuscript census lists specific states of birth within Germany for only two of the five Milwaukee wards (2 and 4), and in 1860 for seven of the nine wards (1, 2, 3, 4, 6, 7, 9). The missing wards in 1860 represent a division and expansion of the missing 1850 fifth ward. In 1850 the large German first ward settlement was the oldest area of German residence, and was reputedly more Catholic than the west side wards for which census data on states of origin exist; thus this ward may have contained a higher proportion of persons from southern and western Germany than Table 5 suggests. The two wards for which no data were available in 1860 were not the main centers of German settlement and were atypical in their employment patterns as well. Owing to a coding error, an estimated ten Pommeranian families in 1860 may have been included in the other German category. The eastern provinces of Prussia were not shaded on Figure 4 to avoid a misleading impression: between 1844 and 1859, emigration from these provinces averaged well under 10 percent of the total Prussian emigration, while Pommerania, Brandenburg, and Saxony each averaged around 10 percent of the total, Westphalia 18 percent, and Rhenish Prussia 33.5 percent; Mönckmeier, *Auswanderung*, 83.

46. Thomas C. Cochran, *The Pabst Brewing Company: The History of an American Business* (New York: New York University Press, 1948), 3-7; Bossert, "Reminiscence," ms., *MCHS*; Conrad, *History of Milwaukee County*, II, 336; III, 32; II, 430, 438; III, 203, 185, 82.

47. Conrad, *History of Milwaukee County*, II, 425.

48. Ibid., III, 12; II, 435; Harry H. Anderson, ed., *German-American Pioneers in Wisconsin and Michigan: The Frank-Kerler Letters* (Milwaukee: MCHS, 1971), 56-57, 38.

49. Henry Stern, "The Life Story of a Milwaukee Merchant," *WMH*, 9 (1925), 63; Obituary, Dr. Eduard Wundsch, *BV*, Sept. 6, 1859; Flower, *History of Milwaukee*,

1152; John Gregory, *A New and Vastly Improved Edition of the Industrial Resources of Wisconsin* (Milwaukee: See-Bote Job Print, 1870), I, 120; Moritz Wagner and Carl Scherzer, *Reisen in Nordamerika in den Jahren 1852 und 1853* (Leipzig: Arnoldische Buchhandlung, 1854), II, 123.

50. Cf. Koss, *Milwaukee*, 155; Joseph Schafer, "The Yankee and the Teuton in Wisconsin," *WMH*, 6 (1922), 139. German settlement in Wisconsin increased from 38,064 in 1850 (12 percent of the Wisconsin population) to 116, 808 in 1860 (14 percent). Milwaukee's share of the German immigration did not keep pace with that of the state as a whole, constituting 19 percent in 1850, 14 percent in 1860, at the same time as the city's share of the total state population declined from 7 to 6 percent. J. D. B. DeBow, *The Seventh Census of the United States: 1850* (Washington, D.C.: Robert Armstrong, 1853), 922; Joseph C. G. Kennedy, *Population of the United States in 1860* (Washington, D.C.: Government Printing Office, 1864), 538-539.

51. Franz Löher, *Geschichte und Zustände der Deutschen in Amerika* (Cincinnati: Eggers & Wulkop, 1847), 277-278.

52. Ibid., 275.

53. See the statistics on arrivals of alien passengers in major ports collected in Robert Greenhalgh Albion, *The Rise of New York Port, 1815-1860* (Hamden, Conn.: Archon Books, 1961), 418.

54. "Letters and Diary of Joh. Fr. Diederichs," *WMH*, 7 (1923-24), 218-237, 350-368; Letter 325, Milwaukee, January 1846, typescript in "Germans in the United States" collection, SHSW; Hermann Haertel to Governor Farwell, 1853, ms. in Wisconsin State Archives, Executive Department, Immigration; Rasmus B. Anderson, ed., "Description of a Journey to North America," *WMH*, 1 (1917), 181; John Remeeus, "Record of a Voyage from Netherland to Milwaukee," trans. Hermann Bottema, MCHS; Joseph Schafer, trans., "Christian Traugott Ficker's Advice to Emigrants," *WMH*, 25 (1941-42), 225-226; Jan-Albert Goris, "From 'Oppressed Flanders' to the 'Most Beautiful Country in the World'," *WMH*, 42 (1959), 276; Johann Diefenthaeler letter, Milwaukee, Jan. 16, 1844, ms. and trans., SHSW; Theodore E. F. Hartwig letter, Sept. 25, 1846, trans. typescript, SHSW; Anderson, *German-American Pioneers*, 69; "Norwegian Immigrant Letters," *WMH*, 15 (1932), 356; Milo M. Quaife, ed., *An English Settler in Pioneer Wisconsin: The Letters of Edwin Bottomley, 1842-1850*, in *Collections*, SHSW, 25 (1918), 29-30; Letters 294, 324, 331, "Germans in the United States" collection, SHSW. See also Fred. W. Horn to Governor Barstow, Aug. 1, 1854, ms., Wisconsin State Archives, Executive Department, Immigration.

55. Conrad, *History of Milwaukee County*, III, 74; Gregory, *Industrial Resources*, I, 121; Flower, *History of Milwaukee*, 1199; Conrad, II, 429; III, 199, 74.

56. Kate Everest (Levi), "How Wisconsin Came by Its Large German Element," *Collections*, SHSW, 12 (1892), 298-334; Hense-Jensen, *Wisconsin's Deutsch-Amerikaner*, I, 119-228; Schafer, "Christian Traugott Ficker's Advice," 228; Wagner and Scherzer, *Reisen in Nordamerika*, II, 110-184; Büchele, *Land und Volk*, 198.

57. Karl Quentin, *Reisebilder und Studien aus dem Norden der Vereinigten Staaten von Amerika* (Arnsberg: H. F. Grote, 1851); Ludwig von Baumbach, *Neue Briefe aus den Vereinigten Staaten von Nordamerika in die Heimath mit besonderer Rücksicht auf deutsche Auswanderer* (Cassel: Theodor Fischer, 1856).

58. Hense-Jensen, *Wisconsin's Deutsch-Amerikaner*, I, 128; J. H. Lacher, "The

German Element in Wisconsin," pamphlet (Milwaukee: Steuben Society, 1925), 10-11; Letter 325, Milwaukee, January 1846, in "Germans in the United States" collection, SHSW.

59. Hense-Jensen, *Wisconsin's Deutsch-Amerikaner*, I, 28-29; *MC*, July 20, 1842; *WB*, March 21, 1846.

60. Theodore C. Blegen, "The Competition of the Northwestern States for Immigrants," *WMH*, 3 (1919), 3-29; letters and reports of the agents, ms. in Wisconsin State Archives, Executive Department, Immigration; *BV*, Nov. 12, 1856; March 11, 1857.

61. The editor and publisher was C. Knobelsdorff, former agent of the "German Society," the city's immigrant protection society. The eight-page paper was scheduled to appear twice monthly to "disseminate in Germany, through an exact representation of the trade, commerce, and agricultural conditions of Wisconsin, and through an apt description of our social and political life, a greater knowledge of our situation, so very favorable as it is for immigrants, and thus guide the immigration more and more towards Wisconsin." The fate of the publication is unclear. *BV*, March 11, 1857.

62. *BV*, June 4, 9, July 27, Dec. 22, 25, 1859.

63. Hense-Jensen, *Wisconsin's Deutsch-Amerikaner*, I, 30-35; Rasmus Sorensen to Governor Barstow, ms., Wisconsin State Archives, Executive Department, Immigration; Diefenthaeler, Jan. 16, 1844, ms., SHSW.

64. Mathilde Franziska Anneke, letter, Milwaukee, April 3, 1850, typescript in Anneke Papers, "Biographical Notes," appendix, SHSW; Anderson, *German-American Pioneers*, 76.

65. Conrad, *History of Milwaukee County*, II, 330, 421; *WB*, March 28, 1846; *SB*, May 20, 1853.

66. Conrad, *History of Milwaukee County*, II, 425, 438, 303; Flower, *History of Milwaukee*, 1268; *Milwaukee: A Half Century's Progress, 1846-1896* (Milwaukee: Consolidated Illustrated Co., 1890), 115; Stern, "Life Story," 65-68.

67. In 1850, 11 percent of the German households included children born in other states, 43 percent of the Irish, and 20 percent of the British; percentages for 1860 were Germans 8, Irish 34, and British 25. The measure is a rough one. The presence in a household of a child born in New York, for instance, does not necessarily mean that the family spent any length of time in that state, nor that the family was together at the time of the child's birth. Moreover, the absence of children born elsewhere is no indication that the family did not make stopovers; nor did all children live with their parents to be recorded in the census as a family unit. Finally, such a measure excludes the large numbers of unmarried or childless migrants who may have had migration paths quite dissimilar to those weighted down with family responsibilities.

68. This relationship held for all age groups. Similar ethnic differences in migration patterns were found by Lawrence A. Glasco in his "Ethnicity and Social Structure: Irish, Germans and Native-Born of Buffalo, N.Y., 1850-1860," Ph.D. diss., State University of New York at Buffalo, 1973, 51-52.

69. Hermann Haertel, Wisconsin Commissioner of Emigration in New York, reported to Governor Farwell in 1853 that increasing efforts were being made to sell emigrants in Europe tickets through to their American destination, thus encouraging early choice of settlement area. Rasmus Sorenson of Tolands Prairie, Wis., wrote to

Governor Barstow in 1854 that most emigrants from Denmark selected their destination under the influence of friends and relatives before leaving home. Both letters in Wisconsin State Archives, Executive Department, Immigration.

70. Fred W. Horn to Governor Barstow, Aug. 1, 1854, ms., Wisconsin State Archives, Executive Department, Immigration; Horn's colleague in Quebec in the same year likewise noted that the Irish and English usually remained in Canada or went to some nearby large city, while the Norwegians went directly west.

71. In 1843, a Milwaukee Irishman, probably John Furlong, wrote a series of letters describing Milwaukee and advising Irish farmers and mechanics of the area's opportunities, though stressing that there was little factory labor and that all outdoors work was seasonal. The consequence was described in *MC*, May 31, 1843: "Handbills have been put in circulation in New York, Jersey City, and other places which state that *three thousand* laborers are wanted upon the harbor works at this place, and in consequence of this, hundreds of poor Irishmen have come on here and landed without a cent to help themselves with, they having expended all their means in their efforts to get here at as early a period in the season as possible." Yet there was little actual work available and "it is presumed that this infamous fraud has been perpetrated by the agents of some of the different canal lines." The letters had been "made a pretext for sending laborers here." For an example of a direct advertisement for canal labor, see *AV*, Oct. 3, 1840.

72. *AV*, June 2, 1841; see also April 17, 1841, April 24, 1844; John G. Gregory, *Industrial Resources of Wisconsin* (Chicago: Langdon and Rounds, 1853); Gregory Papers, MCHS; Robert G. Carroon, "John Gregory and the Irish Immigration to Milwaukee," *HMMC*, 27 (June 1971), 51-64.

73. British Temperance Emigration Society and Saving Fund, *Description of the Wisconsin Territory and Some of the States and Territories Adjoining to It* (Liverpool: C. Cutter, 1844).

74. There were only six Irishmen for whom such information was found, five of whom had lived elsewhere before coming to Milwaukee, for an average interval of 6.1 years.

75. Since nonpersisters in 1860 included those who died, as well as those missed by directory compilers, this crude persistence figure should not be interpreted to imply an out-migration of 61 percent; for a discussion of directory coverage, see Appendix.

76. Cf. Stephan Thernstrom, *The Other Bostonians: Poverty and Progress in the American Metropolis, 1880-1970* (Cambridge: Harvard University Press, 1973), 222-223; for rural turnover summaries, see Michael P. Conzen, *Frontier Farming in an Urban Shadow: The Influence of Madison's Proximity on the Agricultural Development of Blooming Grove, Wisconsin, in the Nineteenth Century* (Madison: SHSW, 1971), 48-51.

77. These figures can be compared with rates of persistence for Poughkeepsie, N.Y, in the 1850-60 decade calculated by Clyde Griffen, in his "Workers Divided: The Effect of Craft and Ethnic Differences in Poughkeepsie, New York, 1850-1880," in Stephan Thernstrom and Richard Sennett, eds., *Nineteenth-Century Cities: Essays in the New Urban History* (New Haven: Yale University Press, 1969), 57: Native, 34 percent, Irish, 21 percent, German, 29 percent, English-Scots, 24 percent. As Griffen suggests, those low persistence rates may reflect changes in Poughkeepsie's rate of growth. Since his figures are based on the total potential adult male working force, they also

probably include a greater proportion of mobile young men than do the Milwaukee rates. But there remains the possibility that, especially for groups such as the Irish, Milwaukee was the last stop—the end of the line for many with a highly mobile past. In more general terms, Peter R. Knights found that the native born of Boston were about twice as persistent as the foreign born; given his sample, foreign born can be considered almost synonomous with Irish. Though the statistics are not strictly comparable, this tends to confirm the suggestion of a greater persistence for the Irish in midwestern as opposed to eastern settings. Knights, *The Plain People of Boston, 1830-1860: A Study in City Growth* (New York: Oxford University Press, 1971), 63-64.

78. Peter R. Knights, "Population Turnover, Persistence, and Residential Mobility in Boston, 1830-1860," in Thernstrom and Sennett, *Nineteenth-Century Cities*, 264.

2. Building Blocks of Community

1. John Remeeus, "Record of a Voyage from Netherland to Milwaukee," trans. Hermann Bottema, ms., MCHS.

2. Bayrd Still, *Milwaukee: The History of a City* (Madison: SHSW, 1948), 47; letter from D. Kennedy, Kansas City, Dec. 2, 1897, in Bleyer Papers, SHSW, Milwaukee Area Research Center, University of Wisconsin; *WB*, Dec. 6, 1852; M. A. Boardman, "Waterfront and Shipping in the '50's," in *Early Milwaukee: Papers from the Archives of the Old Settlers' Club* (Milwaukee: Old Settlers' Club, 1916), 67; Peter Van Vechten, ms., Old Settlers' Club Papers, MCHS; Moritz Wagner and Carl Scherzer, *Reisen in Nordamerika in den Jahren 1852 und 1853* (Leipzig: Arnoldische Buchhandlung, 1854), II, 110.

3. Samuel Freeman, *The Emigrant's Hand Book, and Guide to Wisconsin* (Milwaukee: Sentinel and Gazette, 1851), 115, 116, 142; Wagner and Scherzer, *Reisen in Nordamerika*, II, 111; Harry H. Anderson, *German-American Pioneers in Wisconsin and Michigan: The Frank-Kerler Letters* (Milwaukee: MCHS, 1971), 82, 163. Any city directory contains numerous advertisements for such lodgings.

4. "Letters and Diary of Joh. Fr. Diederichs," *WMH*, 7 (1923-24), 353; Jack J. Detzler, " 'I Live Here Happily': A German Immigrant in Territorial Wisconsin," *WMH*, 50 (1967), 255; Angie Kumlien Main, "Thure Kumlien, Koshkonong Naturalist," *WMH*, 27 (1943), 26; Carlin Family Papers, MCHS; Remeeus, "Record"; Heinrich Bosshard, *Anschauungen und Erfahrungen in Nordamerika* (Zürich: Zürcher und Furrer, 1854), 840; D. Kennedy letter, Bleyer Papers; *BV*, June 21, 1859.

5. See for example, the letters of the Frank and Kerler families collected in Anderson, *German-American Pioneers*.

6. Roughly 28 percent of the 205 biographical subjects of this period in Howard Louis Conrad, ed., *History of Milwaukee County from its First Settlement to the Year 1895*, 3 vols. (Chicago: American Biographical Publishing Co., n.d.), were 30 or over when they arrived. Between 38 and 46 subjects arrived in each of the five-year periods between 1835 and 1859; the proportion over 30 varied between 14 and 31 percent before increasing to 38 percent in the 1855-1859 period. The German proportion ($N=64$) over 30 declined from 31 to 15 percent, averaging 21 percent; the native proportion ($N=118$) averaged 31 percent but rose to 47 and 43 percent in the 1850s.

7. Cf. Jack E. Eblen, "An Analysis of Nineteenth-Century Frontier Populations," *Demography*, 2 (1965), 399-413.

8. Earl S. Pomeroy, ed., "Wisconsin in 1847: Notes of John Q. Roods," *WMH*,
33 (1949), 217.

9. Cf. Adna Ferrin Weber, *The Growth of Cities in the Nineteeth Century*,
reprint (Ithaca: Cornell University Press, 1965), 285-300. The sex ratio is defined as the
number of males divided by the number of females, the result multipled by 1,000.

10. For national fertility ratios see Wilson H. Grabill, Clyde V. Kiser, and Pascal
K. Whelpton, *The Fertility of American Women* (New York: John Wiley and Sons,
1958), Table 6, as reproduced in William Peterson, *Population* (New York: Macmillan
Co., 1961), 211. The number of white children enumerated in each census was
increased by 5 percent in this table to adjust for underenumeration. A similar process
has been performed with the Milwaukee ratios, which were computed from the census
data summarized in Figure 6.

11. However, these native wards were also the wards with the greatest numbers
of servants, many of whom were immigrant females. For ward ethnic composition, see
Figure 9.

12. Chi-square tests indicated no statistically significant relationship between age
and nativity in 1850; results were significant at the .05 level in 1860, but the relationship
was weak.

13. A systematic sample of every twentieth female 15 and over was drawn from
the 1860 federal manuscript census to permit some independent analysis of Milwaukee's
immigrant women. Total sample size was 671.

14. See the comments of the elderly John Kerler on the greater adaptability of
youth: Anderson, *German-American Pioneers*, 100; Kerler's plentiful capital was
undoubtedly a major factor in his own successful adaptation.

15. *WB*, April 4, 1846.

16. Anderson, *German-American Pioneers*, 322.

17. In both 1850 and 1860, 87 percent of all sample households were headed by
married persons. Chi-square tests indicated no statistically significant relationship
between nativity and marriage of heads in 1850; the relationship was significant at the
.01 level in 1860. The percentage married declined for the British from 86 to 81, for the
Irish from 88 to 82; it remained constant at 89 percent for the Germans, and increased
from 85 to 86 among the native born. Married heads of household were defined
by the presence of an apparent spouse in the census enumeration of the household.
There was no way of determining married persons with spouses absent. Unmarried
household heads included not only widowed or deserted partners but single persons
living either alone or in groups. If groups of different nativities exhibited differing pro-
pensities for single persons to form their own households rather than board, a bias
would be introduced which cannot be controlled by this sample.

18. The German pattern may reflect the recency of much of the German immigration; if most women immigrated with parents or husbands, as sex ratio estimates
suggest, and if young immigrant men preferred to postpone parenthood until after they
had established themselves, as some German letters and biographies suggest, the
present pattern could result. The more numerous progeny of older German women
could then be attributed to such factors as the migration of already established families,

births delayed during migration and early settlement, and a later age at which children left home. Laurence A. Glasco, however, found that in Buffalo Germans tended to leave home at an earlier age than others; his findings concerning ethnic variation in relative family size and frequency of marriage among women suggest patterns similar to those in Milwaukee; "Ethnicity and Social Structure: Irish, Germans and Native-Born of Buffalo, New York, 1850-1860," Ph.D. diss., State University of New York at Buffalo, 1973, 197-208, 162-164.

19. The mean number of children for native wives of nonmanual workers was 2.1, skilled manual 1.6, semiskilled and unskilled 1.7; comparable figures for Irish wives were 3.0, 2.9, and 2.4, while the mean was 2.4 children in each of the three categories for German wives and 2.3 in each of the categories for the total sample of wives. The native pattern did not result from age differences between manual and nonmanual workers. Cross-tabulation by age of husband showed that in each age group native white collar husbands had more children than their blue collar counterparts. In the sample as a whole, manual laborers' wives whose husbands were under 40 tended to have more children than wives of nonmanual laborers, a pattern which reversed itself after age 40. Given the probability of sample error owing to small cell size, however, too much stress should not be laid on these results.

20. Anderson, *German-American Pioneers*, 236.

21. John Modell and Tamara K. Hareven, in "Urbanization and the Malleable Household: An Examination of Boarding and Lodging in American Families," *Journal of Marriage and the Family*, 35 (1973), 467-479, discuss the frequency of boarding in nineteenth century cities and suggest its positive roles as family surrogate and family support.

22. See the appendix.

23. Cited in Modell and Hareven, "Urbanization and the Malleable Family," 467-469.

24. Anderson, *German-American Pioneers*, 352.

25. Cf. Glasco, "Ethnicity and Social Structure," 197-216.

26. One percent of sample native heads of household were illiterate in both 1850 and 1860, and 3 percent of the British heads in both years. German illiteracy increased from 4 to 5 percent; Irish illiteracy declined from 27 to 21 percent.

27. In 1860 about 14 percent of Irish households were headed by women, who accounted for more than 19 percent of the illiterate heads of household; comparable figures for 1850 were about 5.5 and 6.5 percent. In 1850, 35 percent of Irish heads of household were 30 or under in age and over 45 percent of the illiterate heads. Compare with 16 and 17 percent in 1860, when the 37 percent of Irish householders 31-40 included 41 percent of the illiterate householders.

28. Anderson, *German-American Pioneers*, 372. The following discussion is based upon the family letters collected in this volume.

29. Cf. Helmut Möller, *Die Kleinbürgerliche Familie im 18. Jahrhundert* (Berlin: Walter de Gruyter & Co., 1969); Friedrich Sengle, *Biedermeierzeit: Deutsche Literatur im Spannungsfeld zwischen Restauration und Revolution 1815-1848* (Stuttgart: J. B. Metzler, 1971), I, 48-63; Mack Walker, *German Home Towns: Community, State, and General Estate, 1648-1871* (Ithaca: Cornell University Press, 1971), 307-353.

3. A Better Livelihood

1. Theodore C. Blegen, ed., *Land of Their Choice: The Immigrants Write Home* (Minneapolis: University of Minnesota Press, 1955), 264.

2. Caroline F. Ware, "Immigration," *Encyclopedia of the Social Sciences* (1930), VII, 590; see also S. N. Eisenstadt, *The Absorption of Immigrants: A Comparative Study Based Mainly on the Jewish Community in Palestine and the State of Isreal* (London: Routledge and Kegan Paul, Ltd., 1954), 2-4, 242-245.

3. D. Bezalel Sherman, *The Jew within American Society: A Study in Ethnic Individuality* (Detroit: Wayne University Press, 1961), 26-29; Eisenstadt, *Absorption of Immigrants,* 250-252.

4. Cf. Guido A. Dobbert, "German-Americans between New and Old Fatherland," *American Quarterly,* 19 (1967), 663-680, who argues that the critical stage in the disruption of Cincinnati's German community arrived when the economically successful moved out of the community, depriving it of leadership and its hitherto heterogeneous character.

5. L. von Baumbach, *Neue Briefe aus den Vereinigten Staaten von Nordamerika in die Heimath mit besonderer Rücksicht auf deutsche Auswanderer* (Cassel: Theodor Fischer, 1856), 261.

6. For discussion of the occupational classification utilized, see Appendix. It is, of course, possible to add a longitudinal dimension by tracing individuals and families from one census to the next in the manner of the studies discussed in Stephan Thernstrom, *The Other Bostonians: Poverty and Progress in the American Metropolis, 1880-1970* (Cambridge: Harvard University Press, 1973), 232-250, or by analyzing age cohorts as surrogate summaries for the experience of different generations over time, as in Laurence A. Glasco, "Ethnicity and Social Structure: Irish, Germans and Native-Born of Buffalo, N.Y., 1850-1860," Ph.D. diss., State University of New York at Buffalo, 1973, 102-139. The latter proceeding involves risks when applied to a city as young as Milwaukee, when there is no way of controlling for pre-arrival experience or length of residence in the city; the former was not attempted.

7. See the appendix. Natives constituted 25 percent of the total workforce and 28 percent of the nonheads; comparable percentages for the Irish were 18 for both, for the British 10 for both, and for the Germans 38 and 33.

8. Rearrangement of the occupational status categories for St. Louis, Jersey City, and Detroit was straightforward. In the St. Louis classification, the professional and merchant categories were combined into nonmanual, the category which also included the Jersey City economic elite, professional, white collar, shopkeepers, and government; and the Detroit government, business, professional, and clerk categories. The Jersey City artisan and building trades categories were merged into the present skilled and semiskilled, as were the Detroit skilled and clothes manufacturers. The original Boston list from the manuscript census included 64 occupational categories compressed from 992 distinct occupations listed in the census. Reclassification of most nonmanual categories was straightforward; all the manufacturers and craftsmen were included in skilled, the transportation workers in semiskilled along with stablers, waiters, barbers, domestic servants, policemen, and watchmen. Some manufacturers

and craftsmen may have been proprietors better appearing in the nonmanual category. Fitting the New York data taken from the 1855 manuscript state census was more complex. The classification included 115 categories only roughly grouped according to industry. Thus a good deal of arbitrary discretion was exercised, and in general the percentage distributions in Figure 7 should be considered comparable only to a very rough degree.

9. A comparative analysis of occupational status in Buffalo, Kingston, and Poughkeepsie, New York; Hamilton, Ontario; and Philadelphia found this same ethnic hierarchy in all five cities; Theodore Hershberg, Michael Katz, Stuart Blumin, Laurence Glasco, Clyde Griffin, "Occupation and Ethnicity in Five Nineteenth-Century Cities: A Collaborative Inquiry," *Historical Methods Newsletter*, 7 (1974), 174-216.

10. Von Baumbach, *Neue Briefe*, 269; Samuel Freeman, *The Emigrant's Hand Book, and Guide to Wisconsin* (Milwaukee: Sentinel and Gazette Power Press Plant, 1851), 92; Fr. Pauer, *Die Vereinigten Staaten von Nord-Amerika . . . mit besonderer Beziehung auf Deutsche Auswanderer* (Bremen: Druck und Verlag von F. C. Dubbers, 1847), 68. Traugott Bromme, one of the most popular compilers of advice to German emigrants, for example, advised such persons as factory operatives, dyers, gold and silver smiths, artists, button makers, parfumiers, and so on, to remain in eastern cities; *Hand- und Reisebuch für Auswanderer nach den Vereinigten Staaten von Nord-Amerika* (Beyreuth: Verlag der Buchner'schen Buchhandlung, 1848), passim.

11. See Appendix. Earliest city tax assessment rolls available were for 1861 and listed property by location rather than by owner's name; the Civil War income tax likewise came too late and included too small a proportion of the city's population to be useful. Information on personal property in the 1860 census was not tabulated, since there was no comparable data for 1850. Lee Soltow, in *Patterns of Wealthholding in Wisconsin since 1850* (Madison: University of Wisconsin Press, 1971), 15-28, demonstrates his confidence in the relative accuracy of the 1860 Wisconsin census property returns.

12. See Edward Pessen, *Riches, Class, and Power before the Civil War* (Lexington, Mass.: D. C. Heath and Company, 1973), 31-45; Stuart Blumin, "Mobility and Change in Ante-Bellum Philadelphia," in Stephan Thernstrom and Richard Sennett, *Nineteenth-Century Cities: Essays in the New Urban History* (New Haven: Yale University Press, 1969), 203-205; Robert E. Gallman, "Trends in the Size Distribution of Wealth in the Nineteenth Century: Some Speculations," in Lee Soltow, ed., *Six Papers on the Size Distribution of Wealth and Income* (New York: Columbia University Press, 1969), 22. Note that the Milwaukee curves do not include personal property.

13. Soltow found that in 1860 the wealth of a given native resident of Milwaukee was on average 8.3 percent greater than that of a person a year younger than himself, with the difference among the foreign born 6.6 percent; *Wealthholding in Wisconsin*, 8.

14. Richard G. Frackelton, ed., *The Milwaukee Guide* (Milwaukee: South Side Printing Co., 1896-97), 17.

15. This was a phenomenon evident in other cities of the period; see Stephan Thernstrom, *Poverty and Progress: Social Mobility in a Nineteenth Century City* (New York: Atheneum, 1969), 115-120; Clyde Griffen, "Workers Divided: The Effect of Craft and Ethnic Differences in Poughkeepsie, New York, 1850-1880," in Thernstrom and

Sennett, *Nineteenth-Century Cities*, 66-68; Hershberg et al., "Occupation and Ethnicity," 202-204.

16. Type of dwelling could be determined from the distinction made by the census taker between the dwelling number and the family number assigned to each household; separate dwelling numbers were applied to separate physical structures, family numbers to dwelling units within such structures. Ninety percent of native households lived in single-family dwellings, 92 percent of the British, 89 percent of the Irish, and 80 percent of the Germans.

17. Twenty percent of the natives living in multi-family dwellings owned property, 30 percent of the British, 27 percent of the Irish, and 30 percent of the Germans.

18. Among Germans living in multi-family dwellings, 3 percent were professionals, 0.1 percent proprietors, 2 percent semi-professionals, 7 percent clerical, about 11 percent petty proprietors, 39 percent skilled, 12 percent semiskilled, 18 percent unskilled, and 7 percent not employed; 50 percent of the German petty proprietors in multifamily dwellings reported property holdings, 34 percent of the skilled.

19. Harry H. Anderson, ed., *German-American Pioneers in Wisconsin and Michigan: The Frank-Kerler Letters* (Milwaukee: MCHS, 1971), 156, 335-336.

20. Among native households with boarders, 18 percent were headed by professionals, 18 percent by proprietors, another 18 percent by petty proprietors, 22 percent by skilled workmen, 9 percent by clerical workers; among German households with boarders, 41 percent were headed by skilled workmen, 17 percent by semiskilled, 14 percent by petty proprietors, and 6 percent by laborers. Renters, of course, also took in boarders to ease rent payments.

21. Since the 1850 census did not require employment information for females, tabulation of households with servants in 1850 is far more approximate than in 1860 (see Appendix). This may have led to undercounting of foreign households with foreign born servants in 1850, making the decline in employment of domestic help among the Irish and the Germans in 1860 all the more striking.

22. Soltow, *Patterns of Wealthholding*, 28-32, 36-43; the two immigrants in the top sixteen were the Scottish banker, Alexander Mitchell, and John Martin Henni, the Roman Catholic bishop.

23. A C. Wheeler, *The Chronicles of Milwaukee: Being a Narrative History of the Town from Its Earliest Period to the Present* (Milwaukee: Jermain & Brightman, 1861), 276.

4. The Industrious Worker

1. Daniel Kennedy, letter to Henry Bleyer, Dec. 30, 1897, in Bleyer Papers, SHSW, Milwaukee Area Research Center, University of Wisconsin-Milwaukee.

2. For the Irish stereotype, see Carl Wittke, *The Irish in America* (Baton Rouge: Louisiana State University Press, 1956), 24-27; Carl F. Niehaus, *The Irish in New Orleans 1800-1860* (Baton Rouge: Louisiana State University Press, 1965), 44-57.

3. Fr. Pauer, *Die Vereinigten Staaten von Nord-Amerika, nach erfolgtem Anschluss der Republik Texas* (Bremen: F. C. Dubbers, 1847), 123; Samuel Freeman, *The*

Emigrant's Hand Book, and Guide to Wisconsin (Milwaukee: Sentinel and Gazette, 1851), 116; Franklin E. Town, *Milwaukee City Directory for 1859-60* (Milwaukee: Jermain & Brightman, 1859), 276. Charlotte Erickson, *American Industry and the European Immigrant 1860-1885* (Cambridge: Harvard University Press, 1957) discusses the general lack of organized sources of job information in America at the time.

4. Rudolf H. Koss, *Milwaukee* (Milwaukee: Herold, 1871), 369.

5. In September of 1856, for example, the society found jobs for 56 persons, in November for 49, but found it impossible to find work for all who applied; in January 1857, only 25 of 36 applicants could be placed. The society actively sought the cooperation of possible employers, as when it advertised for persons who needed woodcutting done; it likewise contacted farmers and was able to place some immigrants in agricultural work. *BV*, Oct. 15, Dec. 10, 1856; Jan. 7, Feb. 4, 1857.

6. The *Seebote*, a newspaper aimed at a Roman Catholic readership, contained a greater frequency of such advertisements than did the other, more liberal papers; e.g. *SB*, Jan. 9, Feb. 2, April 14, May 18, 1854.

7. *AV*, Oct. 3, 1840; Koss, *Milwaukee*, 129; *MC*, May 31, 1843; *SB*, July 8, 1853; R. N. Messenger, letter, Oct. 21, 1853, in Messenger Papers, SHSW; Joseph D. Sprague, letter, April 19, 1855, in Sprague Papers, SHSW; *BV*, Feb. 3, 1858; Freeman, *Emigrant's Hand Book*, 19. For examples of immigrants who used public works projects to acquire a business stake, see Howard Louis Conrad, ed., *History of Milwaukee County from Its First Settlement to the Year 1895* (Chicago: American Biographical Publishing Co., n.d.), III, 214; Frank A. Flower, *History of Milwaukee, Wisconsin* (Chicago: The Western Historical Co., 1881), 1305.

8. Nelson Olin, "Reminiscences of Milwaukee in 1835-36," *WMH*, 13 (1930), 220-221; Benjamin Kurtz Miller, "Recollections of Early Milwaukee," ms., SHSW; James S. Buck, *Milwaukee under the Charter* (Milwaukee: Symes, Swain & Co., 1884), I, 146; *BV*, May 20, 1857.

9. James S. Buck, *Pioneer History of Milwaukee* (Milwaukee: Swain & Tate, 1890), II, 109-110, 183; Conrad, *History of Milwaukee County*, I, 364-365; II, 421, 439; Flower, *History of Milwaukee*, 1352, 1583, 1593, 1661; "Family History," George Abert and Family Papers, MCHS.

10. Moritz Wagner and Carl Scherzer, *Reisen in Nordamerika in den Jahren 1852 und 1853* (Leipzig: Arnoldische Buchhandlung, 1854), II, 110.

11. Pauer, *Vereinigten Staaten*, 119; Buck, *Pioneer History*, II, 110.

12. Margaret Walsh, *The Manufacturing Frontier: Pioneer Industry in Antebellum Wisconsin 1830-1860* (Madison: SHSW, 1972), 171-209; Harry H. Anderson, ed., *German-American Pioneers in Wisconsin and Michigan: The Frank-Kerler Letters, 1849-1864* (Milwaukee: MCHS, 1971), 381; O. B. Messenger letter, May 28, 1849, in Messenger Papers, SHSW; *BV*, Oct. 15, Dec. 10, 1856; Jan. 7, 1857; Letter 294, Milwaukee, Feb. 1846, ms., "Germans in the United States," SHSW; Johann Diefenthaeler, Jan. 16, 1844, letter, ms. and trans., SHSW. Reports of wages for casual labor varied from 46¢ plus board in 1844, to 65¢ without in 1849, from 75¢ to $1.00 without meals in 1852 to the high of $1.50 in 1856; John Remeeus, "Record of Voyage from Netherland to Milwaukee," trans. Herman Bottema, ms., MCHS; Diefenthaeler letter, SHSW; Anderson, *German-American Pioneers*, 71; *BV*, Oct. 15, 1856. For the relationship between laborers' and artisans' wages, see Wagner and Scherzer, *Reisen in Nordamerika*, II, 182.

13. *MC*, May 31, 1843; Anderson, *German-American Pioneers*, 73-74.

14. *SB*, July 10, 12, 1853; Thomas W. Gavett, *Development of the Labor Movement in Milwaukee* (Madison: University of Wisconsin Press, 1965), 7-8.

15. The pages of the German daily newspapers contained frequent notices of such accidents and comments on the consequences for the families of the injured; for mutual benefit associations, see Chapter 6.

16. In one instance, a mason's helper without permanent employment in any one place, whose personal spending habits were not particularly thrifty and who was supporting a wife and four children, was able in the course of five years to buy half a lot and a small house worth about $250, for which he owed $50 plus interest at the end of that period; *BV*, March 13, 1860.

17. The family ultimately prospered: the gift of a cow enabled the mother to start a dairy, and clerkships for the sons with leading Milwaukee merchants led to a dry goods business of their own; Conrad, *History of Milwaukee County*, III, 87.

18. *BV*, March 13, 1860; Charles D. Goff, "The Swill Children of Milwaukee," *HMMC*, 16 (March 1960), 9-11. The *Sentinel* in 1854 referred to these "swill children" as a "saucy, thievish crew" who "dart into every back door of our dwellings, unbidden laying their thievish hands upon everything within their reach"; many householders, however, appreciated the free garbage removal service; quoted in Goff, 9.

19. Flower, *History of Milwaukee*, 1289, 1315, 1527; see also *SB*, April 1, June 25, 1853, for examples of German youths advertising for apprenticeships.

20. Freeman, *Emigrant's Hand Book*, 43-44; see also Pauer, *Vereinigten Staaten*, 123-124. "They pay me no Salary," wrote one young German apprentice clerk, "still my Father don't pay them anything for Boarding and Lodgeing." Anderson, *German-American Pioneers*, 256.

21. Factors other than child labor influenced these figures. For one thing, the city's schools were too few and too small to accommodate all potential students, and were especially inadequate in the fringe areas where many immigrants settled (see Chapter 6). In addition, the census included many transient families present in the city for too short a period of time to consider schooling.

22. According to the sample of females 15 and over in the 1860 manuscript census, 62 percent of the 118 employed women were live-in servants, 18 percent seamstresses; the only other occupations (in order of frequency) were: washerwoman, teacher, boardinghouse keeper, dressmaker, milliner, and typemaker.

23. Freeman, *Emigrant's Hand Book*, 43; Carl de Haas, *North America. Wisconsin. Hints for Emigrants* (original publication, Elberfeld: Julius Bädecker Verlag, 1848; trans. F. J. Rueping, privately printed, 1943), 57; Pauer, *Vereinigten Staaten*, 68-70; Traugott Bromme, *Hand- und Reisebuch für Auswanderer nach den Vereinigten Staaten von Nord-Amerika* (Beyreuth: Verlag der Buchner'schen Buchhandlung, 1848), 415; *BV*, March 13, 1860.

24. Anderson, *German-American Pioneers*, 546, 378, 215.

25. *A Merry Briton in Pioneer Wisconsin* (orig. Anon., *Life in the West*; London: Saunders and Otley, 1842; Madison: SHSW, 1950), 32. Table 25 is based on a special tabulation of all servant girls in Ward 1 in 1850 and Ward 7 in 1860 (formerly part of Ward 1), the wards with the largest numbers of native households with servants. Immigrant households employing servants were not tabulated, in part because it was difficult to distinguish servants from other foreign-born household members in

1850; not until 1860 did the census note the occupations of women.

26. Letter, Sept. 13, 1845, Messenger Papers; de Haas, *North America*, 57.

27. E.g. Charles E. Wendt's advertisement for such land in *BV*, May 23, 1858.

28. In 1849, J. Ambrose of Chicago commented on the absence of vegetable gardens within Milwaukee; such needs were supplied, he said, by surrounding farmers. Quoted in Bayrd Still, ed., "Milwaukee in 1836 and 1849: A Contemporary Description," *WMH*, 53 (1970), 297. Yet by the 1850s, the west side German area particularly was acquiring a reputation for its gardens; William George Bruce, ed., *History of Milwaukee City and County* (Chicago: The S. J. Clarke Publishing Co., 1922), I, 767. See also Anderson, *German-American Pioneers*, 336, 355; "Letters of the Right Reverend John Martin Henni and the Reverend Anthony Urbanek," *WMH*, 10 (1926), 77.

29. Conrad, *History of Milwaukee County*, III, 82. Charles King recalled that in his boyhood the family's milk was supplied daily by an Irish woman from the third ward; "Memoirs of a Busy Life," *WMH*, 5 (1922), 215.

30. *The Milwaukee City Directory, for 1851-52* (Milwaukee: Parsons and Van Slyck, 1851), *xvii*; Bromme, *Hand- und Reisebuch*, 416; Walsh, *Manufacturing Frontier*, 171-209.

31. Wagner and Scherzer, *Reisen in Nordamerika*, II, 183; Pauer, *Vereinigten Staaten*, 99, 78-80, 83; Joseph Schafer, trans., "Christian Traugott Ficker's Advice to Emigrants," *WMH*, 25 (1941), 228; Bromme, *Hand- und Reisebuch*, 419, 422, 424.

32. Bromme, *Hand- und Reisebuch*, 417-426; Pauer, *Vereinigten Staaten*, 83, 84.

33. Bromme, *Hand- und Reisebuch*, 419-430; Pauer, *Vereinigten Staaten*, 84, 101; Diefenthaeler letter, SHSW; Anderson, *German-American Pioneers*, 71-72; Letter 294, Milwaukee, February 1846, and Letter 324, Milwaukee, December 1846, "Germans in the United States," SHSW.

34. Pauer, *Vereinigten Staaten*, 81-126; Bromme, *Hand- und Reisebuch*, 417-424.

35. Robert Ernst, *Immigrant Life in New York City, 1825-1863* (New York: King's Crown Press, 1949), 75; Wagner and Scherzer, *Reisen in Nordamerika*, II, 183; Joseph Schafer, ed., *Intimate Letters of Carl Schurz, 1841-1869* (Madison: SHSW, 1928), III, 139.

36. The careers of such prominent early German settlers as Charles Geisberg, Hermann Haertel, August Greulich, and John Tesch as recorded in the pages of Rudolf Koss' *Milwaukee* are extremes of the pattern of changing occupations which can be traced for many lesser known individuals, both immigrant and native, through the various city directories.

37. Oscar Handlin, *Boston's Immigrants* (New York: Atheneum, 1968), 235.

38. Compare with the ethnic specialization demonstrated for five eastern cities in Theodore Hershberg, Michael Katz, Stuart Blumin, Laurence Glasco, and Clyde Griffen, "Occupation and Ethnicity in Five Nineteenth-Century Cities: A Collaborative Inquiry," *Historical Methods Newsletter*, 7 (1974), 202.

39. These percentages reflect the contributions of other nationalities not tabulated in Table 24.

40. "Letters of the Right Reverend John Martin Henni . . . ," 78, 79.

41. The census did not make consistent distinctions between employers and employees, masters and journeymen; hence, exact ratios of one to the other cannot be calculated.

42. Conrad, *History of Milwaukee County*, II, 476; III, 198; I, 463-464; see also Buck, *Pioneer History*, II, 160; Conrad, I, 477; III, 126, 175, for other examples.

43. Based upon data made available by Margaret Walsh, compiled from the manuscript census of manufacturing for 1860.

44. Walsh, *Manufacturing Frontier*, 173, 175, 198-200; much of the following is based upon summaries of Milwaukee manufacturing by craft made available by Margaret Walsh, further supplemented in the cases of brewers, tanners, butchers, bakers, builders, cabinetmakers, tailors, shoemakers, and coopers by my own extraction of data from the manuscript manufacturing censuses for 1850 and 1860 for firms whose owners had clearly German names.

45. Conrad, *History of Milwaukee County*, III, 62, 99; Flower, *History of Milwaukee*, 394; Charles E. Schefft, "The Tanning Industry in Milwaukee: A History of Its Frontier Origins and Its Development," M.A. thesis, University of Wisconsin, 1938, 26; John G. Gregory, *History of Milwaukee, Wisconsin* (Chicago: The S. J. Clarke Publishing Company, 1931), I, 525.

46. Margaret Walsh, "Industrial Opportunity on the Urban Frontier: 'Rags to Riches' and Milwaukee Clothing Manufacturers, 1840-1880," *WMH*, 57 (1974), 175-194; Gregory, *History of Milwaukee*, I, 525.

47. Walsh, "Industrial Opportunity"; Conrad, *History of Milwaukee County*, II, 430, 438; III, 137; Flower, *History of Milwaukee*, 1243; Buck, *Milwaukee under the Charter*, I, 234.

48. Flower, *History of Milwaukee*, 1457; Koss, *Milwaukee*, 118, 192, 385; Stanley Baron, *Brewed in America: A History of Beer and Ale in the United States* (Boston: Little, Brown and Co., 1962), 186. This discussion, except where otherwise noted, is based upon analysis of brewers listed in the manufacturing census manuscripts, using city directories to confirm ownership changes, site continuity, and occupational backgrounds of brewery owners.

49. Koss, *Milwaukee*, 118, 158-160, 237, 317, 345, 385-386; Buck, *Pioneer History*, II, 116; Flower, *History of Milwaukee*, 1457, 1461; Thomas C. Cochran, *The Pabst Brewing Company: The History of an American Business* (New York: New York University Press, 1948), 5-35; Conrad, *History of Milwaukee County*, I, 334-335; Bayrd Still, *Milwaukee: The History of a City* (Madison: SHSW, 1948), 189.

50. Julius P. Bolivar McCabe, *Directory of the City of Milwaukee, for the Years 1847-48* (Milwaukee: Wilson & King, 1847), 68; Flower, *History of Milwaukee*, 1461; Gregory, *History of Milwaukee*, I, 539; Still, *Milwaukee*, 189; Conrad, *History of Milwaukee County*, II, 336; Koss, *Milwaukee*, 272; *Milwaukee: A Half Century's Progress, 1846-1896* (Milwaukee: Consolidated Illustrating Co., 1890), 222.

51. Koss, *Milwaukee*, 272, 289; Still, *Milwaukee*, 188; Gregory, *History of Milwaukee*, I, 589; Flower, *History of Milwaukee*, 1463; Conrad, *History of Milwaukee County*, II, 327-28.

52. Walsh, *Manufacturing Frontier*, 187; for detailed discussion of the careers of minor as well as major brewers, insofar as they can be traced, see Kathleen Neils Conzen, " 'The German Athens': Milwaukee and the Accommodation of its Immigrants, 1836-1860," Ph.D. diss., University of Wisconsin, 1972, 222-232; the following generalizations are based upon that discussion.

53. Gregory, *History of Milwaukee*, I, 525.

54. Pauer, *Vereinigten Staaten*, 76; Gregory, *History of Milwaukee*, I, 536.

55. Conrad, *History of Milwaukee County*, II, 303, 308; *An Illustrated Description of Milwaukee* (Milwaukee: The Sentinel Co., 1890), 133; Still, *Milwaukee*, 187-188; Walsh, *Manufacturing Frontier*, 190-191.

56. Gregory, *History of Milwaukee*, I, 536-537; Schefft, "Tanning Industry," 26; Flower, *History of Milwaukee*, 1440-1441; Still, *Milwaukee*, 188; *Industrial History of Milwaukee* (Milwaukee: E. E. Barton, 1886), 96; *Illustrated Description*, 13; Koss, *Milwaukee*, 169.

57. Wagner and Scherzer, *Reisen in Nordamerika*, II, 183; the reference to shoe-makers is in some contradiction to present findings.

58. Gregory, *History of Milwaukee*, I, 521.

59. Walsh, *Manufacturing Frontier*, 191-194; Buck, *Pioneer History*, II, 131; Still, *Milwaukee*, 64.

60. Conrad, *History of Milwaukee County*, II, 425; Gregory, *History of Milwaukee*, I, 525; Flower, *History of Milwaukee*, 1229.

61. Koss, *Milwaukee*, 254; Walsh, *Manufacturing Frontier*, 202-203.

62. Koss, *Milwaukee*, 136, 158, 252, 317; Conrad, *History of Milwaukee County*, III, 169; II, 371-372; Flower, *History of Milwaukee*, 1177.

63. For examples, see Conrad, *History of Milwaukee County*, I, 320; II, 318; III, 174; Robert G. Carroon, "Scotsmen in Old Milwaukee, 1810-1860," HMMC, 25 (1969), 32.

64. James Seville, address to the Old Settlers' Club, 1897, quoted in Gregory, *History of Milwaukee*, I, 546.

65. MC, Dec. 28, 1842; Jan. 29, April 16, 1845; Buck, *Pioneer History*, II, 150; Gavett, *Labor Movement*, 4-6; Milwaukee Writers' Project, *History of Milwaukee County* (Milwaukee: Milwaukee Public Library, 1947), 228; MWS, Aug. 1, 1848. Over two thirds of the 27 shipbuilders listed in the 1850 census were native Americans or Canadians.

66. VF, Oct. 26, Nov. 9, 1848; March 15, 1849.

67. VF, Nov. 9, 23, 1848; March 15, May 17, 1849; Koss, *Milwaukee*, 277-278.

68. See Chapter 6.

69. Koss, *Milwaukee*, 337, 381-383; Gavett, *Labor Movement*, 7; "Biographical Notes," 29, Anneke Papers, SHSW; Milwaukee Writers' Project, *Milwaukee County*, 229; SB, March 5, 1853; May 24, 1854; WB, Nov. 20, 1850; May 31, 1854; Jan. 24, 1855.

70. SB, Aug. 26, 1853; Feb. 4, 28, April 4, May 4, 1854; WB, Sept. 14, 28, 1853; Gavett, *Labor Movement*, 8-10; BV, March 10, 30, May 26, 1860; MA, July 27, 28, 31, Sept. 22, 1860.

71. MA, Oct. 19, 23, 1860; BV, Dec. 18, 1859.

72. Cf. P. H. Noyes, *Organization and Revolution: Working-Class Associations in the German Revolutions of 1848-1849* (Princeton: Princeton University Press, 1966); F. A. Sorge, "Die Arbeiterbewegung in den Vereinigten Staaten, 1850-1860," *Neue Zeit* (New York, 1890), 1900-1999 (Bound Copy, SHSW); John R. Commons et al., *History of Labour in the United States*, I (New York: The Macmillan Co., 1918).

73. Dun and Bradstreet agents' reports, available in manuscript at the Baker Library of the Harvard Business School, could profitably be utilized to add another

dimension to this treatment of immigrant mercantile prospects; see the discussion of these reports in Walsh, *Manufacturing Frontier*, 230-232. Not all firms were covered by the reports.

74. Reprinted in Gregory, *History of Milwaukee*, I, 439; other Germans on the list included seven manufacturers, a contractor, two doctors, and a bishop.

75. About 57 percent of the city's retail grocers in 1860 were German, but only 18 percent of its wholesale grocers; Germans in 1859 constituted some 92 percent of the retail tobacconists but only 25 percent of the wholesale tobacco dealers; 65 percent of the retail dry goods dealers, 40 percent of the wholesale. Fifty-nine percent of the wine and liquor dealers, 62 percent of the clothiers and 75 percent of the crockery store owners were German, but only 8 percent of the commission merchants, 15 percent of the lumber dealers, 19 percent of the produce dealers, 25 percent of the hardware, stove, and implement dealers, and 35 percent of the real estate agents (percentages estimated on the basis of names appearing in the classified sections of the 1859 and 1860 city directories).

76. Wagner and Scherzer, *Reisen in Nordamerika*, II, 183-184.

77. L. von Baumbach, *Neue Briefe aus den Vereinigten Staaten von Nordamerika in die Heimath* (Cassel: Theodor Fischer, 1856), 251-255; Bromme, *Hand- und Reisebuch*, 425, 434-435; Anderson, *German-American Pioneers*, 531; Pauer, *Vereinigten Staaten*, 137-146.

78. *WB*, April 4, June 6, Nov. 21, 1846; Daniel S. Curtiss, *Western Portraiture, and Emigrants Guide: A Description of Wisconsin, Illinois, and Iowa* (New York: J. H. Colton, 1852), 341; Koss, *Milwaukee*, 272; *BV*, Oct. 8, 1856. That such careers did not always proceed smoothly is illustrated by the extreme case of one young trained German clerk who could find no job because of his lack of English, whose failure to make a living peddling led to suicide one day on a Milwaukee beach; *WB*, Nov. 21, 1846.

79. Henry Stern, "The Life Story of a Milwaukee Merchant," *WMH*, 9 (1925), 63-79.

80. Anderson, *German-American Pioneers*, 126-127, 153-154, 376, 424.

81. Conrad, *History of Milwaukee County*, II, 429; Flower, *History of Milwaukee*, 1308; Gregory, *History of Milwaukee*, I, 448-449; Buck, *Pioneer History*, II, 89; for other examples, see Gregory, *History of Milwaukee*, I, 519; Conrad, *History of Milwaukee County*, I, 474; II, 339, 368-370, 403-404, 435; III, 91, 102, 203; *Industrial History*, 111; *Half-Century's Progress*, 115, 136; Koss, *Milwaukee*, 272; Flower, *History of Milwaukee*, 1206, 1268; Buck, *Milwaukee under the Charter*, I, 234, 307.

82. Theodore A. Anderson, *A Century of Banking in Wisconsin* (Madison: SHSW, 1954), 22-24.

83. Ibid., 30; Jesse M. Van Slyck, *Milwaukee City Directory and Business Advertiser 1854-55* (Milwaukee: Starrs' Book and Job Office, 1854), 206-207, 209; Koss, *Milwaukee*, 422, 455-456; *Annual Report of the Bank Comptroller of the State of Wisconsin*, 1854, 1855.

84. Flower, *History of Milwaukee*, 1594; Koss, *Milwaukee*, 156, 216, 422; Van Slyck, *1854 City Directory*, 372; *Comptroller's Report*, 1854-57; *BV*, April 22, Sept. 30, 1857; Anderson, *Century of Banking*, 36.

85. Conrad, *History of Milwaukee County*, II, 393; Koss, *Milwaukee*, 215; *Comptroller's Report*, 1856-60; *BV*, June 10, 1857; Jan. 4, 1860. The Comptroller's

Reports also indicate that several Germans were also shareholders in non-German Milwaukee banks.

86. Bruce, *Milwaukee City and County*, I, 375; Koss, *Milwaukee*, 370; *BV*, Oct. 29, 1856; Oct. 14, 1859.

87. Twelve of the 20 sample tavern and hotel keepers in 1850 were German, four Irish, and two British; by 1860, 35 of the 53 were German, none Irish, five British; property averages exclude one extreme holding in each instance.

88. Flower, *History of Milwaukee*, 1491-1496; other tavern keepers included in Flower came into the business from cabinetmaking, farming, a feed store, night watchman, and tailoring.

89. For both groups combined, some 48 could not be located in the 1856 directory, while 22 percent followed some trade other than grocering either in 1856 or 1851.

90. Pauer, *Vereinigten Staaten*, 152; Bromme, *Hand- und Reisebuch*, 437-438; Anderson, *German-American Pioneers*, 317.

91. Enoch Chase, "Reminiscences," ms., SHSW, Milwaukee Area Research Center, University of Wisconsin-Milwaukee; Buck, *Pioneer History*, I, 301; Flower, *History of Milwaukee*, 658, 665, 668; Conrad, *History of Milwaukee County*, III, 147.

92. Koss, *Milwaukee*, 131, 155-157, 272, 289, 363, 386; Georg von Bosse, *Das deutsche Element in den Vereinigten Staaten* (Stuttgart: Chr. Belsersche Verlagsbuchhandlung, 1908), 188-189; Conrad, *History of Milwaukee County*, I, 363; II, 432; John Gregory, *A New and Vastly Improved Edition of the Industrial Resources of Wisconsin* (Milwaukee: See-Bote Job Print, 1870), I, 180. Salomon was for a time Civil War governor of Wisconsin.

93. Conrad, *History of Milwaukee County*, III, 100; I, 372; for biographies of Milwaukee's early physicians, see Louis Frederick Frank, *The Medical History of Milwaukee 1834-1914* (Milwaukee: Germania Publishing Co., 1915), 9-37; Frederick Luening, Johann Guenther (a former member of the Frankfort Parliament), and G. Aigner were others for whom politics and cultural participation took precedence over the practice of medicine in Milwaukee.

94. Francis Huebschmann Papers, MCHS. All but one of the German doctors in the 1859 city directory had their offices in German neighborhoods.

95. Frank, *Medical History*, 117-124; Conrad, *History of Milwaukee County*, I, 447.

96. Frank, *Medical History*, 24-25, 12; Johnson lived among the wealthy Yankees, as did the two English physicians.

97. Ibid., 11, 27; Conrad, *History of Milwaukee County*, III, 91; Buck, *Pioneer History*, II, 126; Gregory, *New Industrial Resources*, II, 90-91; Flower, *History of Milwaukee*, 1657; Carl Wittke, *Refugees of Revolution: The German Forty-Eighters in America* (Philadelphia: University of Pennsylvania Press, 1952), 116; "Biographical Notes," Anneke Papers, SHSW; Wilhelm Schulte, *Fritz Anneke: Ein Leben für die Freiheit in Deutschland und in den USA* (Dortmund: Im Verlage des Historischen Vereins Dortmund, 1961). In *MC*, Oct. 19, 1842, "an educated German Gentleman, lately come into this place" advertised that he wished a chance to learn English more perfectly and so would be willing to work in a store "for any reasonable compensation" or offered to give language lessons to "some good family." Karl Julius Kern, later Milwaukee lawyer and politician, began as a language teacher in 1844, before successively

attempting soapmaking, Latin farming, city speculation, running a starch factory, and finally a Latin Grocery, which was really a saloon; Koss, *Milwaukee*, 155-158.

98. Wilhelm Hense-Jensen, *Wisconsin's Deutsch-Amerikaner bis zum Schluss der neunzehnten Jahrhunderts* (Milwaukee: Im Verlage der Deutschen Gesellschaft, 1900), I, 153.

99. A. C. Wheeler, *The Chronicles of Milwaukee* (Milwaukee: Jermain & Brightman, 1861), 279.

100. William George Bruce, "Old Milwaukee's Yankee Hill," *WMH*, 30 (1947), 291.

5. The Private Residences of Our Citizens

1. Moritz Wagner and Carl Scherzer, *Reisen in Nordamerika in den Jahren 1852 und 1853* (Leipzig: Arnoldische Buchhandlung, 1854), II, 114.

2. See the references in "Introduction," note 13.

3. William G. Bruce, ed., *History of Milwaukee, City and County* (Chicago: S. J. Clarke Publishing Co., 1922), I, 780; Bruce, "Old Milwaukee's Yankee Hill," *WMH*, 30 (1947), 289-291; *MA*, Oct. 18, 1860; Frederika Bremer, *Homes of the New World* (New York: Harper & Brothers, 1853), 615; City of Milwaukee, Department of City Development, *Milwaukee's Land Use Report* (1964), 24; Bill Hooker, *Glimpses of an Earlier Milwaukee* (Milwaukee: Milwaukee Journal, 1929), 27, 68; James S. Buck, *Milwaukee under the Charter* (Milwaukee: Symes, Swain & Co., 1884), III, 135; Henry S. Lucas, "Reminiscences of Arend Jan Brusse on Early Dutch Settlement in Milwaukee," *WMH*, 30 (1946), 88.

4. The index of dissimilarity can be interpreted as indicating the percentage of any one group which would have to move in order that its distribution among areal subunits would resemble that of the group with which it is being compared. Lack of segregation yields a minimum index of 0, complete segregation a theoretical maximum of 100; an index of 25 is generally accepted as a cutoff point, below which little segregation is present. In calculation, the following formula was used: $D = \frac{1}{2} \Sigma / x_i \text{-} y_i /$ where x_i represents the proportion of any total nativity group present in any ward i, and y_i represents the proportion of the total group with which it is being compared which is present in that ward; or, where the index is used as a measure of segregation of one group from all other groups, the proportion of total nongroup members present in that ward. For discussions of the index, see Otis Dudley Duncan and Beverly Duncan, "A Methodological Analysis of Segregation Indexes," *American Sociological Review*, 20 (1955), 210-217; Karl E. and Alma F. Taeuber, *Negroes in Cities* (Chicago: Aldine Publishing Co., 1965), 203-204, 223-238; Stanley Lieberson, *Ethnic Patterns in American Cities* (Glencoe, Ill.: The Free Press, 1963), 30-39.

5. Since the index tends to increase with decreasing size of areal units as it isolates smaller clusters, indices for 1860 were calculated using both 1850 ward boundaries and the new boundaries of 1857. Old ward 2 included new wards 2, 6, and 9; old ward 1 included new wards 1 and 7; old ward 5 included new wards 5 and 8.

6. Lieberson, *Ethnic Patterns*, 76, 84-85, 206-218; Sam Bass Warner, Jr., and Colin B. Burke, "Cultural Change and the Ghetto," *Journal of Contemporary History*, 4 (1969), 184. It is unclear whether the Warner and Burke indices are calculated in a

manner strictly comparable to those of Lieberson and other studies cited in this chapter.

7. Differences in the data used to calculate the indices for the various cities should be noted. Milwaukee indices were calculated for a sample of all heads of household, St. Louis indices for a sample of males 18 or older, Detroit indices from a city directory compilation, Buffalo indices for the entire population, Pittsburgh indices from a count of white males 21 or older, Boston indices for the entire population, and Philadelphia indices apparently for the entire population. Indices based on the distribution of the entire population could be expected to yield lower values, since they include the native born children resident with foreign born parents. Audrey Louise Olson, for example, found a segregation index for the Germans of St. Louis in 1850 of 29.3 using the entire population ("St. Louis Germans, 1850-1920: The Nature of an Immigrant Community and Its Relation to the Assimilation Process," Ph.D. diss., University of Kansas, 1970, 52); when indices of dissimilarity were calculated for the entire population of Milwaukee in 1850 using the Prieger tabulation, the index for natives and Irish dropped to 27.1, for natives and Germans to 24.7, and for Germans and Irish to 44.8. Use of the adult population presents a clearer indication of the role of ethnicity in residential structure, since it is adults who make residential decisions. The Pittsburgh, St. Louis, and Detroit indices were calculated from ward statistics presented in the cited studies; remaining indices were taken directly from those studies. Frederick Anthony Hodes calculated his own indices of dissimilarity for St. Louis but the method of calculation is unclear; he found an index of 14 for the Irish in 1850, 21 in 1860; 21 for the Germans in 1850, 16 in 1860; "The Urbanization of St. Louis," Ph.D. diss., St. Louis University, 1973, 40.

8. Warner and Burke, "Cultural Change."

9. For a house-by-house map of central Milwaukee residence patterns by nativity of head of household for all households in 1850, see Kathleen Neils Conzen, "Mapping Manuscript Census Data for Nineteenth Century Cities," *Historical Geography Newsletter*, 4 (Spring 1974), 1-7; some of the material which follows appeared, with differing emphasis, in Conzen, "Patterns of Residence in Early Milwaukee," in Leo F. Schnore, ed., *The New Urban History* (Princeton: Princeton University Press, 1975), 145-183.

10. See the appendix for a description of how cells were delimited and the criteria by which they were combined into ethnic areas.

11. Methods used in defining ethnic areas created biases toward native-British and German-other combinations; see the appendix.

12. For tables providing a detailed breakdown of patterns within individual areas, see Kathleen Neils Conzen, " 'The German Athens': Milwaukee and the Accommodation of its Immigrants, 1836-1860," Ph.D. diss., University of Wisconsin, 1972, 307, 312, 314, 316, 318.

13. Ibid.

14. Frank A. Flower, *History of Milwaukee, Wisconsin* (Chicago: Western Historical Company, 1881), 143; Rudolf H. Koss, *Milwaukee* (Milwaukee: Herold, 1871), 74, 15, 98, 121; A. C. Wheeler, *The Chronicles of Milwaukee* (Milwaukee: Jermain & Brightman, 1861), 74-76; James S. Buck, *Pioneer History of Milwaukee* (Milwaukee: Swain & Tate, 1890), II, 109; Benjamin Kurtz Miller, "Recollections of Early Milwaukee," ms., SHSW; Robert Davies, "Early Buildings of Milwaukee" and "Life in Milwaukee Fifty Years Ago," *MWS*, Oct. 16, 1895; Edward Hamming, *The Port of Mil-

waukee (Rock Island, Ill.: Augustana College Library, 1953), 24-26.

15. Davies, "Early Buildings"; Robert Sutherland, "Reminiscences of a Twenty Months' Residence in Milwaukee in 1851-52-53," *Evening Wisconsin* (Milwaukee), July 12, 1904; *Milwaukee's Land Use Report*, 12-20; Buck, *Milwaukee under the Charter*, I, 135.

16. Davies, "Early Buildings"; Wagner and Scherzer, *Reisen in Nordamerika*, II, 112; Wheeler, *Chronicles*, 121-122; Samuel Freeman, *The Emigrant's Hand Book, and Guide to Wisconsin* (Milwaukee: Sentinel and Gazette, 1851), 80; John Gregory, *Industrial Resources of Wisconsin* (Chicago: Langdon & Rounds, 1853), 291; *An Exposition of the Business of Milwaukee* (Milwaukee: A. Baylies, 1863), 13-15; Karl Quentin, *Reisebilder und Studien aus dem Norden der Vereinigten Staaten von Amerika* (Arnsberg: H. F. Grote, 1851), 131.

17. For maps detailing these trends, see Conzen, "German Athens," 281-284. I am indebted to Sheila Kaplan Bradford for analyzing the 1850 patterns in a seminar paper, "Milwaukee 1850: A Study of the C.B.D. and the Occupational and Ethnic Residence Locations Related to It," Department of Geography, University of Wisconsin, January 1969.

18. Mapping of sample data; land values derived from 1861 Milwaukee Assessment Roll (MCHS) mapped in Conzen, "German Athens," 289; J. V. Dupré, *Quarter-Sectional Atlas of the City of Milwaukee*, 2nd ed. (Milwaukee, 1884); Koss, *Milwaukee*, 60; *BV*, Nov. 24, 25, 26, 1859; Bayrd Still, *Milwaukee: The History of a City* (Madison: SHSW, 1948), 249.

19. Jesse M. Van Slyck, *Milwaukee City Directory and Business Advertiser 1854-55* (Milwaukee: Parsons and Van Slyck, 1854), 10; Davies, "Early Buildings"; Sutherland, "Reminiscences"; *BV*, Nov. 3, 1858; Jan. 4, 1860; *Daily Milwaukee News*, Sept. 21, 1859. The locations of Milwaukee saloons were obtained from Franklin E. Town, *Milwaukee City Directory, for 1859-60* (Milwaukee: Jermain & Brightman, 1859).

20. Most of the third ward south of Michigan Street was initially under water, and as late as the early 1850s, reed-grown ponds continued to dot the ward; Wagner and Scherzer, *Reisen in Nordamerika*, II, 112; Wheeler, *Chronicles*, 15.

21. *Milwaukee Free Press*, Feb. 19, 1905; Buck, *Pioneer History*, II, 135; *BV*, May 3, 1858; Alberto C. Meloni, "Italy Invades the Bloody Third: The Early History of Milwaukee's Italians," *HMMC*, 25 (1969), 34-35.

22. Koss, *Milwaukee*, 50, 90-92; Wheeler, *Chronicles*, 56.

23. Koss, *Milwaukee*, 103-126, 239, 158-160; Wheeler, *Chronicles*, 128, 142-144; "Life in Milwaukee Fifty Years Ago," *MWS*, Oct. 16, 1895; city maps provide evidence of lot sizes and names of subdividers.

24. Mathias Humann, memoirs in *Erinnerungsblaetter aus der Geschichte der St. Josephs-Gemeinde zu Milwaukee, Wisconsin* (Milwaukee: J. H. Wenzel, 1905), 187; Wagner and Scherzer, *Reisen in Nordamerika*, II, 112-115; Dr. Büchele, *Land und Volk der Vereinigten Staaten von Nord-Amerika* (Stuttgart: Hallberger'sche Verlagshandlung, 1855), 198; *VF*, Aug. 2, 1849; *WB*, July 25, 1846; Lucas, "Reminiscences," 88.

25. Bremer, *Homes of the New World*, 615-616; Bruce, *Milwaukee City and County*, I, 780; Wheeler, *Chronicles*, 279.

26. William G. Bruce, "The Story of a Neighborhood," *MWS*, April 14, (?), undated clipping in "Milwaukee" scrapbook, SHSW; Bruce, *Milwaukee City and County*, I, 767; Koss, *Milwaukee*, 158-160; *Milwaukee Free Press*, May 21, 1911; Philip

Wells, "A Stroll through Old Kilbourntown," undated *MWS* clipping in "Milwaukee" scrapbook, SHSW; Harry H. Anderson, ed., *German-American Pioneers in Wisconsin and Michigan: The Frank-Kerler Letters, 1849-1864* (Milwaukee: MCHS, 1971), 317, 335.

27. See maps in Conzen, "Patterns of Residence," 166-170; manuscript dot maps indicate place of residence by German province of origin. The south side census taker did not list Germans by province of origin, thereby precluding analysis of segregation by province for the entire city.

28. The tradition of religious differences between east and west side Germans depends as much as anything upon the religion of the first settlers: Catholic Rhinelanders and southern Germans on the east side, then several years later the Lutheran Pommeranians on the west side. Church locations confirm these patterns: throughout the period, all but one of the German Protestant churches were located on the west side, while the first west side Roman Catholic church for Germans was not built until 1856.

29. Wheeler, *Chronicles*, 95; Harry H. Anderson, "Early Scandinavian Settlement in Milwaukee County," *HMMC*, 25 (1969), 7-8; "Letters of the Right Reverend John Martin Henni and the Reverend Anthony Urbanek," *WMH*, 10 (1926), 81; James Seville, "Milwaukee's First Railway," in *Early Milwaukee* (Milwaukee: Old Settlers Club, 1916), 89; Buck, *Pioneer History*, III, 135; *Milwaukee's Land Use Report*, 24; Still, *Milwaukee*, 268-269.

30. Bruce, *Milwaukee City and County*, I, 186; Anderson, "Early Scandinavian Settlement," 7-8.

31. Lucas, "Reminiscences," 88-89. According to Brusse, the nucleus of the Dutch community was a squatters' settlement.

32. Wheeler, *Chronicles*, 121; *A Merry Briton in Pioneer Wisconsin* (orig. Anon., *Life in the West*. London: Saunders & Otley, 1842; Madison: SHSW, 1950), 29; Flower, *History of Milwaukee*, 190; Bruce, "Yankee Hill," 289.

33. Wagner and Scherzer, *Reisen in Nordamerika*, II, 113; Quentin, *Reisebilder*, 128-131.

34. Van Slyck, *City Directory*, 10; Büchele, *Land und Volk*, 198; Wagner and Scherzer, *Reisen in Nordamerika*, II, 113; Bill Hasbin, "The Fresh Air Club," *Milwaukee Free Press*, Dec. 16, 1909; Increase A. Lapham, *A Geographical and Topographical Description of Wisconsin* (Milwaukee: P. C. Hale, 1844), 138; Buck, *Pioneer History*, I, 95.

35. Ambrose Wright, 1849, quoted in Bayrd Still, ed., "Milwaukee in 1836 and 1849: A Contemporary Description," *WMH*, 53 (1970), 296; Calvin C. Bayley, "Western Trip," *WMH*, 37 (1954), 238.

36. Van Slyck, *1854 City Directory*, 10; Davies, "Early Buildings"; Buck, *Pioneer History*, II, 110.

37. The term is Warner's; see Sam Bass Warner, Jr., *The Private City: Philadelphia in Three Periods of its Growth* (Philadelphia: University of Pennsylvania Press, 1968), 11.

38. It would take a careful study of the housing market to demonstrate the actual operation of this process. For its operation in Milwaukee later in the century, see Roger D. Simon, "The Expansion of an Industrial City, 1880-1910," Ph.D. diss., University of Wisconsin, Madison, 1971.

39. Lieberson, *Ethnic Patterns*, 3-18; Hildegard Binder Johnson, "Adjustment to

the United States," in Adolf E. Zucker, ed., *The Forty-Eighters, Political Refugees of the German Revolution of 1848* (New York: Columbia University Press, 1950), 60; Joshua A. Fishman, *Language Loyalty in the United States* (The Hague: Mouton & Co., 1966), 145; Amitai Etzioni, "The Ghetto—A Re-evaluation," *Social Forces*, 37 (1959), 255-262.

40. This notion is fundamental to the "ghetto hypothesis"; see also Francis A. J. Ianni, "Residential and Occupational Mobility as Indices of the Acculturation of an Ethnic Group," *Social Forces*, 36 (1957), 65-72.

41. For maps of this process, see Conzen, "German Athens," 321-323.

42. Compare with Boston's immigrant settlement pattern in the streetcar era, as described in Sam Bass Warner, Jr., *Streetcar Suburbs: The Process of Growth in Boston* (Cambridge: Harvard University Press, 1962).

6. Vereinswesen

1. *1860-61 Directory of the City of Milwaukee* (Milwaukee: Starr & Son, 1860); Frank A. Flower, *History of Milwaukee, Wisconsin* (Chicago: The Western Historical Company, 1881), 1308.

2. Oscar Handlin, *The Uprooted* (New York: Grosset and Dunlap, 1951), 170-188; William I. Thomas and Florian Znaniecki, *The Polish Peasant in Europe and America* (New York: Dover Publications, Inc., 1958), II, 1511-1549; Maldwyn Allen Jones, *American Immigration* (Chicago: University of Chicago Press, 1960), 134-137; Judith R. Kramer, *The American Minority Community* (New York: Thomas Y. Crowell Company, 1970), 79-84.

3. Mack Walker, *German Home Towns: Community, State, and General Estate 1648-1871* (Ithaca: Cornell University Press, 1971); see also Theodore S. Hamerow, *The Social Foundations of German Unification 1858-1871: Ideas and Institutions* (Princeton: Princeton University Press, 1969), 44-83; Wolfgang Köllmann, *Sozialgeschichte der Stadt Barmen im 19. Jahrhundert* (Tübingen: J. C. B. Mohr, 1960), 102-130. The German skilled workers of Milwaukee will be considered generally lower middle class, since that was the status they had presumably emigrated to preserve and which their actions indicated that they considered their due in Milwaukee; see also Edward Shorter, "Middle-Class Anxiety in the German Revolution of 1848," *Journal of Social History*, 2 (1969), 189-216.

4. Herbert Freudenthal, *Vereine in Hamburg: Ein Beitrag zur Geschichte und Volkskunde der Geselligkeit* (Hamburg: Museum für Hamburgische Geschichte, 1968), 11-287; Köllmann, *Barmen*, 213-220; Heinz Schmitt, *Das Vereinsleben der Stadt Weinheim an der Bergstrasse* (Weinheim a. d. B.: Weinheimer Geschichtsblatt Nr. 25, 1963), 7-32. For an autobiographical account of the associational life of a brewer and innkeeper in a southwestern German community, see Harry H. Anderson, ed., *German-American Pioneers in Wisconsin and Michigan: The Frank-Kerler Letters* (Milwaukee: MCHS, 1971), 54. Joshua A. Fishman, in his *Language Loyalty in the United States: The Maintenance and Perpetuation of Non-English Mother Tongues by American Ethnic and Religious Groups* (The Hague: Mouton & Co., 1966), 156, noted the role of urbanized immigrants accustomed to "consciously created mechanisms" of urban life in providing organizational models for their inexperienced countrymen; see also "German-American Language Maintenance Efforts" by Heinz Kloss in the same

volume for a discussion of the specific role of middle-class Germans in shaping associational life in America (224-225). In a discussion of the advisability of forming a separate German Democratic organization in 1851, it was argued by a group of Milwaukeeans that desirable though it was to meld the separate nationalities into one people, this was no reason to give up "the German associations and the sociable life to which they were accustomed in the old Fatherland"; *WB*, Sept. 3, 1851.

5. Fishman, *Language Loyalty*, 156; Kramer, *Minority Communities*, 57; Handlin, *Uprooted*, 185-186; Constance Smith and Anne Freedman, *Voluntary Associations: Perspectives on the Literature* (Cambridge: Harvard University Press, 1972), 166-169.

6. See Alexis de Tocqueville's classic statement in *Democracy in America* (J. P. Mayer, ed.; New York: Doubleday & Co., 1969), 513-517; Arthur M. Schlesinger, "Biography of a Nation of Joiners," in his *Paths to the Present* (Boston: Houghton Mifflin Company, 1964), 24-50; Rowland Berthoff, *An Unsettled People* (New York: Harper and Row, 1971).

7. Raymond Breton, "Institutional Completeness of Ethnic Communities and the Personal Relations of Immigrants," *American Journal of Sociology*, 70 (1964), 193-205.

8. Cf. Joseph Lopreato, *Italian Americans* (New York: Random House, 1970), 106; Robert Ernst, *Immigrant Life in New York City 1825-1863* (New York: King's Crown Press, 1949), 176-181.

9. *MWS*, Dec. 28, 1903; James S. Buck, *Pioneer History of Milwaukee* (Milwaukee: Swain & Tate, 1890), II, 128; *A Merry Briton in Pioneer Wisconsin* (Madison: SHSW, 1950), 33; William George Bruce, ed., *History of Milwaukee City and County* (Chicago: The S. J. Clarke Publishing Co., 1922), I, 771; Rudolf Koss, *Milwaukee* (Milwaukee: Herold, 1871), 50; Wilhelm Hense-Jensen, *Wisconsin's Deutsch-Amerikaner bis zum Schluss des neunzehnten Jahrhunderts* (Milwaukee: Im Verlage der Deutschen Gesellschaft, 1900), I, 67; see the city directories for evidence of the ubiquity of taverns.

10. J. A. A. Lacher, "The German Element in Wisconsin," in Milo M. Quaife, ed., *Wisconsin: Its History and Its People, 1634-1924* (Chicago: The S. J. Clarke Publishing Co., 1924), II, 179.

11. Hense-Jensen, *Wisconsin's Deutsch-Amerikaner*, I, 67-68.

12. Letter 324, Milwaukee, December 1846, in "Germans in America" collection, SHSW; Lacher, "German Element," 179.

13. Lacher, "German Element," 179; *BV*, Sept. 3, 1859. For nostalgic descriptions of the stimulating atmosphere and community importance of the best of these saloons, see Hense-Jensen, *Wisconsin's Deutsch-Amerikaner*, I, 67-69; John G. Gregory, *History of Milwaukee, Wisconsin* (Chicago: The S. J. Clarke Publishing Co., 1931), I, 884; Bruce, *History of Milwaukee*, I, 769-770; and the pages of Koss, *Milwaukee*. Any issue of any German newspaper of the period provides evidence for the almost universal use of the tavern as meeting place and ballroom.

14. Koss, *Milwaukee*, 169; *MC*, Aug. 7, July 17, 1844; H. McConnell letter, Milwaukee, Sept. 13, 1845, Messenger Papers, SHSW; Bruce, *History of Milwaukee*, I, 782; *Industrial History of Milwaukee* (Milwaukee: E. E. Barton, 1886), 153; Anderson, *German-American Pioneers*, 161.

15. Koss, *Milwaukee,* 115-118, 170; Joseph Schafer, *Four Wisconsin Counties: Prairie and Forest* (Madison: SHSW, 1927), 188; *MWS,* Aug. 24, 1844.

16. Immigrant letters stressing the importance have been noted in Chapter 1; for the German view of church-going as a sign of respectability in America, see Moritz Wagner and Carl Scherzer, *Reisen in Nordamerika in den Jahren 1852 und 1853* (Leipzig: Arnoldische Buchhandlung, 1854), II, 115; Anderson, *German-American Pioneers,* 346. For anticlerical fears of pastoral influence, see Koss, *Milwaukee,* 352-356.

17. Lacking religious censuses, German religious affiliation is difficult to estimate. Federal censuses provided some information which suggested that Roman Catholics comprised the single largest denomination in Milwaukee in both 1850 and 1860, whether measured in terms of number of churches (29 percent of the city's total in 1850, 30 percent in 1860), church accommodations (54 percent 1850, 41 percent 1860), or church property (25 percent 1850, 39 percent 1860), followed by the Methodists in 1850, the Lutherans ten years later. J. P. B. McCabe, in his *Directory of the City of Milwaukee, for the Years 1847-48* (Milwaukee: Wilson & King, 1847), 57, estimated that about one third of the German population was Catholic; the Reverend A. Urbanek made a similar estimate in an 1853 letter to the Archbishop of Vienna; "Letters of the Right Reverend John Martin Henni and the Reverend Anthony Urbanek," *WMH,* 10 (1926), 89.

18. Peter Leo Johnson, "Milwaukee's First Mass," *WMH,* 27 (1943), 77-78; Johnson, *Stuffed Saddlebags: The Life of Martin Kundig, Priest, 1805-1879* (Milwaukee: Bruce Publishing Co., 1942), 169-175; McCabe, *1847 Directory,* 44; David J. O'Hearn, ed., *Fifty Years at Saint John's Cathedral 1847-1897* (Milwaukee: St. John's Cathedral, 1898), 18-21; *MC,* June 2, 1841. Father O'Kelley wrote in the *MC,* May 15, 1841, that "the Catholics I trust will make a noble and determined effort to fling from among us a vice which alone has brought on us the contempt of a great portion of the world. The time I trust will come when all the sons of our dear native Isle shall assume a proper standing in society. The tide of invective will then be turned from against them, and all will win that degree of approbation from their fellow men, which those of our countrymen that have had advantages of education are distinguished for enjoying."

19. McCabe, *1847 Directory,* 45; Johnson, *Saddlebags,* 175-182; William George Bruce, et al., *St. Mary's Church, Milwaukee: History of a Pioneer Parish* (Milwaukee: St. Mary's Congregation, 1921), 16; Sister M. Justille McDonald, *History of the Irish in Wisconsin in the Nineteenth Century* (Washington, D.C.: The Catholic University of America Press, 1954), 195; Letter 324, Milwaukee, December 1846, "Germans in America" collection, SHSW; O'Hearn, *St. John's,* 170, 192.

20. First officers included Kundig, Juneau, the Swedish owner of a German inn, and an Irish grocer. *MC,* Jan. 4, Feb. 1, March 1, 1843; Johnson, *Saddlebags,* 229-232.

21. *MC,* March 22, 29, 1843; Koss, *Milwaukee,* 135-137; Johnson, *Saddlebags,* 195-196.

22. Johnson, *Saddlebags,* 190-191; O'Hearn, *St. John's,* 21-22, 31; McDonald, *Irish in Wisconsin,* 197; *MC,* May 8, 1844; Peter Leo Johnson, *Crosier on the Frontier: A Life of John Martin Henni* (Madison: SHSW, 1959). Kundig and Henni had come to the United States together and were ordained at the same time; shortly before his friend arrived in May 1844, however, Kundig and Morrissey were transferred to other Wisconsin settlements.

23. Johnson, *Crosier*, 70-72.

24. Bruce, *St. Mary's*, 16-17, 88-89; Johnson, *Saddlebags*, 181; William George Bruce, *Holy Trinity Church, 1850-1925* (Milwaukee: Holy Trinity, 1925), 13-28, 84; *Erinnerungsblaetter aus der Geschichte der St. Josephs-Gemeinde zu Milwaukee* (Milwaukee: J. H. Wenzel, 1905), 10-53, 113-115, 149-163; O'Hearn, *St. John's*, 32-39, 220-235; Harry H. Heming, *The Catholic Church in Wisconsin* (Milwaukee: Catholic Historical Publishing Co., 1895), 331, 1157; Flower, *History of Milwaukee*, 900-903.

25. *Erinnerungsblaetter*, 10-53, 113-115, 149-163; see also Heming, *Catholic Church*, 1080.

26. Parish histories listed in note 24; for a discussion of mutual benefit societies within German Catholic parishes, see Philip Gleason, *The Conservative Reformers: German-American Catholics and the Social Order* (Notre Dame: University of Notre Dame Press, 1968), chap. 1.

27. O'Hearn, *St. John's*, 32-39, 220-235. Jay P. Dolan, in "Immigrants in the City: New York's Irish and German Catholics," *Church History*, 41 (1972), 360-361, noted a similar difference between the German and Irish Catholic parishes of New York.

28. *MC*, March 29, April 12, Sept. 13, 1843; city directories; McDonald, *Irish in Wisconsin*, 235; *SB*, March 18, 1853. Whether this was a mutual benefit association is unclear. It engaged in St. Patrick's day parades, earned no place in the parish history, and apparently disappeared after 1856.

29. Albert Paul Schimberg, *Humble Harvest: The Society of St. Vincent de Paul in the Milwaukee Archdiocese 1849-1949* (Milwaukee: Bruce Publishing Co., 1949), 1-25; city directories.

30. Wagner and Scherzer, *Reisen in Nordamerika*, 163; J. B. Selby, "First Small Pox Epidemic," in *Early Milwaukee* (Milwaukee: Old Settlers' Club, 1916), 114-118; Peter T. Harstad, "Sickness and Disease on the Wisconsin Frontier," *WMH*, 43 (1960), 87, 204-209, 212-214; *WB*, Aug. 21, 1847; Koss, *Milwaukee*, 246; Donald N. Weber, "St. John's Infirmary, 1848-1858: The First Hospital in Milwaukee," B.A. thesis, St. Francis Seminary, Milwaukee, 1946; Peter Leo Johnson, "The Federal Marine Hospital," *WMH*, 30 (1946), 92-97; O'Hearn, *St. John's*, 192-196; Louis F. Frank, *The Medical History of Milwaukee 1834-1914* (Milwaukee: Germania Publishing Co., 1915), 144-146; Leopold Kist, *Amerikanisches* (Milwaukee: Hoffmann Brothers, 1871), 653-655; Johnson, *Crosier*, 98; "Henni Letters," 76, 82.

31. Their consternation and success are reported in *SB*, April 21, 1854.

32. Johnson, *Crosier*, 70-72, 79-81, 126-133; Wagner and Scherzer, *Reisen in Nordamerika*, II, 115-116, 200-201; O'Hearn, *St. John's*, 39; *MC*, Jan. 29, 1845.

33. For a discussion of such issues among the German Protestants of Missouri, see Carl E. Schneider, *The German Church on the American Frontier* (St. Louis: Eden Publishing House, 1939).

34. Koss, *Milwaukee*, 103-104, 137-139, 248; Friedrich Lochner, *Geschichte der Evang. Luth. Dreieinigkeits-Gemeinde zu Milwaukee, Wisconsin* (Milwaukee: Germania Publishing Co., 1897), 3-31; Flower, *History of Milwaukee*, 924; James A. Watrous, ed., *Memoirs of Milwaukee County* (Madison: Western Historical Association, 1909), I, 348-349.

35. Lochner, *Dreieinigkeits-Gemeinde*, 14; "Grace Church 1849-1949" (Milwaukee: Grace Evangelical Lutheran Church, 1949), 13; Koss, *Milwaukee*, 162-163,

196-197, 248-249, 265, 314; Berenice Cooper, "The Contribution of *Die Freien Gemeinde* to Sciences, Arts, and Letters in Wisconsin," *Transactions of the Wisconsin Academy*, 54 (1965), 63-70.

36. Koss, *Milwaukee*, 274, 336, 366; "Grace Church," 9-13, 28.

37. Ruth E. Westermann, "The History of Methodism in Milwaukee 1835-1935," ms. (1935), SHSW, Milwaukee Area Research Center, University of Wisconsin, Milwaukee; "Golden Jubilee Souvenir" (Milwaukee: Friedens Evangelical Church, 1921), 7-18; Watrous, *Memoirs of Milwaukee County*, I, 369; city directories.

38. Lochner, *Dreieinigkeits-Gemeinde*, 3-31.

39. Flower, *History of Milwaukee*, 822, 855, 942, 930-933; Watrous, *Memoirs of Milwaukee County*, 360; Henry S. Lucas, "The First Dutch Settlers in Milwaukee," *WMH*, 30 (1946), 179-182; "The 100th Anniversary Yearbook, 1858-1958" (Milwaukee: Our Savior's Lutheran Church, 1958), 31-32; Harry H. Anderson, "Early Scandinavian Settlement in Milwaukee County," *HMMC*, 25 (1969), 9, 14; Clarence G. Toepfer, "One Hundred Years for Christ 1852-1952" (Milwaukee: Ascension Lutheran Church, 1952), 11-114.

40. Louis J. Swichkow and Lloyd P. Gartner, *The History of the Jews of Milwaukee* (Philadelphia: The Jewish Publication Society of America, 1963), 11-56; Flower, *History of Milwaukee*, 948; Watrous, *Memoirs of Milwaukee County*, 370; John G. Gregory, *History of Milwaukee, Wisconsin* (Chicago: S. J. Clarke Publishing Co., 1931), I, 908; *VF*, Dec. 27, 1849; *BV*, Sept. 30, 1858, May 3, 11, Sept. 13, Nov. 2, 1859; April 7, 10, May 25, 1860.

41. The quotation is from Anderson, *German-American Pioneers*, 161; Koss, *Milwaukee*, 166-169, 190, 242, 287; *MC*, March 13, 1844; *BV*, May 3, 1845; Feb. 23, Oct. 25, 1858; July 18, 1859; Peter Van Vechten ms:, 1894, Old Settlers' Club Papers, MCHS; Hense-Jensen, *Wisconsin's Deutsch-Amerikaner*, I, 65; Elijah Kennedy in *Milwaukee Free Press*, Feb. 23, 1904.

42. Koss, *Milwaukee*, 166-167, 197-198, 277, 332; *WB*, May 3, 1845, Aug. 7, 1847; *VF*, Feb. 22, 1849; Hense-Jensen, *Wisconsin's Deutsch-Amerikaner*, I, 66; the February 1849 article gives December 1842 as the date of its founding, in direct contradiction to the founding notice which appeared in May 1845; some sort of informal organization may well have preceded its official founding. The association was still in existence as late as 1851. No membership lists were found.

43. Koss, *Milwaukee*, 277; *VF*, Oct. 19, 1848; *WB*, July 26, 1854; Hense-Jensen, *Wisconsin's Deutsch-Amerikaner*, I, 66; Wagner and Scherzer, *Reisen in Nordamerika*, II, 140, 199; city directories.

44. In the late 1850s, for example, young Jews, Plattdeutsch, Swabians, and "a group of respectable men" all formed societies of their own. There was also an active German Medical Society in the mid-1850s. *BV*, April 17, 23, Sept. 22, 1858; Nov. 2, 1859; Frank, *Medical History*, 117-124.

45. Koss, *Milwaukee*, 145, 244; Hense-Jensen, *Wisconsin's Deutsch-Amerikaner*, 66; *WB*, Aug. 8, 1846.

46. Koss, *Milwaukee*, 246; *WB*, Dec. 12, 19, 26, 1846; Feb. 20, March 13, May 8, 1847; Jan. 28, 1852; Feb. 28, March 7, 1855; *VF*, Dec. 16, 1847, March 2, Dec. 7, 1848; Feb. 1, 1849; Jan. 24, 1850; *BV*, Dec. 10, 1856; Jan. 26, Feb. 23, March 5, Nov. 27, 1859; *MWS*, Jan. 15, Jan. 20, 1859.

47. Koss, *Milwaukee*, 221, 246-247, 263-264, 287-288.

48. Robert G. Carroon, "Scotsmen in Old Milwaukee, 1810-60," *HMMC*, 25 (1969), 24-31; *MWS*, Oct. 16, 1895; Jan. 15, 20, 1859.

49. *MC*, Jan. 3, 1844.

50. *MC*, June 14, July 12, Aug. 9, Sept. 13, Dec. 13, 1843; March 20, May 1, July 10, 1844; Koss, *Milwaukee*, 133; McDonald, *Irish in Wisconsin*, 241; *MC*, Feb. 23, 1847; Humphrey J. Desmond, "Early Irish Settlers in Milwaukee," *WMH*, 13 (1930), 336; city directories; Heming, *Catholic Church*, 1070-1086.

51. Bayrd Still, *Milwaukee: The History of a City* (Madison: SHSW, 1948), 153; *MA*, Sept. 10, 13, 1860; Milwaukee *Daily News*, Oct. 18, 1860; Charles N. Scanlan, *The Lady Elgin Disaster, September 8, 1860* (Milwaukee: n.p., 1928).

52. Wagner and Scherzer, *Reisen in Nordamerika*, II, 116.

53. Cf. Marcus Lee Hansen, *The Immigrant in American History* (New York: Harper Torchbooks, 1964), 134-140; Hense-Jensen, *Wisconsin's Deutsch-Amerikaner*, I, 69; Anton Eickhoff, *In der neuen Heimath* (New York: E. Steiger and Co., 1884), 368; Sister M. Hedwegis Overmoehle, "The Anti-Clerical Activities of the Forty-Eighters in Wisconsin 1848-1860," Ph.D. diss., St. Louis University, 1941, 47-55.

54. Howard Louis Conrad, ed., *History of Milwaukee from Its First Settlement to the Year 1895* (Chicago: American Biographical Publishing Co., n.d.), I, 372; Buck, *Pioneer History*, II, 129; Hense-Jensen, *Wisconsin's Deutsch-Amerikaner*, I, 108; Carl H. Knoche, "Dr. Franz Huebschmann's Political Career," *MCCH*, 28 (1972), 114-131.

55. Conrad, *History of Milwaukee*, II, 386; Hense-Jensen, *Wisconsin's Deutsch-Amerikaner*, I, 104.

56. Hense-Jensen, *Wisconsin's Deutsch-Amerikaner*, 115-116; Koss, *Milwaukee*, 194, 223-229; Carl H. Knoche, "Alexander Conze: An Early Milwaukee German-American Poet," *German-American Studies*, 5 (1972), 148-162.

57. Koss, *Milwaukee*, passim; Conrad, *History of Milwaukee*, II, 371; Gregory, *History of Milwaukee*, I, 720-721; Conrad, III, 74; Flower, *History of Milwaukee*, 1588; *WB*, April 11, 1855.

58. Koss, *Milwaukee*, 145, 254, 275-277; *MC*, Jan. 11, March 13, 1843; *The Musical Society of Milwaukee 1850-60: A Chronicle* (Milwaukee: Musical Society, 1900), 7; *VF*, Dec. 23, 1847; Feb. 17, 1848.

59. Koss, *Milwaukee*, 278-283; *VF*, Jan. 25, Feb. 1, 15, 22, March 1, 1848.

60. Hense-Jensen, *Wisconsin's Deutsch-Amerikaner*, I, 129-135.

61. Koss, 292-296; Hense-Jensen, *Wisconsin's Deutsch-Amerikaner*, I, 151-153; *Musical Society*, 8-42; Wagner and Scherzer, *Reisen in Nordamerika*, II, 117-118.

62. Koss, *Milwaukee*, 296-299, 327-331, 377-381, 408-412; Francis Magyar, "The History of the Early Milwaukee German Theatre," *WMH*, 13 (1930), 375-386; *BV*, Feb. 20; March 3, 6, 10, 17, 18, 20, 25; Aug. 31; Oct. 1, 18, 1858.

63. Koss, *Milwaukee*, 288, 313; *WB*, Dec. 29, 1849, Sept. 11, 1850. Wilhelm Weitling, a German socialist and New York labor agitator, had acquaintances in Milwaukee: his newspaper was recommended in the Milwaukee press, and its was his version of Utopian socialism which would influence Milwaukee workers and reformers at mid-century, though the limited enthusiasm which he aroused when he spoke before a Milwaukee reform group in 1851 suggests the relative shallowness of Milwaukee socialism at that time. See Carl Wittke, *The Utopian Communist: A Biography of Wilhelm Weitling, Nineteenth Century Reformer* (Baton Rouge: Louisiana State Uni-

versity Press, 1950), esp. 147, 174-175; F. H. Sorge, "Die Arbeiterbewegung in den Vereinigten Staaten, 1850-1860," *Neue Zeit*, 2 (1890), 232-237.

64. Koss, *Milwaukee*, 337; *WB*, Sept. 11, Nov. 27, 1850; May 28, June 4, 11, July 2, 9, 30, Sept. 7, 1851; P. H. Noyes, *Organization and Revolution: Working-Class Associations in the German Revolutions of 1848-1849* (Princeton: Princeton University Press, 1966).

65. *WB*, July 23, 1851; Koss, *Milwaukee*, 337, 368-369; Wagner and Scherzer, *Reisen in Nordamerika*, II, 192; *Milwaukie Flug-Blätter*, Jan. 8, Jan. 22, 1853.

66. See Berenice Cooper, "Die Freien Gemeinde in Wisconsin," *Transactions, Wisconsin Academy of Sciences, Arts and Letters*, 53 (1964), 53-65, and "The Contribution of Die Freien Gemeinde to Sciences, Arts and Letters in Wisconsin," *Transactions, Wisconsin Academy of Sciences, Arts and Letters*, 54 (1965), 63-70; N.J. Demerath and Victor Thiessen, "On Spitting Against the Wind: Organizational Precariousness and American Irreligion," *American Journal of Sociology*, 71 (1966), 674-687.

67. Koss, *Milwaukee*, 336, 366-368; J. J. Schlicher, "Eduard Schroeter the Humanist," *WMH*, 28 (1944), 169-174; Wagner and Scherzer, *Reisen in Nordamerika*, II, 196-197.

68. Schlicher, "Schroeter," 175-183; Koss, *Milwaukee*, 368, 388-400; A. E. Zucker, ed., *The Forty-Eighters: Political Refugees of the German Revolution of 1848* (New York: Columbia University Press, 1950), 316-317.

69. Walter Osten, "History of the Turner Movement" (1950), ms., Turner Society Papers, MCHS; Robert Wild, "Chapters in the History of the Turners," *WMH*, 9 (1925), 123-129; Koss, *Milwaukee*, 318-319, 401-402.

70. Koss, *Milwaukee*, 404-405, 439-441, 459; Schlicher, "Schroeter," 311-314; Osten, "Turner Movement." The *Bund's* activities in 1854 were limited to a few declarations against popery, and it played no political role that year as the idea of a national association of radical Germans, which underlay its founding, gradually died.

71. Koss, *Milwaukee*, 439-441, 459; *BV*, Oct. 9, 14, 23, Dec. 3, 1858; Jan. 26, 1859.

72. Hense-Jensen, *Wisconsin's Deutsch-Amerikaner*, I, 154; Osten, "Turner Movement"; Overmoehle, "Anti-Clerical Activities," 65; *BV*, Feb. 10, 1858; Aug. 19, Sept. 2, 9, 1857; Jan. 26, 28, July 21, 1858; Jan. 26, 1859; Dec. 31, 1858; Jan. 31, 1860.

73. Flower, *History of Milwaukee*, 351, 542; Still, *Milwaukee*, 81-85, 216-220; *BV*, April 23, July 6, Sept. 28, 1858; April 8, Aug. 10, Sept. 15, 1859; *WB*, Oct. 3, 1846; Aug. 14, 1847; *BV*, May 16, 30, 1860. In 1859 it was estimated that the schools in wards 5, 8, and 9 could hold only one third of the eligible children. In 1858 the city council committee for schools estimated that the 47 percent of school-age children who were not in school included about 3,800 who were unemployed, or 60 percent of the total not in school; *BV*, July 6, 1858. The high schools were closed for reasons of economy between 1860 and 1868.

74. Anthony Urbanek to the Archbishop of Vienna, 1853, "Henni Letters."

75. Koss, *Milwaukee*, 217, 276, 314, 352; Lochner, *Dreieinigkeits-Gemeinde*, 25, 31; *BV*, Aug. 18, 1858; Raphael N. Hamilton, S.J., *The Story of Marquette University* (Milwaukee: Marquette University Press, 1953), 9; the description of St. Aloysius' Prospectus is quoted by Hamilton from the *MWS*, Aug. 26, 1857. For general informa-

tion on Catholic education in the antebellum period, see the parish histories cited earlier, as well as Kist, *Amerikanisches*, 653-654; Johnson, *Crosier*, 111; Benjamin J. Blied, "From Munich to Milwaukee by way of Pennsylvania," *American-German Review*, 14 (1947), 21-23, 37; Johnson, *Saddlebags*, 250.

76. *WB*, Oct. 3, 1846; Hense-Jensen, *Wisconsin's Deutsch-Amerikaner*, I, 135-136; Koss, *Milwaukee*, 331-332.

77. Peter Engelmann, "Autobiography," ms., Engelmann Papers, MCHS; the quotation is from comments by "C. ST." in the "Autobiography."

78. Koss, *Milwaukee*, 334-335, 364-366, 405-408; *BV*, Oct. 15, 1856; Jan. 30, Feb. 19, May 7, June 26, Sept. 6, 1858; Jan. 19, Oct. 19, 1859; *BV*, Jan. 10, 12, 1860; Flower, *History of Milwaukee*, 555. Loose soon began suffering from the attacks which would lead to his early death in a New York insane asylum.

79. Koss, *Milwaukee*, 407-408.

80. Ibid., 277, 345-346; *VF*, Oct. 19, 1848; *Musical Society*, 13-14; *SB*, Aug. 19, 1853; Feb. 13, 24, 1854; April 28, July 25, Aug. 29, 1853; Ernest Bruncken, "The Germans in Wisconsin Politics, I: Until the Rise of the Republican Party," *Parkman Club Publications*, 9 (Milwaukee, 1896), 236. For a more extended treatment, see Overmoehle, "Anti-Clerical Activities."

81. Koss, *Milwaukee*, 354-356, 457-458; Anderson, *German-American Pioneers*, 140. Naprstek left blasphemously promising his readers, "In a little while you will not see me, and yet again in a little while you will see me," and in fact did return briefly as agent of the German Immigration Society and accompanied Huebschmann (at the time holding a federal appointment as Indian agent) to Minnesota before returning to Bohemia.

82. Anderson, *German-American Pioneers*, 346, 425; Karl Obermann, *Joseph Weydemeyer: Pioneer of American Socialism* (New York: International Publishers, 1947), 88-100. Weydemeyer, a friend of Marx, was formerly active in the New York labor movement; he moved to Milwaukee in 1856 owing to financial difficulties, was employed as a surveyor and notary, and participated in various workers' and other radical groups; see also *BV*, March 4, 1859.

83. For a recent history of Milwaukee's German press, see Carl Heinz Knoche, "The German Immigrant Press in Milwaukee," Ph.D. diss., Ohio State University, 1969.

84. Albert Strobl, "German Newspaper Publishing in Milwaukee," M.A. thesis, University of Illinois, 1951, 5, 29; Koss, *Milwaukee*, 152-153; Conrad, *History of Milwaukee*, II, 386; Hense-Jensen, *Wisconsin's Deutsch-Amerikaner*, I, 104; Carl Wittke, *Refugees of Revolution: The German Forty-Eighters in America* (Philadelphia: University of Pennsylvania Press, 1952), 269, 350; *BV*, July 14, 1858.

85. Julius Bleyer, "The Milwaukee Press," in W. J. Anderson and Julius Bleyer, eds., *Milwaukee's Great Industries* (Milwaukee: Association for the Advancement of Milwaukee, 1892), 56; Henry Bleyer, "Index to Periodicals," ms., Bleyer Papers, SHSW, Milwaukee Area Research Center, University of Wisconsin.

86. Koss suggested that Roesler's troubles owed much to the fact that there were still too few educated Germans able to depart from party lines in their thinking to support his kind of paper; *Milwaukee*, 339-341, 350, 361; Wittke, *Refugees of Revolution*, 65; Zucker, *Forty-Eighters*, 331. Roesler returned to private life as a notary, declared

for the Whigs and then left to edit a Whig paper in Quincy, Illinois; when the Whigs lost, his backers abandoned him and he died, apparently of drink, shortly after. There appear to be no copies of the *Volkshalle* available; see Donald F. Oehlerts, ed., *Guide to Wisconsin Newspapers* (Madison: SHSW, 1958).

87. Koss, *Milwaukee*, passim; *SB*, Jan. 21, 1854; Strobl, "German Newspaper Publishing," 63-65; Bleyer, "Press," 57; Anderson, *German-American Pioneers*, 140; Flower, *History of Milwaukee*, 114; Conrad, *History of Milwaukee*, II, 460.

88. Koss, *Milwaukee*, 362, 449-456; Bleyer, "Press," 56; Strobl, "Newspaper Publishing," 8, 27; A. C. Wheeler, *The Chronicles of Milwaukee* (Milwaukee: Jermain & Brightman, 1861), 225; J. J. Schlicher, "Bernhard Domschke," *WMH*, 29 (1946), 319-332. Domschke himself served in the Civil War, was imprisoned in Libby Prison in Richmond, and died shortly after returning to Milwaukee.

89. Zucker, *Forty-Eighters*, 333-334; Wittke, *Refugees*, 269, 277, 68-69; *BV*, Dec. 2, 1858; Jan. 25, 1859; March 30, 31, June 21, 22, July 19, 1859; Ruppius returned to Germany in 1862 to devote himself to writing novels about America; the *Grad 'Aus* earned no mention for itself in the histories of Milwaukee journalism, although it certainly provoked the frequent ire of its competitors.

90. Koss, *Milwaukee*, 142; *MC*, Aug. 9, 1843.

91. This evolution followed its own logic, reflecting the changing size and character of the German population, and does not readily fit into theoretical chronologies of immigrant organizational development; cf. W. Lloyd Warner and Leo Srole, *The Social Systems of American Ethnic Groups* (New Haven: Yale University Press, 1945), 282; Donald B. Cole, *Immigrant City: Lawrence, Massachusetts, 1845-1921* (Chapel Hill: University of North Carolina Press, 1963), 138-139.

92. Koss, *Milwaukee*, 163, 199, 222, 243, 358-359, 433-434; *BV*, June 14, 1858; June 29, 1859; *MA*, July 6, 1860.

93. Koss, *Milwaukee*, 221; *BV*, March 4, 1857; Jan. 30, Feb. 15, 16, 18, 1858; March 8, 1859; Feb. 19, 22, 1860.

94. *BV*, Jan. 2, April 28, May 4, June 2, 1858; April 29, May 5, 9, June 21, Oct. 8, Nov. 16, Dec. 4, 1859; Flower, *History of Milwaukee*, 522; Koss, *Milwaukee*, 434.

95. Cf. Still, *Milwaukee*, 127.

96. Cf. Guido A. Dobbert, "The Disintegration of an Immigrant Community: The Cincinnati Germans, 1870-1920," Ph.D. diss., University of Chicago, 1965, and Audrey Louise Olson, "St. Louis Germans, 1850-1920: The Nature of an Immigrant Community and its Relation to the Assimilation Process," Ph.D. diss., University of Kansas, 1970, for similar interpretations.

7. To Stand Firm in the Ranks of Democracy

1. Franz Löher, *Geschichte und Zustände der Deutschen in Amerika* (Cincinnati: Eggers and Wulkop, 1847), 345.

2. Oscar Handlin, "The Immigrant and American Politics," in David F. Bowers, ed., *Foreign Influences in American Life: Essays and Critical Bibliographies* (Princeton: Princeton University Press, 1944), 84-98; Handlin, *The Uprooted* (New York: Grosset & Dunlap, 1951), 206-212; Maldwyn Allen Jones, *American Immigration* (Chicago: University of Chicago Press, 1960), 141-142; Robert A. Dahl, *Who Governs? Democ-*

racy and Power in an American City (New Haven: Yale University Press, 1961), 33.

3. Elmer E. Cornwell, Jr., "Bosses, Machines, and Ethnic Groups," in Lawrence H. Fuchs, ed., *American Ethnic Politics* (New York: Harper and Row, 1968), 194-216; Raymond E. Wolfinger, "The Development and Persistence of Ethnic Voting," Ibid., 163-193; Handlin, *Uprooted*, 206-207.

4. August Greulich, for example, had previously been a Detroit alderman; Howard Louis Conrad, ed., *History of Milwaukee County from Its First Settlement to the Year 1895* (Chicago: American Biographical Publishing Co., n.d.), III, 74.

5. Cf. Stanley Elkins and Eric McKitrick, "A Meaning for Turner's Frontier," *Political Science Quarterly*, 69 (1954), 323-348.

6. American citizenship required five years' residence in the United States; *MC*, Sept. 7, 1842; Bayrd Still, *Milwaukee: The History of a City* (Madison: SHSW, 1948), 36-75.

7. Rudolf A. Koss, *Milwaukee* (Milwaukee: Herold, 1871), 167; *MC*, Sept. 29, 1841; April 6, Sept. 7, 1842; April 6, Aug. 16, Sept. 20, 1843; *MWS*, April 19, 1843; A. C. Wheeler, *The Chronicles of Milwaukee* (Milwaukee: Jermain & Brightman, 1861), 112-114; Frederick I. Olson, "Juneau and the Postmastership," *HMMC*, 9 (September 1953), 12-16. Juneau's replacement, Josiah Noonan, a Democratic politician and *Courier* publisher, attracted German approval by producing a more correct list of German letters and removing the heading "Dutch List" when its offensiveness was pointed out to him.

8. *MC*, May 3, 1843; Sept. 29, 1841; *MA*, Feb. 27, 1841; *MWS*, March 16, 1841; James S. Buck, *Pioneer History of Milwaukee* (Milwaukee: Swain and Tate, 1890), II, 106-107; Koss, *Milwaukee*, 167.

9. Koss, *Milwaukee*, 149-151; *MC*, Dec. 27, 1843; Humphrey J. Desmond, "Early Irish Settlers in Milwaukee," *WMH*, 13 (1930), 371; *MWS*, Dec. 30, 1843; Jan. 6, 1844.

10. Still, *Milwaukee*, 76; in 1845 the residence requirement was extended to six months and a declaration of intent to become a citizen was added.

11. Koss, *Milwaukee*, 152, 163-164; *MC*, March 27, 1844; Desmond, "Early Irish Settlers," 371. At least 38 of the 366 founding members were German.

12. Koss, *Milwaukee*, 152, 163; Wilhelm Hense-Jensen, *Wisconsin's Deutsch-Amerikaner bis zum Schluss des neunzehnten Jahrhunderts* (Milwaukee: Im Verlage der Deutschen Gesellschaft, 1900), I, 65.

13. Koss, *Milwaukee*, 164-167, 192; *MC*, Nov. 6, 1844. The *Banner's* comments upon a similar proposal in Washington county the following spring suggest at least one of the motives in founding the Milwaukee association: "Such an association provides the German immigrant with an easy way of familiarizing himself with the local institutions and his rights and duties in his new homeland. As far as we know, there are many living in Washington County whose longer stays elsewhere in the United States and the conditions which they experienced in other states have already given them sufficient acquaintance with American institutions that they can perform a true service for their fellow countrymen."

14. For the broader context, see Joseph Schafer, "Know-Nothingism in Wisconsin," *WMH*, 8 (1924), 3-21; Ray Allen Billington, *The Protestant Crusade 1800-1860* (New York: Rinehart, 1938).

15. *WB*, March 29, April 5, 1845; *MC*, Aug. 21, Sept. 25, 1844; Jan. 29, Feb. 26, 1845; Still, *Milwaukee*, 105; Koss, *Milwaukee*, 174.

16. *WB*, March 15, 23, 29, May 17, 24, June 14, 1845.

17. *WB*, Aug. 23, 1845; *MC*, March 26, June 11, 1845; *WB*, June 7, July 5, Aug. 30, 1845; Koss, *Milwaukee*, 199; Wheeler, *Chronicles*, 179-180. Voting requirements under the new charter included not only a declaration of intention to become a citizen, but the payment of taxes, the performance of highway labor, or fireman's service in the six months previous to any election, and thus excluded a number of citizens.

18. The graphs were derived as follows: for each individual election, the contest drawing the largest number of voters was isolated; the resulting maximum turnout figures were then plotted separately for city level and for county, state, and national level and compared with the number of estimated eligible voters. This estimate—25 percent of the total population of each ward at each census year—was suggested by census statistics which show that throughout the period, slightly over half the population was male, and slightly over half the males were twenty years of age and older. By 1860 the male proportion had declined somewhat, but a constant estimate was retained. Those disqualified to vote by lack of residency or citizenship may counteract the tendency of the estimate to underrepresent eligible voters in the early years. Estimate accuracy also varied from ward to ward, with greatest probable underestimation in the centrally located first and third wards. Note that for 1858 through 1860 elections, the graphs use the old ward boundaries; the first ward includes the new seventh ward, the second the new sixth and ninth wards, and the fifth the new eighth ward.

19. Cf. Lee Benson, *The Concept of Jacksonian Democracy: New York as a Test Case* (New York: Atheneum, 1964); Ronald P. Formisano, *The Birth of Mass Political Parties: Michigan, 1827-1861* (Princeton: Princeton University Press, 1971); Paul Kleppner, *The Cross of Culture: A Social Analysis of Midwestern Politics 1850-1900* (New York: The Free Press, 1970).

20. This index is a variant of that presented by V. O. Key, Jr., in *American State Politics: An Introduction* (New York: Alfred A. Knopf, 1956), 209-211. While Key worked with average vote per candidate, the present index was calculated directly from percentages; the percentage of all votes cast polled by all Democratic candidates in all the contests in any given election was calculated; the difference between the percentage of the vote garnered by the Democratic candidate in each contest and this overall percentage was then obtained, and an average percent deviation calculated. As with any other mean, this index can easily be biased by extremely deviant cases. Visually, the closer any given point is to the base line, the smaller the amount of ticket splitting in that election. Data were missing for some contests, wards, and elections, as indicated on the graphs.

21. While a comparison with leadership patterns among the natives and Irish is desirable, only German names could be identified by nationality in lists of participants in political events printed in *MC, WB, VF*; occupational information was derived from city directories and Koss, *Milwaukee*. This does not constitute an exhaustive survey of all active political participants, but only those at meetings which were reported in exhaustive detail by the press.

22. Any issue of the *WB* during any election campaign during the 1850s will suggest the large number of German meetings offering a chance for political experience on

all levels. For example, German delegates (35 of a total of 54) sent to the city Democratic convention in early 1859 included one professional, 16 merchants and shopkeepers, 14 craftsmen, and possibly one laborer. The shopkeepers included four saloon keepers and five grocers. A ninth ward investigation of the ward's books and the conduct of its elected officials involved a teacher, an apothecary, a clerk, a notary public, three grocers, two saloon keepers, five craftsmen, and a teamster. *BV*, Feb. 23; Sept. 24, 25, 28, 1859.

23. Koss, *Milwaukee*, 103, 130-131, 154, 211-212; *MC*, Feb. 25, March 4, 1846; *WB*, March 28, 1846.

24. Still, *Milwaukee*, 81; *WB*, April 11, 1846.

25. Koss, *Milwaukee*, 230, 257; *WB*, Aug. 15, 1846; *VF*, Dec. 2, 1847. Still, *Milwaukee*, 78, 81, lists names of Irish delegates different from those given in the newspapers; his source is unclear.

26. Based on the election results printed in *MWS* each spring.

27. James S. Buck, *Milwaukee under the Charter* (Milwaukee: Symes, Swain & Co., 1884), III, 61; *MWS*, April 6, 1848; Still, *Milwaukee*, 138, 142; Enoch Chase Papers, "Reminiscences, 1876," ms., SHSW, Milwaukee Area Research Center, University of Wisconsin, Milwaukee; election returns, *MWS*. There was little change in the occupational characteristics of German candidates between 1848 and 1860. Those running for city office included Geisberg, a merchant; Weydemeyer, a tobacconist; Freulich, a merchant; Kern, a lawyer; Hertzberg, a publisher; Kuehn, a civil servant; Beck, a deputy sheriff; Mayer, a grocer; Schwarting, a grocer; Cotzhausen, a lawyer; von Baumbach, a land agent; and Tesch, a druggist—all men of prominence. Ward office candidates were generally doctors, grocers, saloon keepers, and other merchants before 1854; thereafter, a stronger representation of craftsmen became evident, but businessmen continued prominent.

28. *WB*, March 21, 28, Aug. 29, 1846. However, complaints of factionalism within German ranks over issues of personality rather than principle began early and continued throughout the period; the Germans, noted Bielfeld, too often treated their political opponents as personal enemies; *VF*, Dec. 2, 1847.

29. *WB*, March 21, April 4, 11, 25, 1846; *MC*, March 18, April 1, 3, 6, 1846; Feb. 20, April 14, 1847; Koss, *Milwaukee*, 230; *WB*, Aug. 29, Sept. 26, 1846.

30. *WB*, Nov. 7, 1846; Feb. 6, 20; March 6, 13, 20; April 10, 1847; Koss, *Milwaukee*, 234, 238; *MWS*, March 15, 17, 1847; Still, *Milwaukee*, 137; *MC*, May 12, March 12, 1847; for further discussion over what the Irish leaders did or did not say, see Buck, *Under the Charter*, III, 52-53.

31. Koss, *Milwaukee*, 255-257. By the summer of 1847 the association turned its attention to the exorbitant fees charged arriving immigrants by pier owners, eventually exerting political pressure to obtain a city ordinance setting maximum rates. Some elements in the association, dissatisfied with this activity, reformed it again in 1848, this time as a vehicle for the socialist views of the "working class"; the older element, however, continued to function sporadically as a *Volksverein* to defend specifically immigrant interests, and finally organized themselves formally as a Society for the Support of German Immigrants in 1850. How long that Society lasted is unclear; by 1855 a new German Society was concerning itself with immigrant protection. *WB*, June 12; July 10, 24; Aug. 21, 1847; Feb. 27, 1850; *VF*, Aug. 7, 19, 1847; March 8, 23, 30; April 27, 1848; Jan. 30, 1858.

32. *VF*, March 16, 1848; Koss, *Milwaukee*, 257-258.

33. *VF*, July 15, Sept. 23, 30, 1847.

34. *VF*, April 27, March 30, June 1, 8, Aug. 3, 1848.

35. Koss, *Milwaukee*, 154, 269-270, 313; Still, *Milwaukee*, 137; Buck, *Under the Charter*, III, 122; Ernest Bruncken, "The Germans in Wisconsin Politics: I, Until the Rise of the Republican Party," *Parkman Club Publications*, 9 (Milwaukee, 1896); *MC*, April 3, 1844; *VF*, April 27, May 4, Aug. 31, Sept. 21, Oct. 12, 19, 1848.

36. Buck, *Under the Charter*, III, 168; *VF*, Jan. 11, 18; Feb. 1; April 30, 1849; Jan. 10, 1850; *WB*, May 7, 11; June 25, Aug. 6; Sept. 10, 1851.

37. See the comments by Huebschmann in *WB*, Aug. 27, 1851.

38. Joseph Schafer, "Prohibition in Early Wisconsin," *WMH*, 8 (1925), 283-284.

39. *WB*, Jan. 30, 1850; *VF*, June 28, 1849.

40. *WB*, March 20, 1850; Koss, *Milwaukee*, 303-305; Buck, *Under the Charter*, III, 247; *VF*, May 17, June 28, 1849; Jan. 30, 1850.

41. *WB*, Aug. 7, Sept. 3, Oct. 8, 1851; Joseph Schafer, *Four Wisconsin Counties: Prairie and Forest* (Madison: SHSW, 1927), 188. For German complaints concerning the Yankee attitude toward Sunday, see Letter 324, Milwaukee, December 1846, "Germans in America" collection, SHSW, and Harry H. Anderson, ed., *German-American Pioneers in Wisconsin and Michigan: The Frank-Kerler Letters* (Milwaukee: MCHS, 1971), 161.

42. *VF*, Jan. 10, 1850; Still, *Milwaukee*, 141; Buck, *Under the Charter*, III, 342; *WB*, Oct. 25, 29; Nov. 12, 1851.

43. Bruncken, "Germans in Wisconsin Politics, I," 236; Koss, *Milwaukee*, 392; Buck, *Under the Charter*, III, 316; see also Sister M. Hedwegis Overmoehle, "The Anti-Clerical Activities of the Forty-Eighters in Wisconsin 1848-1860: A Study in German-American Liberalism," Ph.D. diss., St. Louis University, 1941, 123-196.

44. Koss, *Milwaukee*, 357; *WB*, March 10, 1852; Bruncken, "Germans in Wisconsin Politics, I," 236.

45. Buck, *Under the Charter*, III, 398; *WB*, May 26, July 7, Aug. 4, 1852; Bruncken, "Germans in Wisconsin Politics, I," 237. Wagner and Scherzer, *Reisen in Nordamerika*, II, 202-203, suggest that it was Father Ives of the Cathedral parish rather than the German priests who spoke out most strongly against saloons and dancing. Unfortunately, the extant *Seebote* files begin only in 1853, and it is thus impossible to verify the *Banner's* claim that the *Seebote* too had taken up arms against the German Sunday. That Catholics were not alone in objecting to anticlerical attacks can be seen by the comments of a Lutheran layman: "The Democrats here, especially the spokesmen, are for the greater part sort of revolutionaries and German refugees of the past years, and are trying here just as well as there to undermine state and church and change them to suit their views"; Anderson, *German-American Pioneers*, 185. Fratny aimed his barbs at Lutheran as well as Catholic clergy; cf. Koss, *Milwaukee*, 265.

46. *WB*, July 28, Aug. 11, Oct. 5, 1852; Koss, *Milwaukee*, 361; Wagner and Scherzer, *Reisen in Nordamerika*, II, 126; *WB*, Nov. 1, 1852.

47. *WB*, Nov. 4, 5, 6, 1852; *MWS*, Nov. 4, 1852. Scott polled 546 votes to Pierce's 622 in the first ward, 311 to 806 in the second; Greulich polled 627 votes to Hunter's 649 in the first, 347 to Hunter's 830 in the second ward.

48. Bruncken, "Germans in Wisconsin Politics, I," 237-238; *SB*, Feb. 22, 26, March 3, 1853; Still, *Milwaukee*, 144; Koss, *Milwaukee*, 424-425; Buck, *Under the Charter*, III, 416.

49. Buck, *Under the Charter*, III, 416.

50. *SB*, Oct. 3, 6, 14, 31; Nov. 5, 1853; *WB*, Oct. 12, Nov. 2, 16, 30, 1853; Buck, *Under the Charter*, III, 455; Bruncken, "Germans in Wisconsin Politics, I," 237.

51. Schafer, "Prohibition," 296-298.

52. *SB*, March 8, 1854; *WB*, Feb. 8, March 15, 1854; Buck, *Under the Charter*, IV, 29.

53. *WB*, March 15, 1854; Koss, *Milwaukee*, 154, 442-446; *MC*, April 3, 1844; *WB*, Oct. 27, 1849, July 28, Oct. 11, 1852; *VF*, Sept. 21, Oct. 12, 1848; see also Still's discussion, *Milwaukee*, 151-152.

54. *WB*, April 12, July 26, 12, Aug. 16, 1854. It was also charged that the Republicans included "eccentric females who want to reform the world with their ideas of 'women's rights' "; the editor may have had Mathilde Anneke in mind.

55. *WB*, June 7, 1854, Dec. 3, 1856; see also Oct. 3, 5, 1855; *BV*, Nov. 19, 1856. No love was lost on the German Republican side either, if the sentiments of Mathilde Anneke were representative; in connection with the Glover affair, she wrote that "There is just too much 'plebs' in this hole! But almost all the German creatures are common 'plebs' without exception. One doesn't find among them any more principle, consciousness of freedom, or even sense of justice." "Biographical Notes," 50, ms. in Anneke Papers, SHSW.

56. Ernest Bruncken, "The Political Activity of Wisconsin Germans, 1854-60," *Proceedings*, SHSW, 1901 (Madison: 1902), 192-195; Schafer, *Four Wisconsin Counties*, 153-155.

57. *Atlantis*, III, 225, quoted in Bruncken, "Poltical Activity," 201.

58. *Wisconsin Democrat* (Manitowoc), Aug. 17, 1854, quoted in ibid., 196.

59. Koss, *Milwaukee*, 448-449; *WB*, Aug. 16, 1854; *SB*, Nov. 6, 1854; Louis J. Swichkow and Lloyd P. Gartner, *The History of the Jews of Milwaukee* (Philadelphia: The Jewish Publication Society of America, 1963), 16, 466.

60. *WB*, March 14, 21, April 4, 1855; Buck, *Under the Charter*, IV, 110; *MWS*, March 7, 1855; *BV*, Aug. 22, Sept. 7, Oct. 10, Nov. 14, 21, 1855.

61. *BV*, April 9, Sept. 3, Oct. 8, Nov. 12, 1856; Buck, *Under the Charter*, IV, 147.

62. Still, *Milwaukee*, 144-149; *WB*, Aug. 2, 1854; *BV*, Aug. 2, Oct. 29, Nov. 5, Dec. 17, 1856; March 18, 1857. Huebschmann had been occupied elsewhere between 1853 and 1857 as Superintendent of Indian Affairs for the Northwest; his return may have played a role in generating the reform movement.

63. *BV*, Feb. 25, March 4, 14, April 15, Sept. 16, 27, 30, Oct. 21, Nov. 11, 1857; March 31, 1858; Still, *Milwaukee*, 145-147; Bruncken, "Political Activity," 202. Once in the assembly, von Cotzhausen was soon ejected from the Democratic caucus because of his tendency to vote with the Republicans.

64. Still, *Milwaukee*, 145-149; Buck, *Under the Charter*, IV, 222-223; *BV*, Nov. 11, 1857; Jan. 18, Feb. 6, 9, 16, 20, March 2, 3, 10, 13, 15, 16, 17, 24, 31; April 5, 8, 14; Oct. 22, 25, 28; Nov. 4, 1858. It was at this time that the first notices for separate Dutch and Bohemian ward meetings began to appear; all wards continued to meet through the summer and autumn.

65. *BV*, Feb. 26, April 1, 7, Aug. 5, 8, 10, 18, 20, Oct. 15, 18, 22, 25, 27, 29, Nov. 5, 10, 1859. For details of the workers' movement, which accomplished little but suggested the openness of the German workers to experiment on the model of political

organization in hard times, see Kathleen Neils Conzen, " 'The German Athens': Milwaukee and the Accommodation of its Immigrants, 1836-1860," Ph.D. diss., University of Wisconsin, 1972, 435-442; Gavett gives this movement no attention, probably owing to his reliance upon English-language sources; Thomas W. Gavett, *Development of the Labor Movement in Milwaukee* (Madison: University of Wisconsin Press, 1965).

66. Still, *Milwaukee*, 154-155; *BV*, March 13; April 1, 3, 4, 6, 1860.

67. *MWS*, Jan. 17, 24, 1859; *Daily Milwaukee News*, Sept. 21, 1859; *BV*, Sept. 4; Oct. 7, 13, 28; Nov. 10, 1859; Bruncken, "Political Activities," 203.

68. *BV*, June 8, 1860; *MA*, July 6, 12, Aug. 18, Oct. 15, Sept. 4, 7, Nov. 8, 1860; the *Banner* is not available for the election period; the *Atlas* was the German Republican spokesman.

69. See the historiographical introduction by Frederick C. Luebke to his *Ethnic Voters and the Election of Lincoln* (Lincoln: University of Nebraska Press, 1971), *xi-xxxii*.

70. See particularly Paul Kleppner, "Lincoln and the Immigrant Vote: A Case of Religious Polarization," *Mid-America*, 48 (1966), 176-195; Kleppner, *Cross of Culture*, 35-51; Formisano, *Birth of Mass Political Parties*, 138-140; James M. Bergquist, "People and Politics in Transition: The Illinois Germans, 1850-60," in Luebke, *Ethnic Voters*, 196-226. Kleppner's analysis of Pittsburgh voting suggests that the split between German Catholics and Lutherans was already well developed in that city by 1860; however, he assumes that all non-Catholics were Lutherans as well as a stability of parish membership patterns over time, neither of which was true for Milwaukee in 1860.

71. J. H. A. Lacher, "The German Element in Wisconsin," in Milo M. Quaife, ed., *Wisconsin: Its History and Its People, 1634-1924* (Chicago: The S. J. Clarke Publishing Co., 1924), II, 185; Still, *Milwaukee*, 280-283.

72. Bruncken, "Political Activity," 208.

73. For a different interpretation of the south side vote without the full context of citywide German settlement and occupational patterns, see Richard J. Anderson, "The German Vote of Milwaukee in the 1860 Election," M.A. thesis, University of Chicago, 1968. South side German affairs received less attention from the German press than did those of the far larger communities to the north; they also played much less prominent a role in the reform movement within the Democratic party than did the other German wards.

74. E.g., *BV*, Nov. 27, Dec. 21, 1858; Jan. 10, 15, April 20, 21, May 3, Sept. 28, 1859.

75. Buck, no friend of the immigrant, noted payoffs to Irish voters in the form of "professional" jury service and public employment; *Pioneer History*, II, 102; *Under the Charter*, III, 356. Other sources hint at similar connections between the Irish and political office holders, particularly where public works were involved; no such inferences concerning the Germans were found, though the same situation may well have existed.

76. *WB*, March 28, 1846; *VF*, May 4, July 6, 1848; Nov. 15, 1849.

77. *VF*, April 30, Feb. 1, 1849, Jan. 24, 1850; *WB*, May 7, 1851.

Conclusion

1. *BV*, April 27, 1858; see also April 21, 1858.

2. Students of German-American history have stressed the importance of variation in German dialects in discouraging unified action, and in promoting both associational variety and use of English; e.g., Guido A. Dobbert, "The Disintegration of an Immigrant Community: The Cincinnati Germans, 1870-1920," Ph.D. diss., University of Chicago, 1965, 60-63; Heinz Kloss, "German-American Language Maintenance Efforts," in Joshua A. Fishman, ed., *Language Loyalty in the United States: The Maintenance and Perpetuation of Non-English Mother Tongues by American Ethnic and Religious Groups* (The Hague: Mouton & Co., 1966).

While such differences provoked surprisingly little comment from Milwaukee Germans either in the newspapers at the time or in later memoirs, Germans could hardly help noticing them. A Milwaukee historian later noted that at the city market, "The gossip of the town was here diffused in the Mecklenburger and Pommeranian dialects as freely as it was in the Bavarian and Swabian dialects, although every one made an effort to employ high German." "Every German, whatever his dialect might be, made a pretense to a knowledge and use of the written and official language as taught in the schools of his native country, but he did not always succeed in his use of high German in hiding the inflections of his dialect or the jargon of the particular section of the country he came from." William George Bruce, ed., *History of Milwaukee City and County* (Chicago: The S. J. Clarke Publishing Co., 1922), I, 767, 700.

3. Sample data show increasing intermarriage rates for all groups between 1850 and 1860, but intermarriages involving Germans remained particularly rare, increasing from about 2 percent of the sample in 1850 (when almost 11 percent of the sample was unmarried) to about 4 percent in 1860 (11 percent unmarried); about 4.5 percent of the Irish sample in 1850 were married to persons not born in Ireland (12 percent unmarried), and 7 percent in 1860 (18 percent unmarried); native intermarriage rates were 6 percent in 1850 (14 percent unmarried) and 10 percent in 1860 (14 percent unmarried).

4. Symbolic of the alienation between Germans and natives in 1854 was the German formation of an artillery company in response to Know-Nothing sentiment, "with the interests of the Germans, or even better, the interests of the foreign born in view." The Americans then formed "an independent military company composed wholly of Americans" to offset the German and Irish companies and to counter "the feeling of uneasiness among the native-born Americans for their personal safety on 'election days.' " *BV*, Jan. 27, 1859; James S. Buck, *Milwaukee under the Charter* (Milwaukee: Swain and Tate, 1884), IV, 30.

5. A ten year old boy who had emigrated to Milwaukee with his family in 1849 wrote a letter to Germany in English in 1854 "because I am not able to speak, read and write perfectly the German language." Harry H. Anderson, ed., *German-American Pioneers in Wisconsin and Michigan: The Frank-Kerler Letters, 1849-1864* (Milwaukee: MCHS, 1971), 256. By the immediate post-Civil War period, the children's street dialect was reportedly a mixture of both German and English, but then and earlier, fights between gangs of boys of different nationalities were common. Bill Hooker, *Glimpses of an Earlier Milwaukee* (Milwaukee: Milwaukee Journal, 1929), 20; Charles King, "Memories of a Busy Life," *WMH*, 5 (1922), 215; *BV*, June 17, 1860; *MA*, Oct. 24, 1860.

6. Julius Gugler, "Autobiography" (1898), ms., Gugler Papers, MCHS.

7. Anderson, *German-American Pioneers*, 434.

8. Ibid., 200, 100, 255, 383.

9. It should be clear that I do not accept John Hawgood's interpretation of a defensive, isolationist German-America arising out of the Know-Nothing crisis of the 1850s. Cf. Hawgood, *The Tragedy of German-America: The Germans in the United States of America during the Nineteenth Century—and After* (New York: G. P. Putnam's Sons, 1940). Comparison with the work of Dobbert ("The Cincinnati Germans"), Audrey Louise Olson ("St. Louis Germans; 1850-1920: The Nature of an Immigrant Community and its Relation to the Assimilation Process," Ph.D. diss., University of Kansas, 1970), and George Helmuth Kellner ("The German Element on the Urban Frontier: St. Louis, 1830-1860," Ph.D. diss., University of Missouri, 1973) suggests that in Cincinnati and St. Louis also, heterogeneous German communities thrived on a cultural common denominator and internal conflict. Dobbert argues that it was only when suburbanization drew the elite out of the German community and new immigration faded that a self-conscious attempt to create a retentive German-American community developed; Olson found that the strength of the St. Louis German community lay in the tenuousness of its bonds, and that only with prohibition was its social basis destroyed. See also Frederick C. Leubke, *Immigrants and Politics: The Germans of Nebraska, 1880-1900* (Lincoln: University of Nebraska Press, 1969), esp. chap. 3. For the later history of Milwaukee's Germans, see Bayrd Still, *Milwaukee: The History of a City* (Madison: SHSW, 1948), 112-130, 259-267, 453-464.

Appendix

1. U.S. Census Office, *Report of the Superintendent of the Census, December 1, 1851* (Washington, D.C.: Robert Armstrong, 1853), 127.

2. Manuscript schedules for all but the school censuses are available in the State Historical Society of Wisconsin, Madison, where they were consulted.

3. Carroll D. Wright and William C. Hunt, *The History and Growth of the United States Census* (Washington, D.C.: Government Printing Office, 1900), summarizes the various census questions.

4. Francis A. Walker, *The Statistics of the Population of the United States* (Washington, D.C.: Government Printing Office, 1872), *ix-xlix;* Peter R. Knights, *The Plain People of Boston, 1830-1860: A Study in City Growth* (New York: Oxford University Press, 1971), 140-147; John B. Sharpless and Ray M. Shortridge, "Biased Underenumeration in Census Manuscripts: Methodological Implications," *Journal of Urban History,* 1 (1975), 409-439.

5. WB, May 23, 1846; July 3, 1850; VF, Nov. 25, 1847; BV, May 30, 1855; April 6, May 8, June 21, 1860.

6. This pilot project was undertaken to determine the feasibility of a study based upon a universe of all household heads, or of all employed males. Time constraints precluded either alternative, but the results of the pilot serve to reinforce the credibility of the sample, as well as to provide occupational data for nonhousehold heads which are utilized in Chapter 3. Note that female household heads who are included in the heads of household category in Table A.1 are excluded from the figures for employed males 15 and over.

7. For details, see Kathleen Neils Conzen, " 'The German Athens': Milwaukee

and the Accommodation of its Immigrants, 1836-1860," Ph.D. diss., University of Wisconsin, 1972, 516-525.

8. Extended discussion of problems arising in occupational coding may be found in Stuart Blumin, "The Historical Study of Vertical Mobility," *Historical Methods Newsletter*, 1 (September 1968), 1-13; Clyde Griffin, "The Study of Occupational Mobility in Nineteenth-Century America: Problems and Possibilities," *Journal of Social History*, 5 (1972), 310-330; and Michael B. Katz, "Occupational Classification in History," *Journal of Interdisciplinary History*, 3 (1972), 63-88.

9. Stephan Thernstrom, *The Other Bostonians: Poverty and Progress in the American Metropolis, 1880-1970* (Cambridge: Harvard University Press, 1973), 289-302; Knights, *Plain People*, 149-156. I am grateful to Mr. Knights for making his code descriptions available for use in the Milwaukee study. Roger Simon adapted my variant for use in his Milwaukee study, "The Expansion of an Industrial City, 1880-1910," Ph.D. diss., University of Wisconsin, Madison, 1971.

10. Lampard has consistently criticized the use of census occupational titles as proxies for status and income levels, and of occupational changes as measures of "social" mobility, especially in periods of industrial revolution. He suggests that actual income, taxable or probated wealth accumulation, religious confession, schooling, family size, age, and stage of life cycle are also crucial dimensions of individual status. The status which "enters in as a determinant of individual or 'group' behavior in particular communities" is said to be assigned "in a much more circumscribed social system than is ever reflected by five or six layers of a national occupational 'prestige hierarchy.'" Lampard, "Historical Contours of Contemporary Urban Society: A Comparative View," *Journal of Contemporary History*, 4 (1969), esp. 18-25; see also his "The Plain People of Boston: An Afterward," in Knights, *Plain People*, esp. 194-195; "Two Cheers for Quantitative History: An Agnostic Forward," in Leo F. Schnore, ed., *The New Urban History: Quantitative Explorations by American Historians* (Princeton: Princeton University Press, 1975), 12-48.

11. For an extended discussion of the publishing histories and features of these Milwaukee directories, see Conzen, "German Athens," 537-550, which supplements Peter R. Knights, "City Directories as Aids to Ante-Bellum Urban Studies: A Research Note," *Historical Methods Newsletter*, 2 (1969), 1-10; also helpful are the comments in Thernstrom, *Other Bostonians*, 280-288.

12. Coverage was estimated from the average number of names per page multiplied by the total number of pages and divided by the total city population.

13. Franklin E. Town, *Milwaukee City Directory, For 1859-60* (Milwaukee: Jermain & Brightman, 1859), 5; *BV*, Aug. 17, 1859; *MA*, Aug. 7, 1860.

14. Increase A. Lapham's "Map of the City of Milwaukee" (New York: George Harrison, 1855) was used, both because it represented a mid-point between the two census years and because it depicted structures as well as lot lines, ensuring greater accuracy in assigning locations to vague addresses.

15. For a map series illustrating this process in greater detail, see Kathleen N. Conzen, "Mapping Manuscript Census Data for Nineteenth Century Cities," *Historical Geography Newsletter*, 4 (Spring 1974), 1-7.

16. Further refinements were also necessary. All peripheral cells occupied by only one or two sample households were eliminated; likewise, when assignment of a

cell with three or fewer sample households would have created a single-cell ethnic area, the cell was assigned to the neighboring ethnic area regardless of ethnicity. Neither the Dutch nor the British were sufficiently numerous to create ethnic areas of their own, yet they tended to live among the Germans and the native born respectively; in view of the cultural similarity, they were added to the German and American percentages in areas which lacked sufficiently high percentages of other groups to make them truly mixed. Jack P. Gibbs, ed., *Urban Research Methods* (Princeton: D. Van Nostrand Co., 1961), 145-146, contains a discussion of the creation of such areas for statistical purposes.

17. *German-American Pioneers in Wisconsin and Michigan: The Frank-Kerler Letters* (Milwaukee: MCHS, 1971).

18. *Reisen in Nordamerika in den Jahren 1852 und 1853,* 3 vols. (Leipzig: Arnoldische Buchhandlung, 1854).

19. Karl Quentin, *Reisebilder und Studien aus dem Norden der Vereinigten Staaten von Amerika* (Arnsberg: H. F. Grote, 1851) and L. von Baumbach, *Neue Briefe aus den Vereinigten Staaten von Nordamerika in die Heimath mit besonderer Rücksicht auf die deutsche Auswanderer* (Cassel: Theodor Fischer, 1856) were both written by men with direct interests in Milwaukee real estate; an equivalent aimed at the Irish immigrant was John Gregory's *Industrial Resources of Wisconsin* (Chicago: Langdon and Rounds, 1853). The two most useful general immigrant guides in German were Traugott Bromme, *Hand- und Reisebuch für Auswanderer nach den Vereinigten Staaten von Nord-Amerika,* 5th ed. (Beyreuth: Verlag der Buchner'schen Buchhandlung, 1848), and Friedrich Pauer, *Die Vereinigten Staaten von Nord-Amerika, nach erfolgtem Anschluss der Republik Texas* (Bremen: F. C. Dubbers, 1847).

20. 2nd ed. (Madison: SHSW, 1965).

21. Rudolf H. Koss, *Milwaukee* (Milwaukee: Herold, 1871); A. C. Wheeler, *The Chronicles of Milwaukee: Being a Narrative History of the Town from its Earliest Period to the Present* (Milwaukee: Jermain and Brightman, 1861); James S. Buck, *Pioneer History of Milwaukee,* 2 vols., rev. ed. (Milwaukee: Swain & Tate, 1890); *Milwaukee under the Charter, from 1847 to 1853, Inclusive* (Milwaukee: Symes, Swain & Co., 1884); and *Milwaukee under the Charter, from 1854 to 1860, Inclusive* (Milwaukee: Swain & Tate, 1886).

22. Frank A. Flower, *History of Milwaukee, Wisconsin* (Chicago: The Western Historical Company, 1881); Howard Louis Conrad, ed., *History of Milwaukee County from Its First Settlement to the Year 1895,* 3 vols. (Chicago: American Biographical Publishing Co., n.d.); Jerome A. Watrous, ed., *Memoirs of Milwaukee County,* 2 vols. (Madison: Western Historical Association, 1909).

23. William George Bruce, ed., *History of Milwaukee City and County,* 3 vols. (Chicago: The S. J. Clarke Publishing Co., 1922); John G. Gregory, *History of Milwaukee Wisconsin,* 4 vols. (Chicago: The S. J. Clarke Publishing Co., 1931). The most useful of the booster publications were *Industrial History of Milwaukee* (Milwaukee: E. E. Barton, 1886) and *Milwaukee: A Half Century's Progress, 1846-1896* (Milwaukee: Consolidated Illustrating Co., 1890).

24. For a discussion of these "mug books" and their scholarly uses, see Archibald Hanna, "Every Man His Own Biographer," *Proceedings of the American Antiquarian Society,* 80 (1970), 291-298.

Index

Abert, George, 17, 88

Absorption, economic, 2. *See also* Adjustment, personal; Economic integration of immigrants

Abstinence, *see* Temperance

Accommodation: and German community, 225-228; implications of Milwaukee patterns for, 43, 46, 60-62, 63, 148-149, 192, 224; process described, 2-7

Acculturation, 2, 5, 192-193, 227. *See also* Accommodation; Adjustment, personal

Adjustment, personal: and communal life, 154, 158-159, 191, 224, 226; and residence patterns, 126, 148; influence of demographic patterns upon, 42, 45-46, 49, 50, 55, 59, 60-62; influence of economic integration upon, 63-64, 84, 85, 124; process described, 2, 5, 7

Adler, David, 102-103

Adler, Solomon, 39, 102-103

Age structure, 46-47, 49-50, 52-53, 256n6

Aigner, G., 177, 268n93

American Emigration Co-Operative Association, 41

Americans, *see* Native born

Anneke, Fritz, 32, 123

Anneke, Mathilde Franziska, 32, 112, 188, 286nn54, 55

Anticlericalism, German, 183-184, 207, 211, 212, 213, 216, 217, 221, 222, 285n45

Anti-slavery sentiment, German, 204, 209, 214, 215-222

Apprenticeship, 56-59, 91, 110, 263n20

Arbeiter (Milwaukee), 188

Artisans: adjustment to American methods, 96-98; capital, 110; career paths, 98-110; employment of servants, 81; ethnicity, 66-74, 99; political participation, 204; property ownership, 78-79, 99; trade unions, 110-113, 220. *See also* specific trades

Assimilation: and intermarriage, 227; and language, 227, 288n5; and residence, 149-153; theories of, 2-3, 6-7, 245n2. *See also* Accommodation; Adjustment

Atlantis, 188

Atlas (Milwaukee), 187, 287n68

Austrians, 20-21, 161

Baden, immigrants from, 29-31. *See also* Germans

Bakers and confectioners, 96, 97, 109

Balatka, Hans, 32, 123, 175, 177

Balls, German, 158, 174

Banks, German, 118-119

Banner, see *Wisconsin Banner*

Banner und Volksfreund (Milwaukee), 219, 220

Baumbach, Ludwig von, 35, 284n27

Bavaria, immigrants from, 29-31, 161, 288n2. *See also* Germans

Beergardens, 94, 157-158

Beethoven Society, 173

Begging, 90

Belgians, 20

Bertschy, Jacob, 109, 118

Best, Jacob, 31, 104

Bielfeld, A. Henry, 173, 196, 205, 216, 284n28

Blacks, 21, 250n30

Blacksmiths, 100-101, 109

Blatz, Valentine, 104

Bleyer, Henry, 17

B'ne Jeshuran congregation, 167

Boarding and lodging, 55-59, 80-81, 261n20

Bohemians, 20-21, 286n64

Bossert, Gottlob, 32

HARVARD STUDIES IN URBAN HISTORY